STATE AND LOCAL
GOVERNMENT

COLLEGE OUTLINE SERIES

ABOUT THE AUTHOR

Joseph F. Zimmerman received his B.A. from the University of New Hampshire and his M.A. and D.S.S. from Syracuse University. He is Professor of Government at Worcester Polytechnic Institute and also gives several courses, including seminars for planning-board members and town officials, at Clark University. Dr. Zimmerman has acted as a consultant to the Massachusetts Department of Commerce and various city and town officials and is currently a consultant to the Massachusetts Commission on Atomic Energy. He is a member of many national and regional professional and academic organizations and several civic groups. He has edited *Readings in State and Local Government* and has written articles for *The Encyclopaedia Britannica* and a number of journals.

STATE AND LOCAL GOVERNMENT

Joseph F. Zimmerman, D.S.S.

PROFESSOR OF GOVERNMENT
WORCESTER POLYTECHNIC INSTITUTE

BARNES & NOBLE, INC.   •   NEW YORK

PUBLISHERS   •   BOOKSELLERS   •   SINCE 1873

This book is an original work (no. 112) in the original College Outline Series. It was written by a distinguished educator, carefully edited, and produced in accordance with the highest standards of publishing. The text was set on the Linotype in Baskerville and Caledonia by Wickersham Printing Company (Lancaster, Pa.). The paper for this edition was manufactured by S. D. Warren Company (Boston, Mass.) and supplied by Canfield Paper Company (New York, N.Y.). This edition was printed by Hamilton Printing Company (Rensselaer, N.Y.) and bound by Sendor Bindery (New York, N.Y.). The cover was designed by Rod Lopez-Fabrega.

ACKNOWLEDGEMENTS

A state and local government textbook is never the work of one man for the author draws upon numerous sources of information. Although it is not possible to cite all these sources, I wish to acknowledge my indebtedness to the following: Governmental Research Center of the University of Kansas, Committee for Economic Development, Massachusetts Budget Bureau, United States Bureau of the Budget, United States Bureau of the Census, Council of State Governments, International City Managers' Association, Tax Foundation, National Municipal League, Clerk of the United States House of Representatives, and Advisory Commission on Intergovernmental Relations.

I would be negligent if I failed to express thanks to my students at Worcester Polytechnic Institute and Clark University for providing stimulation and for acting as constructive critics of earlier drafts of this book.

Finally, I wish to acknowledge a special debt of gratitude to Dr. Edward Conrad Smith (Professor Emeritus, New York University) and Mrs. Mary F. Johnson (Editorial Staff, Barnes & Noble, Inc.); their many suggestions greatly improved this text.

J.F.Z.

CONTENTS

Tabulated Bibliography to Standard Textbooks

This *College Outline* is keyed to standard textbooks in two ways.

1. If you are studying one of the following textbooks, consult the cross references here listed to find which pages of this *Outline* correspond to the appropriate chapter of your text. (Roman numerals refer to the textbook chapters or units, Arabic numerals to the pages of this *Outline*.)

2. If you are using this *Outline* as your basis for study and want another treatment of the subject, consult the pages of any of the standard textbooks as indicated in the Quick Reference Table on pp. x–xiii.

Adrian, Charles R. *Governing Urban America.* New York: McGraw-Hill Book Company, Inc., 1961.

I–III (1–11); IV (50–63); V–VI (64–86); VII (157–165); VIII–X (149–156); XI (167–173); XII (165–166); XIV (216–224); XV–XVI (225–240); XVII (174–179); XIX–XX (199–206); XXI (179–183)

Adrian, Charles R. *State and Local Government.* New York: McGraw-Hill Book Company, Inc., 1960.

I–IV (1–11); V (12–36); VI (37–49, 157–166); VII (50–63); VIII–X (64–94); XI (140–156); XII (167–173); XIII (108–119); XIV (95–107); XV (120–128); XVI (216–224); XVII (129–139); XVIII (225–240); XIX (184–189); XX (179–183); XXI (199–206); XXII (174–179, 207–215)

Anderson, William; Penniman, Clara; and Weidner, Edward W. *Government in the Fifty States.* New York: Holt, Rinehart and Winston, Inc., 1960.

I–II (1–11); III (12–26); IV (37–49); V (27–36); VI (157–166); VII–IX (50–86); X–XI (95–107); XII (108–119); XIII (129–139); XIV (120–128); XV (216–224); XVI–XVII (225–240); XVIII (174–179); XIX (192–198); XX (199–206); XXI (184–189); XXII (207–215); XXIII (179–183)

Babcock, Robert S. *State & Local Government & Politics.* 2nd ed. New York: Random House, Inc., 1962.

I (1–11); II (37–49); III (79–86); IV (64–79); V (50–63); VI (145–148); VII (140–145); VIII (149–156); IX (167–173); X (129–139); XI (95–107); XII (108–128); XIII (192–206); XIV (174–183); XV (184–189); XVI (207–215); XVII (108–128); XVIII (225–240); XIX (12–36, 157–166)

Grant, Daniel R., and Nixon, H. C. *State and Local Government in America.* Boston: Allyn and Bacon, Inc., 1963.

I (1–11); II–IV (12–36); V (37–49); VI (50–56); VII (56–79); VIII (79–86); IX–X (87–107); XI–XII (108–119); XIII (120–128, 216–224); XIV (225–240); XV (129–139); XVI (140–148); XVII (149–156); XVIII (167–173); XIX (174–179); XX (207–215); XXI (192–206); XXII (179–189)

Johnson, Claudius O., *et al. American State and Local Government.* New York: Thomas Y. Crowell Company, 1961.

I (12–36); II (37–49); III (50–86); IV (87–107); V (108–128); VI (129–139); VII (225–240); VIII (174–215); IX (140–156); X (167–173)

MacDonald, Austin F. *American State Government and Administration.* New York: Thomas Y. Crowell Company, 1960.

I (12–26); II (27–36); III (157–166); IV (37–49); V–VI (95–107); VII (108–128); VIII (129–139); IX (149–156); X–XI (140–148); XII–XIV (50–86); XV (87–94); XVI (216–224); XVII (204–206); XVIII–XX (225–240); XXI–XXIV (174–183); XXV (184–189); XXVI (192–198); XXVII (199–204); XXVIII (207–215)

Maddox, Russell W., and Fuquay, Robert F. *State and Local Government.* Princeton: D. Van Nostrand Company, Inc., 1962.

I (1–11); II (12–26); III (37–49); IV (108–119); V (120–128); VI–VII (95–107); VIII–IX (129–139); X (50–63); XI–XII (64–86); XIII (87–94); XIV–XVI (225–240); XVII (216–224); XVIII, XXIII (157–166); XIX (149–156); XX–XXI (140–148); XXII (167–173); XXIV–XXV (174–183); XXVI (184–189); XXVII (192–206); XXVIII (207–215)

Phillips, Jewell Cass. *Municipal Government and Administration in America.* New York: The Macmillan Company, 1960.

I–II (1–11); III–IV (157–166); VI (167–173); VII (50–63); VIII (64–86); X–XII (149–156); XIII (129–139); XV (216–244); XVI–XVII (225–240); XVIII–XIX (204–206); XX–XXI (174–183); XXII (184–191); XXIII (192–198); XXIV (207–211)

Phillips, Jewell Cass. *State and Local Government in America.* New York: American Book Company, 1954.

I (12–26); II (27–36); III (37–49); IV–VI (50–94); VII–VIII (95–107); IX (108–119); X (120–128); XI (129–139); XII (225–240); XIII (216–224); XIV–XV, XVII (140–156); XVI (157–166); XVIII (167–173); XIX (174–179); XX (184–191); XXI–XXII (192–198); XXIII–XXIV (179–183); XXV (199–206); XXVI (207–215)

Snider, Clyde F. *Local Government in Rural America.* New York: Appleton-Century-Crofts, Inc., 1957.

I–II (1–11); III–IV (157–166); V–X (140–148); XI (64–86); XII (129–139); XIII (174–179); XIV (192–195); XV (179–181); XVI (181–183); XVII (184–189); XVIII (199–206); XIX (225–240)

Swarthout, John M., and Bartley, Ernest R. *Principles and Problems of State and Local Government.* New York: Oxford University Press, 1958.

I (1–11); II (37–49); III (50–86); IV (95–107); V (108–119); VI (129–139); VII (140–156); VIII (120–128, 216–224); IX (225–240); X (207–215); XI (174–206)

Quick Reference Table to Standard Textbooks

(Roman numerals indicate chapters. Arabic figures indicate pages.)

CHAPTER IN OUTLINE	TOPIC	ADRIAN Gov. Urban Amer.	ADRIAN State & Local	ANDERSON, PENNIMAN & WEIDNER	BABCOCK	GRANT & NIXON	JOHNSON
I	Introduction	I-III	I-IV	I	I	I	
II	National-State Relations		77-90	III	342-351	II	1-20
III	Interstate Relations		90-96	V	351-356	46-48	20-27
IV	State Constitutions		VI	IV	II	V	II
V	Suffrage and Elections	IV	VII	127-143 196-202	V	VI 143-147	76-78
VI	Political Parties and Pressure Groups	V	138-151 IX-X	143-150 VIII 177-196	III-IV	126-143	III
VII	Direct Legislation and Recall	83-84 108-116	151-157		18-19 79-82	209-210	124-129
VIII	The State Legislature		289-311	X-XI	XI	IX-X	IV
IX	The Governor		255-278	XII	XII	XI-XII	132-145
X	State Administrative Organization		XV	XIV	XVII	238-245	146-154

Quick Reference Table to Standard Textbooks (Cont.)

(Roman numerals indicate chapters. Arabic figures indicate pages.)

STATE AND LOCAL
GOVERNMENT

1

INTRODUCTION

A distinguishing feature of the American political system is the division of authority among several levels of government. Besides the national government and the 50 state governments, there are approximately 3,000 counties, 17,000 municipalities,[1] and 17,000 townships; more than 47,000 school districts; and about 12,000 other special districts (see p. 147). The number of governmental units in the United States approximates 100,000. (See pp. 278–279.) The development of, the degrees of authority of, and the interrelationships among the various types of governmental units—national and, especially, state and local—form the bases of the study of state and local government.

FORMS OF GOVERNMENT AND THEIR INTERRELATIONSHIPS

All three forms of government—unitary, confederate, and federal—exist, or have existed, in the history of the United States. Here is a brief discussion of the three systems and their interrelationship. (See Appendix, "Systems of Government," p. 244.)

Unitary Government. In the unitary form one central government wields supreme power over all territorial divisions within a state. Provinces, cities, and other units owe their creation and continued existence to the central government, and they possess only such powers as the central government has seen fit to grant them.

Several European countries having unitary forms of government regard local units as administrative subdivisions to carry out national policies and often prescribe in minute detail the work to be done and the procedures to be followed. Since the operations of the administrative units are subject to more or less continuous supervision and control, the unitary organization is

1 This figure includes all active governmental units officially designated as boroughs, cities, villages, or—with the exception of New England, New York, and Wisconsin—towns (see pp. 149–156).

1

able to achieve a degree of national homogeneity, to provide uniformity of policy and administration, and to swiftly and completely concentrate power in time of war. The unitary system has, however, the disadvantage of being inflexible. The same policies and methods are applied to all local conditions regardless of their applicability in specific areas; sometimes they are ideally suited to certain local problems, but other times they are unsuitable and unadaptable. In addition, this system tends to stifle local initiative.

Each state in the United States has a unitary form of government, but here the rigidities inherent in the unitary system are softened by granting varying degrees of local self-government to counties, municipalities, and other units.

Confederation. A confederate system is one in which two or more independent states band together to establish a central government agency designed to accomplish certain common purposes. Usually these purposes include the conduct of foreign affairs and national defense. Each state retains its sovereignty and complete control over all persons and things within its boundaries. In this way, it grants only limited powers to the central government agency.

Confederation is basically and in practice an unstable form of government. Individual states may nullify the acts of the agency and even withdraw at will from the confederation. States may also impose high tariffs and discriminate against citizens of other states. The friction that results from such measures usually destroys the effectiveness of the confederation. Despite its disadvantages, this system of government has been an instrument for co-operation in revolutionary emergencies and has sometimes been a prelude to the establishment of a closer and more stable union. The experience of the United States, which had a confederate form of government in the years from 1781 to 1789, illustrates this point.

Federal Government. In a federal system, such as the United States has had since 1789, all governmental powers are divided between (1) a national government and (2) the several state (province, canton, etc.) governments. The distribution of powers is made by means of a written constitution. The national government and each of the state governments are supreme within the respective fields assigned to them. Both national and state gov-

ernments may levy taxes and enforce their laws against individuals. (See Appendix, "Federalism in the U. S.," p. 243.)
ADVANTAGES OF FEDERAL GOVERNMENT. The four chief advantages of the federal form are: (1) Uniformity of policy and administration can be achieved in national affairs while the states retain control over their own internal affairs. (2) Retention of some powers by the states is a safeguard against undue concentration of governmental authority in the nation, which might result in general policies harmful to some sections of a large country. (3) Individual states may serve as proving grounds for experiments in government which, if successful, may be adopted elsewhere. (4) National safeguards may be established (e.g., in the Fourteenth Amendment or enforced by the courts) to protect citizens against unequal or discriminatory actions by state or local authorities.

DISADVANTAGES OF FEDERAL GOVERNMENT. The three chief disadvantages of the federal form of government are: (1) The federal system is rigid; it can be changed only by constitutional amendment, a process which is always prolonged and usually difficult. (2) Under a federal system the distribution of powers between the national government and the state governments is often unsatisfactory, with uneconomical overlapping of functions. This is especially apparent in times of rapid change when conflicts in jurisdiction may delay or prevent action by either national or state units or both; concentration of authority in one government (as in a unitary state) would result in greater efficiency. (3) Lack of uniformity among the laws of the states of a federal system creates serious problems; laws governing banking, divorce, mental illness, and highway safety, for examples, vary widely among the American states and frequently without justification.

DEVELOPMENT OF AMERICAN STATE AND NATIONAL GOVERNMENT

Government in the United States owes much to English institutions and philosophies of government. The ideas of popular sovereignty, separation of powers, rule of law, natural rights and natural law (a universal law transcending man-made laws) were well developed—though not always in effect—in England and were transplanted by early settlers in the thirteen colonies.

Revolutionary Government. At the beginning of the American Revolution each colony organized a *de facto* government [2] and sent representatives to a Continental Congress. Although no written document invested this Congress with governmental powers, it raised armies, made treaties with foreign powers, and borrowed money. On July 4, 1776, it issued the Declaration of Independence. At the same time, it called upon every state to draft a written constitution.

Written State Constitutions. By 1780 eleven states had drafted constitutions, and Connecticut and Rhode Island had converted their royal charters into constitutions. These written constitutions recognized that governments emanate from the people and derive their powers from the consent of the governed. They included bills, or declarations, of rights which protected individuals against arbitrary acts of the government. As an additional guaranty of popular liberties, the state constitutions provided for separation of powers among the three branches of government. Although the primacy of the legislature was common, definite powers were allotted to the executive and judicial branches in order that each branch might guard against unreasonable or capricious actions by the others. Thus, the rule of law rather than of men—the limitation placed on the future actions of the government—was implicit in the written state constitutions.

Articles of Confederation. In 1777 the Continental Congress submitted the Articles of Confederation and Perpetual Union to the states for ratification. This document, which was ratified in 1781 by the last of the thirteen states, stipulated: "Each state retains its sovereignty, freedom and independence, and every power, jurisdiction and right, which is not by this confederation expressly delegated to the United States, in Congress assembled." Under the Articles, the central agency consisted of a unicameral Congress whose members were appointed by the state legislatures. Few powers were delegated by the states to the Congress. Nevertheless, it could raise an army and a navy, negotiate treaties, declare war, coin money, borrow money, establish a postal system, regulate Indian affairs, and fix standards of weights and measures.

The national government under the Articles suffered from three principal defects: (1) The Congress was dependent for

---

[2] A *de facto* government actually governs, though it lacks constitutional authority.

funds upon the states, which frequently failed to send their contribution quotas to the Congress. (2) The Congress lacked the power to regulate commerce, and to make matters worse the states erected trade barriers which strangled commerce. (3) The Congress lacked authority to enforce its laws, for the states were under no legal obligation to obey them. Because of the general weakness of its position, the Congress was unable either to suppress domestic disorder or to enter into commercial agreements with foreign governments in order to restore foreign trade.

Creation of the Constitution of the United States. Dissatisfaction with government under the Articles set in motion a train of events which resulted eventually in the substitution of a federal form of government for the Confederation.

In 1785 the boundary commissioners of Virginia and Maryland suggested that all the states send delegates to a meeting at Annapolis in 1786. This body, composed of delegates from only five states, petitioned Congress to call a convention the next year at Philadelphia to reform the Confederation. Congress approved the resolution, reluctantly.

Delegates from all the states except Rhode Island attended the Constitutional Convention, which was in session in Philadelphia from May to September, 1787. Following five days of negotiation, the delegates decided, instead of revising the Articles, to draft a constitution for the United States. After considering various proposals and agreeing to compromises concerning sectional and other interests, the delegates completed the new constitution and reported it to Congress with the recommendation that the constitution should be ratified by conventions to be called in each state.

In certain large states vigorous opposition to the new constitution developed. Several conventions voted to ratify by only slight majorities, and some (such as those in Massachusetts, New York, and Virginia) voted for ratification on the condition that a bill of rights be added to the document after it went into effect. In June, 1788, the ninth state (the number necessary for ratification) voted to ratify, and early in 1789 the new federal government actually came into existence.

The Constitution provided for a bicameral legislature, an independent judiciary, and a vigorous executive. Under the Articles the legislature of the Confederation was only able to make requests of the states, but under the Constitution the national government was able—independent of the states—to govern individuals: The Congress was given the authority to enact laws affecting and controlling the actions of individuals, the federal courts were empowered to interpret the application of these laws to individuals, and the national executive was given the responsibility of seeing that these laws were observed by individuals. This new government was given the power to regulate interstate commerce, to levy taxes on individuals, to raise military forces and require service in them, and to enforce its laws. The federal government was now strong, yet a vast residuum of governmental powers was left to be exercised by the states.

Permanence of the Federal System. The text of the Constitution left unanswered the question of whether states might secede from the Union and nullify federal laws. In controversies which soon arose, nationalists argued that the Constitution had been made by the people and that it bound the states to adhere to the Union. They pointed to the words, "We, the People," in the Preamble to the Constitution and to the fact that its ratification was not by the state legislatures, but by conventions elected by the people of the several states. Their opponents argued that the Constitution was a compact between states which at the time were sovereign and could not convey their sovereignty to another body. In 1832 South Carolina was prevented from nullifying a federal law only by President Jackson's threat to use military force. At the height of the slavery controversy in 1861, eleven states seceded and set up the Confederate States of America. The military victory of the federal government settled the argument. In the words of the Supreme Court, "The Constitution, in all its provisions, looks to an indestructible Union, composed of indestructible States." [3]

Growth of Democracy. It is in the state constitutions that the growth of American democracy has been most evident. During the nineteenth century the majority of the states drafted new constitutions, often two or more times. Their purpose was to make all branches of government more responsible and more responsive to the wishes of the people. They did this in several ways—among them, by extending the suffrage and increasing the number of elective officers at both state and local levels. Toward

[3] *Texas* v. *White,* 7 Wallace 700 (1869).

the end of the century several states experimented with the initiative and referendum, which gave the voters a means of legislating directly, and with the recall, which enabled them to dismiss unfaithful or unpopular officers. (See Chapter 7, "Direct Legislation and Recall.")

Growth of Big Government. In the twentieth century, growth in population and industry created problems which could no longer be solved under the principle of *laissez faire,* which had prevailed in the nineteenth century. There arose an insistent demand at all levels for new government services and for protection of persons and property. As a result, the sphere of federal activities was expanded to meet critical national problems, among them World War I and the depression of the thirties. At the same time, state and local governments substantially increased their activities in welfare, etc., and assumed new functions in areas, such as housing and conservation, which had formerly been left in private hands.

DIFFERENCES AND SIMILARITIES OF THE STATES

The most outstanding characteristic of the fifty states is their diversity. Different conditions—area, natural resources and industrialization, population, and per capita income—in the various states present special governmental problems and determine, to a considerable extent, the particular matters to which some of the states attend. All the states exhibit certain basic similarities, however, in their governmental structures.

Area. A glance at a map of the United States reveals how greatly the states differ in size. They range in area from 571,065 square miles for Alaska to 1,058 square miles for Rhode Island. Compare the total area of the six New England states (63,126 sq. mi.) with that of Texas (262,840 sq. mi.), Nevada (109,788 sq. mi.), or Wyoming (97,411 sq. mi.). (See Appendix, p. 245.)

Population. The population growth of the country has been so great that today the population of any one of ten states exceeds the population of the United States in 1790. Recently, the number of people living in the industrial states of the Pacific Coast has rapidly increased, and, at the same time, the number of people living in a few primarily agricultural states has decreased. The states of the Southwest have experienced a tremendous population influx; between 1950 and 1960 the populations of California and Arizona increased 48.5 and 73.7 per cent, respectively. Moreover, the center of population has been moving steadily westward and has now almost reached the Mississippi River. Alaska, the largest state, with a population of about 200,000 is the most sparsely populated, whereas Rhode Island, the smallest state, with approximately 860,000 persons is the most densely populated; thus in 1960 the country's population density varied from .4 in Alaska to 749.5 per square mile in Rhode Island. (See Appendix, pp. 244, 245.)

The populations of the states vary not only in rate of growth and density, but also in composition. The inhabitants of each state differ in many ways, among them the race, nationality, education, labor skills, and occupation. The Negro population of Vermont, for instance, is less than 1 per cent of the total; in Mississippi it approaches 50 per cent.

Natural Resources and Industrialization. Although many states are well endowed with natural resources, others are relatively lacking in mineral wealth and fertility of land. In different sections of the United States the relative importance of agriculture and manufacturing varies considerably. Agriculture is the source of 14.6 per cent of total income in the northwestern states but of only 1.2 per cent in the middle eastern states. Manufacturing accounts for 33.4 per cent of total income in the New England states, but for only 11.5 per cent in the northwestern states. Only 1.5 per cent of the population of Rhode Island is employed in agriculture, compared with 44.4 per cent in North Dakota. Again, 44 per cent of the population of Rhode Island is employed in manufacturing industries; but only 2.9 per cent in North Dakota. (These percentages apply to 1960 statistics.)

Per Capita Income. The development of natural resources and the status of industrialization are reflected in the per capita income of a state or region. The total per capita income differs from state to state and substantially between certain states. In 1960, the annual per capita income was lowest ($1,162) in Mississippi and highest ($2,946) in Delaware. Throughout the country as a whole, the average individual income has been rising rapidly, from less than $600 in 1940 to more than $2,000 in 1960. Per capita income varies not only from state to state, but also from region to region; usually the variance is greater between different regions than between states within regions. Per capita income is a factor of prime importance in determining the ability of states to raise revenue and hence to provide school facilities and other governmental services. (See Appendix, p. 245.)

Governmental Powers and Structure. Regardless of how much they differ in physical characteristics and wealth, the states are constitutionally equal: a recently admitted state or one of the original thirteen each has the same powers and rights under the Constitution of the United States. The states also exhibit certain basic similarities in governmental powers and structure. Each state has a written constitution; each has executive, legislative, and judicial branches of government, with organization and powers that are everywhere similar. The states perform similar major functions, although from state to state their relative importance varies.

DEVELOPMENT OF LOCAL GOVERNMENT

Although each colony had a governor, a legislature, and a system of courts, the colonists found it expedient to establish self-government on the local level. These local governments were patterned closely on English models and were created under the authority of the king or colonial governor. The English *shire,* which was the unit for judicial administration, law enforcement, and highway maintenance, became the American *county.* The English *parish,* which was the unit for the maintenance of the established church, charities, and local roads, became the American *town* or *township.* The English *borough,* a thickly populated area which had received a charter from the king in order that it might engage in business as well as governmental enterprises, was the prototype of the American *municipality.*

The earliest state constitutions gave the state legislatures full authority to create local units and to modify the boundaries, powers, and organizations of existing units. In the course of time, new counties and townships were created from the territory of existing ones. Municipal corporations were set up to provide special services which counties and townships were unable or unwilling to provide. Later, characteristics different from English forms were added to local government. A bewildering array of special districts was formed, each to provide for one function, such as education, irrigation, drainage, flood control, or electrical service.

Despite the serious problems of overlapping and conflicting

jurisdictions, the foundations of local autonomy were deeply planted in the American system. Concern for local affairs and actual experience in administering them have long been regarded as essential in training for good citizenship.

DIFFERENCES AND SIMILARITIES IN LOCAL GOVERNMENT

The varying needs of different parts of the country have produced notable differences in the development and functions of local government. In the South, for example, the plantation system was adapted not to the town, but to the county. In New England the town was encouraged by small farming and fishing ventures and by the protection its concentration afforded during the Indian wars. Later adaptations in local forms were made to handle the conditions and problems of special areas. Cities required more services than rural areas and were able to tax their property-holders to provide them. Considering the diversity of this vast country, however, it is surprising that so many similarities exist in the organization and the powers of local units.

Variation in Rural Units. In New England the town is the principal unit of local rural government, and the county exists mainly for judicial administration. In the South the county is the principal unit, and rural subdivisions of counties, if they exist, have few functions. In the region from the middle Atlantic states to the Pacific Coast both counties and townships are important units of government.

With few exceptions, counties are fairly equal in area. An old rule used to be that the county seat should be within one day's journey from the most remote part of the county. In population, counties vary from a few thousand in sparsely settled sections to several million where they include one or more large cities. Nowadays the less populous counties find it difficult to support the governmental functions which people expect from them.

Variation in Municipalities. The populations of municipalities vary from a few hundred in an incorporated village to nearly eight million in the city of New York. Municipalities rarely enclose more than the developed area in which their inhabitants live and work. Great disparities exist in the functions performed by municipal governments. For instance, the government of a coastal city must provide wharves and docks; the government of a city in a freezing weather zone has heavy expenses for maintaining streets and sewers. In general, it may be said that the functions assumed by the city depend on its size, its physical environment, and the variety of its industries, but there is also the important element of human choice. The people of one city may be satisfied to have their government perform relatively few services. The people of another city may demand many services —even including the municipal ownership of transportation and other public utilities. Thus, the powers and the forms of government vary in accordance with local desires and the decisions of the state legsislature.

IMPORTANCE OF STATE AND LOCAL GOVERNMENT

The dramatic activities of the federal government often overshadow the activities of the state and local governments. But state and local government are also "big government," because of their important powers and functions, their employment of millions, and their sometimes enormous budgets. (See Appendix, p. 293.)

It is the governments of states and local communities by which our individual activities are most regulated. True, we fulfill the requirements of federal laws in many ways, such as paying taxes on our incomes, but the laws of the state and local governments more closely govern the lives of average citizens, for it is these governments which issue licenses—to own a dog, to operate a motor vehicle or airplane, to marry, to practice law and medicine, to form a corporation, etc.—certificates—of birth, death, etc. —permits—to burn trash, paint a house, obstruct a road or sidewalk, and so on.

State and local governments recognize and regulate so many of the "ordinary" activities and events of our lives that, taken together, they employ approximately twice as many employees as the federal government. The revenues of state government approximated, in 1960, 20 billion dollars annually; municipal government, 10 billion dollars. It is staggering to realize that the budget of the city of New York in that same year was about two and one-half billion dollars and was second in size only to the national budget. Two states, California and New York, each had annual budgets in excess of two billion dollars.

2

NATIONAL-STATE RELATIONS

The Constitution of the United States is the instrument that divides governmental powers between the national government and the state governments, the partners in the federal system. It does this by (1) granting a number of powers to the national government, (2) providing that all other powers shall be exercised by the states or by the people, and (3) prohibiting the national government and the states from doing certain specific things to the detriment of each other or of the people. Each level of government has supreme power in the fields assigned to it by the Constitution, but in Article VI, the Constitution provides that it and all laws made in accordance with it and all treaties shall be the supreme law of the land.

POWERS OF FEDERAL GOVERNMENT

Most of the powers of the federal government are delegated to Congress in Article I of the Constitution. Others, such as the conduct of foreign relations and of military operations, are assigned, by Article II, to the President. Still others have been entrusted, by Article III, to the Supreme Court. An early strict interpretation, which would have confined federal powers to the literal wording of the Constitution, has gradually given way to a liberal view of the scope of federal powers. Thus, the powers of the federal government have been expanded to meet the needs of a growing country.

Delegated Powers. In Article I of the Constitution Congress is granted the power to tax, borrow money, regulate foreign and interstate commerce, prescribe rules of naturalization, regulate bankruptcies, establish standards of weights and measures, coin money, punish counterfeiting, establish post offices and post roads, issue copyrights and patents, punish piracies and felonies committed on the high seas, declare war, raise armies, maintain a navy, provide for organizing, training, and calling forth the militia, and govern the nation's capital and the territories.

Additional *delegated* federal powers are found in Article II. The President is commander in chief of the army and navy and, when it is in the service of the United States, of the militia. Through the power to appoint and receive diplomatic representatives he has charge of relations with foreign countries. With the consent of two-thirds of the Senate the President also makes treaties.

Under Article III, the judicial power of the United States extends to all cases arising under the Constitution and the laws and treaties of the United States, to suits between states, to suits between citizens of different states, and to all cases affecting ambassadors or arising on the high seas.[1]

Implied Powers. *Implied powers* are those not expressly stated in the Constitution, but which exist because they are necessary and proper to carry out expressly granted powers. The "elastic clause" of the Constitution (Article I, Section 8, Paragraph 18) grants Congress power "To make all laws which shall be necessary and proper for carrying into execution the foregoing powers, and all other powers vested by this constitution in the government of the United States or in any department or officer thereof." This provision serves as the basis for the doctrine of implied powers, the liberal interpretation of which has resulted in greatly augmenting the powers of the federal government. This doctrine originated in the famous case of *McCulloch* v. *Maryland,* in which the Supreme Court ruled: "Let the end be legitimate, let it be within the scope of the constitution, and all means which are appropriate, which are plainly adapted to the end, which are not prohibited, but consistent with the letter and spirit of the constitution, are constitutional." [2] Appropriate means which Congress may use vary widely, including the creation of national banks and many other institutions not mentioned in the Constitution, the formation of agencies regulating business, labor, and agriculture, and almost innumerable activities based on the authority to levy taxes to provide for the national defense and general welfare.

1 Some of the less important powers which the Constitution places within the federal sphere have been omitted here. For a complete list consult Articles I, II, and III of the Constitution of the U. S.

2 *McCulloch* v. *Maryland,* 4 Wheaton 316 (1819). For a summary of this case, see Harold C. Syrett, *American Historical Documents* (Barnes & Noble, Inc., 1960), pp. 167ff.

Expansion of Federal Powers. From the very beginning of its existence, the federal government has expanded the scope of its expressed and implied powers, and it has added others. This expansion has occurred through judicial interpretation, statutory enactment, and formal amendment of the Constitution.

JUDICIAL INTERPRETATION. The Supreme Court established its own power as final interpreter of state and federal legislation. With the exception of a few brief periods, the trend in Supreme Court decisions has been toward a broad interpretation of the powers granted to the federal government by the Constitution. Many of these decisions were promulgated under special circumstances, such as those which resulted from the country's growth in area, population, and technology. As new methods of transportation and communication were developed, the court enlarged the meaning of "interstate commerce" to include railroads, telegraphs, telephones, airplanes, radio, and television, which were all nonexistent in 1788 (when the Constitution was ratified). When large-scale manufacturing processes crossed state and national boundaries, the Court brought them within the scope of federal control. Moreover, the Supreme Court has interpreted the power to raise and support armies to include selective service for men of military age, and rationing and price-fixing for the civilian population. Under the treaty-making power, the court has even upheld an act of Congress to prevent the killing of migratory birds. Judicial interpretation has added flexibility to the Constitution and obviated the need for formal constitutional amendment.

STATUTORY ENACTMENT. At various times in the past seventy-five years, Congress has enacted statutes—especially in the fields of commerce, money, and taxation—based on hitherto unused powers. An example is the interstate commerce power which was brought to life with the enactment of the Interstate Commerce Law of 1887, dealing with the regulation of railroads. Again, by means of statute Congress created the Federal Reserve System and through it controls credit.

Congress cannot make regulations for the general welfare—that power belongs to the states—but it does have the power to "lay and collect taxes . . . for the general welfare." Under this power it has spent and is continuing to spend billions of dollars for agriculture and for old age insurance, which have traditionally been considered within the domain of the states. This same power has justified federal grants of money to the states to assist them in many activities, among them road-building, slum clearance, and education. This is an excellent example of statutory enactment based on a power which has come into existence through gradual development. In its earliest days the federal government made it a practice to give federal lands to the states for purposes of development (and reclamation); this resulted in the building of canals, roads, railroads, schools, and so on. In 1836 a federal treasury surplus was distributed among the states; in 1862, federal lands were again allotted to the states by Congress for the establishment of agricultural and mechanical colleges. In the twentieth century various kinds of grants-in-aid from the federal government to state governments became accepted practice. The main difference between earlier and present-day grants is the addition of "conditions," emphasizing the co-operative nature of the program. Nowadays when a state accepts a grant-in-aid, as it nearly always does, it is usually obliged to match the awarded amounts, dollar-for-dollar, and to conform to rigidly enforced standards set by the federal government.[3]

CONSTITUTIONAL AMENDMENT. Formal amendment of the Constitution has increased the federal government's power to protect individual rights and has strengthened its financial resources. The Fourteenth Amendment, a product of the Civil War, was originally designed to protect the rights of the former slaves against infringement by state governments. It extends the protection of federal courts to all persons who are denied due process of law or the equal protection of the law by state legislatures or state courts.

The Sixteenth Amendment granted Congress power to levy income taxes and, thus, provided the principal financial resources, which enabled Congress to expand federal activities. The Eighteenth Amendment granted the national government power to prohibit "the manufacture, sale, or transportation of intoxicating

3 These conditions are commonly imposed: (1) The grant must be spent only for the purpose specified. (2) The state must provide an agency which will work with federal officials in administering the grant. (3) Federal engineering and professional standards must be satisfied. (4) The personnel employed on the program must be selected by the merit system. (5) The state must submit reports on the progress of the program. (6) The program is subject to federal inspection.

liquors," but these provisions were repealed by the Twenty-first Amendment.

Limitations on Federal Powers. Although the breadth and depth of federal powers have been expanded greatly, the exercise of federal powers is strictly limited by various provisions of the Constitution. Here are five of the most important limitations. The first set of limitations occurs in the Bill of Rights (the first ten amendments), which contains a great many guarantees against encroachment by the federal government. They include the guarantees of freedom of speech, of the press, of religion, of petition, and of assembly and detailed procedures for the protection of persons accused of crime. The second major limitation on federal powers is the privilege of the writ of habeas corpus, which cannot be suspended except in instances of rebellion or invasion Article I, Section 9, Paragraph 2). This writ is a court order designed to prevent arbitrary imprisonment by directing a jailer to bring a prisoner into court and explain under what authority the prisoner is being confined. The third restriction appears in Article VI and provides that "no religious test shall ever be required as a qualification for any office or public trust under the United States." The fourth major limitation appears in Article I, Section 8, and provides that "all duties, imposts, and excises shall be uniform throughout the United States." This means that with the exception of the income tax, direct taxes must be apportioned among the several states according to their respective populations. Finally, by Article I, Section 9, Paragraph 6, Congress is forbidden to give preference to ports of one state over ports of any other state.

POWERS OF STATE GOVERNMENTS

Conceivably, the framers of the Constitution might have enumerated all state powers as well as federal powers. They chose, however, to mention only the powers of the national government and leave the remaining government powers, with some restrictions, to be exercised by the states. In actual fact, the great number and variety of fundamental powers reserved to the states are often overlooked. These powers are inherent and original and to a great extent undefined; the police power, the establishment and maintenance of public services, and the control of local governments, however, reside basically with the states. It is not always easy to determine the dividing line between national and state powers in a number of fields. In case of dispute the Supreme Court determines the limits of federal and state powers. Later, we shall see the ways in which the reservoir of unsurrendered state powers has been increasingly utilized as the demands of society for governmental action and services have grown.

The Police Power. The importance of the police power of the states cannot be overemphasized, since it serves as the basis for a vast amount of social legislation. The police power as broadly interpreted by the Supreme Court is the power to limit personal and property rights in order to protect public safety, health, morals, convenience, and welfare. Mr. Justice Holmes stated that "the police power extends to all great public needs. It may be put forth in aid of what is sanctioned by usage, or held by the prevailing morality or strong and preponderant opinion to be greatly and immediately necessary to the public welfare." [4]

The police power may be exercised by the enactment and enforcement of a law or it may be summarily wielded by public officials to cope with emergencies, such as epidemics and fires. Local governments exercise the police power as instrumentalities of the state.

Since the turn of the century, the police power has been used with increasing frequency by the enactment of laws on a multitude of subjects. Although the police power is undefinable in precise terms, these five categories of state activities are indicative of its scope: (1) *Public safety:* the requirements of vaccination, construction standards, inspection of buildings, motor vehicle rules, safety devices on trains, and the destruction of buildings to prevent the spread of disease or fire. (2) *Public health:* the regulations governing the destruction of diseased animals, the quarantine laws, licensing of the medical profession, the inspection and distribution of food and drugs, the inspection and maintenance of sewage and water facilities and public hospitals, and the draining of marshes. (3) *Public morals:* the enactment of fraud laws, the prohibition of prostitution and the use of narcotics, the regulation of the sale of alcoholic beverages, and the suppression of obscene literature. (4) *Public convenience:* zoning regulations, the regulation of public transportation and related

4 *Noble State Bank* v. *Haskell*, 219 U.S. 104, 111 (1911).

facilities, and the construction and maintenance of highways and parks. (5) *General welfare:* the prohibition of child labor and of monopolies in restraint of trade, the regulation of utilities, hours of work, and uses of billboards and outdoor signs.

Public Services. Most of the numerous public services of state governments are provided independently of the federal government. These services are described in greater detail in later chapters; only the general nature of the classifications of state public services will be indicated here: (1) One of the major state functions, and one constantly increasing in importance, is *education.* Institutions of higher education and special schools are maintained by state governments; the public school system is operated by local authorities under state supervision. (2) One of the oldest governmental services and one performed by all levels of government is *public protection.* Many organizations exist for the protection of the public; among those controlled by the state are the National Guard, state police, highway patrols, and civil defense organizations. (3) Among the newer governmental functions are many *public health services.* Aid for crippled children, dental clinics, water pollution control, and mental health programs are just a few of the public health services provided by the state governments. (4) Although they have originated only recently, state *public welfare services* have assumed a major role in state public service activities. States commonly provide institutional facilities for indigent persons, special programs for the aged, and child welfare services. (5) Another state public service of increasing importance is the *construction and maintenance of highways.* (6) All states have supported *agricultural and conservation programs* by agricultural research, improvement of water resources, conservation of fish and game, soil conservation, and reforestation, as well as by the county agent system (which provides demonstration of improved agricultural methods on the farmer's own land).

Control of Local Government. Although a federal relationship exists between the federal government and the states, the relationship between a state and its local governments is unitary. Local governments are creatures of the state and possess only such powers as are delegated to them by the state constitution and laws. Unless the state constitution provides to the contrary, the state legislature has complete control over local government.

States exercise administrative supervision over their local governments by means of advice, reports, personnel controls, inspections, grants-in-aid, administrative rule-making, and substitute administration. (See Chapter 14, "State and Local Relations.")

Increased Use of State Powers. The expansion of the powers of the federal government has been accompanied by an increase in the states' use of their own powers. Since the states possess all powers not granted to the federal government by the Constitution, they may assume hitherto unused functions in order to meet the needs of a changing society.

The states have expanded their powers primarily by undertaking novel functions in many fields and secondly by vastly increasing the scope of their regulatory activities. Regulation of businesses, motor vehicles, and public utilities and the provision of educational and public health facilities are examples of areas in which the states have extended their activities. Marked increase in the size of state budgets and in the number of state employees attests to the broader use of state powers and to the continuing vigor of state government. The increase in state activities has alleviated to a great extent the fear that the growth of federal powers has endangered states' rights.

Limitations on State Powers. The powers of the states are restricted in eight important ways by the federal Constitution, as specified in Article 1, Section 10, and in the First, Fourteenth, Fifteenth, and Nineteenth Amendments: (1) Foreign affairs are the province of the national government. States are forbidden to "enter into any treaty, alliance, or confederation." Without the consent of Congress a state may not enter into a political agreement or compact with another state of the union.[5] (2) Troops or ships of war may not be kept by states during peacetime. A state militia or national guard may be maintained, however, to preserve law and order.[5] (3) Some early colonial and state laws forbade creditors to bring suit to collect debts. To protect creditors, the Constitution stipulates in a contract clause that "No State shall . . . pass any . . . law impairing the obligation of contracts." [5] The due process (of law) clause of the Fourteenth Amendment is invoked in suits to protect property rights more frequently today than the contract clause. (4) States are forbidden

5 See Article I, Section 10, of the Constitution of the United States.

to "coin money; emit bills of credit; make anything but gold and silver coin a tender in payment of debts." Although the national government has exclusive monetary powers, banks may be chartered by the states. (5) States are forbidden to "lay imposts or duties on imports or exports, except what may be necessary for executing their inspection laws." Such imposts and duties may be controlled and revised by the Congress. (6) The broadest limitations on the powers of the states are found in the Fourteenth Amendment, which stipulates that "No State shall make or enforce any law which shall abridge the privileges or immunities of citizens of the United States; nor shall any State deprive any person of life, liberty, or property, without due process of law; nor deny to any person within its jurisdiction the equal protection of the laws." The courts have invalidated a number of state laws enacted under the police power, because they were contrary to the due process of law or equal protection clauses of the Fourteenth Amendment. Recently, the courts have interpreted the privileges and immunities clause to include the First Amendment's guarantees of freedom of speech, press, religion, assembly, and petition; therefore, these guarantees are protected against infringment by either the state or the federal government.[6] (7) Two amendments limit the states' control over suffrage: The Fifteenth Amendment forbids the states and the national government to restrict the rights of U.S. citizens to vote on the grounds of "race, color, or previous condition of servitude"; the Nineteenth Amendment forbids both states and the national government to restrict the voting franchise on the basis of sex. (8) Neither a state nor the national government may pass *ex post facto laws*—criminal laws which declare previous acts to be crimes or increase punishments for crimes after they have been committed.

CONCURRENT POWERS

In certain areas of government the federal system and the states have *concurrent powers*—that is, governmental powers which may be exercised by either the federal government or the state governments. For example, both have the power to levy taxes and to borrow money; furthermore, the states may, and often do, tax the same items that the federal government taxes,

6 *Gitlow* v. *New York*, 268 U.S. 652 (1925).

such as tobacco products, alcoholic beverages, gasoline, and personal incomes. Other examples of concurrent powers include the powers to establish courts, construct highways, and charter corporations.

The delegation of powers to Congress by the federal Constitution does not necessarily exclude the states from exercising these powers, for not all powers delegated to Congress are exclusive in nature. Thus, a state may exercise its police power in federal fields if Congress has not legislated or if congressional action is insufficient. Even though the regulation of interstate and foreign rail and air travel and transportation falls within the area of federal power, it is common practice for the states to license pilots and to regulate safety devices on interstate railroads in order to promote public safety and convenience. When, however, Congress passes new laws in federal fields of activity and there is conflict between state and federal power, the existing state laws are superseded. The effect of such legislation is apparent in regard to bankruptcy, which was regulated primarily by the states until the end of the nineteenth century, at which time congressional legislation on this problem superseded state legislation. Note the ruling of the U.S. Supreme Court that in the absence of congressional legislation the judicial function extends only to an inquiry as to whether the state, in enacting a law, has acted within its province and whether the regulations are reasonable.

FEDERAL GUARANTEES TO THE STATES

The federal Constitution not only reserves powers to the states, but also contains five provisions which protect the states and guarantee their integrity.

Territorial Integrity. The boundaries of a state must be respected by the federal government. Article IV of the Constitution guarantees that no territory may be taken from a state to form a new state without the consent of the state legislature and the Congress. Again, without their own consent two or more states may not be combined by Congress into one state.

Protection against Foreign Invasion and Domestic Violence. The United States, according to Article IV of the Constitution, will protect each state against invasion and, on application of the legislature or the governor if the legislature cannot be convened, against domestic violence. The federal government considers the invasion of any state by a foreign power to be automatically an invasion of the United States. While invasion is a threat to a state or nation from without, domestic violence is a rebellion, or condition of riotous resistance, to state authority from within the state. When a state is unable to suppress it, the legislature or the governor may request federal troops to help quell the uprising. The President may refuse to dispatch troops to the state if he concludes that the situation does not warrant such action. On the other hand, the President may send troops into a state if a federal function, such as the mail or interstate commerce, is interfered with, even though the state legislature and governor protest against the dispatch of federal troops.

Republican Form of Government. Article IV of the Constitution also guarantees each state a republican form of government. Although it is not defined in this document, the U.S. Supreme Court has defined a "republican form of government" as a representative government; that is, one in which the power rests with the legislators chosen by the people. In considering Oregon's initiative and referendum, the court held that provisions for direct legislation (see Chapter 7) do not impair the republican form of government.[7] This decision opposed the views of those who held that since republican government is representative government, the laws passed by popular vote were in violation of the constitutional guarantee of a republican form of government. An interesting sidelight to this case was the declaration of the Supreme Court that Congress in accepting the representatives elected by the state had approved their manner of election—affirming the view that direct legislation did not contravene republican principles.

Equality of Senate Representation. In order to safeguard and perpetuate the original equality of the states, the Constitution specifically provides in Article V that "no state, without its consent, shall be deprived of its equal suffrage in the Senate." In other words, on this one point it would be impossible to amend the Constitution without the unanimous concurrence of the states—and such an event is all but impossible.

Immunity from Suits by Private Citizens. The Eleventh Amendment prohibits the federal courts from considering suits

[7] *Pacific State Telephone and Telegraph Co.* v. *Oregon*, 233 U.S. 118 (1912).

against a state by citizens of another state. The courts have interpreted this Amendment as prohibiting the federal courts from
considering suits against a state by its own citizens and citizens
of foreign countries as well as suits against a state by citizens of
another state.[8] A state may be sued with its consent, but only in
its own courts.

FEDERAL DEPENDENCE ON STATE ACTION

Without the full co-operation of the states the federal government could not function. Two responsibilities of the states readily indicate federal dependence on them: (1) they conduct the
election of federal officers, and (2) they must consent to amendment of the Constitution before it can be formally accomplished.

Elections. Subject to the limitations of the Fifteenth and
Nineteenth Amendments, the states possess complete authority
to determine the suffrage requirements for the voters who choose
presidential electors and members of Congress. The qualifications
of these voters are determined in each state by the state constitution. State officials determine the form of the ballot, conduct
the elections, count the votes, and certify the results of the
elections.

Amending the Constitution. Affirmative state action is necessary before the Constitution of the United States can be
amended. Under the method which has thus far been used,
amendments are proposed by a two-thirds vote in each house of
Congress. To become effective they must be ratified either by the
state legislatures or by specially chosen conventions in three-
fourths of the states. The Constitution provides for an alternative
method: At the request of two-thirds of the state legislatures
Congress must call a convention for the purpose of proposing
amendments. The proposals made at such a convention would then
have to be ratified by the legislatures or conventions in three-
fourths of the states.

Co-operative Federalism. The federal system of government
provides material for a study in contrasts. Legally it is a system
of sharply divided powers and mutual guarantees designed to
preserve a delicate balance. In practice the relationships between
the states and the federal government have developed into co-

---

[8] *Hans* v. *Louisiana*, 134 U.S. 1 (1890) and *Principality of Monaco* v. *Mississippi*, 292 U.S. 313 (1934).

operative activity in many fields. Under its interstate commerce power, Congress has prohibited the transportation across state lines of kidnaped persons, stolen automobiles, and wild game killed in violation of state laws and has made it a federal crime for felons to flee from one state to another to avoid prosecution. Under their police powers the state legislatures have passed laws to aid the federal government in promoting public health, public housing, farm credit, and rural electrification. Furthermore, the federal government has made available to the states the findings of its numerous research agencies and, in turn, has benefited from state research.

GRANTS-IN-AID. Earlier in this chapter *grants-in-aid* were mentioned as devices by which the federal government expanded its powers. It is necessary now to illustrate how these grants have inured to the benefit of both states and nation. Highway grants have resulted in the construction, not only of state roads, but of a system of national highways paid for in part by the states. Grants to the poorer states have tended to raise the national average in public health, maternity and child care, and vocational education. Federal grants to cities for airport construction have provided, partly at local expense, landing fields for airplanes engaged in interstate transportation. State and local administration of the grants-in-aid allows flexibility and adjustment to special conditions, thus avoiding the strait jacket of national uniformity. (See Appendix, p. 295.)

TAX CREDITS. Through the device of *tax credits* the federal government has effected partial equalization of certain tax burdens (of citizens) which would otherwise vary widely among the several states. Two examples may be cited: (1) The Revenue Act of 1926 authorized estates which paid a state inheritance tax to credit the amount paid to the state, up to 80 per cent of the federal estate tax due. (2) The Social Security Act of 1935 permitted employers to credit their state unemployment compensation taxes up to 90 per cent of the federal unemployment compensation tax due.

ADMINISTRATIVE PARTNERSHIPS. Federal and state organizations and officers have to all intents and purposes formed informal *administrative partnerships* in order to expedite many programs. One of the most important of these programs is the co-operation among federal and state law enforcement agencies in the prevention and detection of crime. In this way members of the Federal Bureau of Investigation work with state and local police officers; and local officers assist in enforcing the federal revenue laws. Federal and state officers also work together in issuing licenses. The federal government will not issue many kinds of licenses to individuals and corporations unless they have complied with state laws. Many states reciprocate by requiring dual compliance with their own and federal laws; for example, certain states require airplane pilots to obtain federal licenses, although the pilots fly only within the state.

ADMISSION OF NEW STATES

Subject to two restrictions, Congress has full discretion to admit new states to the Union: Without the consent of the legislatures of the states concerned a state may not be divided, and two or more states may not be combined. Since the thirteen colonies declared their independence, thirty-seven states have been admitted to the Union. Three of these were the results of lawful separation from other states; Kentucky and West Virginia were formed from Virginia in 1792 and 1863 respectively, and Maine was formed from Massachusetts in 1820. In 1845 the independent Republic of Texas was admitted as a state by Congress. With the exceptions of Vermont in 1791 and California in 1850 the other new states were required, before admission, to go through a territorial stage.

Admission Procedure. During the past century Congress has set up a fairly uniform procedure for the admission of new states: (1) The residents of the territory, through their territorial legislature, petition Congress for admission. (2) If Congress receives the petition favorably, it passes an "enabling act," which specifies the conditions for framing a constitution. (3) The voters of the territory elect a constitutional convention, which drafts a constitution for the new state. (4) The draft constitution must then be approved by a majority vote in the territory. (5) If Congress approves the constitution, it passes a joint resolution of admission. (6) The voters elect officers for the new state. (7) When everything is in order and the new government is ready to operate, the President of the United States issues a proclamation declaring that the state is a member of the Union.

Conditions of Admission. Congress sometimes imposes on the territory conditions with which it must comply before admission. If the conditions imposed by Congress concern federal property in the new state, or grants of land or money to the state to be used for specific purposes, they are judicially enforceable.[9] On the other hand, if these conditions restrict the state in its internal organization and government, the state may safely ignore them after its admission. For instance, in annexing Oklahoma Congress stipulated that for a definite period the capital of the new state should be at Guthrie; but, before the period expired, Oklahoma moved its capital to Oklahoma City. In this matter, the Supreme Court ruled that "the power to locate its own seat of government, and to determine when and how it shall be changed from one place to another, . . . are essentially and peculiarly state powers. That one of the original thirteen states could now be shorn of such powers by an act of congress would not for a moment be entertained." [10]

Legal Equality of States. Under the Constitution every state is legally equal to every other state. Alaska and Hawaii have the same reserved powers guaranteed by the Tenth Amendment as any of the original thirteen states. The only distinction which the Constitution makes among states is in the number of representatives in Congress and of presidential electors, a distinction based upon population.

[9] *Sterns* v. *Minnesota,* 179 U.S. 223 (1900); *Ervien* v. *U.S.,* 251 U.S. 41 (1919).
[10] *Coyle* v. *Smith,* 221 U.S. 539 (1911).

3

INTERSTATE RELATIONS

The states are obliged to co-operate not only with the federal government but also with each other. Article I, Section 10, of the Constitution governs compacts between the states, and Article III, Section 2, invests the powers of jurisdiction over state controversies with the federal courts. Moreover, Article IV, called the "interstate article," regulates three important relations of the states: the full faith and credit provision, the interstate citizenship provision (also affected by Section I of the Fourteenth Amendment), and the interstate rendition provision. In recent years it has been necessary, owing to the number of extra-constitutional contacts between the states, to try by various means to improve the performance of their mutual obligation.

SUITS BETWEEN THE STATES

In anticipation of disputes that might arise between states, the founding fathers granted the Supreme Court, in Article III (Section 2, Paragraphs 1 and 2) of the federal Constitution, original jurisdiction in such cases. Although relations between states are generally good today, interstate conflicts have occurred over boundaries, water pollution, and debts.

Disputes over Boundaries and Water Rights. Commencing with a controversy between New York and Connecticut in 1799,[1] the Supreme Court has adjudicated on the basis of international law a number of boundary disputes between states. Ambiguous boundaries in land grants, errors in surveying, and natural changes in the courses of boundary rivers have been responsible for several boundary controversies.

The Supreme Court has also been called upon to settle a number of conflicts arising out of the use of water. For example, in 1906 Missouri sued Illinois because a drainage canal of the Chicago sanitary district emptied sewage into a tributary of the

[1] *New York* v. *Connecticut,* 4 Dallas 1 (1799).

Mississippi River, causing the pollution of one of Missouri's water sources.[2] In 1907, Kansas sued Colorado for diverting water for irrigation from the Arkansas River, to the detriment of Kansas farmers. In the same year, the Supreme Court ruled that little damage had thus far been done by diversion of the river water.[3]

Conflicts over Debts. The most famous controversy between states is the West Virginia debt suit begun in 1906 and finally adjudicated in 1918.[4] This dispute originated in the loyalty of the northwestern counties of Virginia to the Union during the Civil War and in the condition imposed when the new state of West Virginia, comprising these counties, was admitted to the Union in 1863: it would "take upon itself a just proportion of the public debt of the Commonwealth of Virginia, prior to January 1, 1861." Virginia attempted for years to secure from West Virginia a settlement of the amount due, but West Virginia disputed the amount. Consequently, Virginia in 1906 filed suit against West Virginia for a court determination of the amount due. West Virginia contended that the Supreme Court lacked jurisdiction and therefore could not enforce a judgment should it render one. The court ruled that it had jurisdiction in the dispute and permitted West Virginia to answer the complaint in the next term of the court. Following numerous technical pleas by West Virginia and the filing of additional suits by Virginia, the Supreme Court in 1918 ordered West Virginia to pay the bondholders $12,393,929.50—the sum which had been determined by the Supreme Court in an earlier decision. In 1918 the Supreme Court postponed a final decision by scheduling for argument at the next term of the Court the question of the specific methods to be used to enforce the judgment against West Virginia.

The 1918 decision is of particular interest since the Supreme Court suggested several means that might be utilized to enforce its judgment against West Virginia. Among others, the court mentioned as a possible remedy "an order in the nature of mandamus commanding the levy by the legislature of West Virginia of a tax to pay the judgment." The legislature of West Virginia

---

[2] *Missouri* v. *Illinois,* 200 U.S. 496 (1906).
[3] *Kansas* v. *Colorado,* 206 U.S. 46 (1907) and earlier citations.
[4] *Virginia* v. *West Virginia,* 246 U.S. 565 (1918).

meeting in special session in 1919, enacted a law providing for payment of the amount determined by the Supreme Court.

INTERSTATE COMPACTS

The Constitution of the United States expressly forbids states to enter into any treaty, alliance, or confederation. This provision was included in the Constitution to prevent states from splitting the Union by forming alliances among themselves which might be directed against the Union or against other states. However, Article I, Section 10, Paragraph 3, of the Constitution authorizes a state, with the consent of Congress, to enter into political agreements or compacts with another state or states.

Political and Nonpolitical Compacts. States may make nonpolitical compacts without the consent of Congress, but interstate compacts of a political nature must be approved by Congress before they become effective. In the final analysis Congress decides whether a compact is political in nature, and its decision is final. For example, if the boundary line between two states were in dispute, the states could agree to have the boundary line surveyed without the consent of Congress; however, a change in a boundary line would require the approval of Congress if as a result of the boundary change the number of representatives from one or both states would be altered.

The Constitution does not indicate at what stage congressional consent must be given to a compact or whether the consent must be express or implied. Congress has occasionally approved an interstate agreement before the completion of negotiations; but it usually takes a long time to secure the approval of the states concerned and of Congress, so that a compact is a slow method of securing interstate co-operation.

Types of Compacts. Prior to 1900 only seventeen interstate compacts were approved by Congress; since that time, however, over one hundred have received congressional approval. Within recent years interstate compacts have been an important means of furthering regional development. An example of this type of regional co-operation is the Port of New York Authority, which was established, by an interstate compact, to develop and operate the port facilities of New York and New Jersey. Flood control, the prevention and elimination of water pollution, the protection of wildlife, and the establishment of regional educational

30   STATE AND LOCAL GOVERNMENT

institutions are other problems which states have attempted to solve by this method. Interstate agreements may be administered by special interstate agencies created for that purpose or by regular agencies within each state covered by the compact.

FULL FAITH AND CREDIT

Article IV, Section 1, of the federal Constitution provides that "Full faith and credit shall be given in each State to the public acts, records, and judicial proceedings of every other State. And the Congress may by general laws prescribe the manner in which such acts, records, and proceedings shall be proved, and the effect thereof." The public acts mentioned here are the statutes passed by the state legislatures. The records involved are documents such as deeds, mortgages, and wills. Judicial proceedings are civil court judgments. (This provision does not include public acts, records, or judicial proceedings of foreign countries.)

With the exception of two very general laws Congress has failed to clarify the full faith and credit obligations of the states. Furthermore, the Supreme Court has only partly clarified the provision by ruling that state constitutions are public acts entitled to full faith and credit, and that the federal constitutional provision (of full faith and credit) applies only to civil acts and proceedings and not to criminal acts. It follows, then, that courts in one state are not required to enforce the criminal laws of any other state, but each state must recognize the legal acts of every other state. Decisions of courts in one state must be accepted by the courts of every other state, provided that the court which made the decision has jurisdiction over the subject matter and the parties to the dispute. The important question of jurisdiction frequently arises. Sometimes, for example, the courts of one state may refuse to recognize as valid a divorce decree of a court in another state on the ground that the court granting the divorce did not have jurisdiction over the parties, because they had not properly fulfilled the residence requirements.[5]

EQUAL PRIVILEGES AND IMMUNITIES

Article IV, Section 2, Paragraph 1, of the Constitution of the United States provides that "The citizens of each State shall be

[5] *Williams* v. *North Carolina*, 325 U.S. 226 (1945).

entitled to all privileges and immunities of citizens in the several States." Section 1 of the Fourteenth Amendment contains a similar provision: "No State shall make or enforce any law which shall abridge the privileges or immunities of citizens of the United States." The Constitution does not define "privileges and immunities," but the Supreme Court has ruled that the clause relieves citizens "from the disabilities of alienage in other states; it inhibits discriminatory legislation against them by other states; it gives them the right of free ingress into other states and egress from them; it insures to them in other states the same freedom possessed by the citizens of those states in the acquisition and enjoyment of property and in the pursuit of happiness; and it secures to them in other states the equal protection of their laws." [6] Numerous Supreme Court cases have arisen under the privileges and immunities clause, because states have attempted to favor their own citizens over citizens of other states.

Exclusion from Beneficial Services. There are, however, exceptions to the privileges and immunities clause. The Supreme Court has held that this clause does not apply to beneficial services—those resources and institutions in which the state has property rights. Thus, a state may require out-of-state students to pay a higher tuition rate at its college or university. It may exclude nonresidents from, or limit their use of, state property which it makes available to its own citizens. Hunting and fishing license fees are commonly higher for nonresidents than for residents. Also, a state may refuse to admit nonresidents to its public hospitals and refuse to provide them with public assistance.

Exclusion from Political and Other Privileges. Political privileges are also an exception to the privileges and immunities clause. A state may require that a new resident dwell in the state for a specified period of time before he will be allowed to vote or to hold office. Again, an individual may not compel a state to recognize special privileges granted to him by his home state, (e.g., the right to practice law). Through comity, privileges (e.g., recognition of expert witnesses from other states in court) may be granted.

Special Position of Corporations. The Supreme Court has said that a corporation "must dwell in the place of its creation, and can not migrate to another sovereignty." [7] Although corpora-

---

6 *Paul* v. *Virginia*, 8 Wallace 168 (1869).
7 *Bank of Augusta* v. *Earle*, 13 Peters 519 (1839).

tions are legal entities possessing many of the characteristics of natural persons, they are not considered citizens. Consequently, a state may discriminate against foreign corporations by imposing higher license fees and by levying heavier taxes on them than on domestic corporations, or by prohibiting them from conducting business in the state.[8]

INTERSTATE RENDITION

A person accused of a state crime can be tried and punished only by the state in which the crime was committed. Article IV, Section 2, Paragraph 2, of the Constitution provides for interstate rendition, or extradition. "A person charged in any State with treason, felony, or other crime found in another State shall on the demand of the executive authority of the State from which he fled, be delivered up to the State having jurisdiction of the crime." Interstate extradition is essential to prevent criminals from escaping trial simply by crossing state lines.

Procedure in Rendition. An act of Congress passed in 1793 regulates the manner of interstate rendition. The first step in the procedure is the *indictment*—a formal written accusation charging an individual with having committed a crime. Police officers in the state from which a fugitive has fled often make an informal request that the police in the asylum state hold the fugitive until necessary formalities can be completed. The governor of the requesting state then submits to the governor of the asylum state a formal request for rendition together with a certified copy of the indictment against the fugitive or a copy of the record of the trial if the fugitive has been convicted of a crime. The governor of the requesting state is required by Congressional statute to send an officer to the asylum state to bring back the fugitive.

The governor of the asylum state examines the documents concerning the accused and may call upon the attorney general for advice. He frequently holds a hearing before making a decision on the extradition request. By act of Congress, all expenses incurred in the arrest, including transportation of the fugitive, must be paid by the requesting state. Once the fugitive has been returned to the requesting state, he is subject to the normal legal procedures in criminal cases.

[8] A corporation operating within the state which chartered it is called a *domestic corporation;* a corporation operating within the state but chartered by another state is called a *foreign corporation.*

Rendition Not Mandatory. The act of Congress regulating interstate rendition appears to make it mandatory that the governor of the asylum state return the fugitive to the requesting state. However, Chief Justice Taney, speaking for the Supreme Court, said that it "is of the opinion, the words—'it shall be the duty'—were not used as mandatory and compulsory, but as declaratory of the moral duty which this compact created, when congress has provided the mode of carrying it into execution." [9] The court has ruled that it has no power to force the governor to return a fugitive from justice since no penalty is imposed for his failure to act. Consequently, the decision of a governor to return or not to return a fugitive from justice is final.

Governors have refused extradition requests when they have believed fugitives to be innocent or that fugitives would not be given fair trials in the state from which they fled. A governor occasionally has refused to return a fugitive from justice because in the past the requesting state has failed to honor a rendition request from his state. There have been relatively few occasions when governors have refused to return fugitives, but the exceptions have created ill feeling.

Other Considerations in Rendition. If a fugitive from justice commits a crime in the asylum state, he will be tried and, if convicted, must serve his sentence before being surrendered to the requesting state. Certain states allow police officers from adjoining states in hot pursuit of fugitives to pursue them across their borders.

Congress has enacted a statute which makes it a criminal offense for an individual to travel to another state or to a foreign country in order to avoid prosecution or imprisonment by a state for specified felonies. Violators of this statute are returned to the federal judicial district where the felony was alleged to have been committed and may be turned over to state officers.

INTERSTATE TRADE BARRIERS

Although the founding fathers granted to Congress (in Article I, Section 8, Paragraph 3 of the Constitution) the power to regulate interstate commerce, the states have been able through police and other powers to erect interstate trade barriers.

[9] *Kentucky* v. *Dennison*, 24 Howard 66 (1861).

Barriers Based on Police Powers. Many states have attempted to use their police powers (see Chapter 2) to discriminate against persons and goods from other states. In some places the sale of milk from outside the state has been prohibited for the ostensible purpose of protecting the health of the public. Again, certain states have enacted laws which allow only eggs produced within the state to be marked "fresh eggs." Because it is possible for heavily loaded trucks to damage highways, the police power has also been used in many states to limit the size and weight of trucks operating on their highways. Of this practice the Supreme Court declared: "The fact many states have adopted a different standard is not persuasive. The conditions under which highways must be built in the several states, their construction and the demands upon them, are not uniform. . . . The legislature, being free to exercise its own judgment, is not bound by that of other legislatures." [10]

Many acts of states under their inspection laws are legitimate; others are not. For example, California's quarantine and automobile regulations in the depression of the 1930's were but subterfuges to prevent the immigration of impoverished persons.

Barriers Based on License, Tax, and Proprietary Powers. The licensing and taxing powers are extensively used by states to erect trade barriers. Many states have enacted laws requiring itinerant vendors to obtain licenses, have imposed discriminatory license fees and taxes on foreign corporations, and have subjected chain stores to special taxes (frequently based on the total number of stores in the national chain). In states where dairying is an important occupation, special taxes have been levied on oleomargarine in order to protect dairy farmers. States purchase huge supplies of materials and hire thousands of employees, and often discriminate against other states by purchasing only supplies produced or sold within their own borders and by limiting public employment to their own citizens. Adjacent states may retaliate with similar measures against the selfish state.

Means of Removing Barriers. Interstate trade barriers may sometimes be removed by acts of Congress, judicial decisions, or reciprocal legislation. State regulation of matters such as truck transportation might be replaced by a federal law that would be

---

[10] *South Carolina State Highway Department* v. *Barnwell Brothers*, 303 U.S. 177 (1937).

uniform throughout the United States. If Congress did regulate truck transportation, it would apparently be under a moral obligation to construct and maintain highways adequate for heavy trucks.

Certain statutes of the states that restricted interstate commerce have been declared unconstitutional by the Supreme Court. For example, the court held unconstitutional a Florida cement "inspection" law, which required all imported cement to meet minimum standards of quality, because the law applied only to the imported product and not to cement produced in Florida.[11]

Through reciprocal arrangements states have extended privileges and relaxed discriminations in return for the same treatment from other states. For instance, a number of states have incorporated reciprocal provisions in their tax laws in order to protect citizens against double taxation. A familiar result of interstate comity is the general recognition of state automobile and drivers' licenses throughout the country.

INFORMAL CO-OPERATION AMONG STATES

In recent years state officers have met regularly to discuss regional and national problems and to co-operate in solving them. In almost all matters the methods used have been extraconstitutional and much progress has been made.

Uniform State Laws. Since each state may legislate for itself, diversity rather than uniformity has been typical of laws on the same problem in different states. In an effort to eliminate, or at least to reduce, conflicts among laws of the states, the National Conference of Commissioners on Uniform Laws was founded in 1892. This conference is held annually for approximately one week's duration and is attended by three commissioners (all lawyers) appointed by the governor of each state. This organization has drafted and recommended many "model" acts—especially in the fields of business and traffic laws—to the state legislatures. Finding them appropriate, many legislatures have enacted model acts into law.

Conferences of Administrative Officials. National and regional groups of administrative officers have met in recent years

---

11 *A. B. Hale,* et al. v. *Binco Trading Co., Inc.,* 306 U.S. 466 (1939).

to try to solve the problems common to the states. The Governors' Conference, which has been held annually since 1908, has had for its major purpose the bringing about of closer relations between the states. Moreover, many groups of state administrative officials, including, among others, attorneys general, purchasing agents, budget officers, and secretaries of state, have organized national associations to promote closer co-operation among the states. Co-operation has been more successfully fostered, however, by regional conferences of governors and other state officials, meeting to deal with the problems common to a particular area.

Council of State Governments. Another organization which has given impetus to the movement for interstate co-operation is the Council of State Governments. This body is composed of the commissions on interstate co-operation created by each of the states; an individual commission is commonly composed of ten legislators and five administrators. Control of the Council of State Governments is exercised by a board of managers composed of one representative from each state, eighteen ex-officio members, and ten members at large. The prime function of the Council is the researching and dispensing of information. Every two years it publishes a volume entitled *The Book of The States*,[12] which contains special studies on important state problems (administrative and electoral problems included) and up-to-date information on changes in constitutions and laws affecting state politics and administration. Furthermore, the Council of State Governments works with the National Conference of Commissioners on Uniform Laws and acts as a central secretariat for the following associations: The American Legislators Association, The Governors' Conference, The Conference of Chief Justices, The National Association of Attorneys General, The National Association of State Budget Officers, The National Legislative Conference, The National Association of State Purchasing Officials, and the Parole and Probation Compact Administrators.

---

12 *The Book of the States, 1960–1961* (Chicago: The Council of State Governments, 1960).

4

STATE CONSTITUTIONS

The state constitution is the fundamental law in the sphere of state activity; through it all offices are created and their powers are delimited. Within the restrictions imposed on state powers by the federal Constitution, each state may draft and amend its own constitution. Originally the state constitutions were designed as a limitation on the powers of the state legislatures so that citizens would be protected against legislative oppression. The early state legislatures possessed residual rather than enumerated powers, but the recent tendency has been to enumerate legislative powers as grants from the people.

DEVELOPMENT OF STATE CONSTITUTIONS

The constitutional history of states is a study in the limitation of legislative powers, democratization, and the expansion of governmental activities. Constitutions have been increased greatly in length by the insertion of provisions specifying in detail the powers of the different branches of government and permitting the expansion of state services to meet the changing requirements of society.

Original State Constitutions. The majority of the early state constitutions were drafted by the state legislatures or special assemblies and were not submitted to the people for ratification. These documents were brief, confined to the fundamentals, and, for the most part, consisted of limitations on the state legislatures, which exercised all the powers that were not denied to them nor assigned to others. They varied in length from five to sixteen pages. The New Jersey constitution of 1776 was the shortest, consisting of less than 3,000 words. The Massachusetts constitution of 1780 was the longest, containing approximately 12,000 words; it was also the first to be ratified by the voters themselves and is the oldest written constitution still in use in the world.

POPULAR SOVEREIGNTY. Early state constitutions stressed that all governmental powers emanate from the people. The government was based upon the principle of the consent of the governed. Thus, the people were to possess the power to change the constitution and, hence, the government. There was, however, an apparent inconsistency between this concept and the limitation of the suffrage to property-holders.

LEGISLATIVE SUPREMACY. The relationship of legislatures and governors under the early state constitutions is traceable to the experience of the colonists: before the Revolution the popularly elected colonial legislature was an instrument to check the tyranny of the royal governor. Following this pattern, the early state constitutions were designed to provide strong legislatures and weak governors. The first constitutions in all states except Massachusetts and New York provided for the election of the governor and other officers by the state legislature. The term of office for the governor was short, only one year in seven states. The governor of Massachusetts alone possessed the power of a qualified veto. The governor of New York could exercise the same power with the consent of his council.

SEPARATION OF POWERS. In all the early state constitutions governmental powers were distributed among three branches of government—legislative, executive, and judicial. In addition, the constitution of each state, except Pennsylvania and Georgia, provided for the division of the legislature into two houses.

A major criticism of the early state constitutions has been the difficulty of amending them. Many framers of these constitutions apparently thought that the documents would be permanent. Thus, five state constitutions made no provision for amendment; the others provided for constitutional amendment by the state legislature or by constitutional convention.

Constitutional Development, 1781-1860. During the eighty years following the Revolution nearly every state rewrote its constitution one or more times. A significant feature of constitutional revision in the states was the movement to provide checks and balances by strengthening the governorship and by limiting the power of the legislature. The impact of frontier democracy also led to extension of the suffrage and provision for the popular election of state officers.

STRENGTHENING OF EXECUTIVE POWER. Gradually, after the revolutionary period, the governor gained his independence of the legislature and was able to claim many of the prerogatives that had been denied him. His independence increased as his term of office was lengthened. Pennsylvania increased the governor's term from one year to three years in 1790; other states followed this example until all governor's terms were two, three, or four years. The governor in each state also gained strength with the disappearance of the governor's council, which had checked his authority, and the removal of the restrictions on his eligibility for re-election. A qualified veto was granted the governor by several states, including Pennsylvania in 1790, New Hampshire in 1792, Georgia in 1798, and New York in 1821. By 1825, all state governors were popularly elected.

LIMITING OF LEGISLATIVE POWER. The state legislatures did not live up to the great trust placed in them by the people (in the early state constitutions). Abuses of legislative power became more and more frequent in the nineteenth century. Under corrupt influences, many legislatures disposed of land and other properties and enacted laws granting valuable franchises to private corporations. Public confidence in the state legislatures was further lessened by the disastrous consequences of reckless financing of internal improvement projects, such as canals and roads.

As the prestige of the legislature declined, its lawmaking powers, which were relatively unrestricted by the early state constitutions, were limited by the adoption of constitutional amendments and new constitutions. Two types of limitations—*substantive* and *procedural*—were imposed upon state legislatures. Substantive limitations forbade the state legislatures to create debts and vigorously circumscribed their authority in other matters. Procedural restrictions limited the frequency and length of sessions and prescribed in great detail the methods which the legislature must follow in enacting laws.

DEMOCRATIZATION. Remarkable democratization of all institutions was an important feature of the westward movement. Class distinctions were dissolved and equality became fact on the frontier. Here the great faith in the governing ability of the common man was soon reflected in the extension of the suffrage and of local self-government, in the popular election of officers, and in the constitutional referendum.

Extension of the Suffrage. Prior to the nineteenth century there was strong agitation for the removal of property qualifications for voting and officeholding) from state constitutions. For a time taxpaying requirements were substituted, but just after the middle of the nineteenth century white manhood suffrage was practically universal in the United States.

Popular Election of State Officers. The democratic wave associated with Jacksonian democracy (1829–1837) resulted in the direct popular election of most state officials—including the governor, members of the legislature, judges, and many administrative officials. Jacksonian democracy was premised on the belief that all public officers should be elected for short terms and that their eligibility for re-election should be restricted so as to ensure rotation in office. Even judges did not escape the impact of Jacksonian democracy: in the majority of states their indirect election was gradually abandoned in favor of direct popular election; life tenure, in favor of limited terms.

Extension of Local Self-Government. A notable feature of the process of democratization was the extension of local self-government. Constitutions began to stipulate that city and county officials were to be elected locally. The Louisiana constitution of 1812 contained such a provision, but it was limited to New Orleans. The first constitution of New York vested the appointment of mayors and county officers in the governor and council; the 1821 constitution required that the mayor in all cities be appointed annually by the city council, but an amendment in 1833 provided for his direct popular election. The 1822 charters of Boston and Saint Louis, the 1824 charter of Detroit, and the 1833 charter of Baltimore called for the direct popular election of the mayor. Constitutional provisions for popular election of local officers were adopted in 1848 by Wisconsin and in 1850 by Kentucky, Michigan, and Virginia.

The Constitutional Referendum. With the exception of the Massachusetts constitution of 1780, none of the early state constitutions was submitted to the voters for ratification. Maine in 1820 followed the example of Massachusetts by requiring that the constitution drafted by the convention should be ratified in a popular referendum. Other states adopted the principle that changes proposed by conventions or legislatures must be approved by the voters before they became effective. By 1860 the

principle was well established in most of the northern states.
Constitutional Development, 1860-1900. The Civil War and
the rapid industrialization of the United States greatly influenced
constitutional development during the last four decades of the
nineteenth century. Southern states were required by Congress
to amend their constitutions to bring them into conformity with
the Thirteenth and Fourteenth Amendments. Constitutional
changes were also required to permit the expansion of state services necessary in a growing urban and industrial society.

CONSTITUTIONAL CHANGES IN THE SOUTH. At the end of the
Civil War, a provisional governor was appointed for each state
that had seceded. His duties included the calling of a constitutional convention to be composed of delegates selected by citizens
who had not participated in the rebellion. The conventions were
required to prepare the states for readmission to representation
in Congress and other federal privileges. They were also required
to ratify the Fourteenth Amendment and to remove from the
former constitutions all discriminations among different classes
of citizens. Provisions for Negro suffrage and for a system of public schools were characteristic of post-bellum constitutions in the
South. It was not until 1870 that all the seceded states were re-
stored to their full privileges in the Union.

Beginning about 1890 another movement to revise state constitutions spread throughout the South. Its most noteworthy
characteristic was the restriction of Negro suffrage. The southern
states could not, of course, discriminate on the basis of "race,
color, or previous condition of servitude," for discriminations on
these grounds had been outlawed by the Fifteenth Amendment.
The southerners attempted to secure the same results by reviving
taxpaying qualifications, by imposing excessively long residence
requirements, and by requiring voters to pass tests of literacy or
of "understanding" the state constitution. To salvage the suffrage
for many illiterate whites, several constitutions provided that
former soldiers and their descendants might be permanently
registered to vote—the notorious "grandfather clause" (p. 53).

CONSTITUTIONAL CHANGES IN THE NORTH. The new constitutions adopted in the North during this period were characterized
by provisions for state regulatory activities and for additional
state services. The railroads, which had acquired a virtual monopoly of transportation, were subjected to regulation of rates and

services. Activities of other corporations were limited in order to control or break up existing monopolies. The development of the germ theory of disease necessitated comprehensive reorganization of public health services. Rapid urbanization caused more exact definitions of the relations between the state and municipal corporations. Social welfare activities were expanded to include the establishment of charity boards. State activities in the fields of education and agriculture were greatly extended.

Constitutional Development since 1900. During the present century only a few states have adopted wholly new constitutions, but constitutional change has proceeded by other means. Several states, notably Massachusetts and New York, have made large-scale revisions in the texts of existing constitutions, and other states have added one or more amendments nearly every year. Two innovations are of special importance.

The first was the adoption of constitutional provisions for the statutory initiative and referendum, beginning with South Dakota in 1898. This innovation is based on the principle that the electorate should have the right to enact laws directly and to veto laws passed by the legislature. Direct legislation resulted from continued dissatisfaction with the performance of state legislatures, which had often refused to enact laws of urgent public importance but had enacted laws to promote the interests of pressure groups at the expense of the public. (See Chapter 7 for a more detailed discussion of the initiative and referendum.)

The second important innovation was the movement to centralize the executive power of the state in the hands of a strong governor. It began in Illinois in 1917 and has since made remarkable gains. In many states the governor has been made the chief executive in fact as well as in name. Many elective state executives have disappeared or have lost their essential powers; they have been replaced by officers appointed by the governor and subject to removal by him.

STATE CONSTITUTIONS TODAY

The average state constitution is presently more than seventy-five years old. If confined to fundamental principles, an old constitution is still a usable framework of state government. But, a state constitution which assumes the character of a detailed legal code hinders the future development of the state government.

Tendency toward Excessive Detail. The recent trend, especially in southern and western states, has been toward longer and more detailed constitutions. The New Jersey constitution, which became effective in January, 1948, is an exception in that it is only 12,500 words in length. Another exception is the brief Alaska constitution adopted in 1956. The constitution of Vermont (1793) is the shortest—8,000 words long—whereas the constitution of Louisiana (1921) is the longest—over 201,000 words long. In 1960 the state constitutions averaged about 15,000 words in length, almost twice the length of the federal Constitution. Long constitutions usually need frequent amendment, because they contain many ephemeral provisions. (See Appendix, pp. 246f.) Often included is material of a statutory nature such as detailed stipulations of the duties and salaries of officials and regulations concerning economic and social affairs. Such matters are best entrusted to legislatures for change as the need arises.

Arrangement of Contents. Though state constitutions differ greatly in length and provisions, the basic arrangement of their contents is everywhere similar. In contrast to the federal Constitution, the state constitutions place the bill of rights in the most prominent position.

PREAMBLE. The *preamble* is a statement of the sources of the constitution and the reasons for its adoption. It is usually not regarded as part of the constitutional law of the state. The preambles of the Massachusetts constitution (1780) and the federal Constitution have served as models for a number of states. Only three state constitutions—those of New Hampshire, Vermont, and West Virginia—do not contain preambles.

BILL OF RIGHTS. The preamble is followed by an extensive declaration of the rights of citizens. This *bill of rights* is designed to protect what the authors of the Declaration of Independence called "life, liberty, and the pursuit of happiness." For example, the constitution of Alaska provides "that all persons have a natural right to life, liberty and the pursuit of happiness, and the enjoyment of the rewards of their own industry." This section in older constitutions commonly includes a statement of the political theories that were generally accepted in the late eighteenth century.

Among other matters, bills of rights guarantee indictment by a grand jury, trial by jury, a speedy trial, and freedom of speech, press, assembly, and religion. Some constitutions forbid the establishment of a state church or the appropriation of money to aid any religious group or sectarian institution. Other prohibitions include bills of attainder, ex post facto laws, laws impairing the obligation of contract, excessive bail, imprisonment for debt, double jeopardy, unreasonable searches and seizures, and the taking of private property for public use without just compensation. The bill of rights in certain constitutions contains a provision to the effect that the enumeration of rights and privileges shall not be construed to impair or deny others retained by the people. The courts have held that the freedoms guaranteed in state constitutions are relative and not absolute. Consequently, limitations can and have been placed on them. Generally the guarantees and prohibitions of state constitutions are similar to those found in the Constitution of the United States, which was based on existing state bills of rights. As a result, the rights of citizens are doubly protected against federal and state infringement.

BODY. The *body* is the heart of the constitution and, among other things, outlines the framework and powers of the legislative, executive, and judicial branches of the government and provides for local government. It sets forth the qualifications, duties, methods of selection, and terms of office of state officials, and it also sets forth the limits on their powers and their methods of operation. Also specified are legislative immunity and the procedure for filling vacancies, as well as the impeachment procedure. Some state constitutions specify the procedure to be followed by the legislature in enacting a law. The Nebraska constitution, for example, provides that "Every bill and resolution shall be read by title when introduced, and a printed copy thereof provided for the use of each member and the bill and all amendments thereto shall be printed and read at large before the vote is taken upon its final passage." Articles customarily cover the suffrage and elections, stipulating the qualifications for voting and the dates of election. The article on local government spells out the forms and powers of local governments, as well as the types of charters, and may make provisions for local home rule.

Other articles in the body of many constitutions treat major functions of the state government, such as the development or improvement of agriculture, education, finance, public health, and social welfare. Also found are general principles regulating corporations and relatively complicated provisions relating to the public debt, revenue, and taxation.

AMENDING ARTICLE. Each current state constitution contains an *amending article,* which states the procedure by which the constitution may be formally amended. Often the amending article provides for two, or even three, different means of changing the constitution.

THE SCHEDULE. The *schedule* is the implementing article of the state constitution. It specifies the method, the time, and the place of establishing the government which is provided by the constitution.

AMENDMENTS. Finally, it must be recognized that a great part of the constitutional law of the states consists of *amendments* which have been appended to the original text, and which add to, subtract from, or otherwise change its provisions.

METHODS OF AMENDMENT

In some states the amending articles are easily implemented, whereas in other states almost insurmountable barriers in the amending articles prevent desirable changes. The federal Constitution has been amended only twenty-three times since 1787, but many state constitutions have been amended much more frequently. For instances, the constitutions of California (1879) and Louisiana (1921) have 372 and 376 amendments, respectively. On the other hand, the constitution of Tennessee (1870) was not amended until 1953, at which time eight amendments were adopted.

The formal procedure for changing state constitutions varies greatly among different states. Four methods of proposing amendments to state constitutions are now in use: by constitutional convention, by proposal in the legislature, by constitutional commission, and by popular initiative. In all but a few states popular approval in a constitutional referendum is necessary before a proposed amendment becomes effective.

Constitutional Convention Proposal. Originally a constitutional convention could make a constitution on behalf of the people; now it has developed, with few exceptions, into a body which only proposes a new constitution or parts of a constitution for popular approval.

In thirty-eight states the constitution provides for the calling of a constitutional convention to propose amendments when extensive constitutional revision is desired. In New Hampshire this is the only legal method of amendment. The constitutions of Georgia and Maine permit the legislature by a two-thirds vote of each house to call such a convention. Thirty states require both legislative action and a popular referendum in order to call a constitutional convention. The requisite popular vote in seventeen of these states is a majority of those voting in the election, and in the other thirteen states it is a majority of those who vote on the question of calling a convention. The constitutions of five states require that the question of convoking a constitutional convention be periodically submitted to the voters, at intervals ranging from seven to twenty years.

Although sometimes elected at large, delegates to a constitutional convention are commonly elected by districts. (Ballots in these elections may be partisan or non-partisan.) Prior to the convention, much information—in the form of judicial interpretations of the constitution, copies of the constitutions of other states, and other important documents—is assembled for use by the delegates. The convention opens with the election of officers, the adoption of the rules of procedure, and the establishment of committees. Hearings are conducted by the committees which report their recommendations to the delegates. Suggestions for important changes are usually debated on the floor of the convention; voting may often be by roll-call.

The proposed constitutions or amendments are customarily submitted to the voters for ratification, but only in twenty-one states is such action mandatory. The 1921 constitution of Louisiana, for example, was not placed before the voters for confirmation. In sixteen states approval is secured by a majority of the electorate voting on the intended amendments; in five states by a majority of the electorate voting in the election. The constitution of New Hampshire requires that amendments must be accepted by a two-thirds vote in town meetings.

Proposal of amendments by a constitutional convention rather than by the state legislature can be supported on two grounds: (1) Public opinion on constitutional change is more accurately reflected in a convention especially chosen for the purpose of proposing amendments. (2) The convention can give more concentrated attention to constitutional problems than can the legislature, whose main function is lawmaking. The principal disadvantage of the convention method is its expense; this objection generally rules out the holding of a convention for the consideration of one or only a few amendments.

Legislative Proposal. Constitutional amendment by legislative action is relatively simple, yet the requirement of extraordinary votes for approval reduces the danger of radical changes.

In forty-five states the constitution may be amended by a legislative proposal ratified by a popular vote in a referendum. The size of the legislative and popular vote required to complete the amending process varies from state to state: In twenty-seven states a two-thirds or three-fifths vote of the legislature and a simple popular majority vote are required; in nine states a simple majority of the legislature and of the citizens voting on the amendment is sufficient; in nine other states a simple majority of the legislature at two successive sessions followed by a simple majority (three-fifths in Rhode Island) in the popular referendum is necessary.

The constitution of Delaware may be amended by a two-thirds vote of the members elected in two successive sessions of the legislature; in order to defeat an amendment the voters must choose legislators to replace the members who voted for it. The constitutions of Mississippi and South Carolina require the legislature to submit proposed amendments to the electorate between the two legislative sessions at which the amendments are to be considered; however, the popular vote is only advisory, for the legislature may adopt an amendment that has been rejected by the voters, or vice versa.

Constitutional Commission. Occasionally during the past century commissions have been created as agencies of the legislature to propose constitutional amendments. A *constitutional commission* is a small group of from three to thirty-five persons appointed by the governor and having legislative authorization to recommend constitutional amendments. Since a commission of this sort is not provided for in any state constitution, its reports serve only as the basis for amendments to be proposed in the manner stated in the constitution.

A constitutional commission has four advantages over a constitutional convention: (1) it is less expensive, (2) its smaller

membership permits informal discussion instead of formal debate, (3) its membership is likely to be composed of constitutional
experts, and (4) it is less subject to popular pressures than an
elected body. On the other hand, the constitutional commission
suffers from two principal disadvantages: (1) Its appointment by
the governor is less democratic than a popularly elected constitutional convention; in this way, it may not be truly representative
of the people and may be composed of individuals having the
same political philosophy. (2) Since the commission derives its
life from the legislature, its freedom of action may be limited by
the necessity of pleasing the legislature.

Popular Initiative. More than a quarter of the states allow
constitutional amendment by popular initiative, as well as by
legislative proposal. On petition of a certain number or percentage of the voters (usually 8 to 15 per cent), the proposed amendment must be placed before the voters. Ratification is commonly
by a majority of those voting on the amendment, but a few
states require the approval of a majority of those voting in a
general election. Amendment by popular initiative has been used
extensively in California and Oregon.

It is a common error to think of a constitution as a written
document consisting of a number of pages of printed text. In
actual usage many provisions of written constitutions are found
to be inapplicable and become mere nullities. Then, too, the
legislatures may enact statutes which are just as fundamental as
many provisions of written constitutions. Though the supreme
court of each state is more strict than the federal Supreme Court
in holding members of the legislature and executive officers to
the terms of the written document, court decisions are often a
potent means of constitutional alteration. The living constitution consists of *applicable* provisions of the written document as
formally amended and as modified by usage, by statute, and by
judicial decisions.

THE MODEL STATE CONSTITUTION

In order to provide a critique of existing state constitutions
and suggestions to states contemplating a constitutional revision,
the National Municipal League's Committee on State Government has drafted a model state constitution. (See Appendix, pp.
296ff.) The draft incorporates many of the best provisions of ex-

isting constitutions together with recent proposals of scholars for reforms in state government. In contrast to the trend toward detailed constitutions, the model state constitution emphasizes fundamentals.

Among the more distinctive features of the model state constitution is the provision that the legislature is to be a unicameral body, the members of which are to be elected for terms of two years; executive authority is to be concentrated in the governor. The judiciary article provides for the appointment of the chief judge and the associate judges of the supreme, appellate, and general courts by the governor with legislative approval and for initial terms of seven years. Upon reappointment judges serve during good behavior.

The model state constitution provides for three methods of proposing amendments: by the legislature, by a convention, or by the initiative. Before submitting the question or holding a constitutional convention to the voters, the legislature is required to create a special preparatory commission whose purpose it is to assemble information on constitutional questions and to inform the voters. If the voters authorize a convention, the preparatory commission is continued in order to advise the convention during its deliberations. Whether amendments are proposed by the legislature, by initiative, or by convention, they must be promptly submitted to the electorate, and to take effect they must be approved by a majority of those voting on the amendments.

5

SUFFRAGE AND ELECTIONS

A widespread suffrage is everywhere considered the most fundamental characteristic of a democratic society. Government by the people cannot be said to exist unless all persons competent to participate intelligently in the choice of officials are admitted to the suffrage. No one should be deprived of the vote on account of his race, religion, or economic status. But a widespread (or universal) suffrage is of little value unless elections are free and honestly administered. When voters are marshaled to the polls in huge numbers merely to approve an official slate, as in a dictatorship, only a travesty of popular government exists. It is essential in a true democracy that voters have a choice between real alternatives, that they exercise their choice without fear or compulsion from either public officials or private persons, and that elections be honestly administered and the votes fairly counted. (See Appendix, pp. 260–261.)

THE SUFFRAGE

Suffrage is the franchise, or privilege, granted by the state to individuals which allows them to elect candidates for office and approve or disapprove of proposals submitted to them. Through the suffrage franchise individuals become participants in the governmental process. Too often the suffrage is regarded as a means by which individuals may protect or promote their own private interests. It should rather be regarded as a solemn duty to be fulfilled for the benefit of the society to which they belong.

Because the framers of the federal Constitution were unable to agree on a uniform national suffrage, they left the suffrage to the determination of the individual states. Each state has complete discretion to admit or exclude persons from the suffrage, subject to the following restrictions: Members of the House of Representatives must be elected by those persons who are eligible to vote for the members of the most numerous branch of the state legislature; the Seventeenth Amendment contains the same requirement for those who vote for senators. Article II of the Constitution also provides that presidential electors may be chosen in the manner determined by the state legislatures. Under these provisions presidential electors and congressmen might be chosen by different voters. For example, Illinois in 1913 allowed women to vote for presidential candidates, but denied them the privilege of voting for state and national representatives. Nearly all the qualifications for voting for local, state, and national officers are set forth in state constitutions.

Extension of the Suffrage. The early American colonists brought with them the prevailing English theory that the suffrage should be exercised by those who had a "stake in society." At first only holders of real estate and, in some colonies, members of the established churches were enfranchised. In the colonial and revolutionary periods the suffrage was extended by degrees to persons who held a considerable amount of personal property. But, it is estimated that by 1789 only about 2 per cent of the adult male population was legally entitled to vote.

Soon a movement to liberalize the suffrage began. Its proponents asserted that persons who supported the government by paying taxes had a stake in society, too. A taxpaying qualification was substituted for the property qualification by New Hampshire in 1782, by Georgia in 1789, by Connecticut in 1818, by Massachusetts and New York in 1821, and by Rhode Island in 1842. Next, it was argued that taxpayers were not limited to those whose names appeared on the assessor's rolls, for nearly everyone who rented a house or consumed taxable articles paid taxes indirectly. It was also urged that veterans of the Revolutionary and Indian wars had made a contribution to society by their service and, therefore, had earned the vote. Finally, many advocates of suffrage extension boldly asserted that the suffrage is a natural right of all men that no government should withhold.

WHITE MANHOOD SUFFRAGE. More than fifty years of effort was required before the agitation for male suffrage extension was completely successful. When Vermont entered the Union in 1791, her constitution provided the suffrage for all men of "quiet and peaceable behavior." A year later, the new state of Kentucky allowed suffrage for all men who met a residence requirement of two years. New Hampshire and Georgia abolished their taxpaying requirements in 1792 and 1798, respectively. In 1809, Maryland granted manhood suffrage without property-owning or taxpaying qualifications. In 1821 New York enfranchised all white residents of one year who had paid taxes or served in the state militia, and all others who had lived in the state for three years; it retained the property qualification only for Negroes. In many others and particularly frontier states the movement toward full manhood suffrage made rapid progress until, by 1860, property-owning requirements had disappeared everywhere and taxpaying prerequisities were negligible.

Before white manhood suffrage was a reality, however, a reaction set in. Alarmed at the rapid increase of illiterate immigrants in their populations, Connecticut in 1855 and Massachusetts in 1857 amended their constitutions by requiring that all voters be able to read.

NEGRO SUFFRAGE. Prior to the Civil War, few Negroes were enfranchised. Maine, New Hampshire, Vermont, Massachusetts, and Rhode Island had granted the suffrage to Negroes; in New York a Negro could vote if he possessed a freehold. Until 1835 North Carolina permitted free Negroes who met other requirements to vote. Immediately after the Civil War, the movement to extend the franchise to Negroes gathered momentum and was implemented by two constitutional amendments. The Fourteenth Amendment, ratified in 1868, provided that a state's representation in the House of Representatives could be reduced in the proportion that it denied the suffrage to male citizens twenty-one years of age or over. The Fifteenth Amendment, ratified in 1870, prohibited the United States or any state from denying the suffrage on account of race, color, or previous condition of servitude. The latter amendment was designed to enable Negroes in the South to protect their newly acquired freedom.

Neither radical Republicans in Congress who proposed the Fifteenth Amendment nor the members of the state legislatures who ratified it had foreseen the political effects of the sudden enfranchisement of illiterate former slaves. As a result, corruption became common in state governments of the South. Public funds were squandered or pocketed by unscrupulous "carpetbaggers" who controlled the Negro vote. Southerners at first sought to alleviate the evils by equally unscrupulous methods. Members of the Ku Klux Klan terrorized Negroes to keep them from the polls, and others stuffed ballot boxes to insure white majorities. Beginning about 1890, the southern states sought more legal methods of disenfranchisement. They revived the taxpaying qualification by requiring a person to present poll tax receipts, sometimes for many years, before he could vote at an election, lengthened the residence requirement to debar transient Negroes, and introduced the literacy test, which required a voter to read or at least "understand" the Constitution. These provisions struck at white, as well as colored, voters. In order to preserve the suffrage for illiterate whites, southerners invented the notorious "grandfather clause" which permitted the permanent registration of all persons who had themselves served in the Army of the United States or the Confederate Army or were descendants of veterans.[1] Negroes were effectively excluded from the nominating process by the "white primary," which debarred Negroes from the Democratic party's primary elections. The white primary was finally declared unconstitutional in 1944.[2]

WOMAN SUFFRAGE. The movement for woman suffrage began in the period of Jacksonian democracy (1829–1837). Advocates of extending the franchise to women argued that: (1) under the theory of natural rights women are as much entitled to political privileges as men; (2) women possess as much natural intelligence as men; (3) women are especially interested in educational opportunities and moral conditions which affect the rearing of their children; and (4) the enfranchisement of women would improve the moral tone of politics. Against woman suffrage it was argued that (1) woman's place is in the home and not in the rough-and-tumble game of politics; (2) women lack the experience and ca-

---

[1] The grandfather clause was declared unconstitutional by the Supreme Court in the case of *Guinn* v. *United States*, 238 U.S. 347 (1915).

[2] An act of the Texas legislature excluding Negroes from the Democratic party's primary was declared unconstitutional because it violated the equal protection clause of the Fourteenth Amendment (*Nixon* v. *Herndon*, 237 U.S. 536 [1927]). The same fate befell a statute which gave the state party's committee power to determine party membership since the committee was held to act as agent of the state (*Nixon* v. *Condon*, 286 U.S. 73 [1932]). When Texas repealed its laws thus making it possible for the party to act in a private capacity, the party's exclusion of Negroes from membership was at first upheld (*Grovey* v. *Townsend*, 295 U.S. 45 [1935]). This exclusion was later declared unconstitutional because a state could not cast its laws in such fashion as to allow a private organization to practice racial discrimination in elections (*Smith* v. *Allwright*, 321 U.S. 649 [1944]).

pacity to evaluate public issues; (3) the enfranchisement of women would only increase the expense of elections without affecting the result, because they would vote as did their husbands and fathers; and (4) most women did not want the suffrage and would not vote if they had the privilege.

During the nineteenth century the woman suffrage movement made little progress. Kentucky, in 1838, allowed widows and unmarried women whose property was assessed for taxation to vote in school elections. In 1861 Kansas permitted all women to vote in school elections; this example was followed before 1880 by Colorado, Massachusetts, Michigan, Minnesota, and New Hampshire. The territory of Wyoming allowed women to vote in all elections in 1869 and continued the provision for universal suffrage when it was admitted as a state in 1890. The twentieth century witnessed a redoubled effort by advocates of woman suffrage, and many new conditions favored their cause: (1) statistics showed that a greater number of girls than boys finished grade school and high school; (2) many women owned property and managed it successfully; (3) during World War I the number of women wage earners vastly increased. Public demonstrations in many cities and the picketing of the White House convinced the doubtful that women did, indeed, want the suffrage. In twenty-nine states, by 1918, women had gained the suffrage for some or all elections. The Nineteenth Amendment, which forbade suffrage discriminations on account of sex, was ratified in time for women in every state to vote in the presidential election of 1920.

Present Suffrage Requirements. Although they vary in detail, the basic suffrage requirements are similar in every state. With four exceptions they are the same for national, state, and local elections. (See Appendix, "Qualifications for Voting in the States and Territories," pp. 250–253.)

CITIZENSHIP QUALIFICATIONS. Although a few states formerly permitted aliens with first papers to vote, all states now restrict suffrage to citizens of the United States. In six states a foreign-born person is eligible to vote after a specified period of time following his naturalization—one month in Pennsylvania; ninety days in California, Minnesota, New York, and Utah; and five years in Connecticut.

AGE REQUIREMENTS. Forty-six states require an individual to be twenty-one years of age before he is permitted to vote in general elections. Georgia and Kentucky lowered the voting age to eighteen in 1943 and 1955, respectively. The Alaska constitution, adopted in 1956, and the Hawaii constitution, adopted in 1950, set the voting age at nineteen and twenty years of age, respectively. Proponents of lowering the voting age to eighteen argue that a man who is old enough to fight for his country is old enough to vote, and that good citizenship is promoted by early participation in elections.

RESIDENCE REQUIREMENTS. Residence requirements for voting are considered essential so that (1) voters may become familiar with new political conditions and (2) time may be allowed for proper registration of voters in order to prevent gross election frauds. Every state now insists on a period of residence, which varies from six months to two years in the state, thirty days to one year in the county or town, and ten days to four months in the election precinct.

EDUCATION OR LITERACY REQUIREMENTS. At present, nineteen states about equally distributed in the Northeast, the West, and the South have literacy requirements. Through a literacy test, a voter is asked to demonstrate his reading or writing ability or his understanding of the state constitution before he is allowed to vote. The literacy test in Hawaii is either in English or in the Hawaiian language. In several of the states a satisfactory alternative to a literacy test is the presentation of a grammar school certificate or a high school diploma. The New York law of 1923 placed the administration of educational qualifications and literacy tests in the hands of the school authorities, rather than in election boards. One of the principal advantages of the New York system is uniformity and fairness in literacy test administration. In the South discriminatory administration of literacy tests by election officers is a common method of preventing Negroes from voting.

OTHER QUALIFICATIONS. In Alabama, Arkansas, Mississippi, Texas, and Virginia, the payment of a poll tax of one to two dollars is the prerequisite for voting in state and local elections. Other states levy such a tax, but payment of it is not a requisite for voting. The poll tax has been used extensively in the South in order to disfranchise Negroes and poor whites.

States commonly disfranchise felons, idiots, insane persons, immoral persons, and paupers. Less commonly, exclusion from vot-

ing extends to persons convicted of bribery or other election offenses, as well as to deserters from the armed forces.

Problems of Suffrage. There has been little popular response
to suggestions that the Constitution of the United States be
amended so as to require a uniform national suffrage. The lack of
a uniform national suffrage has been decried mainly by citizens who
find themselves disfranchised when they move from one state to
another. More numerous condemnations have been based on the
continued existence of the poll tax in five southern states and
the unfair administration of literacy tests by southern election
boards. The House of Representatives has on three occasions approved bills to outlaw the poll tax, but—possibly owing to constitutional reasons—the senate has refused to concur. Neither
house has sought to invoke the provisions of the Fourteenth
Amendment by which the representation in Congress of states
denying the franchise to some of their citizens could be reduced.
By such action Congress could also strike at the literacy requirements of New York, California, Massachusetts, and the southern
states. Conditions could be at least improved if Congress and the
states placed the administration of literacy tests in the hands of
the educational authorities. Advocacy of lowering the minimum
age for voting to eighteen has achieved comparatively little
success.

ELECTIONS

An *election* is the choice by qualified voters of an individual
to hold a public office. Normally several elections occur at the
same time. The regulation of elections to exclude those who
are disqualified, prevent fraud and intimidation, and insure an
accurate count of the votes is the subject of numerous detailed
laws.

Constitutional and Legal Provisions. The Constitution of the
United States specifically grants to Congress the power to fix
the time at which federal officials are to be chosen. Congress, in addition to fixing a uniform date for national elections, has passed
laws requiring voting by ballot and prohibiting bribery, intimidation, the excessive use of money, and other corrupt practices. Subject to the foregoing limitations, the states have complete discretion in enacting election laws and in the conduct of
elections. The provisions for state and local elections in the state

constitutions are similar, though New Jersey stipulates that "all questions submitted to the people of the entire state shall be voted on at general elections"; and Nebraska requires that "all votes shall be by ballot." Other constitutional provisions are permissive; in Alaska, for example ,"the legislature may provide a system of permanent registration for voters."

Election Administration. The conduct of an election necessitates careful planning and elaborate organization. Though a few states have established centralized control over nearly all the procedures, the responsibility for election administration is usually dispersed among state, county or town, and precinct officers.

STATE OFFICIALS. The secretary of state or a state election commission is charged with the general supervision of elections. This function includes the determination of whether candidates are eligible for the offices they seek and whether or not they have been properly nominated; in several states it extends to the registration of voters, and the preparation of the ballot and the letting of contracts for printing it. In Kansas, Louisiana, Maryland, Missouri, New Jersey, and Pennsylvania the governor may appoint election officials in the more heavily populated cities and counties. After the election a state authority canvasses the returns and issues certificates of election to successful candidates. The secretary of state is the official custodian of election returns.

COUNTY OR TOWN OFFICIALS. The administration of elections is entrusted to the boards which conduct county or town governments, or in a few states and large cities to specially constituted boards of election commissioners. The county, town, or city board divides the area into election precincts; designates a polling place in a public or private building; appoints registrars, precinct boards, and clerks; provides for the printing and distribution of ballots, or for voting machines; and makes a preliminary canvass of the returns.

PRECINCT OFFICIALS. In each precinct (an area in which from 150 to 1,500 persons vote) there is a precinct election board consisting of from two to four persons, one or two of whom are usually affiliated with the minority party. This board reviews the qualifications of voters before admitting them to polling booths and may directly challenge a voter. Each political party is entitled by law to have in each precinct one watcher, who may dispute the right of any voter to participate; the board summarily makes a decision when a voter is challenged. At the close of the election the precinct board in most places is responsible for counting the votes—a long and exacting task when paper ballots are used. In some states, separate counting boards are provided. The precinct board is assisted by one or more clerks.

Registration of Voters. Registration prior to elections was devised in order to eliminate the abuses of colonization (introduction of voters from other areas), repeating (voting more than once), and personation (voting in the name of another person). It provides a means by which police officers and party workers can check the lists of voters before an election and prepare to challenge those who lack one or more of the requirements for voting. Massachusetts, in 1800, was the first state to establish a voter registration system. Now every state, except Arkansas and Texas, which rely on poll-tax receipts, has a system of either periodic or permanent registration.

PERIODIC REGISTRATION. Under the system of periodic registration voters are registered before every election or at somewhat longer specified intervals. This is accomplished in two ways: (1) the voter appears in person before the precinct board, or (2) registrars are employed to canvass the district and list the names of qualified persons. The periodic system of registration is expensive, inconvenient to voters, and subject to abuses from the carelessness or partisanship of temporary registration workers and boards.

PERMANENT REGISTRATION. Thirty-four states now use permanent registration in all areas; eleven states, in some areas. Under this system the voter registers only once, and his name remains on the list until he dies, moves away, or fails to vote. The system is administered by a permanent office which constantly checks the voting lists, using vital statistics, records of public utility companies, and similar sources. If a voter changes his residence (within the state) he has only to notify the office, and his registration is changed to the proper precinct. Permanent registration provides fewer opportunities for fraud than does periodic registration.

Ballots and Voting Machines. In the early days of America elections were often conducted under the *viva voce* system in which a voter publicly announced his choice among candidates. This procedure encouraged bribery—the vote buyer could be sure that what he paid for was delivered—and subjected voters to intimidation. Though *viva voce* voting persisted in Kentucky until 1891, most of the states by 1850 required paper ballots. These were generally printed and distributed by each party and contained only the names of the party's candidates. Since the voter obtained his ballot outside the polling place it was often possible to determine for which party he voted.

AUSTRALIAN BALLOT AND VARIATIONS. In 1888 the Kentucky legislature provided for the Australian ballot in municipal elections in Louisville, and its use rapidly spread to other states. The *Australian ballot* has four characteristics which previous ballots lacked: (1) it is prepared by a public authority; (2) it contains the names of candidates regularly nominated by all political parties, and usually blank spaces in which the voter can write other names; (3) it is distributed only within the polling place; and (4) it must be marked in secret and deposited in the ballot box before the voter leaves the polls. The Australian ballot appears in different forms in various states. In the *Indiana* or *party-column ballot* the names of party candidates are arranged in columns and a party circle is usually placed at the top of each column. By placing an X in the party circle a voter may vote a straight party ticket; by placing an X opposite the name of each candidate he prefers, he may split his ticket. In the *Massachusetts* or *office-block ballot* the names of all candidates for each office are grouped together, and the voter must mark each of his preferences separately. Although the Indiana ballot has been more widely used, the Massachusetts ballot is preferred by most political scientists because it is conducive to independent voting.

VOTING MACHINES. The first use of voting machines was in Lockport, N. Y., in 1892. At present their use is mandatory or optional in forty-five states, though they have actually been used in only thirty-eight states.

When a voter enters a booth containing a voting machine, the closing of a curtain behind him unlocks the machine. Before him on the machine are the titles of referendum proposals and the names of candidates arranged by office and party. Above each proposal and each name is a small lever which the voter may pull down to register his choice. When he has finished, he pulls a large lever which simultaneously counts all his votes, locks the machine, and opens the curtain. The voting machine is accurate, saves voting time, and can be tampered with only by collusion among members of the precinct board. When election day ends, the members of the board have only to unlock a panel at the back and read the total number of votes cast for each proposal and candidate. The chief objection to voting machines is their initial cost, but over the years they save substantial sums of money that would otherwise be spent for printing and counting paper ballots.

Contested Elections. A candidate who has been defeated by a narrow margin may file notice of a contest and demand a recount. If his demand is granted, the courts, legislative committees, or election authorities hear charges of fraud or irregularities in the precincts, and the ballots are examined and recounted. The process is costly and may consume many weeks or months. Sometimes the expense is assessed against the candidate.

Corrupt Practices. Both the Congress and the state legislatures have passed laws prohibiting corrupt practices in elections. The early laws prohibited bribery, personation, betting on elections, and the payment of one voter's poll tax by another person. All civil service reform acts have forbidden the assessing of officeholders as a means of raising party campaign funds.

More recent statutes have been directed at curbing the excessive use of money in elections. They have established the maximum permissible amount of campaign contributions and expenditures and often restrict the source of campaign funds. Thirty states outlaw campaign contributions by corporations; Colorado, Indiana, New Hampshire, and Wisconsin forbid contributions by labor unions, but allow contributions by all union members as individuals. Twenty-nine states restrict the purpose for which money may be spent; thirty-one, the total expenditure of each candidate. Eighteen states limit the amount spent in behalf of a candidate, and most laws prohibit expenditures for treating voters and transporting them to the polls.

The enforcement of corrupt practices laws leaves much to be desired. Many states demand that candidates or their managers (in a few states, all persons active in the campaign) file statements of campaign receipts and disbursements. Reports of receipts are required of party committees in twenty-eight states and of candidates in forty-three states. During election campaigns candidates may sometimes denounce the financial reports of their rivals in order to impress the voters. After the election, however, these records are usually of little interest to anyone. Although the reports of receipts and disbursements are often incomplete and difficult to understand, candidates and members of party committees are rarely prosecuted and the penalty of loss of office is seldom applied.

Failure to Vote. On a nation-wide average only about 50 per cent of Americans of voting age participate in elections. This is far less than in democratic European countries, where often more than 80 per cent of the qualified voters attend the polls. Only in a few of our northern states, which have vigorous two-party systems, is this high percentage of participation frequently reached. At the opposite extreme are the one-party states in the South, where few citizens vote in the general elections and not many more in the primaries.

Surveys indicate these reasons as the most common causes of nonvoting: illness, absence from home on election day, congestion at polling places, disqualification on account of literacy or residence requirements, disgust with party politics, inability to distinguish any difference between opposing parties or candidates, and willingness to allow others to determine the results. Certain of these excuses illustrate a general political apathy among Americans. This apathy is greater in some groups and in certain types of elections than others. Men vote more often than women, and older voters participate more frequently than younger ones. Those with high incomes and a high level of education participate more often in elections than those with little education and low incomes. National elections bring out more voters than state elections, and local elections show the least participation. More votes are cast for candidates than on measures proposed by means of the initiative and referendum.

SEPARATION OF ELECTIONS. Many states have recently decided that elections for state offices should occur midway between presidential elections and that municipal elections should be held only in odd-numbered years. In justification, it is argued that national issues and candidates absorb the attention of voters, with the result that state and local issues are neglected; there is also the fear that the latter are often determined by straight party voting. Despite the lower participation that results, the movement for the separation of elections is apparently growing.

SHORT-BALLOT MOVEMENT. In the early nineteenth century Jacksonian democracy was responsible for measurably increasing the number of elected officers. At the state level they included many with almost purely administrative duties, among them the treasurer, the comptroller, and the superintendent of education. At the county level they added the sheriff, the coroner, the assessors, recorders, clerks of courts, and others. On numerous occasions the ballot has contained the names of two hundred or more candidates as well as several referendum proposals. Obviously the average voter has faced an almost impossible task in attempting to make intelligent choices among so many candidates.

In 1909 the National Short Ballot Association was formed for the purpose of reducing the number of elective offices. It has called attention to four points regarding lesser offices: (1) Most state and local offices involve the use of little political discretion and present no issues on which candidates may appeal for votes. (2) The qualifications for these offices are personal and technical, and since most voters are unacquainted with the candidates and cannot properly judge their technical qualifications, these offices should be appointive. (3) In this situation, the appointing officer possesses the resources to determine and to evaluate the technical qualifications of applicants and may be held responsible for the conduct of those whom he appoints. (4) Elective offices should be confined to those which determine policies, including the governor, members of the state legislature, members of the county board, and the city council. In spite of the cogency of these arguments the short ballot has met with only partial success. Its greatest successes have been attained in council-manager cities (where the council appoints the manager, and the manager appoints the other officers).

ABSENTEE VOTING. During the Civil War several northern states permitted soldiers who were in the field to vote. In World War II absentee ballots were provided under national and state laws. In 1896 Vermont became the first state to permit civilians to vote *in absentia;* its example has been followed in all the states except Alabama, Louisiana, Mississippi, New Mexico, and South Carolina.

Absentee ballots are issued to qualified voters who expect to be absent from their homes on election day; the ballots must be marked in the presence of a notary and must be sealed and returned to the proper office before the election. A few states also extend this privilege to invalids. Not many persons, however, take advantage of the opportunity to vote in this way.

COMPULSORY VOTING. It has sometimes been proposed that the voter be compelled to attend the polls under the penalty of a fine. In Australia, where the amount of the fine is substantial, compulsory voting provisions have resulted in a great increase in voting. In other countries, where the fine is small, there has been indifferent success. Forcing the electorate to the polls often causes resentment and has resulted in the casting of blank or meaningless ballots.

Compulsory voting does not exist in any state in the United States, because there is a general belief that one who votes under compulsion will not make the effort to inform himself about candidates and issues before he goes to the polls. Many are of the opinion that compulsory voting violates a citizen's freedom of choice, which may be to refrain from voting when he wishes to mildly rebuke his party, feels incapable of voting wisely, or lacks interest in public affairs. The problem of nonvoting will not be solved until, by civic education, voters are impelled to assume an attitude of responsibility in exercising their franchise.

6

POLITICAL PARTIES AND PRESSURE GROUPS

In the democratic process both parties and pressure groups exercise a predominant influence. They have no official standing as parts of the government, but they have developed under protection afforded by state and national constitutions, and they perform important functions in present-day American political life. Guarantees of freedom of association and assembly allow groups to organize for legitimate purposes. Freedom of speech and press permits private groups, as well as individuals, to disseminate their views on public questions. The freedom to petition for redress of grievances includes the right to bring influence to bear on legislatures and other branches of government and on officials. By forming organizations, numerous individuals may concentrate their efforts effectively. Through political parties, nominations for office are made; political campaigns are conducted; and party representatives who are elected to office may conduct the government co-operatively in accordance with a party program. Through pressure groups the interests of various segments of the population may be effectively brought to public attention and presented to legislative and other offices of government. In the United States the two great political parties operate on the national, state, and local levels and bring about co-operation among them. And great associations that represent different economic and social interests are organized at all levels to make their programs effective.

POLITICAL PARTIES

A *political party* is an organized body of voters that seeks to secure control of government by the election of its candidates to office. American political parties are extraconstitutional institutions; the federal Constitution and the early state constitutions made no mention of them. State election laws usually describe a political party as an organization that polled a specified number or percentage of the votes cast for governor in the preceding general election. Small parties that failed to poll the required number or percentage of votes are not recognized as legal political parties, but as independent political associations.

A political party performs these basic functions: (1) It facilitates the election process by recruiting candidates for public office. (2) It develops programs of action and works for their adoption. (3) Its campaigns generate interest in public affairs, inform the public of the issues, and increase the attendance of voters at the polls. (4) When out of power it performs a watchdog function by criticizing the party in power and exposing inefficient administration and corruption. (5) It assists citizens in their efforts to secure various public services. Although all political parties perform these five functions, they have not performed them with equal effectiveness.

Composition of American Parties. Is there a significant difference or similarity between the two American political parties?

Parties may be classified on the basis of political or social philosophies. They may be conservative—opposing rapid changes in the old order—or liberal—supporting moderate changes. The two major American parties appear to be similar when both, for example, are controlled by liberals. On the other hand, the differences between the two are plainly evident if, for instance, the Republican Party is controlled by its conservative wing and the Democratic Party by its liberal wing.

Parties in general may also be classified on the basis of the economic interests and social classes of their memberships. However, American political parties are similar in composition in that each has attracted to its membership men and women from all the classes and interests of society. Thus, American parties are not class parties. Rather, they are parties of opinion, since they are more interested in the practical conduct of government than in political and social philosophies.

Usually there is a correlation between a person's income and his party affiliation. For example, businessmen, members of professions, and wealthy individuals tend more frequently to be Republicans than Democrats. Individuals with low incomes, union members, and unskilled workers tend more frequently to be Democrats than Republicans.

NATIONAL PARTY DIVISIONS. The adoption of the federal Constitution in 1788 gave rise to the Federalist Party, which favored a loose interpretation of the Constitution and a strong national government, and an opposition group, later called Jeffersonian Republicans, which advocated a strict interpretation of the Constitution and states' rights. Alexander Hamilton was the leading Federalist advocate of a strong central government; in order to increase and consolidate the power of the national government, he proposed funding the Revolutionary War debt, assuming state debts, establishing a national bank, and levying an excise tax on distilled liquors and protective tariff duties. Thomas Jefferson led the anti-federalist attack on Hamilton's policies. He did this by uniting the small back country farmers from Maine to Georgia in the Democratic-Republican Party. Jeffersonian democracy emphasized the natural and equal rights of all citizens and the reserved powers of the states.

The Federalist Party disappeared in 1820 and the Democratic-Republican Party began to split into factions during the early 1820's: the supporters of John Quincy Adams called themselves the National-Republicans, and the supporters of Andrew Jackson called themselves Democrats. These two parties opposed each other in the election of 1828. In 1834 the National-Republican Party was succeeded by the conservative Whig Party—representing to a great extent the mercantile and financial interests of the North, the tobacco interests of Virginia, and the rice planters of South Carolina—which engaged in an unequal contest with the Jacksonian Democrats, composed of the people in lower-income groups, especially in the frontier areas. Jacksonian democracy was characterized by the democratization of political institutions: universal manhood suffrage, popularly elected state and local officials, short terms of office and frequent elections, and the dethroning of "king caucus" by the delegate convention.

The rise of the Republican Party in 1854 was associated with the slavery issue. The major reason contributing to its rise was dissatisfaction with the Kansas-Nebraska Act, which opened Kansas to slavery and thereby alienated many northern Democrats from their party. Also, the Whig Party was hopelessly divided on the slavery problem, and most of its members deserted it to join the Republicans. The combination of former Whigs and Democrats resulted in a predominantly Northern party, which borrowed many of its principles from all the earlier parties.

In the past, party divisions have been affected by "hereditary" allegiance. National, as well as state, party alignments, still reflect forces of abolitionism in the rural North and of the Civil War and reconstruction throughout the South.

Following 1860 the manufacturing interests of the North became allied with the agricultural interests of the Midwest in the Republican Party. The South became solidly Democratic and found allies in northern urban centers. Several third parties in succession attempted to find support for agrarian principles but, meeting with little success, eventually drifted to the Democratic Party. In recent years, sectionalism has been weakening under the impact of national issues. Voters have tended to discard hereditary allegiances, to vote independently, and to split their tickets. The Republicans, for example, are not as strong as formerly in the Northeast and the solid South has shown signs of independence, particularly in presidential contests. In order to elect a president, a party must adopt a compromise program which will permit the formation of a coalition of sectional and other interests.

STATE PARTY DIVISIONS. In each state there is a separate party system composed of one or more parties which nominate candidates for state offices. Though all the state party systems operate under national party names, state issues and candidates for office exercise a profound influence on the results of national elections. Some observers go so far as to declare that national parties are merely coalitions of state parties.

One of the strongest forces in state politics is the mutual antagonism between great cities and rural areas, with the result that rural and urban areas are commonly controlled by opposite parties. Cities are underrepresented in state legislatures and constantly complain of domination by rural majorities: their corporate powers are unduly circumscribed, they are subjected to unworkable provisions of general state laws, they pay a greater proportion of taxes and receive a lesser proportion of the benefits of state government; rural legislators do not understand urban problems. So run the complaints which in many cases are increasingly justified as urban population increases and rural population declines. New York City has threatened to ask for separate statehood if its interests are not recognized by New York

State. Chicago and Cook County, after long domination by down-state legislators, finally succeeded in 1954 in obtaining a compromise constitutional amendment whereby the Illinois house of representatives is controlled by Cook County and the Illinois senate is controlled by the downstate area.

The rivalry is not always between rural residents and city residents, but between economic interests. Business interests may find rural overrepresentation advantageous, since they often can obtain greater support for their programs from rural than from urban representatives. The Los Angeles Chamber of Commerce in 1948, for example, successfully opposed a constitutional initiative to increase urban representation in the state senate; this measure would have increased from one to ten the number of senators from Los Angeles County. In recent years organized labor has emphasized political action as a means of obtaining advantages and has thrown its support to candidates, generally of the Democratic Party, who are elected on a state-wide basis. Its greatest strength is in heavily industrialized states such as New York, Pennsylvania, and Michigan. Other factors—racial, religious, and social —may determine the loyalty or opposition of citizens to state political organizations.

As a rule, one party in a state is conservative and the other is a liberal, or a reform, party. The Democratic Party, for instance, may be simultaneously a conservative party in some states and a reform party in others.

LOCAL PARTY DIVISIONS. In municipalities many citizens are conservative and others are disposed to support reform movements. Although a city may be under the control of a corrupt "boss" or a "machine," many citizens apparently are not concerned; others, however, attempt to improve the conduct of the government by organizing a reform movement. Conditions of local government do not always present cause for two such opposite alignments. Local party divisions more commonly reflect the fact that citizens demand either more or less in the way of public works and services, depending on their outlooks. The latter may be rationalizations of benefits expected or tax burdens to follow: residents of established neighborhoods may demand relatively little in the way of public works and thus strive to keep the tax rate low, while residents of newer neighborhoods are more concerned with the need for public works and services than with the tax rate. Often conflicts between different sections of a city may assume a partisan nature: inhabitants of high-income areas tend to be republican, whereas inhabitants of low-income areas tend to be democrats. These conflicts between the various sections of a city may be intensified by the election of the city council members by wards rather than at large.

The Two-Party System. The American system of politics has been somewhat unique in that the two-party system has prevailed since the early days of the country. Though third parties have dominated certain states and cities for brief periods of time, they have rarely had marked impact on the two major parties or been of national importance.

FUNCTIONS OF THE PARTY IN POWER. The political party in power is responsible for the conduct of public affairs. It has a continuing responsibility to the voters, who can sweep it out of office for failing to govern in accordance with their wishes. In theory, the political party in power has guaranteed that its candidates are qualified men of integrity who will work for the implementation of the party platform. It must accept the blame should any of its elected candidates prove to be incompetent or corrupt. Under these circumstances there is a strong compulsion for the party to constrain its executive and legislative representatives to work together. If the governor is the leader of his party, he may exert great pressure through party mechanisms over the majority in each legislative house.

FUNCTIONS OF THE PARTY IN OPPOSITION. An active opposition party is essential to the success of democratic government. It criticizes the party in power, exposes corruption and inefficient administration, prevents excessive use of power, stimulates the majority party to greater activity in some areas, slows its too-rapid moves in other areas, and reminds the party in power of its promises and policies. The watchfulness of the opposition party encourages administrators and legislators of the majority to be honest and efficient, By championing good government, the opposition party hopes to win the voters' favor, so that it may itself be returned to power. It has little chance of gaining office if it simply engages in negative criticism; it must present a reasonable alternative policy and convince the public of the superiority of its program.

FUNCTIONS OF MINOR PARTIES. Third or minor parties have at times been powerful in certain states and cities. The Farmer-Labor Party was once strong in Minnesota, and the Progressive Party, under the La Follettes, controlled Wisconsin for many years. The Socialist Party has elected its candidate mayor of Bridgeport, Connecticut, a number of times. Elsewhere a third party has occasionally held the balance of power in elections and consequently has been able to force the acceptance of one or more of its proposals by one of the major parties.

The nomination of candidates is generally not so important a function of third parties as the formulation of policies. Minor parties focus public attention upon issues that the two major parties may have dodged or shunned as too controversial. If an issue raised by a minor party receives considerable public support, it often is adopted by one or both of the major parties. For instance, most of the planks in the 1892 platform of the Populist Party were subsequently taken over by the two major parties and are now law. An additional function of a minor party is to provide an outlet for the expression of views by discontented elements who may organize reform parties in a state or community to defeat the entrenched major party. Generally speaking, however, minor parties have had short lives and have represented special interests to a larger extent than have major parties.

Party Organization. Decentralization of party control is a distinguishing feature of American political parties. Each of the two major political parties is a loose federation of state and local political organizations. The national party organization has relatively little control over the state and local party organizations. The strongest party discipline exists on the state and local levels.

HIERARCHY OF COMMITTEES. The two major political parties have adopted the same basic hierarchal pattern of organization.

The Precinct Captain. The party member in most intimate contact with the average voter is the precinct captain or committeeman. It is his function to carry the precinct for his party on election day. He ingratiates himself with residents of the precinct by acting as an intermediary to secure the reduction of property assessments and the quashing of summonses, to disburse charity, and to obtain other benefits for citizens in general and party members in particular. An efficient precinct captain maintains a card file containing information on every person in his precinct. By means of this file, he is able to direct an effective appeal to each voter.

The Local Committee. The town or city, township, or ward committee is the next level in the party hierarchy. It supervises the precinct captains, aids in getting the party's voters to the polls, and is the basis of representation for higher party committees. In most large cities there are party committees which assist candidates in their campaigns for municipal offices.

The County Committee. The county committee is commonly composed of town committeemen. If this committee is very large, an executive committee is appointed to act on problems which arise between meetings of the entire group. Although the county committee usually has a certain amount of supervisory authority over the local committees, it is not itself supervised to any great extent by the state central committee. The county committee is frequently a powerful organization, owing to the amount of patronage available to the party controlling the county government.

The District Committee. In some states district committees exist in the party hierarchy intermediate between the county committees and the state central committee. It is the responsibility of these committees to work for the election of congressmen, state senators, and others who are elected on a district basis.

State Central Committee. The focal point of power rests in the state central committee in a state party organization. The number of members of a state central committee varies from ten or twelve to several hundred. If this group is large, an executive committee may be selected to perform many of its functions. The duties of the state central committee include directing state-wide campaigns, assisting the national committee in the conduct of the presidential election campaigns, and in some states drafting the state party platform.

The National Committee. At the apex of the party pyramid is the national committee. The Democratic National Committee is composed of one man and one woman from each state. The Republican National Committee is similarly constituted except that the state party chairman serves as a third member when the state has returned a Republican plurality in the most recent presidential or gubernatorial election or has chosen a majority of Republicans in its Congressional delegation. In both parties the

presidential candidate designates the chairman of the national
committee, and the committee selects the other committee officers.
The national committee arranges for the national convention,
raises funds, and helps conduct the presidential campaign. This
group meets only three or four times between national conventions and seldom interferes with state and local party organizations. (See Appendix, p. 249.)

SELECTION OF COMMITTEEMEN. In several states precinct captains or committeemen are required by law to be elected by the
rank and file of the party in a direct primary. In other states they
are chosen by the county or district committee or are elected at
precinct caucuses. The ward and city or town committees usually
are composed of the precinct captains or persons recommended
by them. County committeemen are selected in party primaries,
or in party conventions, or by the city and town committees.
The district committee generally is composed of representatives
chosen by the county committees. The method of selecting
members of the state central committee is determined by law in
most states. Members may be chosen in party primaries, or local
conventions, or they may be county or district chairmen. Members of the national committee are elected by the state party
convention or in primaries and the choice is officially accepted
by the national convention.

INFLUENCE OF CHAIRMEN. The influence of the chairmen of
the different party committees varies considerably. Ward chairmen frequently have a considerable amount of power since they
supervise precinct captains and commonly serve on the city committee. If a boss controls a city, he may either serve as chairman of the city committee or appoint and control the chairman.
The county chairman usually exercises great influence because
of the amount of patronage he controls when his party is in
power. The chairman of the state central committee often is designated by the party's candidate for governor and may in fact
conduct the state campaign.

BOSSES AND MACHINES. "Bosses" and "machines" often are associated with municipal governments and occasionally with state
governments, but there has never been a national "boss." These
terms are loosely defined: The politician who has the greatest influence in the selection of candidates and the operation of party
machinery frequently is called a *boss*. A political *machine* is com-

monly defined as the group which controls the government, but the principal members of the machine usually do not hold public office. Bosses and machines are sometimes referred to as the "invisible government." The spoils system keeps the political machine oiled by rewarding faithful workers and their relatives with government jobs if the machine wins the election. Since most public officials are indebted to the boss for their positions, he may influence appointments made by executive officials, votes in the city council or state legislature, and judicial decisions. Corruption in the letting of contracts, in the construction of public buildings, and in police administration is common in boss or machine dominated areas. The power of the machine is greatest in one-party cities and states where there is no effective opposition party. In such an area a boss or machine may with impunity nominate party hacks in every election.

In recent years the power of bosses and machines has been weakened as a result of three developments: (1) the introduction of efficient civil service systems (see Chapter 21) in state and municipal government; (2) the assumption, after 1933, of many welfare functions by government agencies, which made unnecessary the charitable activities previously performed by or through machines in return for the recipients' gratitude at the polls; (3) the decline in the percentage of foreign-born persons, who were as a group especially susceptible to machine influence.

Nominations. The importance of the nominating system cannot be overestimated, for it is the first step in the election process. *Nomination* is a preliminary selection of a candidate for a public office by a party or other group, and is a principal reason for the existence of parties.

EARLY NOMINATING METHODS. The caucus and the unregulated convention were the principal nominating methods during the greater part of the nineteenth century. A *caucus* is a meeting of party leaders for the purpose of selecting their party's candidates for public office. It was an undemocratic method because the great majority of party members were excluded from participation in the nomination. Later, this method was replaced by the nominating convention system, which in theory had a popular basis. Mass meetings of party voters in towns, townships, and wards nominated candidates for local offices and elected delegates to attend conventions in counties and larger units. The choice of delegates was often rigged by leaders, with the result that the higher conventions were unrepresentative of the voters. At its best the convention was rarely free from boss control either in the precinct or in the higher levels. The widespread abuses of nominating conventions led states—beginning with California in 1866—to attempt to regulate the convention system by law. Their efforts met with indifferent success. The convention system survives today in national party affairs and in a few states where it is limited to making nominations for only a few officers, drafting a party platform, or adopting a preprimary slate of candidates in order to guide members in the primary election.

THE PRIMARY ELECTION. The *direct primary* is an election, conducted by public officials, in which registered voters may make a choice between candidates for the party's nomination for office in a forthcoming general election. A direct primary is conducted under the same regulations as a general election. (See pp. 56–61.) Although the direct primary was used in the nineteenth century for the nomination of candidates for local offices, Wisconsin in 1903 was the first state to adopt it for use on a statewide basis; all but four states had adopted it in some form by 1913. Today every state provides for the direct primary, at least for the selection of the parties' candidates for local offices. In a few states a candidate may, by "cross-filing," seek the nomination in primaries of two or more parties. In one-party states, the direct primary is of greater importance than the general election; the winner of the Democratic Party's primary in most southern states is almost always certain of success in the general election. In approximately four-fifths of the states the use of the primary is mandatory of all parties; in the remaining states its use is optional, at the discretion of a party. In Colorado, Massachusetts, New Mexico, and Utah, preprimary conventions endorse slates of candidates to be voted on in forthcoming direct primaries. This device enables party leaders to make their preferences known to party members.

Candidacy in the Primary Election. In order to get his name on the primary ballot, a person must file his candidacy with a designated public official by a specified date. Usually he is required to submit a supporting petition signed by a small number of voters or to pay a nominal filing fee which rarely exceeds fifty dollars even for the highest office. An aspirant for office has only to file his candidacy in Delaware, Indiana, Oklahoma, and West Virginia.

Forms of the Primary Election. There are four forms of primary elections in general use: (1) A *closed primary,* the most common form, is confined to members of a particular party who have declared their party affiliations in advance. (2) An *open primary* is one in which any eligible voter may participate. He is given the ballots of all parties; he then selects and marks the ballot of the party of his choice, places it in the ballot box, and puts the unmarked ballots in a second receptacle. The open primary has the advantage of preserving the secrecy of a voter's party affiliation. It may be abused, however, when a party, united on its candidates, sends many of its regular members to vote in the primary of the opposition party and thus to nominate the weakest opposition candidates. (3) The *blanket primary* is used in the state of Washington. The ballot for this primary contains the names of all candidates for office and their party affiliations. A voter may mark the names of any candidates. The candidates who stand highest in their respective party votes are nominated. (4) Several states use the *non-partisan primary* for the nomination of candidates for judicial and local offices. The names of all candidates for these offices appear on the ballot without party designation; the two candidates for each office receiving the highest votes in the primary election oppose each other in the subsequent general election (which is also a non-partisan election).

Majority or Plurality Nominations. The plurality principle is generally followed in direct primaries; that is, the candidate for each office who receives the most votes in the primary becomes the official party nominee. To prevent the nomination of candidates by a minority, a "run-off," or second, primary is held in ten Southern states when no candidate for an office has received a majority of the votes cast in the primary. In a run-off primary all but the two candidates who stand highest are eliminated. The winner of the run-off primary becomes the official party nominee. (In Virginia a run-off primary is conducted only if requested by the candidate who received the second largest number of votes. In Iowa or South Dakota, if no candidate for a nomination has received 35 per cent of the vote cast in the primary, the nomination must be made by a party convention. In such cases, it is the practice of the convention to nominate the candidate who has received the most votes in the primary.)

Criticisms of the Primary Election. The direct primary is attacked on six grounds: (1) The cost of nominating candidates for public office is measurably increased by holding a direct primary, for the state must then finance two elections—the primary and the general—and the candidates are faced with the expenses of two campaigns. The additional campaign expenses incurred may make it impossible for individuals with modest incomes to compete for public office. (2) When three or more candidates aspire to the party's nomination for one office in a state where no run-off primary is held, the nominee may not be the majority choice. (3) The primary is a contest among persons who may or may not agree with the principles and program of the party. Thus, party responsibility is weakened because active party members cannot control the party's nominations. (4) The average voter cannot become acquainted with the qualifications of all the candidates whose names appear on the primary ballot. (5) In the closed primary it is impossible to design an adequate party-membership test which will exclude interference by members of other parties. (6) "Machine" and "boss" rule have not yet been eliminated by the direct primary.

Proponents of the direct primary freely admit the validity of most of the foregoing objections. They point, however, to the vast improvement that has taken place since the direct primary was substituted for the convention system in states and cities. Though bosses and machines may still manipulate the primary, they must act circumspectly. The rank and file of party members may dislodge them more easily through the direct primary than through any other nominating method. In spite of expenses and other difficulties, independent candidates do often succeed in winning nominations and elections. In primary campaigns, party affairs as well as public affairs are subject to the scrutiny of the voters. Though primary campaigns often result in unbalanced party tickets, and so impair party responsibility, the successful candidates are usually better qualified to conduct public affairs than those nominated by conventions.

In 1950 the National Municipal League drafted a model primary law which: (1) provides for a preprimary convention through which party leaders may submit a slate for the approval of party members; (2) requires a direct primary for all parties that polled more than 10 per cent of the popular vote at the last election; (3) prohibits cross-filing; and (4) provides for the closed, open, or blanket primary at the option of a particular state.

Political Campaigns. Without intensive campaigning by parties and candidates it is doubtful that many citizens would vote. No two political campaigns are ever exactly alike, yet there is a basic similarity in techniques. In national elections, each party concentrates its efforts in doubtful states and does little campaigning either in areas dominated by itself or by its chief rival. In state and local elections, parties campaign intensively throughout the whole area because every vote contributes toward the plurality necessary for election.

CAMPAIGN ORGANIZATION. Organization is essential to a campaign if the party is to be successful. Volunteers and salaried full- and part-time workers are pressed into action. To supplement the regular party organization, special committees are formed. These committees promote the special appeals designed to capture such groups as labor, Negroes, veterans, women, and young voters. Auxiliary organizations with nonpartisan names are established in an attempt to attract groups of voters who would not respond to, or assist, the regular party organization. Headquarters are set up in cities and principal towns. Speakers are supplied to all types of organizations. And transportation to the polls is arranged by volunteer workers.

CAMPAIGN TECHNIQUES. Candidates attempt to be all things to all people by appealing to occupational, ethnic, racial, religious, and other special-interest groups; they ask for the support of voters on both individual and mass bases. A candidate may make an individual appeal by a direct personal approach such as doorbell-ringing, visiting workers in a factory, and writing personal letters. The direct approach is the most effective campaign technique.

Nowadays radio and television appearances are of paramount importance in keeping or winning the support of voters. It is unlikely, however, that they will entirely supplant campaign meetings. Indoor meetings are attended chiefly by party workers and, though they convert few voters, they do heighten enthusiasm among party workers and members. Outdoor meetings have certain advantages over indoor meetings: they are less expensive and they may be the means of converting members of the opposition party, the undecided, and the indifferent to the party. Many other techniques are employed to convince or beguile the electorate. Debates which are sometimes arranged with representatives of the opposition party often help to clarify the issues in the campaign. Comic books, political cartoons, movies, and billboards promote platforms and candidates, as do endorsements by prominent citizens and bolters from the opposition party. Appointment to public office may be promised and public contracts may be offered in exchange for votes. Parades, dances, barbecues, clambakes, coffee and tea parties, and the distribution of campaign literature, buttons, ribbons, and souvenirs have also been used with varying degrees of success.

CAMPAIGN EXPENSES AND FINANCES. The average voter is generally ill-informed regarding the cost of conducting a state or local political campaign. He is apt to be shocked at the publication of the total amount of money spent by a party. The plain truth is that in order to make effective appeals to the voters, parties must spend large sums. Campaign headquarters must be rented, staffs must be hired, and campaign literature must be printed and distributed. The advent of radio and television, which are very expensive, has greatly increased the cost of campaigning. Other expenses have increased with the rapid growth of population and the cost of living. In a large state expenses run into millions of dollars in each election, and in a large city more than a million dollars may be spent in one municipal election. The sources and uses of funds are more important than the total amount, impressive though it may be.

Legitimate Expenditures. Legitimate campaign expenditures include the maintenance of party headquarters; the salaries of campaign workers; and the cost of printing, stationary, postage, advertising in newspapers and periodicals, telephone bills, radio and television programs, transportation of candidates and speakers, rental of meeting halls, campaign buttons and ribbons, and payment of watchers at the polls.

Illegitimate Expenditures. Many types of campaign expenditures clearly are not legitimate. Bribery, treating, loans, and gifts in exchange for an individual's vote or support are abuses and are prohibited in most places by law. (See Chapter 5 for a discussion of corrupt practices acts.) It is, of course, impossible to determine the extent of illegitimate campaign expenditures, but it is reasonable to conclude that it is considerable. Treating voters to cigars and tobacco, clothing, drinks, liquor, and entertainment is covertly or openly done in an effort to win votes. Candidates occasionally contribute to fraternal, religious, and eleemosynary institutions or buy tickets to various public affairs such as dances, fairs, and theatrical programs in order to win or avoid losing votes. The support of newspapers and periodicals may be purchased through paid political advertising which masquerades as news.

Sources of Funds. The financing of a campaign is the responsibility of the party treasurer, who is usually assisted by a finance committee. The sources of campaign funds are known to be many and varied, but complete information about them is lacking. The contributions of candidates account for only a small percentage of the total campaign funds. Wealthy individuals, special-interest groups, officeholders, party members, and supporters of candidates all contribute to campaign treasuries. Contributions from business firms, including public utility companies, are important for their size and dependability. In state and local elections, corporations and contractors may contribute to the campaign funds of all parties in order to be certain of friendly relations with the elected officials regardless of which party and candidates win the election. Business interests are apt to contribute to the Democratic Party in a Democratic city or state and to the Republican Party in a Republican area. In cities, the underworld, which wants police protection and immunity from prosecution, may be a major source of campaign funds; gambling and vice interests have much to gain from a friendly local administration. In some places political assessments are levied on state and local government employees, who may lose their jobs if they fail to contribute to the party's campaign fund.

PRESSURE GROUPS

Like political parties, *pressure groups* seek to create a favorable public opinion and influence the conduct of government. They are to be distinguished from parties in three important respects: (1) they are limited in membership; (2) they are interested in one or a few phases of government and are not concerned with the great bulk of governmental activities; and (3) they do not nominate candidates for office. They may and often do publicly or privately endorse candidates nominated by parties, and contribute to party campaign funds. But they try to evade positive identification with any one party in order that they may influence officers of government, no matter which party is in power.

Kinds of Pressure Groups. There is an almost endless variety in the kinds of pressure groups, yet they may be placed in one of two broad categories—groups that are predominantly concerned with the private interests of their members, and other groups, like good-government associations, that are devoted to the improvement of civic affairs.

The business community has organized a number of pressure groups. Several of these organizations, such as the Chamber of Commerce, represent the entire business community; others, such as the National Association of Manufacturers, the United States Brewers Association, and the Association of American Railroads, represent more limited sections of the business community. Business pressure groups are united on the need for creating a favorable attitude toward free enterprise, low business taxes, and favorable labor laws, but they differ on many matters—among them, the tariff question. Banks, public utilities, and insurance companies are active in pressure organizations because they are closely regulated by state governments. Contractors co-operate in pressure groups owing to their concern with such problems as building codes and zoning regulations. Real-estate organizations try to influence property assessments and obtain public improvements.

Taxpayers' associations are active on both the state and the local levels; their chief concerns are with the achievement and maintenance of efficient government and the lowest possible taxes. Often they work closely with business pressure groups. Professional and occupational organizations are among the most effective pressure groups. The prestige of certain professions, such as law and medicine, gives their associations considerable political power. Accountants, architects, barbers, chiropractors, dentists, engineers, lawyers, nurses, pharmacists, physicians, and plumbers have their own organizations, many of which are particularly interested in legislation regulating entrance into their occupations and professions.

Among the most powerful pressure groups are the American Farm Bureau Federation, the State Grange, and the Farmers Union. They have obtained special financial aids from the states for rural roads and schools, and they have successfully thwarted the reapportionment of legislative districts, when such reapportionment would result in a reduction of rural representation.

The role of labor unions as pressure groups has increased markedly in importance since the middle 1930's. Naturally, labor is most influential in industrial states and cities. Samuel Gompers, the first president of the American Federation of Labor, established the policy that organized labor should not attempt to form an independent labor party, but should follow the policy of rewarding its friends and punishing its enemies. One should not think of organized labor as a unified pressure group; many unions are outside the AFL-CIO and the political interests of craft and industrial unions differ.

Veterans' organizations have been powerful pressure groups for almost a hundred years. The first substantial organization of veterans was the Grand Army of the Republic, composed of former soldiers of the Union Army in the Civil War. Nowadays the American Legion and the Veterans of Foreign Wars, with posts in every city, are the two largest veterans' groups. The local posts and state organizations of these groups are active in attempts to secure increased benefits for veterans and their dependents, including hospital facilities, bonuses, pensions, and veterans' preference in public employment.

Wherever foreign-born first-generation Americans are concentrated, there are ethnic pressure groups which work to advance the interests of their nationality groups. Ethnic groups often advocate the teaching of their languages in public schools and the removal of discriminations against their members. Racial pressure groups are also active in many states and cities. One of the best known is the National Association for the Advancement of Colored People.

In recent years associations of public employees have become important pressure groups. For example, associations of policemen and firemen in many states exert considerable influence over legislation affecting their interests. Other pressure groups are composed of city clerks, city treasurers, county clerks, and county sheriffs.

Within the past sixty years, a number of associations of teachers and school administrators have been formed. These organizations are mainly concerned with improving standards of education, but they also have a lively interest in increasing salaries and fringe benefits in the educational field, in raising requirements for teaching certificates, and in establishing or improving tenure and retirement systems.

Good-government associations have played a major part in reform movements and have operated primarily on the local level. Generally these are composed of members of all political parties and are frequently identified with the council-manager form of municipal government, nonpartisan elections, civil service reform, and municipal home rule. These associations often endorse slates of candidates for office. Examples of good-government associations include the Cleveland Citizens' League, the Citizens' Plan E Association of Worcester, the City Charter Committee of Cincinnati, and the Citizens' Association in Kansas City (Missouri). The Citizens' Association was formed specifically to challenge the machine of the late Tom Pendergast and the corrupt government in Kansas City. The League of Women Voters is an example of a good-government association that operates on national, state, and local levels.

Functions of Pressure Groups. Pressure groups perform the legitimate function of representing various interests before legislative bodies and administrative officials. Even when a legislative district is composed of persons who have primarily the same interests, the representative of the area will often be grateful for information supplied to him by organized groups in his district. A number of pressure groups operate competent research bureaus which make their findings available to legislators, administrators, and the general public. Experts employed by these organizations provide valuable assistance to legislators and administrators. A large percentage of the bills introduced in legislative bodies are prepared by pressure groups.

Representatives and other officials must be alert to the tendency of pressure groups to advance their special selfish interests at the expense of the public need. Group representatives rationalize their own interests as public interests. Thus, special concessions to manufacturers are said to create employment, and increased wages for labor are said to create additional purchasing power. The motive for such arguments is, of course, rarely altruistic.

Organization of Pressure Groups. Many pressure groups are organized on all three levels of government; others, on only one or two levels. No standard organizational pattern is adhered to by pressure groups, but certain features are common to all.

PERMANENT HEADQUARTERS. The large pressure organizations maintain permanent headquarters and representatives at the national and state capitals. Smaller pressure associations send representatives to testify before committees of the state legislatures and city councils. Members of the permanent headquarters staff of a major pressure group are commonly assigned to such divisions as legislative relations, public education, and finance. Temporary workers may be added to the permanent staff whenever the pressure group is conducting an all-out effort to achieve an immediate goal.

PUBLIC RELATIONS. Large groups employ experts to promote good relations with the public. These experts conduct educational campaigns to create a favorable and sympathetic public opinion for the interests they represent. Public relations men prepare weekly and/or monthly periodicals and other publications the purpose of which is to inform the membership and to influence the public. Considerable time is devoted to the preparation of news releases for newspapers and radio and television broadcasts. Many pressure groups advertise heavily and also prepare speeches for legislators and editorials for newspapers.

PAID LOBBYISTS. Pressure associations also employ paid agents or lobbyists, who attempt to influence legislation and administration in the state capitals and city halls. Many of the lobbyists operating at the state level are lawyers who have served in one or both houses of the legislature. Certain lobbyists may represent more than one pressure group. Lobbyists not only maintain close relations with legislators, but also keep up close contact with insurance commissions, public utility commissions, and other regulatory agencies possessing quasi-legislative powers. Although lobbyists are associated in the public mind with bribery and corruption, they often provide valuable assistance to legislators and administrators.

Methods of Pressure Groups. Pressure groups utilize many and varied techniques to influence legislation and administration. Frequently one group will co-operate with other groups that have similar interests. Another favorite method of pressure associations is logrolling or backscratching; that is, one group agrees to support a bill favored by a second group provided that the second group reciprocates by supporting a bill favored by the first.

PRESSURE ON PARTY LEADERS. Pressure groups work diligently to have planks favorable to their interests placed in party platforms. Since party leaders exercise considerable influence over party nominations, pressure groups urge party leaders to work for or oppose the nomination of certain candidates for public office. Many times the co-operation of party leaders is forced by the group's promise to provide or threat to withhold contributions to campaign funds. The interests of pressure groups extend to the organization of state legislatures and city councils; here, again, party leaders are pressured so that representatives amenable to the desires of the groups are appointed to key posts and committees.

ENDORSEMENT OF CANDIDATES. The policies of pressure groups toward the question of endorsing candidates for public office vary considerably. As a rule, most of these organizations do not openly endorse candidates. The value of a public endorsement by a pressure group cannot be determined precisely. Although many pressure groups insist that they can deliver a block of voters, there is considerable evidence to the contrary. Furthermore, an open endorsement by a pressure group has often caused many voters to rally to the opposing candidates.

Good-government associations in cities frequently endorse candidates. The Citizens' Plan E Association of Worcester is a typical example of the procedure followed by such associations. It invites all candidates for the city council and school committee to a public interview and also examines their records carefully before deciding on its endorsed slate of candidates. There is considerable evidence to indicate that the endorsement of a good-government association carries with it a large number of votes. Although the League of Women Voters does not endorse candidates, it does, by means of interviews and questionnaires, ascertain and publicize the views of candidates, for state and local offices, on important issues. Many pressure groups inform their membership and the general public of the voting records of candidates for public office.

PRESSURES ON PUBLIC OFFICIALS. Pressure groups not only exert pressure on party leaders but also on legislators and administrative officials. Group representatives attempt to force legislative bodies to pass favorable legislation and to reject unfavorable legislation. They often press for the vigorous enforcement of legislation to their liking and seek to weaken the administration and enforcement of other laws. They appear before legislative committees that are conducting hearings on bills and also see to it that legislators and committees that are considering bills are flooded with letters and telegrams. In addition, pressure groups use newspapers, radio, and television to enlist public support for legislation. The larger groups maintain files on the interests and views of every legislator so they may more effectively deal with and present their views to the legislators. Once a law is passed, pressure organizations turn their attention to influencing the preparation of the administrative regulations, for in modern legislation the details of statutes are completed at this point. Agents of pressure groups have not always confined their activities to the presentation of information and to a show of political power; in far too many instances they have been involved in the bribery of both legislators and administrators.

Regulation of Pressure Group Activities. All states regulate the activities of pressure groups in some manner. Massachusetts in 1890 became the first state to enact a law which required lobbyists to register, and its example has been followed by more than half of the states. The registration laws require lobbyists to identify their employers and to reveal the amount of their compensation. The lobbyists may also be required to file a list of the groups they represent. Several states have also forbidden pressure groups to pay lobbyists on a contingent basis.

In several states pressure groups are required to file reports covering their activities, the sources of their funds, and the purposes for which funds were used. Legislative committees investigate lobbyists and publicize their names and the groups they represent, the ways in which they are attempting to influence certain legislation, and the amount of money spent by pressure groups. The theory behind the publicity given to pressure group activities is the belief that an informed public will be able to counter their influence.

Unfortunately the registration laws are poorly enforced. The reports filed by pressure groups are seldom carefully scrutinized to determine their accuracy. It is obvious that the reports should be carefully examined and analyzed if they are to serve a useful purpose. Swift punishment should follow the willful filing of false reports or any other violations of law.

7

DIRECT LEGISLATION AND RECALL

Every governmental system has the problem of keeping its officers continuously responsible for their acts. When the framers of the early state constitutions provided for the election of officers, it was expected that these officers would carry out their duties in accordance with the popular will. If a legislative body failed in its trust, its members might be replaced by others at the end of their terms. If executive officers were guilty of crimes or misconduct they might be removed on impeachment or on legislative address (a request that the governor remove a public official from office). But no method was provided by which voters could reverse the course of legislation or remove incompetent officers before the expiration of their terms. During the progressive movement at the beginning of the twentieth century, the initiative, the referendum, and the recall were introduced in an effort to enforce continuous political responsibility to the voters.

DIRECT LEGISLATION

Direct legislation permits voters to supplement the actions of a legislature. Through the initiative they may enact measures which a legislature has refused to consider or to pass; through the referendum, they may veto laws enacted by the legislature. Both devices supplement the work of the legislature and are not intended to supplant it. The number of measures submitted to the voters has rarely exceeded twenty-five and is usually only two or three. Certain subjects such as religion, the courts and judges, and private rights usually are not subject to the initiative and referendum.

The initiative and referendum as instruments of direct legislation are commonly found together; however, they are separate instruments and one may be used independently of the other.

The Referendum. *The referendum* is a type of direct legislation which is negative in character and which permits the voters to pass upon proposed state constitutions, proposed constitutional amendments, and laws enacted by the state legislature. The referendum has had a long history of use with respect to constitutional revision (constitutional referendum), creation of local governments, and bond issues. A relatively new development in the use of the referendum is the extension of its use to prevent unpopular statutes enacted by the legislature from going into effect. South Dakota (in 1898) was the first state to adopt the statutory referendum, which is now used in more than twenty states. San Francisco (in 1899) was the first major American city to provide for the referendum.

COMPULSORY REFERENDUM. In most states proposed constitutional amendments must be submitted to the voters for their approval; the means of submission to the voters is called *compulsory,* or *mandatory, referendum.* An extramajority affirmative vote often is required for the adoption of a constitution or a constitutional amendment. State constitutions and laws frequently require that proposed bond issues and the revisions of city charters must be submitted to the voters concerned for their approval.

OPTIONAL REFERENDUM. The *optional,* or *advisory, referendum* permits a legislative body, at its discretion, to submit an issue to the voters. The measures referred to the voters by a state legislature or a city council frequently are highly controversial. They may include, for instance, the question of whether or not the sale of intoxicating liquor should be permitted in a local area. A legislative body, fearing to offend important segments of the voting population, may shift the responsibility by referring the issue to the voters for their approval or rejection.

STATUTORY REFERENDUM. Sometimes called the *protest referendum,* the *statutory referendum* permits the voters to delay and possibly prevent a law enacted by the legislature from going into effect. A waiting period usually of ninety days is provided before a legislative act is effective. Within this period objectors to the law may circulate petitions for a popular referendum on the law. If the required number of voters—5 to 10 per cent in different states—sign the petitions, the measure must be submitted to the voters at a special or general election. In the interval before the election the publicizing of referred measures is required by law. In Iowa, Nebraska, and South Dakota the full texts, with arguments for and against measures, must be published in newspapers. In eight other states the same information, in pamphlet form, is mailed to every registered voter. If the majority of those voting on a law cast their votes against it, the law is rejected. Several state constitutions declare that emergency measures are not subject to the referendum and may go into effect when passed by the legislature. To avoid legislative abuse of the emergency provision, some states require that the declaration of emergency must be made by an extraordinary majority of the legislature. Other states list subjects that may not be classified as emergency measures. Despite these precautions, legislatures have often declared statutes to be emergency measures without sufficient justification.

The Initiative. The *initiative* is a type of direct legislation which is positive in character; it is a means by which voters may enact laws or constitutional amendments without action by the legislature. A measure may be proposed by a petition signed by a specified number or percentage of voters. The measure then goes on the ballot at the ensuing general or special election. If adopted it becomes part of the state constitution or laws. The governor is not permitted to veto initiative measures. Moreover, measures proposed by initiative and approved by the voters generally cannot be amended or repealed by the state legislature. The initiative is also an important instrumentality in municipal government. In a number of cities it may be used to enact charter revisions and ordinances.

In 1960 twenty-one states were using the initiative, but Alaska is the only one to provide for it since 1920. The initiative may be direct or indirect, statutory or constitutional.

DIRECT AND INDIRECT INITIATIVE. The *direct initiative,* which exists in thirteen states, allows citizens by means of a petition containing the signatures of a specified number or percentage of voters—usually 5 to 8 per cent—to place a proposed law on the ballot. The petitions must be submitted to a designated public official who scrutinizes the signatures and certifies the sufficiency of the petitions. The direct initiative requires that the proposed law be submitted to a vote. A majority of those voting on an initiative proposal is required for the adoption of the proposed law in most states, although Massachusetts and Nebraska require that the vote must be equal to at least 35 per cent of the total votes cast in the election for the initiated measure.

The *indirect initiative,* used in seven states, allows citizens by means of petitions to propose bills which must be considered by the legislature. If the legislature at its next session fails to enact a bill that has been proposed in this way, the bill is submitted to the voters. If approved by a majority, the bill becomes law.

STATUTORY AND CONSTITUTIONAL INITIATIVE. The initiative may be further classified as statutory and constitutional. The *statutory initiative* is used in eighteen states to pass an ordinary law. It was apparently adapted from provisions in the laws of Switzerland where it had been in use for many years. The first effective use of statutory initiative in the United States was in South Dakota in 1898. Fourteen states provided for the *constitutional initiative,* which allows the voters to propose amendments to the state constitution. Oregon in 1902 was the first state to adopt the constitutional initiative.

Evaluation of Direct Legislation. Direct legislation has been the subject of much controversy, especially in the early decades of this century. The validity of several of the arguments for and against direct legislation is questionable. It has neither lived up to the high expectations of its proponents, nor has it resulted in the dire consequences predicted by its opponents. In fact, the number of unwise laws adopted by direct legislation has been small.

ADVANTAGES OF DIRECT LEGISLATION. Proponents of direct legislation believe it has four major advantages. (1) Direct legislation is the purest form of democracy, for the people have an opportunity to reverse the actions of their representatives. Through it citizens are able to initiate and adopt laws which pressure groups have blocked in the legislature and to veto laws that are not in the public interest. (2) Direct legislation stimulates the legislators to action. They become more responsive to public opinion, because they know that if they fail to act the voters have the power to initiate action. (3) Campaigns associated with the use of the initiative and the referendum generate public enthusiasm and interest in governmental affairs, although voters naturally are more interested in the candidates than in the proposals which appear on the ballot. (The total vote for candidates tends to be 25 to 50 per cent larger than the total vote on referred proposals on the same ballot). (4) Direct legislation fosters the movement for shorter constitutions and city charters for it obviates the need for detailed restrictions on legislative power.

DISADVANTAGES OF DIRECT LEGISLATION. The validity of the

arguments claimed for direct legislation is challenged by its opponents who believe that it has seven principal disadvantages. (1) The voters may lack the necessary information and training to pass intelligently on the proposals of a highly technical nature which appear on the ballot. (2) Initiated measures are often incompletely considered and poorly drafted. Voters are limited to a choice of yes or no. Furthermore, once the petitions are signed the direct initiative provides no opportunity for amendment or for the reconciliation of conflicting interests, which are important advantages of legislative procedures. (3) Direct legislation adds to the length of a ballot that is already generally too long. (4) The proposals which appear on the ballot may be adopted or rejected by a small minority of voters because many voters, being unwilling to give thorough consideration to measures, prefer to abstain from voting on them. As few as 25 per cent of the registered voters have sometimes been responsible for adopting or defeating measures. To prevent legislation by a small minority, several states specify that proposed measures shall not become effective unless approved by a specified percentage of those voting in the election. (5) Special or sinister interests may utilize direct legislation for their own advantage. They have greater financial resources than citizens' groups and can better afford the expense of collecting signatures on petitions and conducting campaigns for the adoption or rejection of measures. Thus, direct legislation may permit pressure groups to secure legislation that they could not secure from the legislature. (6) Governmental costs are increased by the necessity of printing and distributing the texts of proposals and arguments for and against their adoption, and also when direct legislation necessitates special elections. (7) Laws passed by direct legislation tend to be inflexible because they generally cannot be amended or repealed by legislative bodies. Once on the statute books, the laws remain there until repealed or amended by the electorate through the long and difficult process of amendment by initiative or repeal by referendum.

THE RECALL

The *recall* is a means by which citizens may petition for a special election to determine whether a public official should be removed from office prior to the expiration of his term. It differs from other methods of removal in two important respects: (1) the decision to remove a public official is made directly by the voters; and (2) unlike impeachment, removal may be made for reasons other than a crime or a misdemeanor—the reasons may be inefficiency or popular disappointment with the official's conduct or program. The recall is designed to enforce a continuing political responsibility of officers to the electorate.

Los Angeles (in 1903) was the first governmental unit in the United States to adopt the recall, and Oregon (in 1908) was the first state to adopt it. Although the recall has been adopted by fourteen states, Alaska is the only state which has provided for it since 1920. Judges in six of the fourteen states are not subject to the recall and the judicial recall has seldom been used in the other states. Kansas is the only state to provide for the use of the recall against appointed officials. In thirty-nine states, certain cities are authorized to use the recall; it is most commonly used in cities with commission and council-manager governments.

Provisions for the recall are similar wherever it exists. Public officials generally cannot be removed from office by the recall during the first few months of their terms of office; they are given the opportunity to prove themselves during this period. Furthermore, in several states an official may not be subjected to a vote for recall twice during his term of office. The recall is not primarily directed at members of the legislature; rather it is a method of removing executive officers and sometimes judges.

Procedure in Recall. The first step in the recall procedure is the circulation of petitions stating the reasons why the official should be removed. (The official commonly is allowed to place a statement of defense on the petition or on the ballot.) The petition must contain the signatures of 10 to 35 per cent of the eligible voters—25 per cent is the most common requirement. The process of collecting signatures on a recall petition is both difficult and expensive. If the required number of signatures is obtained, the recall petition is filed with a specified official—usually the secretary of state—who checks to see whether all the requirements of the recall provision have been met. If the official subject to the recall petition does not resign within a specified period of time, the question of removing him is placed upon the ballot. Unless a general election is scheduled for the near future, a special recall election is held. In certain states and cities the voters merely decide whether the official shall be recalled from office. If the public official is recalled, an election is subsequently held to select a successor. In other states and cities the question of whether a public official shall be removed from office and the choice of his successor, in the event of his removal from office, are placed on the same ballot. This arrangement permits an official to be removed from office and returned to office simultaneously, for the majority who removed the official may not have united on one candidate to succeed him. Hence, the removed official may be returned to office by a plurality vote. To prevent this occurrence, some states and cities do not permit the name of the official involved to be included in the list of candidates to fill the office in the event of removal.

Evaluation of Recall. Although the recall was hailed as introducing a new era of governmental responsibility, it has not lived up to its promise. On the other hand, it has not disrupted government as was predicted by its opponents. It has been rarely used. When it has been used, officials have been removed for both major and minor reasons.

ADVANTAGES OF RECALL. Proponents of the recall cite four arguments for it. (1) The recall provides a means by which voters may remove officials simply because they have lost confidence in them. (2) The recall improves the performance of public officials by constantly reminding them that corruption and inefficiency will be punished by removal from office. The theory of the recall is that public officials must be responsive to popular opinion at all times rather than only at election time. This is the "gun behind the door" theory. (3) The recall increases popular interest in public affairs because it permits citizens to participate more directly in them. Citizens are better informed when public officials take pains to explain the reasons for an important governmental action before it is initiated. (4) Political scientists agree that the terms of office of public officials generally are too short and should be lengthened. Voters who traditionally have been in favor of frequent elections, are inclined to agree to longer terms if they are able to recall officials.

DISADVANTAGES OF RECALL. Opponents of the recall advance five major arguments against it. (1) The recall imposes an additional burden upon the voters and lengthens a ballot that already is too long, and also increases the number of elections. (2) Dynamic public officials may be unduly restrained and their independence weakened. The recall forces them to consider the immediate public reaction to a program rather than its long-term effect. An official may hesitate to initiate an action that is in the public interest for fear that the action may be misunderstood by the voters. Furthermore, competent individuals may refuse to run for public office because they dislike having the recall held over their heads like the sword of Damocles. (3) Governmental expense is increased if special elections are held. (4) The recall is superfluous, since other constitutional provisions and laws permit the removal of public officials for cause by less expensive and less fickle methods. (5) The recall may be utilized for partisan purposes. A party which has lost an election by a close margin may be tempted to invoke the recall at the first opportunity in order to win an office.

8

THE STATE LEGISLATURE

The legislature with powers that exceed those of other branches of government is the principal policy-making branch of a state. It is officially called the "legislature" in twenty-six states, the "generally assembly" in nineteen states, the "general court" in Massachusetts and New Hampshire, and the "assembly" in Montana, North Dakota, and Oregon. Just as its name varies among the states, so does its composition: the New Hampshire general court has the largest membership with 424 members; Nebraska's unicameral legislature, the smallest with 43 members.

POWERS OF THE LEGISLATURE

The powers reserved to the states by the federal Constitution are exercised by the state legislatures subject to certain prohibitions contained in the federal and state constitutions. (See Chapter 2 for a discussion of the reserved powers of the states.) The reserved or residual powers of a state legislature fall into six categories: legislative, constituent, judicial, executive, electoral, and administrative. The legislative or statute-making power is the power to determine public policy by the passage, repeal, or modification of statutes. As an incident to law-making, the legislature may conduct investigations into subjects of proposed legislation. Under the constituent power the legislature may ratify amendments to the federal Constitution, call state constitutional conventions, and propose amendments to state constitutions. Through its judicial power the legislature may impeach, try, and remove from office, members of the executive or judicial branch of the state government. An executive power of the legislature is the confirmation of gubernatorial appointments. The legislature exercises an electoral power when it chooses state administrative officers and boards. In two states the legislature may choose the governor when no candidate has a majority of the popular vote. Finally, through appropriations, investigations, and other means the legislature exerts control over the state administration.

The powers of state legislatures are subject to four major limitations: (1) those contained in the federal Constitution and laws of Congress enacted in accordance with it (see Chapter 2 for a discussion of the restrictions on state powers contained in the federal Constitution); (2) those contained in the state constitutions (see Chapter 4 for a discussion of the limitations on the powers of the legislature contained in state constitutions); (3) judicial review of legislation by the Supreme Court of the United States or the state courts; and (4) action of the people in approving or disapproving legislative acts by means of the initiative and referendum.

STRUCTURE OF THE LEGISLATURE

The legislature in forty-nine states is composed of two houses and is said to be bicameral in structure. Four states have tried the one-house, or unicameral, plan but only Nebraska has retained it. All the upper houses and the single chamber in Nebraska are called "senates." The lower house is called "house of representatives" in forty-one states, the "general assembly" in New Jersey, the "assembly" in California, Nevada, New York, and Wisconsin and the "house of delegates" in Maryland, Virginia, and West Virginia. Lower houses vary in size from thirty-five members in Delaware to four hundred in New Hampshire. The membership of state senates ranges from seventeen members in Delaware and Nevada to sixty-seven in Minnesota. (See Appendix, pp. 262f.)

Bicameralism and Unicameralism. *Bicameralism* is a vigorous survival of a long course of historical development. Its continuance is often justified by the argument that separate consideration of measures in two houses reduces the possibility of hasty and ill-considered legislation. Many reformers advocate *unicameralism* on the grounds of economy of money and time, the concentration of the popular will in one house, the elimination of deadlocks between houses, and the greater certainty in fixing responsibility for legislative acts or failures to act. In addition, it is supposed that membership in a unicameral legislature carries greater prestige and thus attracts more able men than membership in one of the houses of a bicameral legislature. Despite the successful experiment of Nebraska with a unicameral legislature since 1937, no other state has seriously considered adopting this system since Vermont abandoned it in 1836.

Apportionment. In all states, the basic unit of representation for both houses of the legislature is the single member district. The boundaries of districts are coterminous with those of counties or other subdivisions. State constitutions frequently specify that each county or town, no matter how small, shall return at least one representative. Such antiquated constitutional provisions have resulted in rural overrepresentation and urban underrepresentation; through these provisions rural representatives have retained their favored position and thus control over the amendment process despite the rapid growth of urban population. The Supreme Court ruled in 1964 that both houses of a state legislature must be apportioned on a population basis.

Many state constitutions provide for apportionment, and in Delaware and Maryland these apportionments are permanent. The other states allow reapportionment by the legislature, but rural members, owing to their numerical strength, are often able to prevent reapportionment of the seats. A number of legislatures have not reapportioned seats for several decades. In a few states another body may reapportion the state if the legislature does not act. In Illinois, for example, the governor may appoint a bipartisan commission to apportion anew the seats in the legislature.

Legislative districts, in theory, should be compact and approximately equal in population. Sometimes, however, a new apportionment fails to achieve these results because of *gerrymandering,* the redistricting of the seats in an effort to continue the majority party's control of the legislature. District lines are redrawn so that voters of the opposition party are concentrated in few districts, making it possible for the party in power to carry the others. Consequently, gerrymandered districts are generally grotesque in shape and greatly unequal in population.

Sessions. Most state constitutions do not allow the legislatures sufficient time in which to complete their work. Biennial sessions are still the general rule, though there is a growing trend toward annual sessions. Expanding state programs and rapidly changing financial and administrative needs require frequent attention. Moreover, the legislatures are generally limited to a relatively brief regular session, the most common limitation being sixty days. Often it is necessary to call a legislature into special session —sometimes at the end of the regular session—in order to pass appropriation bills and other necessary legislation. Special sessions are also sometimes restricted; the maximum length allowed varies from fifteen days in certain states to sixty days in others.

The *split session*, which encourages the systematic consideration of business, was first adopted in California in 1911 and is now used in four states. Under this plan the legislature at first meets for a limited period during which bills are introduced and referred to committees. It then must adjourn for a specified number of days to allow its members to confer with their constituents and its committees to visit state institutions. After the legislature reconvenes, additional bills can be introduced only by extraordinary majorities. This second part of the session is devoted to consideration, debate, and passage of bills. (See pp. 264–265.)

Special or extraordinary sessions of the legislature may be called by the governor. In a few states the legislature itself may call a special session or may force the governor to call one. Generally the purpose of the special session must be specified in advance. By naming one or a few subjects, the governor may focus public attention upon them.

Qualifications of Members. In several states all qualified voters are eligible to hold legislative office; other states prescribe a higher minimum eligible age. (See pp. 54–56.) All states require a minimum period of residence within the state and a few insist on moral qualifications. Each house of the legislature is the judge of the election returns and qualifications of its members and may expel a member by a two-thirds vote. In most houses standing committees hear evidence and recommend decisions in cases of contested seats.

Terms of Office. State senators usually serve four-year terms; representatives, two-year terms. In Nebraska, members of the unicameral legislature serve for two years. (See pp. 254–259.)

Political scientists generally agree that a two-year term is too short to allow a legislator to gain the necessary experience for the important decisions he is called upon to make. Moreover, the legislator who wishes to run for re-election must devote part of his time to campaigning in the primary and general elections. Owing to the rapid turnover of membership in many state legislatures, the average legislator is relatively inexperienced.

Compensation. The salaries paid to legislators by most states are small. The same amount is paid members of both houses of the state legislature. In 1960 thirty-four states were using the salary plan, with biennial salaries ranging from $200 in New Hampshire to $15,000 in New York; these states were also paying for special sessions on a per diem basis. In that year three states were providing a combination of biennial salary and daily pay. The other sixteen states were using daily-pay plans which varied from about $5 to about $50 a day. (See Appendix, pp. 254ff.)

In a number of states legislators receive expense allowances. All states grant legislators a travel allowance, usually of ten cents per mile. In a few states the members' expense allowance exceeds the daily pay. Compensation for legislators is set by the constitution in some states and by statute in others; it is set in a few states by a combination of constitution and statute. Several states provide legislators with retirement pensions through the system established for civil service employees.

Privileges and Immunities. State constitutions grant legislators privileges and immunities which are similar to the privileges and immunities provided in the federal Constitution. Generally, legislators are immune from arrest during and going to and from sessions of the legislature, except in cases of treason, felony, and breach of peace. Legislators are also immune from suit for slanderous remarks made in debate on the floor of the house or in the confines of the committee room.

Occupational Distribution. Although the occupational distribution of members in the legislature differs from state to state, in most places all occupations are represented; lawyers usually form the largest group and farmers, the second largest. When a pressure group wishes to secure the enactment of a law, it often promotes the election of one or several of its members to the state legislature.

ORGANIZATION OF THE LEGISLATURE

Numerous officers and committees are necessary in order to provide for orderly procedure and to efficiently subdivide the work of the state legislature. Their actions are subject to scrutiny and to control by the legislative house by which they were appointed.

Presiding Officers. The *speaker* is the presiding officer of the lower house in all states (including the unicameral Nebraska legislature) and is chosen from the members of the lower house.

The *lieutenant governor,* elected by the voters, is the presiding officer of the senate in thirty-five states. In the remaining fourteen states the senate chooses a president from its own membership to preside over its sessions.

The speaker exerts great influence over the house because he can (1) appoint committees, (2) refer bills to committees, (3) recognize members who wish to address the house, (4) administer rules of the house. When the senate elects its own presiding officer, his powers are similar to those of the speaker of the house. The lieutenant governor is rarely vested with power to appoint committees, and his influence is slight. The efficient functioning of a legislative house depends on the ability and hard work of its presiding officer. His influence may often smooth the road to legislation.

Other Legislative Officers. Each house of the state legislature has several officers in addition to the presiding officer. Clerks, the sergeant-at-arms, and the chief doorkeeper usually are chosen by the legislature on nomination by a caucus of the majority party. Selection of these officers by the merit system would be a desirable substitute for the present system.

Legislative Committees. The legislature is organized into committees to facilitate the lawmaking process. The median number of house committees was twenty-three in 1960; the number varied from eight in South Carolina to sixty-three in Missouri. The median number of senate committees was twenty-one; New Mexico with seven had the smallest number and Mississippi with forty-six had the largest.

Committees are classified as standing, joint standing, special (or select), and interim. A *standing committee* is a permanent committee entitled to consider all bills which pertain to its area of legislation. The province of a standing committee may be a subject like appropriations or education or an aspect of procedure like rules or the review of government operations. A *joint standing committee* is a permanent committee which draws its membership equally from both houses of the legislature. Twenty-seven states utilize one or more joint standing committees. In Connecticut and Massachusetts all bills introduced in either house are referred to joint standing committees which conduct hearings and make recommendations to both houses of the legislature for the passage or defeat of bills. A *special,* or *select, committee* is temporary in nature, and its function is to investigate and report on only one subject. An *interim committee,* which may be either separate or joint, conducts investigations between sessions of the legislature. (See Appendix, "Legislative Procedure," pp. 266–267.) The existence of so many committees gives rise to several problems. Members of both houses are appointed to too many committees; the attention of the legislators is divided among so many committees that it is difficult to find a convenient time at which all members of a particular committee may meet. Worse still, a legislator's effort is distributed not only among too many problems but also among problems too varied in nature by membership in such a large number of committees, and his time (as well as effort) is frequently wasted by the duplication of committee functions. To further complicate the situation, the jurisdiction of committees sometimes is not clearly drawn and, as a result, disputes arise over which group should consider a certain bill. These and other problems thwart the hopes and purposes of many committees and call for thorough reconsideration and reorganization of the committee system in the majority of state legislatures.

Party Organization. Though party organization is not officially a part of legislative organization, it is influential. The principal party organ in each house is the caucus. Each major party organizes a caucus which is composed of all party members elected to the house.

Before the house is organized, the caucus is busy nominating its candidate for speaker and candidates for the other offices and sometimes preparing a preliminary slate of committees. Each party caucus also chooses a floor leader to lead the debate on behalf of the party and to defend its policies from attack. The floor leader is often assisted by whips who attempt to induce caucus members to support party bills. After the legislature is organized, the caucus is sometimes called into session to thrash out matters on which there is disagreement and to decide on a program which members of the party will support. Usually, however, policies are determined by party leaders.

LEGISLATIVE PROCEDURE

The number of bills introduced in a state legislature during each session varies from a few hundred in some states to four or five thousand in others; however, the process of lawmaking is similar in every state. The state constitution commonly contains procedural requirements, such as the following: that each bill, except appropriation bills, shall be confined to one subject, which shall be clearly expressed in its title; that each bill shall be read by title when introduced; that each bill shall be read on three separate days in each house; and that the *yeas* and *nays* shall be recorded on demand of a specified number of members. At its first session each house of the legislature adopts rules containing detailed provisions; ordinarily they are the rules of the preceding house, with perhaps a few revisions. The rules systematize legislative procedure from the introduction of a bill to its final passage. (See Appendix, p. 268.)

Introduction and First Reading. Individual members or committees of either house may *introduce* bills on most subjects. Revenue bills, however, must originate in the lower house. Although individual legislators are the official sponsors, most of the bills introduced are drafted by private individuals and organizations. In recent years the governor has become an important source of legislative proposals.

When a bill is introduced it is read by a clerk; this constitutes the *first reading.*

Reference. After its introduction the presiding officer refers a bill to an appropriate committee. The power of *reference* is an important one for the following reasons: certain bills may lie within the scope of two or more committees; the fate of the bill may very well depend on the presiding officer's decision: one committee may report a bill favorably and another may refuse to report it at all. An interested committee may sometimes successfully appeal to the house to change the reference.

The Committee Stage. The functions of a legislative committee are to examine the details of bills, determine underlying facts, and report its conclusions to the house. With rare exceptions committee meetings must be held when the house is not in session. After the public hearing, which generally is held on a bill of importance, the committee meets behind closed doors to consider the bill. The committee report may recommend (1) that the bill be passed as it stands, or (2) that it be passed with amendments, or (3) that a substitute be passed, or (4) that the bill be indefinitely postponed.

Owing to their great number, it is impossible for the committee to give adequate consideration to all bills. The chairman selects the most important ones for committee consideration. The power of committees to "pigeon-hole" bills varies from state to state. A few states require that all bills must be reported by the committee after a specified period has elapsed; in others the committee may hold the bill indefinitely unless the legislative house, by a majority or extramajority vote, withdraws it from committee and brings it to the floor for consideration.

Debate on the Floor. Bills reported favorably by committees are placed on the calendar along with other measures. Usually they are considered in the order in which they appear on the calendar. When its turn comes, the bill comes up for a second reading either in the house or in the committee of the whole. The procedure is less formal in the committee of the whole: numerous roll calls are avoided, speeches are short, and questions may be asked and answered. The second reading may be either of the bill as a whole or only of section titles. As each section is read, amendments may be offered and passed. When the discussion ends the speaker of the house takes the chair and the chairman of the committee of the whole reports to the house. The house then votes whether to approve the actions of the committee. Whether or not the committee of the whole is used, there is a time limit on debates. If this time limit is not fixed by prior agreement, the previous question may be moved at any time; this action brings the bill to an immediate vote. A decision may be reached by a voice vote, a standing vote or—on demand of a group of members—a record vote.

Engrossment and Passage. After being passed on second reading, the bill is sent to the engrossing room where a completely new copy, including all amendments, is prepared. Engrossed bills are placed on the calendar for the third reading, which is usually only a formality. Amendment, with the exception of striking out the enacting clause (which kills the bill), generally is not permitted. At the end of the third reading a vote is taken on the final passage of the bill.

Action in the Second House. A bill that passes one house is transmitted to the second house, where all the procedural steps are repeated. Should the second house vote amendments to the bill, the bill is returned to the first house for concurrence. If the first house refuses to adopt the amendments proposed by the second house, a conference is arranged at which representatives of the two houses attempt to work out a compromise that will be acceptable to both houses. If either house rejects the conference report, the bill is lost. If the bill is passed in identical form by both houses, it is transmitted to the governor for his approval.

Executive Action. In every state except North Carolina the governor possesses the *veto,* that is, the power to refuse to sign a bill and to return it with his objections to the house in which it originated. The vote necessary to override the governor's veto varies from state to state. In twenty-four states it may be overridden by a two-thirds vote of all members elected to each house; in thirteen states, by two-thirds of the members present (assuming a quorum); in a dozen other states, by three-fifths or a majority of all members elected to each house.

The governor is given a specified period of time, three to fifteen days, to consider a bill. If he fails to act within the specified period, the bill becomes law without his signature. In seventeen states the governor possesses the *pocket veto:* the power to kill a bill by failing to sign it within the specified number of days, three to forty-five, subsequent to the adjournment of the legislature. Bills killed by a pocket veto may be repassed by an ordinary majority vote in each house during the next session of the legislature and submitted to the governor a second time for his approval.

In forty-one states the governor may use the *item veto:* the power to refuse to approve separate items of appropriation bills. Even the President of the United States does not possess this important power. Through its use the governor may protect his fiscal program against legislative logrolling and prevent the insertion of extraneous legislation (riders) in appropriation bills. In Alaska, California, Hawaii, Massachusetts, New Jersey, and Pennsylvania, the governor may reduce the amounts of items in appropriations bills, and in Washington he may veto sections in general bills. The item veto may be overridden in the same manner as an ordinary veto.

The governor of Massachusetts, New Jersey, or Virginia may return an act with proposed amendments to the legislature with the assurance that he will sign the act if it is amended in accordance with his suggestion. If the legislature refuses to adopt the amendments proposed by the governor, the act is returned to the governor and he must then approve or veto it.

LEGISLATIVE AIDS

Legislators often lack the time and the competence to gather and analyze information needed for lawmaking, and relatively few are qualified to draft bills in proper form. Many states have created staff agencies to provide legislators with assistance in these matters.

Legislative Reference Bureaus. Wisconsin generally is given credit for establishing (in 1901) the first legislative reference bureau, although New York in 1890 had created such a bureau as a branch of the state library. In forty-five states legislative reference services now provide pertinent and reliable information to members of the legislature. At the request of a member or a committee, the professional researchers on the bureau's staff prepare digests of information. The services of legislative reference bureaus have substantially reduced the burden of legislators and have permitted them to function more effectively.

Bill Drafting Services. Laws should not be ambiguous; their meaning must be clear. Bill drafting requires legal training and highly technical skills. Until the early 1900's most legislators who wished to introduce bills depended for assistance in bill drafting on lawyers and lobbyists. To prevent abuses, legislatures in all states except Idaho, Vermont, and Wyoming have provided some sort of official *bill drafting agency*. It is sometimes the attorney general's office, but more often it is a group of experts who may be assigned to the reference bureau. An efficient bill drafting service not only drafts bills in correct form for legislators but also provides information as to the constitutionality of proposals and their effect on other laws that are already on the statute books. Since official bill drafting services were introduced, the technical quality of bills has greatly improved.

Legislative Councils. A *legislative council* is a more or less permanent body composed almost entirely of legislators, which studies legislative problems between sessions. A professional research staff of the council prepares a comprehensive program for the consideration of the legislature. Kansas (in 1933) was the first state to create a legislative council; its lead has been followed by over thirty-five states. The councils vary in size from five mem-

bers in South Carolina to two hundred and sixty members in
Pennsylvania. All legislators are members of the council in Nebraska, Oklahoma, Pennsylvania, and South Dakota.
Reviser of Statutes. The position of reviser of statutes has
been created in a number of states to eliminate obsolete or unconstitutional provisions and to prepare editions of the collected
laws of the state. (The collected laws are called the revised statutes in some states and codes in others.) Statute revision in
some form or other has now been undertaken by more than
thirty states.

CONTROL OF ADMINISTRATION

The legislature, as the basic policy-making branch of government, determines in what activities the state will engage and
how they shall be carried out. Through the exercise of various
powers it may maintain general oversight of state administration.
Statutory Control. Many of the departments of state governments owe their existence to statutes passed by the legislature.
By means of these statutes, the legislature defines their powers,
their organizations, and their methods. If the legislature is not
satisfied with the way in which state administration is carried
out it may abolish agencies and create new ones to do the work.
Investigations. Legislative investigating committees determine
whether the laws are being carried out by administrators, whether
corruption exists, or whether the administrator is competent.
They also collect information which is useful in passing new
laws designed to correct administrative abuses and to generally
strengthen administration. Unfortunately, legislative investigations are frequently used for partisan purposes. An investigation
may be conducted to embarrass the administration if it is controlled by the opposition party, or to whitewash a poor administration if it is controlled by the party in power.
Financial Supervision. Through its annual or biennial appropriation bills, the legislature exercises control by granting or
withholding funds to administrative departments and agencies.
It may specify in great detail how funds may be spent. In ten
states the legislature elects the post auditor to examine the accounts of administrative officers and agencies and determine
whether or not funds have been spent in accordance with legislative directions.

Requirements of Reports. The requirement that administrative departments and agencies must submit periodic reports to the legislature provides the legislature with much information that enables it to control administration. Required reports have a salutary effect upon administrative departments and agencies by forcing them to plan and execute programs with care. Unfortunately, the reports submitted by administrative departments and agencies often are incomplete and of poor quality. Then, too, the reports sometimes gather dust because the legislature does nothing with them.

Appointments and Removals. Most state constitutions require senatorial approval of gubernatorial appointments. The constitution in a number of states permits the governor to remove public officials from office only upon address of the legislature. *Address* is a formal request of the legislature that the governor remove a public official from office.

Impeachment. Executive, judicial, and administrative officials may be removed from office by impeachment in every state except Oregon. In forty-seven states the lower house votes *impeachment,* a formal written statement of charges against an official; and the state senate acts as a court to try him. (In Alaska, the role of the two houses is reversed; in Nebraska, the supreme court acts as a court of impeachment.) Conviction usually requires a two-thirds vote and results in the removal of the official from office. The impeachment process is slow and costly and not always effective. State administrative officials have been infrequently removed from office by this method.

9

THE GOVERNOR

The governor is by far the most important officer in state government. He occupies a position of dignity and influence, represents the state on ceremonial occasions both within and outside the state, and wields considerable power both in legislation and in administration. In state constitutions he is often called the "chief" or "supreme" executive; a better title might be "principal" executive because there are other elective executive officers who occupy secure positions from which they sometimes oppose and harass the governor. Nevertheless, a courageous, resourceful, and energetic governor can find means to exercise a dominant influence throughout the state government. Many former governors have become United States senators or have been appointed to high offices in the national government. At least ten Presidents of the United States served as state governors at some time during their early careers.

HISTORICAL DEVELOPMENT OF THE OFFICE

The office of governor as it exists today is the product of a curious historical development. In colonial days the governor of a royal colony was the personal representative of the king and, as such, exercised all executive powers and many legislative and judicial powers as well. He was frequently in conflict with the popularly elected colonial assembly. When royal authority ceased and state constitutions were adopted, the state governor was generally subordinated to the legislature. In eleven states the governor was elected by the legislature; only Massachusetts and New York provided for popular election of the governor. His term of office was fixed at one year in ten states and at two or three years in the others. In several states he was limited in the number of terms he could serve. The governor was not empowered to recommend legislation, nor to call special sessions of the legislature, nor to veto legislation except in two or three states. His appointive power was limited; important appointments were generally made by the legislature. Furthermore, most of the powers exercised by the governor were granted to him by acts of the legislature.

During the early part of the nineteenth century two important influences were at work to strengthen the governor's position. These were (1) popular loss of confidence in the legislature and (2) the prevailing idea of Jacksonian democracy that public officials should be elected by popular vote. Through constitutional amendment the governor's dependence on the legislature was lessened, and he was given a qualified veto over legislation. By 1825 all governors were elected by the people. Through the same two influences, other state officials were also made popularly elective and were given independent powers. The dispersal of executive powers, thus embedded in the constitutions, could be altered only with great difficulty.

As the states assumed new governmental functions during the latter half of the nineteenth century, additional offices and boards were created. Certain of these were made elective, but many of the more important ones were made appointive by the governor with the consent of the state senate. Many members of boards served for long terms and could be removed only with difficulty; thus, the governor's ability to direct the officers he appointed was often limited.

The early twentieth century witnessed the birth of the administrative reorganization movement which had as a principal object the strengthening of the administrative powers of the governor. In more than half the states the governor's term of office has been lengthened, restrictions on his eligibility to succeed himself have been removed, his powers of appointment and supervision have been broadened, and he has been provided with staff assistance in budgeting, managing personnel, planning, and purchasing. Single offices and boards have been grouped together into departments under the immediate supervision of the governor. (See Chapter 10 for a discussion of the administrative reorganization movement.)

ELECTION OF THE GOVERNOR

The constitutions of all the states go to great lengths in trying to prevent the election and continuance in office of persons who are improperly qualified for the responsibilities of the governorship. If the provisions are mostly negative, it is because the positive qualifications of fitness are so various as to defy enumeration.

Qualifications for Governorship. The most common qualifications attempt to assure that only mature persons who have sufficient experience with the problems of the state will be eligible for the office of governor. Thirty-six states set thirty-five as the minimum age in 1960. In Oklahoma the governor must be thirty-one years old; in Alaska, thirty; in four other states, twenty-five; and in eight, the governor must be of voting age. United States citizenship is a requisite in all states, although it is specifically mentioned in only thirty-eight constitutions. A minimum period of residence within the state, usually of from five to ten years, is customarily required. These minimum qualifications are seldom operative, because most candidates for governor have had long experience in state political life.

Term of Office. In order to secure frequent oversight by the electorate, the two-year term was until recently the general rule. In 1961 the governor's term was four years in thirty-three states and two years in only seventeen states. Most political scientists (and the model state constitution) recommend a four-year term, for a new governor can scarcely become acquainted with the complexities of the office and govern effectively in a shorter term.

Election and Re-eligibility. In all states a popular vote for the election of the governor is required. A plurality is sufficient for election in all but four states, which require a majority of the popular vote for election. If, in these four states, no candidate receives a majority of the popular vote, the final choice is made as follows: by the legislature meeting in joint session in Georgia or Vermont; by the lower house alone in Maine or Mississippi.

Fifteen states (in which the chief executive is elected for a four-year term) have adopted the practice of scheduling gubernatorial elections in years when there is no presidential election; this is desirable in order that state issues, rather than national issues, may be uppermost in the minds of the voter when a governor is elected.

A bare majority of the state constitutions place no limit on the number of times a governor may be successively re-elected. When a governor has made a good record in office the voters may properly reward him with another term. In some states where the fear of executive tyranny or machine rule persists, constitutional provisions limit the governor to one or two terms or make him ineligible for re-election until one full term has intervened. (See Appendix, pp. 274–275.)

Removal from Office. In every state except Oregon the governor may be removed from office by impeachment (See Chapter 8), but usually only for high crimes and misdemeanors. A governor convicted on an impeachment charge may also be declared ineligible to hold any other office in the future. Since the Civil War, only a few governors have been removed through impeachment proceedings and since 1929 no governor has been removed. In twelve states the recall may be utilized to remove the governor either for misconduct or for political reasons. Lynn J. Frazier of North Dakota (1921) has been the only governor to be removed by recall.

Vacancy and Succession. The constitutions of thirty-eight states provide for the popular election of a lieutenant governor who will succeed to the governorship in the event of the governor's death, disability, or removal from office. The lieutenant governor must possess the same qualifications as the governor. In the other states the governor is usually succeeded by the president of the senate. To provide against the possibility of further vacancy the state legislature may establish a line of succession by statute.

The constitutions of several states provide for the exercise of gubernatorial powers by the lieutenant governor or another officer when the governor is temporarily absent from the state. Only the constitution of Alabama fixes the period of temporary absence; it provides that the lieutenant governor shall assume the duties and powers of the office when the governor has been absent during a period of twenty days. In certain other states occasional incidents have occurred when the lieutenant governor has taken advantage of the governor's absence for a few hours to issue pardons and to sign bills passed by the legislature.

All the state constitutions provide for the assumption of the governor's powers by the lieutenant governor or other officer when the governor is unable to discharge the duties of his office. Few constitutions have defined "inability," however, or set up a method of action. In Alaska the legislature may prescribe the procedure for declaring the office vacant if the governor has been absent from his office or unable to perform his duties during a

period of six months. The Three states provide that the highest
state court shall determine the question when it is submitted:
in Mississippi, by the secretary of state; in Alabama, by any of two
of six specified officers; and in New Jersey, by a two-thirds vote of
all members of each house of the legislature. The Alabama
provision seems to be preferable, because it both protects the
governor's interests and provides for prompt action in a serious
emergency.

Salary and Emoluments. Considering the duties and responsibilities of his office, the governor is probably the most poorly
paid executive in America. In 1960 the annual salary ranged from
$9,000 in North Dakota to $50,000 in New York. Only eight states
paid $25,000 or more; thirty-one states paid $15,000 or less. There
is a tendency to allow the legislature to fix the governor's salary;
for example, the constitution of Hawaii stipulates that "the
compensation of the governor . . . shall be prescribed by law, but
shall not be less than $18,000." Four-fifths of the states provide
an official residence for the governor and all provide allowances
for his official expenses. (See Appendix, pp. 274–275.)

POWERS OF THE GOVERNOR

The governor possesses no inherent powers. The state constitution is the principal source of the governor's powers, but other
powers may be granted by the legislature through statute. Though
the duties of the governor are mainly executive, he has important legislative and judicial powers.

Executive Powers. The governor is usually charged with responsibility for the faithful execution of the laws. In states where
no major administrative reorganization has occurred, the governor's executive powers are inadequate to direct the whole administration of the state. He must share administrative powers
with a number of elected officers who are responsible only to
the law and to the voters. The governor has no direct control
over their departments except that in thirty-seven states he may
require them to submit formal reports. In many states there are
officers and boards which, though appointed by the governor,
are nearly independent of his control. The enforcement of many
laws has been vested in county and town officers who are elected
by the people. The governor rarely is given the power to remove

them. Nevertheless, the governor may indirectly exert influence over all these officers by mobilizing public opinion against certain of their policies and in favor of policies he recommends.

APPOINTMENT OF OFFICIALS. Under the state constitution and the laws, the governor may generally appoint heads of departments and members of commissions created by statute, but his appointments must be confirmed by others. Approval by the senate is required in forty-six states; by the legislature in joint session in Alaska; and by the executive council (a relic from the colonial period) in Maine, Massachusetts, and New Hampshire. Several political scientists have suggested that the appointing power should be vested solely in the governor, because securing confirmation has often resulted in political bargains in which the governor has agreed to appoint friends of senators in return for their support of his legislative program.

REMOVAL OF OFFICIALS. The governor is in most states without power to remove elective officials, though he may suspend them from office to await action by the legislature or the courts. He may usually remove appointive officials for legal cause, though senate or council approval is almost everywhere required. In some states certain specified officers may be removed only on address of the legislature. Recently there has been a trend toward granting the governor the unqualified power of removal. It is justified on the ground that the governor cannot be expected to enforce the laws if he cannot remove a subordinate who ignores or defies his orders. The constitutional provision which most simply and effectively expresses the recent trend is a contribution of the State of Alaska: department heads serve at the pleasure of the governor.

SUPERVISION OF ADMINISTRATION. One of the chief difficulties of the governor's position is that he is expected to be responsible for efficient administration without having the requisite powers. The threat of suspension or removal may sometimes be adequate to induce an administrative officer to do his duty as the governor sees it. The requirement of reports from administrative officers can be a powerful tool *if* the governor insists upon their adequacy and takes proper action when deficiencies in administration are apparent. The governor often has investigatory powers over officers and departments, and can bring pressure to bear by publicizing the results. If corruption is uncovered the governor can file charges against those who are responsible. He may also institute judicial proceedings to compel negligent officials to perform their duties.

FINANCIAL CONTROL. Though the governor's financial powers are mostly legislative in nature, certain aspects are useful in administrative control. When the governor is preparing the executive budget for submission to the legislature, he may strike out or reduce items of expenditure recommended by department heads. Without the governor's approval it is difficult if not impossible, for the department head to secure the desired appropriation. After the legislature has granted appropriations the governor is, in many states, empowered to allot funds on a periodic basis to the departments. The power to specify the amount that a department may spend during a given period enables the governor to exercise some control over all departments.

MILITARY POWERS. The governor is commander in chief of state units of the national guard except when they are called into the service of the United States. He also directs, in thirty-six states, the state police, which has general law-enforcing responsibility, and, in the other states, the highway patrol. The national guard may be called out by the governor to suppress riots and other disorders. If a serious emergency occurs the governor may request the President to send a detachment of federal troops into the state.

EXTERNAL RELATIONS. The governor is the official spokesman for the state in her relations with the federal government and with other states. When the speaker of the federal House of Representatives informs him that a vacancy exists in the state's representation, the governor is required to issue writs of election for the choice of a congressman. If a dispute arises between two states, the governors enter into negotiations to settle it. In the event of failure, one of the governors may institute a suit on behalf of his state in the Supreme Court of the United States. Governors have full discretion in rendition proceedings (see Chapter 3) for the return of fugitives from justice. (One governor may address a formal request to another governor for the return of a fugitive for trial. The governor addressed decides whether or not to order the fugitive's return.) In less formal relationships, the governor may confer with the President of the United States or the governor of another state, or attend governors' conferences at which problems of common interest are discussed.

Legislative Powers. During the past 180 years the governor has gradually advanced from a position of subordination to the legislature to a position of legislative leadership. Among the causes of this development have been the relative inexperience of legislators, short sessions, and the consequent inability of the legislature to generate a comprehensive legislative program. On the other hand, the governor is a full-time official, constantly made aware of state problems, and expected by the people to assume large responsibilities for the government of the state. His relative weakness in administration is an incentive for the governor to attempt to accomplish results through legislation.

LEGISLATIVE PROGRAM. The constitutional requirement that he must inform the legislature of the condition of the state has been utilized by the governor to present a more or less complete legislative program. Before the legislature meets, the governor, with the assistance of his staff, prepares a message outlining the principal state problems and proposing legislative solutions. He delivers this message at the opening session of the legislature and thus focuses legislative and popular attention on his program; later he may send messages emphasizing the importance of passing particular bills. The governor may also draft bills in complete form for introduction in the legislature. If the legislature appears to be reluctant to accept his program, he may confer with leaders or members individually and may appeal to the people through radio, television, and platform appearances to bring pressure on their representatives. If his party has a majority in the legislature, he may bring the pressure of the party organization to bear. During the period when the legislature is in session the average governor devotes his energies almost exclusively to the accomplishment of his legislative program.

CALL OF SPECIAL SESSIONS. All the state constitutions empower the governor to call special sessions of the legislature whenever in his judgment the need arises. Constitutional limitations on the length of the regular session may prevent the legislature from completing its work, in which case the governor may call a special session immediately after the regular session. If a financial or other emergency arises, the governor is expected to call a special session. In about thirty states the legislature is limited in special sessions to the subjects mentioned in the governor's call; by mentioning only one or a few subjects the governor may concentrate legislative and popular attention on important reforms.

ADJOURNMENT OF THE LEGISLATURE. In about twenty states the governor has the power to adjourn the legislature for a limited period, if the two houses are unable to agree on a time for adjournment. The governor's power of adjournment is seldom used and is of no importance except to break deadlocks between the houses and to provide an opportunity for informal agreements among the leaders.

POWER OF VETO. The *veto power* (see Chapter 8) is negative in effect: It enables the governor to prevent the passage of legislation. Early governors used the veto chiefly on grounds of unconstitutionality or encroachment on the governor's powers. Today a governor vetoes bills if, in his judgment, their passage is not in the best interest of the state or its people. In New York the legislature hurriedly passes numerous bills during the last few days of its session, but the governor on the average vetoes one-fourth of them. At the opposite extreme the governor of Massachusetts customarily vetoes only a few bills during the entire legislative year. In several states the governor's veto is seldom overridden because of two factors: the extraordinary majority required by the constitution before this can be done; and the habit of many legislatures to pass most of their bills at the very end of the legislative session. Statistics of bills vetoed and set aside provide only a partial means of estimating the effect of the veto power. A governor's threat to veto a bill has resulted in the quiet pigeonholing of many a bill in the legislature.

PREPARATION OF THE BUDGET. A relatively recent addition to the governor's powers is the constitutional or statutory authorization to prepare a budget for submission to the legislature. The budget is a balanced estimate of the state's receipts and expenditures during the approaching fiscal year. In preparing the budget the governor takes the responsibility for recommending taxes as well as for setting down in detail the amounts and purposes of proposed expenditures. The legislature, when it considers the budget, must take the same responsibility and must justify its deviations from the governor's budget figures.

ISSUANCE OF ORDINANCES. The increasing volume of legislation during recent years has resulted in the practice of passing brief statutes which embody only the broad outlines of policy concerning a subject. The legislature leaves the details to be filled out by the governor through the issuance of ordinances or rules. Generally these ordinances are designed to apply the principles of the law with greater precision than was possible when the legislature passed detailed statutes. As long as they do not exceed the powers granted in the statute, these ordinances have the same force as law. The use of the ordinance power saves the time of the legislature and provides for administrative flexibility in law enforcement.

Judicial Powers. Decisions on applications for executive clemency are probably the most trying and difficult duties of the governor. They always involve the prisoner's liberty and often his life. In most of the states clemency may be granted by the governor only upon the recommendation of an officer, board, or council. In nine states it may be granted by a board of which the governor is one of the members. In nine other states the governor has sole responsibility.

Executive clemency may be granted in several forms. A *pardon* is a release from the legal consequences of a crime and a remission of the penalties imposed. It has the effect of restoring an accused or convicted individual to his position in society as if no crime had been committed. Sometimes it is granted after a sentence has been completed in order to restore voting and other privileges. Most states provide that pardons may not be issued to persons convicted by impeachment or to other persons prior to conviction by a court. A *commutation of sentence* is a reduction of the penalty imposed; for instance, the substitution of life imprisonment for the death penalty, or a reduction in the total number of years to be served in prison. A *parole* is a release from confinement in prison, conditioned on the prisoner's future good behavior. He is usually required to report at intervals to a parole officer. Violation of the parole subjects the prisoner to reconfinement. A *reprieve* is a temporary stay of execution, usually limited to thirty days, which is sometimes granted in order that new evidence may be presented on behalf of the prisoner.

THE GOVERNOR'S INFLUENCE

In preceding sections numerous statements appear concerning ways in which the governor may enhance his constitutionally granted powers by the use of his influence upon others. It is desirable now to consider the sources of the governor's influence. They are not altogether to be discovered in strength of character, personality, or tireless energy, though these are desirable requisites for any executive position. Sources of influence are also to be found in party organization and in the prestige of the highest office of the state.

Leadership of the Party. At the time of his nomination the candidate for the office of governor is almost certain to be prominent in the councils of his party, though he is rarely the dominant party leader. His nomination may, or may not, have been dictated by a party boss or machine, but he must have the support of the party organization to be elected. As candidate for the governorship he at once acquires great prestige in the party, and he is almost certain to be consulted in the formulation of the party platform. During his campaign he amplifies the principles of the party in a series of personal pledges of his own and assists legislative and other state candidates of his party who in turn recommend him to the voters. The gubernatorial candidate's victory at the polls is usually a party victory.

After his election the governor finds a general disposition among party leaders to co-operate with him in the government of the state. Party government is, of course, a two-way street. The governor will do well to consult party leaders before announcing a program, and he will be expected to make some concessions in return for support. He must learn to give credit to others for their accomplishments. Above all he should impress party leaders with the idea that his program is sound and that their own political futures will be advanced by supporting it. If harmonious party relationships are maintained, the governor's problems will be immeasurably lightened.

Leadership of the State. The great prestige attached to the governor's office is a source of influence and power. The governor is regarded as the leader not only of his party but also of the whole population of the state. Under the condition of rural overrepresentation in the legislature, the people who live in the cities especially look to the governor as almost the only means by which their interests may receive recognition and support in state government. The state's citizenry want the governor to be informed at first hand of their problems. For this reason they invite him to attend public functions of all sorts where he may present his views on public matters and in turn may perceive the reactions of his audiences. His interest in their economic welfare is especially appreciated. By making himself accessible to the people and by establishing good public relations, the governor may obtain valuable support beyond the confines of his own party.

The existence of powers and opportunities for leadership is no guarantee that they will be exercised. Many conscientious governors have failed to realize their full opportunities because of personal limitations or the activities of more adept and powerful leaders in the state. Unfortunately there have been numerous examples of governors who have forfeited both party and popular leadership by supinely accepting the dictation of the party machine.

10

STATE ADMINISTRATIVE ORGANIZATION

In the beginning the state governments performed only a few functions directly and, therefore, needed only a simple administrative organization. Their few officers were usually elected by popular vote. In 1860 Massachusetts, for example, had only three agencies in addition to the elective officers. It was not until after the Civil War that the administrative activities of the states began to multiply. Industrialization and advances in technical knowledge created a popular demand for the states to assume new functions. The states complied and generally the result was the creation of a separate new agency to administer each function. The unplanned proliferation of agencies created a serious organizational problem. Overlapping, duplication, and rivalry among agencies resulted in waste both of money and of administrative effort. Despite vigorous efforts toward administrative reorganization during the present century, many elements of the traditional administrative structure are found today in most of the states.

PRINCIPAL OFFICES AND AGENCIES

The officers and agencies of state administration may be classified in several different ways. Probably the most useful classification is according to the methods by which they were created and their powers conferred. All offices and agencies have been created either by the state constitution or by statute.

Constitutional Offices. The oldest, but not necessarily the most important, state offices are those which owe their existence to the state constitution. Usually they are headed by single officers elected by popular vote. In addition to the powers granted by the constitution the legislature has often conferred important powers by statute. The constitutional officers occupy a fairly secure position because their positions can be abolished only by constitutional amendment. They are rarely subject to the governor's orders and are frequently at loggerheads with him and with each other. The number of constitutional officers is commonly six, though several states have more than this number, and several states have none at all or only a few. (See pp. 270–271.)

LIEUTENANT GOVERNOR. Thirty-eight state constitutions provide for a *lieutenant governor* to be elected by popular vote on a statewide basis. In Tennessee the position is created by statute and is filled by an election in the legislature. In thirty-five states, the lieutenant governor's principal duty is to preside over the senate. He does not head an administrative department as do the other constitutional elective officers, but in several states is a member of one or more administrative ex officio (by virtue of his office) boards.

SECRETARY OF STATE. The constitutions of forty-one states provide for a *secretary of state,* who is elected by the voters in thirty-eight states and by the legislature in Maine, New Hampshire, and Tennessee. The secretary of state is the custodian of all official documents and records. In each state he proclaims and publishes laws, and, as custodian of the official seal, affixes it to documents, commissions and other papers. Additional duties in many states include issuance of corporation charters, administration of elections, registration of motor vehicles, and other duties prescribed by the legislature. He executes policy, but generally is not a policy-making official. It is difficult to justify the independent status of the secretary of state. The governor's control of administration would be strengthened and the ballot would be shortened if the secretary of state were appointed by the governor.

STATE TREASURER. The office of *state treasurer* is created by the constitution in forty-five states and by statute in Alaska, Hawaii, New Jersey, and Virginia. In New York the Department of Taxation and Finance performs the duties of the treasurer. He is elected by popular vote in forty-two states, by the legislature in three states, and he is appointed by the governor in four states. The state treasurer's functions are the receipt, custody, and disbursement of state funds. He possesses little discretionary authority and disburses funds only when authorized by an administrative official and the state controller.

AUDITOR OR CONTROLLER. Every state has either an *auditor* or a *controller* (often officially spelled *comptroller*) whose function is to scrutinize the state's financial transactions and accounts;

three-fifths of the states have both an auditor and a controller. Though the terminology of statutes sometimes confuses and even juxtaposes the distinction between them, properly speaking an auditor has the function of post-auditing, and a controller has the function of conducting a current audit. In current-auditing, the controller examines vouchers submitted by spending agencies and, before any money can be disbursed, must certify that the expenditure is covered by a legislative appropriation made in accordance with law. In post-auditing, the auditor examines accounts to determine whether they have been accurately kept and whether officials have been honest and have conformed to law in spending the state's money. The auditor in most states has the authority to prescribe accounting systems for state departments and agencies. He is granted access to the accounts, books, and records of all state departments and agencies. In a few states he examines the accounts of specified county officials annually. In some states the auditor is responsible for the supervision of banks, state land, and state property.

Most of the auditors and about half the controllers are popularly elected. Administrative experts recommend that current-auditing be performed by a controller appointed by the governor and post-auditing by an auditor elected by the legislature and subject to its control. The state auditor should not be appointed by the governor, because the auditor's chief function is to scrutinize expenditures made by the governor or made under his direction.

ATTORNEY GENERAL. The constitutions of forty states provide for an *attorney general;* in the other states his position has been created by statute. He is elected by popular vote in forty-two states and by the legislature in Maine. In the other seven states he is appointed. Administrative experts recommend that the attorney general be appointed by the governor rather than be elected.

As its chief legal officer, the attorney general represents the state when it is a party in a court case. In a few states the attorney general supervises local prosecutors and law-enforcement officers. He is the legal adviser to the governor, administrative departments and agencies, and the legislature. In fifteen states he provides bill-drafting services for the legislature and in approximately one-quarter of the states he gives legal advice to local officials. The opinions of the attorney general on constitutional and legal matters are of great importance in law enforcement.

SUPERINTENDENT OF PUBLIC INSTRUCTION. Every state provides for a *superintendent of public instruction* or a *commissioner of education*. He is popularly elected in twenty-three states and is appointed by the board of education in twenty-two states. The superintendent of public instruction is appointed by the governor in five states. In Vermont the governor must approve the selection made by the board of education.

The primary function of the superintendent of public instruction is the administration and enforcement of the state school laws. He is frequently an ex-officio member of the state board of education or its secretary. The superintendent of public instruction and the board of education are concerned with building construction, equipment, courses of instruction and their content, qualifications of teachers, selection and purchase of textbooks, and other matters. It is generally agreed that the superintendent of public instruction should be appointed rather than be popularly elected, but opinions are divided as to whether he should be appointed by the governor or by the state board of education.

Statutory Offices and Agencies. In creating new administrative offices and agencies the state legislatures have acted without plan and without sufficient consideration of the problems of state administration as a whole. Several of the statutory agencies, such as the public utility commission and the public health department, exercised more important powers than some of the constitutional officers. (See Chapters 16–20 for a consideration of the duties and functions of the principal state officers and agencies.) The importance of other statutory agencies ranged downward to comparative insignificance. The greatest possible variety was exhibited in the structure of administrative agencies. Some were headed by a single officer empowered to act alone; some by a single officer who could act only with the concurrence or advice of a board; others by a board or commission which employed a full-time administrative officer; still others by a board acting alone. An equal variety existed in methods of filling administrative positions. Some were elected by the legislature or by popular vote; some were appointed by the governor with, or without, the

consent of the senate; others were appointed by boards and commissions; and still others were composed of constitutional or
elective state officers who acted ex officiis. (See pp. 270–271.)

COMMISSIONS AND BOARDS. Administration by commissions is
justified when the function requires the exercise of quasi-legislative or quasi-judicial powers. Public utility regulation, for instance, presupposes hearings and the weighing of evidence prior
to the determination of rates to be charged and standards of
services to be provided. It is, however, difficult to justify the use
of boards for matters which involve more or less routine administrative duties. When members of a board represent different
interests and points of view, the points of view tend to cancel
each other out. The result is unimaginative and often tardy performance, instead of the vigorous and prompt action which is
the essence of good public administration. As usually constituted,
boards are less susceptible to executive control than departments
headed by single administrative officers. Staggered terms for
members are often the rule, in order to secure continuity of
administrative policy. Sometimes the terms are five, seven, or
more years in length. A governor, especially if his term is only
two years, can hardly hope to make a sufficient number of new
appointments to influence the board's policies.

LACK OF INTEGRATION. The very number of existing agencies,
which in some states exceeded one hundred at one time, would
have made executive supervision difficult under the best of circumstances. In this period few attempts were made toward the
functional integration of agencies. The end results of administrative disorganization were often extravagance, waste, duplication
of effort, corruption, and inefficiency in the administration of
state activities. (See Appendix, p. 248.)

THE ADMINISTRATIVE
REORGANIZATION MOVEMENT

Credit for beginning the *administrative reorganization movement* is usually given to the work of a commission on efficiency
and economy, appointed by President Taft in 1911, and to administration surveys conducted in fifteen states within the next
half dozen years. The first state to effect a fairly thorough reorganization was Illinois, where the legislature in 1917 consolidated the principal administrative functions under nine depart-

ments, each directly responsible to the governor. Several other states soon followed with either statutory or constitutional reorganizations. The movement was further stimulated by the reports of federal commissions in 1937 and 1949, and by numerous state commissions popularly known as "little Hoover commissions." At least thirty states have adopted more or less comprehensive reorganizations, and some of the others have acted to reorganize important portions of their administrative systems. Only four or five states have been able to effect complete administrative reorganizations. (See Appendix, pp. 247, 296f.)

Principles of Reorganization. Experts in the field of state administrative organization generally agree upon six basic principles of reorganization: concentration of responsibility in the governor, functionally integrated departments, assistance of expert staff, elimination of boards, uniformity of organization, and institution of independent audit. These principles may be applied separately, but the best results may be expected when they are used together.

CONCENTRATION OF RESPONSIBILITY. The strengthening of the governor's position is a major objective of the reorganization movement. As the chief elective officer, the governor is expected to assume responsibility for the administration of state government. Thus, it is reasonable that he should have authority commensurate with his responsibilities. Clear lines of authority should run from the governor, at the apex of the hierarchical pyramid, through departments, divisions, bureaus, and offices, to the base of the structure. He should have complete power to appoint and remove department heads in order that he may enforce responsibility throughout the administration.

FUNCTIONAL INTEGRATION. Departments should be organized according to major function. All agencies concerned with a particular operation should be grouped together in one department. Successive subdivisions of departments should be composed of similar groupings. The concept of a span of control influences the determination of the number of subdivisions to be created at each level. Depending upon the subject matter, experts estimate that one officer can supervise from three to seven immediate subordinates. However, the number of subordinates an executive can properly supervise depends upon the ability of both the executive and his subordinates. Most state reorganizations have provided for from ten to twenty departments.

STAFF ASSISTANCE. The governor cannot adequately supervise the complex administration of the modern state without expert staff assistance. The staff agencies in the governor's office should include: a *budget office*, to control the financing of departments and thereby supervise their operations; a *personnel office*, to study the operation of the state civil service system and the conditions under which state employees work; a *planning office*, to study the present and future needs of the state and recommend suitable new legislation and administrative adjustments; and a *central purchasing office*, to set proper standards and eliminate extravagance in procuring supplies for the state.

ELIMINATION OF BOARDS. Effective administration requires the elimination from the administrative structure of all boards which exercise little or no discretionary authority. Boards are expensive, less efficient than single administrators, inclined to shift responsibility, and relatively unresponsive to administrative direction. The commissions which exercise important quasi-judicial and quasi-legislative functions should be retained, but their purely administrative tasks should be transferred to appropriate departments.

UNIFORMITY OF ORGANIZATION. In order to eliminate confusion among many different organizational forms, it is desirable to effect a uniformity of structure and terminology throughout the state administration. Divisions, bureaus, and offices should have the same relative position in all departments. The titles of officers should also be brought into conformity with a basic pattern.

INDEPENDENT AUDIT. Administrative experts recommend that current auditing should be performed by a controller appointed by the governor and subject to his supervision. Since the governor is charged with the responsibility of administration he should be armed with this service of administrative control. Post-auditing, however, should be independent of the governor's control, and the results of the post-audit should be reported by the auditor to the legislature and to the public.

Criticism of Principles of Reorganization. Several political scientists have expressed doubts as to the validity of many of the principles set forth by administrative reformers. They ask such questions as the following: Why is it preferable to require administrative agencies to be personally responsible to the governor rather than to the law? Can popular election always result in the choice of a good and capable governor? Can any governor actually supervise all the multifarious activities of the modern state? Are not administrative reformers too much concerned with creating a structure which, though perfect in outline, or theory, may fail to satisfy the actual requirements of different functions and situations? Is there not danger that the concentration of all the agencies of state government in a few departments will result in combinations of unrelated functions, some of which will almost surely be neglected or unskillfully administered? Should not independent agencies be continued for the exercise of functions that ought to be divorced from politics? These are questions that deserve serious study when administrative reform is proposed. The answer to them will depend somewhat on the underlying political situation in a state.

Methods of Reorganization. Various methods have been used for the complete or partial reorganization of the administrative structure. (1) Reorganization by constitutional amendment is the best method, but it is also the slowest and most difficult because entrenched interest defend their positions at every opportunity in the amendment process. (2) Legislative reorganization may be accomplished with somewhat fewer difficulties, but no one can be sure that it will remain in effect. Pressures by interested parties may afterward result in the repeal of essential elements of the program. (3) Initiation of reorganization plans by the governor has been authorized in several states. The governor of Michigan is empowered to submit proposals for reorganization to the legislature which will become effective ninety days after the session unless in the meantime one or both houses object. This method appears to have two advantages: it is based on administrative experience; and it speeds up the process of reorganization. It should be recognized that reorganization is a more or less continuous process. New programs are created in response to new needs, and old programs are reduced in scope or eliminated.

Results of Reorganization. The administrative reorganization movement has had varying success in different states. In several states it has resulted in the elimination of all but one or two of the constitutional officers and the transfer of their functions to departments. In a majority of the others the essential services have been placed within integrated departments responsible to the governor. The movement has had to contend both with powerful vested interests and with deeply-rooted beliefs in the traditional system of popular election. Though every state has now improved financial control and has completed reforms in other matters, boards and elective officers still continue to clutter the administrative system. Whether or not administrative reorganization has resulted in increased efficiency and economy is sometimes disputed. Such matters are not easily susceptible of proof. When charges of extravagance are made the figures presented need to be examined with great care and with due allowance for the change in the value of the dollar and the value of the new services the state performs for its people.

11

THE STATE JUDICIARY

Law and courts are essential to the existence of organized society. Through a well-developed legal system the rights, privileges, and duties of individuals are established. Through a judicial system controversies are authoritatively settled. Depending on the types of cases brought before them, the courts adjudicate disputes, decide the guilt or innocence of persons accused of crime, protect personal and property rights, and determine the constitutionality of laws.

In terms of the number of courts and the number of cases adjudicated, the court systems of the fifty states are more important than the federal court system. Most of the commoner crimes, like murder, assault, burglary, and robbery are violations of state laws and hence are triable in state courts. The law relating to contracts, wills, inheritances, damages to persons and property, and commercial and personal relationships is likewise state law and, for the greater part, is enforced by state courts. When the litigants are citizens of different states and the amount involved is more than $10,000, federal courts may try cases related to such subjects; but the federal court is required to follow state law as determined authoritatively by decisions of the higher state courts. The state courts constitute an independent judicial system; they are in no way dependent on the federal court system.

TYPES OF LAW

With the exception of Louisiana, whose law is based on the Napoleonic Code, all the states have adhered to the Anglo-American legal system which is based largely on common law and equity.

Common Law. *Common law,* the oldest component of the Anglo-American legal system, began to be developed when early English judges decided cases on the basis of the prevailing customs of the people. When later cases arose it was common practice for the justices to decide them on the principle of *stare decisis*, which means to follow the precedents set in cases that had already been decided. In the absence of much legislation by Parliament, the common law gradually came to occupy the field of civil and criminal law. It crossed the Atlantic with the first settlers of the New World.

Equity. In the eleventh or twelfth century, *equity* was de-veloped as a supplement to the common law and a corrective of some of its rigidities. Chancery (or equity) courts did not need to wait until a wrong had been committed; they could issue a writ of injunction to prevent a threatened wrong. They were not limited in their remedies to requiring the payment of damages for a wrong; they could require specific performance of a con-tract or a restitution in kind. These are only the most outstand-ing characteristics of a rather complicated body of rules of equity. Violation of the order of a court was punishable by heavy fine or imprisonment at the discretion of the judge.

At present only Delaware, Mississippi, and Tennessee con-tinue to maintain separate courts of law and equity. A few states have placed the two remedies of equity and law under one court, but have required different procedural rules for each. In most states both law and equity are administered by the same courts and the remedies of both are available to the parties in the same case.

Statute Law. In contrast to common law and equity which were developed by the courts, *statute law* consists of acts passed by a legislative body. Statutes are superior in authority to com-mon law and equity and are often passed to modify or repeal some of their provisions. Almost all of the common law concern-ing crimes has been superseded by statutory law.

Constitutional Law. In American legal usage, a written con-stitution is superior to any other form of law; *constitutional law* supersedes common and statute law and equity. A legislative act passed in contravention of the terms of the state or national constitution may, under the famous principle of judicial review, be declared void and of no effect by the courts. If a state law may seem to violate some part of the federal Constitution, like the due process clause or the equal protection clause, the Supreme Court of the United States has final authority to determine the constitutionality of the state law, but the Court will refuse to accept it for review until all state judicial remedies have been exhausted; in other words, an appeal can be taken to the Supreme Court of the United States only from the highest state court having jurisdiction over a subject. The state supreme court is the final arbiter in any case in which a law is said to be repugnant to the provisions of the constitution of the state.

Both the federal and the state supreme courts have declared that they will not invalidate a law merely because they consider it unwise or inexpedient. Many people, nevertheless, believe that both federal and state supreme courts have at times been swayed by judges' political and economic philosophies. The invalidation of popular laws on technical or purely legal grounds has created much resentment. When the invalidation is by a margin of one vote, critics of the courts invariably insist that there must have been good reasons on both sides and that the popular will, as expressed by the legislature, should not be thwarted by the opinion of one judge. In Nebraska, North Dakota, and Ohio, the state constitutions require an extraordinary majority vote of the judges in order to invalidate acts of the legislature.

Criminal Law. The definition and punishment of offenses against the peace and order of the state constitute the bulk of *criminal law*. Crimes fall into two categories, felonies and misdemeanors. Though the dividing line between the two varies from state to state, a felony is always the more serious crime and is usually punishable by at least a short term in prison. Conviction for misdemeanor ordinarily is followed by a fine or a jail sentence. In many states minor traffic violations and other lesser offenses apparently constitute a third category, not sufficiently serious to be called misdemeanors. Prosecution for offenses is invariably brought in the name of the state or its people against an accused defendant.

Civil Law. Laws declaring the rights and duties of individuals in their relationships with each other are commonly called *civil laws*. An individual may enforce his rights by bringing a civil case against another person.

JUDICIAL ORGANIZATION

The organization of the courts in various states exhibits such great diversity as almost to defy classification. Many states have relatively complicated judicial systems with four or more levels of courts. On the other hand, relatively simple court structures are to be found in certain states. The principal levels of courts are, in ascending order: (1) minor courts in both rural and urban areas, (2) county courts with limited jurisdiction, (3) general trial courts, (4) intermediate courts of appeal, and (5) supreme courts. (See Appendix, pp. 272–273.)

Minor Courts. At the bottom of the judicial scale lie the courts of justices of the peace in rural areas and the magistrates' courts, with their specialized offshoots, in the cities. The jurisdiction of the minor courts is limited to the trial of civil cases in which the matters in dispute are of small value, and of criminal cases in which persons are accused of minor offenses. To the average litigant, however, such cases are of great personal importance. It is desirable that they be settled speedily, inexpensively, and justly.

THE JUSTICE OF THE PEACE. In rural areas and in small cities, a crude and uneven type of justice is dispensed by the *justice of the peace.* With a few exceptions, he has had no formal legal training; he is elected by the voters in a town or township for two or four years; he holds court whenever a case is brought before him; he keeps few and scanty records; he receives no salary but is compensated by the fees he collects in cases before him. If he is mercenary, he may maintain speed traps or decide cases in favor of those who bring him business. (The initials, "J.P." are sometimes said to stand for "judgment for the plaintiff.")

Experts in legal administration are unanimous in advocating the abolition of the office of justice of the peace or at least of the fee system. In Missouri justices of the peace have been replaced by magistrates, who are required to be lawyers. In Virginia and Maryland, though the title of justice of the peace remains, the incumbent is paid a salary and is required to have legal training. The office has been abolished in one or more cities of a dozen states and in at least one county in Alabama, Oregon, Tennessee, and Wisconsin.

THE CITY MAGISTRATE. *Municipal, police,* or *magistrates' courts* are at the base of the legal hierarchy in cities. They are authorized by the city charter or by law to enforce municipal ordinances, and usually they are granted, in addition, the civil and criminal jurisdiction of the justice of the peace. Judges of these courts are either popularly elected or appointed by the

mayor and council. Except in very small cities they have some
legal training. They are paid salaries, but the amounts are too
small to attract capable lawyers. Magistrates' courts are often
dingy, crowded, lacking in dignity and order, and are conducted
with undue haste.

SPECIALIZED COURTS. State legislatures and city councils have
created a number of specialized courts to hear particular types
of cases. The presiding judge is an expert and is often permitted
to follow less formal procedures than are required in other
courts. Common forms of specialized courts are *traffic courts* to
handle minor traffic violations, *police courts* to dispose summarily of cases arising from minor infractions of the law, *juvenile courts* to hear cases of minors accused of crime, *domestic
relations courts* to reconcile or to settle differences between es-
tranged spouses, and *small claims courts* to provide inexpensive
means of disposing of civil cases in which small amounts of
money are in dispute.

County Courts. In a majority of the states the next step in
the judicial hierarchy is occupied by courts of limited jurisdiction. In nineteen states such a court is called a *probate court* and
is solely concerned with the probate of wills, the selection of
guardians for orphans, and the appointment of administrators
of estates of deceased persons. In nineteen other states it is usually
called a *county court.* In addition to probate work the county
court may hear appeals from justices of the peace and magistrates courts, and it has original jurisdiction to try civil cases
of middling importance and criminal cases in which persons are
accused of misdemeanors. In addition, the judges in some states
perform a few purely administrative duties like the issuance of
hunting licenses.

General Trial Courts. The first state court with general jurisdiction is variously called the *superior court, district court, circuit court,* or *court of common pleas.* Under whatever name, it
has original jurisdiction to try persons accused of felonies and
other serious crimes and to hear all but the less important civil
cases. In a few states civil and criminal cases are heard by separate courts or by divisions of the *general trial court.* Customarily the general trial court has some appellate jurisdiction to
examine and review the decisions of the courts below it.

Each court is in charge of one judge. In a rural area his district or circuit may include two or more counties, in each of which he holds court four times or more a year. In criminal cases —and sometimes in civil cases—he is assisted by a jury. Complete stenographic records are kept of all proceedings; hence when appeals are taken to a higher court it is unnecessary to re-examine witnesses or hold another jury trial.

Intermediate Courts of Appeal. *Appellate courts,* intermediate between the general trial courts and the highest state court, have been established in fourteen states. Their appellate jurisdiction is complete except for cases on specified subjects which go directly from the trial court to the supreme court. A few intermediate courts have original jurisdiction over cases such as those concerning contested elections. The purpose of the intermediate court is to provide a re-examination of a case and to relieve the highest state court of the burden of hearing a great many appeals. In some matters the decisions of the intermediate court are final.

The intermediate appellate courts are composed of three or more judges who sit together, examine the records sent up from the lower courts, read the briefs of attorneys, hear oral arguments, and render decisions.

Supreme Courts. The highest court in the state judicial hierarchy is called the *supreme court* in forty-three states; *the court of appeals* in Kentucky, Maryland, and New York; the *supreme judicial court* in Maine and Massachusetts; and the *supreme court of appeals* in Virginia and West Virginia. In Texas the *supreme court for civil cases* and the *court of criminal appeals* are the two highest courts. Aside from the issuance of specified writs, only a few supreme courts possess original jurisdiction. Their appellate jurisdiction is fixed by the state constitution or statute. All these courts, of course, may hear appeals on any question involving the interpretation of provisions of the state constitution whether or not the issue has previously been considered in an intermediate appellate court.

The highest state courts have from three to nine justices; usually they have five or seven justices. In recent years the increase in the number of cases appealed to state supreme courts has resulted in a tendency toward increasing the number of justices. Though a few states require the supreme court to hold sessions in several cities of the state, most supreme courts sit only at the state capital. The decisions of the state supreme court are final in all questions concerning the constitution or laws of the state.

JUDICIAL PERSONNEL

No judicial system can be superior to the individual judges who compose it. The chief problem of judicial administration is to secure and retain the services of able men who will be alert to the changing needs of society and yet will be completely independent of political pressures.

Selection of Judges. During the colonial and early federal periods state judges were appointed to serve during good behavior. In the democratic movement which swept over the country in the nineteenth century nearly every state amended its constitution so as to provide for the popular election of judges for relatively short terms. At present the method of selecting judges differs among the states and even within different levels of courts in the same state. Popular election is the preferred method in forty states; appointment by the governor with the consent of the senate or the council, prevails in six states; and election by the legislature is the rule in Rhode Island, South Carolina, Vermont, and Virginia. In California the governor appoints judges for twelve-year terms, at the end of which each judge may seek to continue in office by running in a general election without opposition. If the vote goes against him, another judge is appointed. Similar plans are in effect in Alaska, Kansas, and Missouri.

Most judicial authorities are in favor of the appointment of judges—usually by the governor, subject to senatorial confirmation. Three principal arguments are advanced against the popular election of judges: (1) successful candidates are likely to be popular men or political figures rather than legal experts; (2) qualified lawyers hesitate to run for office because of the uncertainty of election and the "smear" tactics used in some campaigns; and (3) incumbent judges, in order to win re-election, may cast their decisions in favor of a more popular side.

Judicial Tenure. Throughout the United States great variations exist in the tenure of judges. (See Appendix, pp. 272f.) Only in Massachusetts and Rhode Island do judges serve for life or during good behavior. In New Jersey the initial appointment of a judge to one of the higher courts is seven years, but he may be reappointed. In Pennsylvania judges of the supreme court are elected for terms of twenty-one years, but are ineligible for re-election. In other states the terms are twelve, ten, eight, seven, or six years. The Vermont legislature elects judges for two-year terms, but the habit of successive re-election practically amounts to life tenure.

Legal experts generally agree that long tenure is conducive to judicial independence. In order to avoid poor judicial perform-ance resulting from the infirmities of old age, Alaska, Connecti-cut, Hawaii, New Hampshire, and New York require judges to retire at the age of seventy.

All state constitutions contain provisions for the removal of venal judges by impeachment. In eight states the recall of judges is available to the voters, but it is seldom used. Other methods of removal in several states are by resolution of the legislature, by the governor on address of the legislature, and by the abolition of a court on which a judge is sitting.

Judicial Salaries. In 1960, the salaries of judges on the highest state courts ranged from more than $35,000 in New York down to about $10,000 in Vermont; the median salary was about $17,000. For judges of general trial courts the median salary was about $12,000. In a large number of states, judicial salaries are too low to attract competent men; thus, the administration of justice suf-fers in the lower courts.

THE JURY SYSTEM

In early English law the *jury* at first was a body of witnesses. It later became differentiated into a grand jury and a petit, or trial, jury. Both are chosen by lot from a list of citizens compiled by jury commissioners.

The Grand Jury. The *grand jury,* composed of from twelve to twenty-three persons, is summoned prior to the opening of a term of court. Its function is to hear evidence concerning the existence of crime in the county and to formally accuse indi-viduals. It may either draw up a presentment on its own motion or approve, as a "true bill," an indictment drawn by the prosecu-ting attorney. On the basis of either document an accused person may be tried for the criminal offense named.

The present usefulness of the grand jury is seriously questioned. It is often no more than a compliant tool in the hands of the prosecuting attorney. In several states a formal accusation before a magistrate, called an "information," may be substituted for an indictment.

The Trial Jury. The *petit* or *trial jury* is composed of twelve men. Its function is to hear the evidence presented in court and to determine the guilt or innocence of an accused person. At common law a unanimous verdict is required for conviction.

Jury trial is often criticized as expensive, tedious, and uncertain. In attempting to improve its effectiveness several states have provided for a jury of less than twelve members or have permitted verdicts by votes of five-sixths or three-fourths. A number of states permit waiver of jury trial in all but the most serious criminal cases. In civil cases concerning complicated business transactions or technical matters, the parties usually agree to accept the decision of the judge alone.

JUDICIAL REFORM

For many years both lawyers and political scientists have recognized the need for judicial reform in the states. In many of them the court system is excessively complicated. Overlapping jurisdictions make it difficult to determine where a case should be tried. Even within the same court the burden of cases is unequally divided among judges; some have relatively little business, while others are overburdened. In trial courts of large cities little effort is made to segregate cases and permit judges to develop specializations in criminal and the various kinds of civil cases; instead every trial judge is compelled to be a Jack-of-all-trades. The heavy costs involved in bringing cases to court and making appeals work hardships, particularly on poor litigants. Many technical grounds for appeals exist which have little or nothing to do with the guilt or innocence of the accused in criminal cases or with the fundamental rights of parties in civil cases. As a consequence, some appellate courts have four or five year backlogs of cases. To correct these conditions several proposed reforms have been suggested.

The Unified Court System. The most drastic reform is the *unified court system* which was first brought forward in 1909 by a committee of the American Bar Association. Under this system every court and judicial officer from top to bottom in the state hierarchy would be integrated into one great court with three divisions. At the top would be a genuinely supreme court with authority to maintain a sound and uniform course of decisions in the lower divisions. Next would come a general trial division which would have original jurisdiction over important civil and serious criminal cases. A third divison organized at the county level, would supersede the present magistrates, justices of the peace, and other judges of courts of limited jurisdiction. The whole system would be under the direction of a chief justice, elected by the voters of the state. He would have authority to appoint all the other judges and assign them to duty where, and as, they are needed.

Under the judicial reorganization in New Jersey, effected in 1947, a chief justice appoints a chief administrator who has power to assign and transfer judges according to rules made by the supreme court. The New Jersey system has been widely adopted. At present twenty states have chief administrative officers. In some of the larger cities considerable progress has been made in the unification of municipal courts.

The Judicial Council. A second proposed reform is the creation of a *judicial council,* to be composed wholly of judges, or of judges, lawyers, and legislators. Its principal function would be to make continuing studies of the judicial system and to recommend corrective action to the legislature. In addition, it might be given power to make rules for the administration and procedure of the courts, to propose lists of persons eligible for appointment to judicial vacancies, to remove justices and court employees for cause, and, in general, to supervise the administration of the courts.

Thus far, thirty-six states have created judicial councils. Most of these councils can only make recommendations, though a few are empowered to take remedial action. In California, for example, the council may reassign judges to relieve court congestion and, within limits, may adopt procedural rules. No state has thus far made a sweeping reform of antiquated rules of procedure which, while ostensibly guaranteeing the rights of litigants to a fair trial, actually increase court costs and impose unnecessary delays in the disposition of cases.

Declaratory Judgments. A third suggested reform is the *declaratory judgment*—a declaration by a court, in an actual controversy, of the rights of parties under a statute, will, contract, or other document. This declaration is binding on the parties; if issued before a lawsuit arises, it saves the expense and time which might be spent in litigation. Forty-six states and the federal government have enacted laws which permit courts to issue declaratory judgments.

Advisory Opinions. A reform which is designed to do away with uncertainty as to the constitutionality of a statute or a proposed law is the *advisory opinion.* The constitutions of ten states permit the governor to obtain advisory opinions from the highest court prior to the passage or the enforcement of a statute. In seven of these states the legislature may similarly request an opinion, as a guide to enacting, amending, or repealing statutes. Except in Colorado, where they are binding upon the court in cases which may afterward arise, advisory opinions are regarded merely as the personal opinions of individual judges, and thus have no legal effect.

Conciliation and Arbitration. The avoidance of litigation through conciliation and arbitration is common in European countries and is being increasingly advocated in the United States. *Conciliation* consists of the efforts of a friend of both parties who brings them together, suggests terms of settlement, and aids them in arriving at a compromise. Proceedings before conciliators are less formal and less encumbered by delays and technicalities than proceedings before courts at law, and the parties are in no way bound to accept the conciliator's judgment. In *arbitration* the parties agree in advance to submit their claims to a friendly third party and to be bound by his decision. Both conciliation and arbitration have been successfully used in the settlement of disputes between employers and employees.

12

RURAL LOCAL GOVERNMENT

In every governmental system regional subdivisions have been necessary for convenience in administration. In the United States the general policy has been for the states to grant the territorial subdivisions a wide degree of self-government. In different sections of the country the powers and organization of the local units have been adapted to the customs and peculiar needs of the people. There is no American system of local government organization. Instead there is a wide variety of local government units, which can only be roughly classified by type of organization and geographical section.

The most common unit of rural government is the county. The county as a governmental unit is especially important in the southern and western parts of the country, for in these sections subdivisions of the rural county are either nonexistent or practically negligible. Rural government below the level of the county includes the New England town, township government in many states, and special districts for the performance of single governmental functions. The New England town performs most of the work of local government and the larger county possesses few powers. In the central and northwestern states the functions of local government are fairly equally divided between counties and their subdivisions, commonly called townships. In every section, but especially in the South and West, special districts have been created each to perform a special function without regard to the boundaries of the regular governmental subdivisions.

THE COUNTY

With the exceptions of Alaska, Connecticut, and Louisiana, all states are subdivided into counties. The principal subdivisions are called *boroughs* in Alaska, and *parishes* in Louisiana, but they have the same general organization and functions as counties. In Rhode Island the county is a judicial district and there is no organized county government.

By recent count there are over 3,000 counties in the United States. The number of counties within a state varies from 3 in Delaware to 254 in Texas. The area, functions, and population of counties differ greatly. Arlington County, Virginia, with an area of twenty-five square miles is the smallest; San Bernardino County, California, with an area of 20,131 square miles is the largest. The population of counties varies from about two hundred persons in Hinsdale County, Colorado to more than five million in Cook County, Illinois. Baton Rouge, Boston, Denver, New Orleans, and Philadelphia are city-counties.

Functions. Counties possess only enumerated powers; they may perform only the functions granted them by the state constitution and the legislature. The functions of counties fall into nine categories. (1) In thirty-seven states, counties perform important fiscal duties, such as drafting and approving the county budget, appropriating funds, levying taxes, and borrowing money. (2) The county is the principal subdivision of the state for the administration of justice. (3) It maintains public records such as deeds, mortgages, and wills in the county courthouse. (4) In an increasing number of states it is becoming the principal unit for educational administration. (5) Though the state has taken over the principal highways, the county is usually responsible for the construction and maintenance of secondary roads and bridges. (6) The county is important in the provision of welfare assistance to the aged, the blind, and dependent children. (7) Within each county the sheriff and his deputies, or the county policemen, are responsible for law enforcement. (8) In most states, counties perform electoral functions: the county board determines precinct boundaries, provides polling places, appoints electoral officials, prepares local ballots, and canvasses returns. (9) Within recent years counties have assumed responsibility for important services, such as conservation and the operation of airports, hospitals, libraries, parks, and public utilities.

County Board. In each county the principal governing authority is a board called in various states by twenty-seven different names: common titles are *board of common freeholders, board of revenue, board of supervisors, county commissioners, county court,* and *fiscal court.* The county board possesses primarily administrative powers; its legislative powers are few and are generally limited to the powers to tax and appropriate funds.

County boards generally are of two types. (1) The large boards, usually called *boards of supervisors,* may have fifteen to more than one hundred members. The members are commonly elected by the voters in the townships. As individuals, they are supervisors or administrators of their respective townships. Boards of this type are found in Michigan, New York, Wisconsin, and parts of Illinois. (2) The small board, usually called the *board of county commissioners,* may have from three to seven members, who generally are elected from the county at large. It is found in the southern and far-western states and in New England, Pennsylvania, Ohio, and Indiana. In twenty-seven states all county boards are required to have the same number of members regardless of differences in the area, population, and other characteristics of counties. Predominantly the membership is composed of farmers.

Terms of office for members of county boards vary from one to eight years: four-year terms are the most common. Frequently the terms are staggered in order to provide continuity of experience. County board members usually are paid on a per diem basis—$5 to $25 a day. The presiding officer is commonly selected by the board from its own membership for a one-year term. The procedure is informal. The boards hold public or private hearings before deliberating.

The administration of counties generally is inefficient. The board is unwieldly, unskilled in the conduct of affairs assigned to it, and unable to control a number of elective county officers, each of whom governs a little administrative dominion of his own. (See Appendix, p. 275.)

Other Boards and Commissions. In many states separate boards and commissions have been created to perform a single function within the county, such as education, health, welfare, or planning. Their members are generally appointed by the county board for overlapping terms of from three to five years. Sometimes they are popularly elected. The chief justification for the existence of such boards is that some of them provide expert nonpolitical administration in matters requiring technical knowledge.

County Officers. Counties generally have a large number of popularly elected administrative officials. Some officers perform mainly state functions; others perform strictly local functions;

but few are subject to much direct supervision by either state officials or county boards. Few county officers possess important discretionary authority. The *sheriff*, with his deputies, maintains order, apprehends criminals, and executes the orders and processes, both civil and criminal, of the courts of the county. He usually has custody of the prisoners in the county jail. A few large counties have set up professional county police forces. The *coroner*, an appointive officer, is responsible for determining the causes of death when the deceased was not attended by a physician. When foul play is suspected, the coroner summons a jury to hear the evidence. In progressive communities a qualified *medical examiner* has replaced the coroner. The *prosecuting attorney*, sometimes called the *state's attorney* or the *district attorney* (the "D.A."), is the legal representative of the state in the prosecution of persons accused of crimes. He appears with witnesses before grand juries or magistrates and endeavors to obtain indictments or informations. Afterwards he conducts the trial before the court and endeavors to secure a conviction. An additional duty, which is sometimes onerous, is to give legal advice to the county board and county officers. A *clerk of the court* maintains the records of the court and issues processes and writs. A *county clerk* is secretary of the county board and performs certain miscellaneous duties. In about half the states he issues marriage licenses and keeps records, such as vital statistics, land titles, and deeds. In approximately half the states a *register of deeds* maintains records of land titles and keeps other public records. The *county treasurer* is responsible for the collection, custody, and disbursement of county funds. The *county assessor* determines the valuation of property for the purpose of tax levies by the county and other governmental units. The *county auditor*, provided for in a third of the states, inspects financial records to insure that county and other local government funds are expended as authorized. The *surveyor* undertakes surveys of lands in dispute and charges a fee for his services. In a number of states the *county engineer* acts as the surveyor, but his main function is to oversee the county's major construction projects.

Criticisms of County Government. County government has been criticized on the following grounds: (1) There are too many counties, some of which are too small and sparsely populated to possess adequate resources for the proper execution of their functions. (2) The lack of an executive is a major weakness of county government. Administrative authority is scattered among a relatively large number of boards and officials, consequently, there is little central direction of administration. (3) The organization of county governments makes it difficult to fix responsibility, so that "buck passing" is common. (4) The long ballot permits the popular election of many officials whose duties are concerned wholly with routine administration. They are in each other's way and if they are personal enemies or members of opposite political parties they may nullify each other's efforts. (5) Many counties are tightly controlled through special legislation by the state legislature. Since the constitutional and legal rules often are constrictive, counties in many states may be unable to initiate the action needed without first securing the approval of their state legislatures.

Reform of County Government. Counties generally are the weakest units in state government and the most in need of reconstruction. Among many reforms which have been proposed, the following are especially worthy of consideration. (1) Reduction in the number of counties in each state through the combining of existing counties; thus, fewer but larger counties would have the financial and other resources to cope with contemporary problems. (2) Functional consolidation in which two or more counties enter into co-operative arrangements to provide a single service such as a hospital or a welfare institution. (3) Transference of some county functions to a state agency, which could perform them more efficiently; in many places highway construction has already been transferred to the state. (4) Extension of the principle of county home rule through effective constitutional or statutory provisions granting counties broad powers of self-government. (Home rule is discussed in more detail in Chapter 14.) (5) Abolition of large county boards and concentration of authority in the hands of a small board with adequate powers. (6) Abolition of special purpose boards and commissions in order to centralize policy-making and administration in the county board. (7) Reduction in the number of elective officers and provision for the appointment of all officers whose duties are mainly administrative. (8) Extension of civil service reform to county government. (9) General adoption of the county-manager plan to overcome the principal weakness of county government—the lack of a chief administrator. Because the functions of counties are almost entirely administrative in nature, the county-manager plan is particularly applicable to county government. Under this plan the county board would determine policy and employ an experienced administrator to direct the affairs of the county. Since the county manager, would appoint all officers and employees, the traditional long county ballot would be greatly shortened. Only fifteen counties in the United States have thus far adopted the plan. In practice the county manager has not been authorized to appoint all officers: the county attorney, the sheriff, and other officials continue to be popularly elected or appointed by the governor. As a result, the manager must share some administrative authority with those officers. The county-manager plan is opposed by a few who advocate increasing state control over counties and also by politicians who would be deprived of political power if the county-manager plan superseded the present jungle of elective offices. (10) Provision for the chief administrative officer to supervise department heads who are appointed and subject to removal by the council. This plan has been successful in Los Angeles County, California since 1938.

THE NEW ENGLAND TOWN

The principal unit of rural government in New England is the *town,* not to be confused with small urban communities called "towns" in other sections of the United States. In New England, towns perform most of the local government activities; the county is either nonexistent or is of strictly secondary importance. New England towns are quasi-corporations deriving their powers from general laws and not from charters. They usually have small populations, for the legislature ordinarily incorporates a town as a city when the population becomes large.

Town Functions. The functions of New England towns are generally similar to those of municipalities, but on a smaller scale. The administration of public safety, public health, public works, taxation, and sanitation are typical town functions. In New England the administration of education is also a normal responsibility of town government, although in other sections of the country special districts are often set up for the purpose of directing the systems of public instruction.

The Town Meeting. In theory the New England town is an example of direct democracy. A *town meeting,* an assembly of qualified voters, is held once a year, usually in the spring, to decide the basic policies of the town; special town meetings are called as needed. A moderator presides over the town meeting. During the first part of the meeting policy matters and town finance matters are debated and decided by vote; later in the meeting town officials are directly elected. In large towns two town meetings may be held: one to conduct town business and one to elect town officials. Every voter may attend the town meeting and has the right to express his views and vote on issues.

In some of the larger towns in Massachusetts a limited or representative town meeting has been adopted. Under this plan, representatives elected from districts, into which the town is divided, debate and vote on the issues selected for consideration and action. Other citizens may attend the town meeting, but they do not possess the right to vote.

Selectmen and Other Officers. At the town meeting a board of three or five selectmen is elected usually for a one-year term. *Selectmen* maintain town property, issue licenses, award contracts, prepare the town budget, and oversee the activities of town officials. Between town meetings they act as a town executive committee.

The *town clerk,* elected by the town meeting, keeps the records of the town and performs miscellaneous functions; he is the principal town official. The function of the *town treasurer* is the receipt, custody, and disbursement of town funds. The *road surveyor, tax assessor, auditor, constable, pound keeper* (dog catcher), and *public weigher* are typical of the other town officials. In some of the larger towns the town meeting elects, or the moderator appoints, a *finance,* or *budget, committee* of three to twelve members to prepare the town budget and present it at the next regular town meeting.

The Town Manager. In any New England state except Rhode Island a town meeting may adopt the town-manager plan. Under this plan, the *town manager* is appointed by the board of selectmen and is the chief administrative officer of the town. Thus far, one hundred and sixty towns have put this type of plan into operation. Maine has more towns operating under town-manager government than any other state. (See Appendix, p. 276.)

THE TOWNSHIP

The *township* is an important subdivision of the county in the rural areas of New York, New Jersey, Pennsylvania, and twelve of the North Central states. Most townships are small. Two-thirds of the approximately 17,200 townships have populations of less than 1,000; less than 500 townships have populations in excess of 10,000.

Township Functions. Since the townships operate as subdivisions of counties and not as separate entities, they have fewer functions than New England towns. Public safety, roads, libraries, relief, and parks are typical areas of township responsibility; and in some states townships operate schools. The importance of the township is steadily diminishing. For greater economy and efficiency township functions are being transferred to the county.

Township Government. Direct democracy exists in approximately half the township states, much as it does in the New England town; all qualified voters may attend township meetings, vote on general policies, and elect officers. A representative form of government is found in the remaining half of the township states. In all townships, supervisors or boards elected by the voters at the township meeting or in a regular election are responsible for township administration. A popularly elected board, usually of three members, is the governing body in half the township states; in the other township states the township supervisor is the administrative official. Other officials may include an assessor, a clerk, constables, and a treasurer. Twenty townships have adopted the manager form of government.

SPECIAL DISTRICTS

Special or *ad hoc* districts, each of which is limited to the performance of one or a few functions, are found in every state. Their boundaries may include only a fraction of a rural county or may comprise several cities and intervening areas. At least fifteen *special districts* comprise portions of two or more states.

There are four principal reasons for the creation of a special district: (1) Development of a need for a special service which no existing local government is able to fulfill; examples are special water supply, sanitation, and park districts in metropolitan areas and specifically the Port of New York Authority. (2) Willingness of a part of a local government area to provide and pay for the service which it needs; examples are drainage, irrigation, and levee districts. (3) Existence of a popular demand to remove a particular subject from politics—this probably accounts for the creation of many school districts. (4) A desire to evade constitutional restrictions on the taxing and borrowing powers of the regular units of government is responsible for the existence of many special districts.

Types and Number of Special Districts. Most special districts were created to perform one function, but some perform a variety of functions. Common types of special districts are those created to deal with school, fire, drainage, soil conservation, cemeteries, and housing.

School districts account for approximately 80 per cent of all special districts: there were about 45,000 school districts in 1960, a decrease from 63,000 in the past twenty years. The number of other special districts has been increasing rapidly and totals in excess of 12,000 districts. California, Illinois, Kansas, Missouri, Nebraska, New York, Oregon, Texas, and Washington each have more than 500 special districts besides school districts.

Government of Special Districts. Special districts generally are governed by a board of three to seven members, who usually are popularly elected, but may be appointed. The board determines policy, levies taxes, borrows money, and appoints administrators. Frequently it hires a full-time administrator who carries out the policies established by the board.

School districts often are organized in a manner similar to the council-manager form of municipal government (see Chapter 13). A school district commonly is under the control of a popularly elected school committee which is considered to be an agency of the state. It provides for the construction and maintenance of school buildings, the transportation of pupils, and the employment of teachers. The committee also selects a superintendent who administers the school department.

13

MUNICIPAL GOVERNMENT

The development of the United States has been characterized by rapid urbanization. The census of 1790 revealed only six cities with a population greater than 8,000, whereas the census of 1960 revealed that the population of each of five cities exceeds 1 million persons. The population of New York City is close to 8 million and is greater than the population of each of forty-three states. Approximately 70 per cent of the population of the United States is urban; the urban population of the states varies from about 25 per cent in North Dakota to about 85 per cent in New Jersey. (See Appendix, p. 269.)

The importance of municipal government is indicated by the size of municipal budgets and the number of persons employed by municipalities. Annual expenditures of municipal governments total approximately $14 billion and employees number 1.5 million persons. Municipal government is of prime importance to the average citizen because of his dependence upon it for essential services.

MUNICIPAL CHARTERS

Three conditions are essential for the creation of a city or other urban unit of government: (1) a thickly settled population which needs more efficient government and more public services than a county is able or willing to supply; (2) a request by the inhabitants for incorporation; and (3) the granting of a charter by the state legislature or another state authority. "Incorporation" means that the inhabitants are formed into one artificial legal person for the purpose of conducting a local government and supplying public services. A *charter* is the formal written document which creates the city, enumerates the powers which it is permitted to exercise, and specifies in great detail the organization of the city's government. It determines the form of government, the titles, qualifications, and duties of the city's

149

principal officers, and the methods by which they are to be elected. Very frequently the charter contains provisions concerning municipal finance, the civil service, and the organization of city departments. It is the fundamental constitution of the city and the basis for its operation. The provisions of the charter are strictly interpreted by the courts. (See Chapter 14 for a discussion of the legal relationship of the city to the state.)

In the laws of the states there is considerable variation in the titles of the smaller municipal corporations. In New York and Pennsylvania only municipalities with populations of 10,000 or more may be called "cities." In all other states the minimum is less and is only 500 in California. In some states "incorporated towns" (not to be confused with towns in New England), "incorporated villages," and "boroughs," have greater powers and more complicated governmental structures than some small "cities." Whatever a municipal corporation is called, the element that distinquishes it from other local units is its charter of formal incorporation.

THE MAYOR AND THE COUNCIL

In the colonial period the government of a city or other incorporated place was conducted by a council elected by the freeholders of the corporation. The council enacted ordinances, raised and appropriated money, hired employees, and directly or through committees supervised the details of city administration. The mayor, usually appointed by the royal governor, presided at council meetings and represented the city on ceremonial occasions, but possessed no real powers.

Following the establishment of national and state governments with their emphasis on the principle of separation of powers, it was practically inevitable that municipal governments should be reorganized on the same principle. For a time in many cities the council became bicameral and was forced to share the administration of the city with other officers. The mayor was given some executive powers, subject to various limitations in the city charter. In many cities other officers including heads of some departments were made elective.

The Mayor. Like a governor, a *mayor* possesses administrative, legislative, and judicial powers. The mayor's powers of appointment and removal give him considerable control of administration and over administrative officers. He is charged with the responsibility for enforcing state laws and city ordinances. In most cities he is required to prepare and submit a budget to the city council. In all cities the mayor is empowered to make recommendations to the council and thus may summon public opinion in support of his program. Two-thirds of the mayors in cities with a population in excess of 5,000 possess the veto power which may usually be overridden by a two-thirds vote of the city council. In one large city, Chicago, and many small cities the mayor still presides over the council, but usually does not have a vote except in the event of a tie. In certain small cities the mayor presides over a court in the trial of offenders against municipal ordinances.

The qualifications prescribed for mayor vary considerably; he must be a qualified voter and may be required to be of a specific age and a resident of the city for a minimum period of time. Mayors are popularly elected for terms of one to four years; taking all cities together the two-year term of office is the most common, but in large cities the four-year term is more usual. In a few states or cities the mayor may be subject to a recall election. In some other states he may be removed by the governor for cause with or without the preferment of charges and a public hearing. The salaries of mayors vary greatly; except in a few large cities, they are generally underpaid.

The City Council. With the exception of four cities, which have bicameral chambers, the *city council* is a unicameral legislative body with a relatively small membership. The method by which council members are elected varies: they are elected at large, or by wards, or by proportional representation. Their terms vary also, but a two-year term is the most common. A councilman's salary may be only a nominal sum or as much as $12,000 annually; usually his salary is higher when he has administrative, as well as legislative, duties.

The council is the principal municipal policy-making body, especially in weak-mayor cities and in other cities having a commission form of government (treated later in this chapter). Everywhere the council enacts ordinances, imposes taxes, and makes appropriations. The use of its power to investigate the administrative branch is a principal activity of councils, especially in cities with council-manager and strong-mayor governments.

City councils customarily meet weekly on a day which is
frequently prescribed by the city charter, but special sessions
usually may be called by a minority of the members. Unless the
charter designates a chairman, the council commonly elects its
own presiding officer. It may adopt its own rules of procedure
subject to the limitations contained in the city charter and state
laws; the rules of procedure are similar to those of the state
legislature. (See Chapter 8 for a discussion of state legislative
procedure.)

FORMS OF MUNICIPAL GOVERNMENT

When deficiencies in the balanced form of city government
became apparent, new forms were developed. At present three
principal types of municipal government exist throughout the
United States: the mayor-council form, the commission form,
and the council-manager form. (See Appendix, p. 274.)

The Mayor-Council Form. The oldest kind of municipal government is the *mayor-council form,* which is patterned after the
structure of the state and federal governments. More than 50
per cent of the nearly 3,000 cities with populations of over 5,000
operate under the mayor-council form of government (see Appendix, p. 274). It is the most popular form of municipal government in the very large and the very small cities. The mayor-
council form of municipal government may be classified into two
principal types—according to whether the mayor may be termed
"weak" or "strong"—but many gradations between the two types
are provided for in so-called "compromise charters."

WEAK MAYOR-COUNCIL FORM. The *weak mayor-council form*
of municipal government provides for a large and fairly strong
council and a mayor with few powers. The mayor is elected by
the voters at large and the council usually is elected on a ward
basis. Council domination and decentralization of administration
are prominent characteristics of this form of municipal government. Many of the administrative departments are headed by
popularly elected boards and commissions which generally are
independent of both mayor and council. The relatively few appointments that the mayor is authorized to make must be confirmed by the council. The mayor commonly possesses the veto
power, but in many cities the council may override his vetoes by
a two-thirds vote. The weak-mayor plan is similar to an early

plan of state government which subordinated the governor to the state legislature; the mayor is charged with the supervision of administration, but possesses relatively little power to carry out this responsibility. (See Appendix, p. 277.)

The weak-mayor plan suffers from three principal defects. (1) Central direction of administration is lacking, because there is no official who qualifies as the chief executive of the municipality. (2) This plan diffuses responsibility among the mayor, the council, and the independently elected boards and commissions. (3) Since under this plan many boards and commissions are independently elected, the ballot is a long one, making it difficult for the average citizen to become acquainted with the qualifications of all the candidates for office.

STRONG MAYOR-COUNCIL FORM. The *strong mayor-council form* of municipal government partly eliminates the defects of the weak-mayor plan by strengthening the mayor's position. The powers scattered among nearly independent department heads and others are centralized in the mayor. The mayor appoints and removes the heads of most municipal departments without council approval, and he is made responsible for preparing the annual budget. The city council determines only policy; in theory, it does not interfere with administration. Since independently elected boards and commissions are eliminated or greatly reduced in number, the ballot is shortened considerably. In some small cities the mayor is the presiding officer of the council and may vote in case of a tie. In large cities the mayor is not a member of the council, but may recommend measures and call special meetings of the council.

The strong mayor-council plan has four major advantages. (1) It provides for a mayor with power to give central direction to administration, and it strengthens administration by facilitating the introduction of sound administrative control devices, such as an adequate budget system and the merit system. (2) The council's control over policy formation is strengthened by the elimination of independently elected boards and commissions which in weak-mayor cities exercise policy-making as well as administrative powers. (3) The ballot is shortened by the elimination of independently elected boards and commissions, thus allowing the average voter to become better acquainted with the qualifications of the candidates for the various offices. (4) The shifting of responsibility is reduced, because responsibility for administration rests with the mayor.

The strong mayor-council plan suffers from two defects. (1) The popularly elected mayor is often a political figure who possesses little administrative leadership or ability. (2) The separation of powers inherent in the plan tends to create conflicts between the mayor and the council with resulting confusion, inaction, and deadlock.

The Commission Form. Generally credited with being the first city to do so, Galveston, Texas, in 1901 adopted the *commission form* of municipal government. (The city had experienced a tidal wave, which killed 5,000 inhabitants and destroyed many of the streets and public works and really caused a state of emergency.) Civic leaders proposed and the state legislature enacted a new charter which provided for government by a powerful five-man commission. The success of the plan in Galveston attracted the attention of other cities. In 1907 Des Moines, Iowa adopted the plan with the addition of initiative, referendum, and recall provisions, and by 1914 more than four hundred cities were being governed under the commission form of municipal government. Since that time, however, few cities have adopted the plan and a number of commission-plan cities subsequently abandoned the commission plan in favor of the council-manager (including Galveston) or mayor-council plans. About 9 per cent of the cities with a population in excess of 5,000 presently operate under the commission form of municipal government.

The commission form provides for a popularly elected commission of, most commonly, five members who serve for two- or four-year terms. As a body the commission acts as the municipal council and exercises legislative powers. Each member of the commission either supervises or actively administers one of the three to seven city departments. The Galveston charter provided for appointive department heads, each to be supervised by a commissioner. Many other commission plan charters vest active administration of one or more administrative departments in an individual commissioner. Finance, health and welfare, public affairs, public safety, and public works are typical departments in a city with five commissioners. Some commission plans provide for a mayor who is the chairman of the commission and the ceremonial head of the city. (See Appendix, p. 276.)

Proponents cite five major advantages of the commission form
of municipal government. (1) Checks and balances—and hence
opportunities for stalemate—are eliminated. (2) At elections the
voters' task is confined to making a choice among candidates for
membership on the commission. (3) By consolidation, the separate departments are reduced to a manageable number. (4)
Through election at large of a small body of commissioners ward
politics is eliminated. (5) The simplicity of the plan promotes
understanding and citizen participation in civic affairs.

The commission plan has the following disadvantages. (1)
Responsibility for administration is divided among commissioners
of equal rank and therefore co-ordination is lacking. (2) The
popularly elected commissioners are often not administratively
competent. (3) Relatively short terms of office necessitate frequent
campaigning and limit the acquisition of administrative experience. (4) Legislative criticism of administration tends to disap-
pear: a commissioner hesitates to criticize the department of
another commissioner for fear of retaliation. (5) Budgetary control frequently is inadequate because of log-rolling among commissioners. (6) The arbitrary grouping of all municipal functions
into a specified number of departments may not be in the best
interests of a city. (7) The commission is too small to adequately
represent all groups in a large city.

The Council-Manager Form. Staunton, Virginia, in 1908, was
the first small city and Dayton, Ohio, in 1914, was the first
large city to adopt the *council-manager plan*. Among all cities
with populations in excess of 5,000, about 38 per cent have
adopted the plan; only 4 per cent of the cities which adopted
the plan subsequently abandoned it. Dallas, Texas is the largest
city operating under this plan.

The distinctive feature of the council-manager plan is a council elected by the voters and a professional manager appointed
by, and responsible to, the council. The council's function is to
determine policy; it passes ordinances, approves projects, and
appropriates funds. The manager's function is to execute the
policy determined by the council; he appoints all subordinate
administrators and employees, and supervises every aspect of the
city's activities. The code of his profession requires him to abstain from all political activities. (See Appendix, p. 277.)

In selecting a manager the council seeks a man with technical administrative training and experience. Though great pressure is often exerted for the selection of a local man, records show that 80 per cent of city managers are not local men.

The manager is appointed for an indefinite term; his tenure averages about seven years. Many charters provide that before he can be removed from office the council must give the manager a public hearing if he requests it. Some charters prohibit his removal during his first six months in office. A manager's average salary in towns with populations under 5,000 is about $6,400; in cities of more than 250,000, approximately $22,000.

The manager attends council meetings, supplies information, and answers questions. He is required to prepare the budget and defend his estimates of expenditures. From time to time he may be asked to present special reports and he may exert considerable influence on policy. Sometimes friction develops because the council feels that the manager is encroaching on its policymaking functions or the manager thinks the council is interfering with administration.

Normally the council chooses its own presiding officer who, in about half the council-manager cities, has the title of mayor and receives a somewhat higher salary than other councilmen. He has no appointive, administrative, or veto powers.

The council-manager plan has four advantages. (1) The direction of administration is completely centered in one professionally-trained individual. (2) The plan is simple and the governmental processes are readily followed by all voters. (3) Responsibility may be enforced—by citizens upon the council and by the council upon the manager. (4) The deadlocks and delays encountered in other forms of municipal government are avoided.

The chief charge directed against the council-manager plan is that it fails to develop policy leaders in the council. Dynamic political personalities, such as "strong" mayors, are absent and the council-manager city may cease to be progressive. It also has been argued that the manager has too much power for an official not directly responsible to the voters. Like other forms of government the council-manager plan may be perverted by a lackadaisical citizenry, by a corrupt or complacent council, or by a compliant or incompetent manager.

14

STATE AND LOCAL RELATIONS

Local self-government is deeply rooted in the American tradition. It is a school of democracy, an exercise in public responsibility, an opportunity for residents of local units to provide for their own needs in their own way. It must be noted, however, that local units are also agencies for the decentralization of state administration. This fact is most evident in such matters as the administration of elections and the educational system, and the enforcement of criminal laws. It is less apparent in a wide variety of purely local functions; yet the state may be concerned with them, at least to the extent of ascertaining how local units raise and spend money and keep accounts.

The proper division of functions between the state and the local units is a difficult problem. How much freedom should be accorded to the local units? This question has never been answered to the satisfaction of both the state government and the local units. Futhermore, the problem has become more difficult with the increase in both state and local activities.

LEGAL STATUS OF LOCAL GOVERNMENTS

All units of local government owe their existence and the continued exercise of their powers to the state. Though they differ in legal status, all local units are legally inferior to the state.

Classification of Local Units. Local governments may be classified in two broad categories—as municipal corporations and as quasi-municipal corporations. *Municipal corporations* are cities, towns, and incorporated villages which have received charters from the state legislature. The charter establishes the city as an artificial legal person and outlines its organization and powers. Unless the state constitution provides to the contrary, a municipal corporation continues to be subject to the control of the state legislature through ordinary legislation or charter revision. *Quasi-*

municipal corporations are nonchartered units—counties and their subdivisions—which nevertheless are legal entities.

Municipal and quasi-municipal corporations differ in four major ways: their manner of creation, their functions, their legal responsibility, and their sublegislative powers. (1) A municipal corporation is formed by the legislature at the request of a majority of the voters who live in the area. A quasi-municipal corporation is created by the legislature usually without the consent of the residents. (2) In addition to performing governmental functions as an agent of the state, a municipal corporation engages in a wide variety of proprietary, or business, functions. A quasi-municipal corporation exercises few or no proprietary functions; it is almost entirely an agent of the state. (3) A municipal corporation is liable to suit when it is performing proprietary functions; it is immune from suit only when performing governmental functions. A quasi-municipal corporation has generally the same immunity from suit as the state itself. (4) A municipal corporation has relatively broad sublegislative powers to enact ordinances. A quasi-municipal corporation has relatively little ordinance-making power.

Judicial Interpretation of Municipal Powers. In interpreting the powers granted to municipal corporations, the courts in every state now adhere to a rule of strict construction laid down in 1868 by Judge John F. Dillon. "Dillon's Rule" states, in part: "Municipal corporations owe their origin to, and derive their powers and rights wholly from the legislature. It breathes into them the breath of life, without which they cannot exist. As it creates, so may it destroy. If it may destroy, it may abridge and control. Unless there is some constitutional limitation . . . the legislature might, by a single act, if we can suppose it capable of so great a folly and so great a wrong, sweep from existence all the municipal corporations of the state, and the corporations could not prevent it.[1] Judge Dillon declared that municipal corporations possess only powers expressly granted by charter or by law and implied from or incident to the expressly granted powers indispensable to accomplish the declared purpose of the municipal corporations.

Judge Dillon's opinion was challenged in 1871 by Judge

[1] *City of Clinton* v. *Cedar Rapids and Missouri Railroad Co.,* 24 Iowa 455 (1868).

Thomas M. Cooley who ruled that some rights of local self-government are inherent in municipalities.[2] Among other things, Judge Cooley maintained that state legislation should be general and not special or discriminatory in application. His ruling was followed for a time by the courts in Indiana, Iowa, Kentucky, and Texas, but it is not followed at present in any state.

The state courts are frequently called upon to hear cases brought by individual taxpayers and others who claim that the activities of a county or city are in excess of the powers granted by law. In deciding these cases the courts exercise some supervision over local governments.

Municipal Liability. The liability of a municipality for its acts depends upon the type of function it is performing. Cities perform two principal types of functions—governmental or public functions, and corporate or private functions. Education, fire protection, health, police protection, and welfare usually are classified as public functions. When cities are performing these functions they are said to act as agents of the state, and they may not be sued without the consent of the state legislature.

In the performance of private, or proprietary, functions, such as the operation of a municipal golf course, a city may sue and be sued like any private corporation. It is liable for its contracts, whether they are concerned with governmental or private functions. However, it is not liable for torts—civil wrongs committed by its officers and employees when performing governmental functions. There is no sharp boundary between governmental and proprietary functions; a particular function has been designated as proprietary by the courts of one state and as governmental by the courts of another state.

CREATION OF LOCAL GOVERNMENT UNITS

Few of the present units of local government can claim a very early origin. Most of them have been created by the state out of pre-existing units; and the process of creating new units still continues.

Creation of Rural Units. Counties, towns, townships, and other rural units of government are usually created by the passage of brief special acts of the legislature which give the unit

2 *People* v. *Hurlbut*, 24 Michigan 44 (1871).

a name, establish its boundaries, and provide that its officers shall have the usual powers and duties specified by the state constitution and laws. As a rule, a temporary clause provides for commissions to select the seat of government and supervise the election of the first officers of the new unit.

Creation of Urban Units. The procedure in the creation of a city or incorporated town is somewhat more complicated. The usual steps are (1) petition of a number of the inhabitants for incorporation; (2) a special state-supervised election to determine that the proposed corporation is approved by a majority of its inhabitants; (3) the issuance by the state of a charter which confers upon the unit the power to act as a corporation.

According to the methods by which they are granted, charters are said to be special, general, classified, optional, or home rule charters.

SPECIAL CHARTERS. The *special charter*, the oldest type, is granted to a city by a special act of the state legislature. In theory a special charter is custom-tailored to the city, granting it exactly the kind of government organization and the powers it needs. In practice, the special charter system suffers from two major disadvantages: (1) The legislature often acts capriciously, forcing upon cities unwieldy or burdensome governmental structures and imposing limitations on city action which only rural legislators would consider desirable. (2) The excessive time expended by state legislatures on local problems leads to neglect of state problems. For both these reasons the constitutions of many states have been amended to prohibit the granting of special charters.

GENERAL CHARTERS. Under the *general charter system,* each city, large or small, is granted exactly the same charter. In theory, the system provides for equal corporate privileges for all cities; in practice, it is grossly unequal for it burdens small cities with administrative paraphernalia they do not want and deprives large cities of urgently needed powers and facilities. It fails to take into account local political conditions, geographical considerations, and economic differences. Though the general charter system is useful in facilitating the incorporation of smaller cities, it is impractical in general use and is not now used exclusively in any state.

CLASSIFIED CHARTERS. In order to avoid the defects of both special and general charters, the *classified charter system* has been adopted in several states. Under it, cities are classified according to population, and a uniform charter is provided for all cities within the same population class. Unfortunately, a classification has often been made in order to evade constitutional prohibitions against the issuance of special charters. If the law states that "the following charter shall apply to all cities with populations in 1960 between 70,001 and 80,000," it is safe to assume that the charter will apply to only one city. In some states each of the largest cities is in a different population class and has a different charter. Even with a reasonable classification, the classified charter system has the following defects: (1) it fails to take account of different environmental characteristics of cities with nearly the same populations, and (2) it requires a change of charter—no matter how satisfactory the existing one is—if a city's population increases or declines beyond the limits of its class.

OPTIONAL CHARTERS. In 1913 Ohio adopted an *optional charter plan* which has been copied by fourteen other states. Under this plan the state legislature draws up a number of different charters; and the voters of a city, by means of a referendum, may adopt the particular charter which seems best fitted for the city's needs. For example, cities in Massachusetts, except Boston, may choose among six different charters—three mayor-council charters, two council-manager charters, and one commission charter. The optional charter system has the advantages of securing a degree of uniformity and at the same time permitting some local self-determination.

HOME RULE CHARTERS. *Home rule* is the privilege granted to cities to draft, adopt, and amend their charters. The provision is contained in the constitutions of thirty states and in legislative acts in five states. Constitutional home rule grants localities greater protection than legislative home rule, because the state constitution is more difficult to amend than state law.

The Missouri constitution of 1875 was the first to contain a municipal home rule provision, but home rule was limited to cities with a population in excess of 100,000. (At that time St. Louis was the only city of that size in Missouri.) Constitutions specify the matters that are subject to local control, but a major problem in the home rule states is the one of distinguishing between local and state or general affairs. It must be pointed out that the interests of the state are paramount and are not subordinated to those of the city or county under home rule. In cases of dispute the courts decide whether a function is of local or general concern; judicial interpretation of the scope of local affairs has everywhere been narrow.

Advantages and Disadvantages of Home Rule Charters. Proponents of home rule cite four main advantages. (1) Home rule eliminates or greatly reduces legislative interference in city affairs; such interference is especially troublesome when rural areas are overrepresented and urban areas are underrepresented in the legislature. (2) It permits citizens to determine the form and administrative organization of their local government. (3) Home rule relieves the state legislature of the time-consuming burden of special legislation and allows it to devote itself to state problems. (4) Home rule permits citizens to have a greater voice in the determination of local governmental policies and thus encourages many more citizens to become interested in local affairs.

Opponents of home rule cite three main disadvantages. (1) Frequent changes in the charter may cause instability in local government. (2) Owing to proposals to change the charter, the ballot may be lengthened at each election. (3) Under home rule local political machines may enjoy increased freedom from state interference.

Freedom under Home Rule. The amount of freedom granted to cities under home rule varies greatly from state to state. Cities in Michigan are subject to relatively little state control, whereas cities in Ohio have relatively little freedom from state control. Home rule cities generally have considerable liberty in such matters as form of government, creation or consolidation of departments, method of electing members of the council, and salaries of officers. They have little freedom in the field of municipal finance. The courts have ruled that state-imposed debt and property tax limits are applicable to home rule cities.

Formation of Home Rule Charters. In home rule states the city charter is usually drafted by a charter commission of ten to twenty members, who are commonly elected at large. It is then submitted to the voters of the city for approval. Although in most places, the charter may be adopted by a majority vote, a few states require a favorable vote by an extraordinary majority. Amendments to a home rule charter may be proposed by the city council or by the use of the initiative petition and must be approved by the voters.

Adoption of Home Rule Charters. The number of cities that have adopted charters under home rule provisions is relatively small: of 6,400 cities, qualified by population to set up home rule charters, only 1,400 have. Indifference, liberality of state laws, difficult procedures for acquiring charters, and lack of implementing laws keep others from doing so.

LEGISLATIVE CONTROL OF LOCAL UNITS

Under early state constitutions the legislature had practically unlimited power to control local governments. It chose to exercise this power directly rather than through state administrative agencies. By statute the legislature has granted additional powers to local units, has withdrawn or has reduced previously granted powers, has provided new local administrative agencies, and has specified the manner in which local units perform their activities. Legislative control has been exercised principally through special and general legislation.

General Legislation. Extensive bodies of *general legislation—* statutes applying to local government problems wherever they occur—have been developed in every state. These statutes are largely concerned with police and fire protection, public health, welfare, financing of local units, civil service and standards of official performance, in all of which the state as a whole has an undoubted interest. General legislation has three principal advantages: (1) it is usually more carefully drafted and considered than special legislation; (2) it is satisfactory for almost all the problems of most of the cities of a state; and (3) it clearly conforms to contemporary practices in statute-making wherein the legislature passes laws in broad general terms and grants considerable discretionary authority to executive officers in applying them to specific situations.

Special Legislation. Through special laws the legislature recognizes that local units differ in many respects, such as population, topography, climate, transportation, and industry. A special law is created to apply to only one locality. Unfortunately, experience has shown the many ways in which *special legislation* has been abused. It has been used by legislatures as a means of arbitrarily controlling cities and towns. Special legislation is often traceable to the activities of special interests; they often obtain the election to a state legislature of persons who are willing tools and who work for the passage of laws favorable to the special interests and against the public interest. Bribery has sometimes been suspected. A further disadvantage of special legislation is the fact that state legislators frequently are not familar with the needs of the localities involved and must rely on the statements of the legislators from the cities and towns concerned.

These and other abuses led a number of states, early in the nineteenth century, to adopt constitutional measures prohibiting their legislatures from passing special laws on certain subjects— among them, selection of local officials, salaries of local officials, and the location of local roads. At present the constitutions of more than forty states ban special legislation by provisions similar to this one from the Alaska constitution (Art. II, Sec. 19), "The legislature shall pass no local or special act if a general act can be made applicable." In many states, constitutional prohibitions against special legislation apply only to municipal corporations; only a few constitutions contain provisions which prohibit special legislation for counties, towns, and special districts.

In practice the constitutional prohibitions against special legislation have been circumvented. One method is for the legislature, without mentioning a city by name, to pass a law applying to "all cities" within a narrow population classification, when only one city can possibly fit the description. The supreme court of Ohio has, for more than a century, refused to permit this subterfuge, but the courts in other states have complacently accepted all classifications which appear to be "reasonable." In Texas and California especially the courts have shown a disposition to approve what are in effect special laws couched in general terms. A second means of avoiding the constitutional prohibition of special legislation is to pass an act creating a new special district and transferring to it one or more functions of an existing municipality.

In eleven states the constitutions require that localities which will be affected by a proposed special law must be notified well in advance of legislative committe hearings on the bill. The localities will thus have time to prepare arguments why the proposed law should be approved, amended, or defeated. In a few states, cities are granted the power to veto special legislation that affects them; a special law becomes effective only when the city approves it. A constitutional amendment in Illinois (1904) granted such a veto power to the Chicago electorate, and an amendment to the Michigan constitution (1908) granted a similar power to all cities. Some political scientists are of the opinion that the limitation rather than the prohibition of special laws is a better way to avoid abuses.

STATE ADMINISTRATIVE SUPERVISION

In recent years the state legislatures have provided for administrative supervision of local governments by creating departments or bureaus especially for that purpose or by placing certain aspects of local administration under the charge of appropriate state administrative departments.

Administrative supervision of local governments is superior to legislative supervision in two respects. (1) The administrative supervision system has greater flexibility, for administrative rules can be amended more readily than state laws. (2) Administrative supervision is supervision by qualified personnel; for example, the state board of health, which is composed of public health experts, is more competent to supervise local health activities than would be most members of the state legislature.

The degree of supervision and the activities examined vary considerably from state to state. The greatest degree of supervision is over the educational, health, financial, highway, personnel, and welfare functions of local governments. The legislature determines the general policy to be followed and permits the administrative agency to work out the details.

Advice to Local Governments. Advice from a state agency is a noncoercive means of control. It is nevertheless effective in improving the performance of local units of government. This is particularly noticeable in the smaller units which lack facilities to gather information on governmental problems. Local administrators are especially receptive to advice on technical matters. This kind of assistance is of less importance to large cities and counties, which maintain research organizations.

Requirement of Reports. The reports required by state agencies are not only a source of information but also a means of control. Required reports may reveal unsatisfactory conditions, which necessitate corrective action by a state administrative agency or by the state legislature.

Financial Controls. The most common, and the oldest, state administrative supervision is in the area of finance. *Financial controls* include limits upon taxes and debts and review of local assessments and budgets. Through local financial and other inspections state agencies obtain information and insure the observance of state laws and regulations. Since 1930 state inspection of local accounts has increased greatly.

Control of Personnel. To a certain extent state officials exercise control over the personnel of local governments. In some states the governor may remove county officials for cause (that is, for corrupt or improper performance of duties or for neglect of duties). The administrators of special state functional programs have the authority to appoint and remove local personnel. The state commonly establishes standards for local government employees; for example, the state department of health may prescribe the minimum qualifications for local health officials.

Grants-in-Aid. *Grants-in-aid* with eligibility requirements are an increasingly popular type of control device. The state will not extend financial aid to a local government unless specified conditions are met. The state, for example, may refuse to grant funds to localities for the construction of schoolbuildings unless the plans for the new buildings meet state requirements.

Administrative Rule Making. State agencies may exact obedience to their regulations from local governments and may request the courts to compel compliance. Many state legislatures have authorized administrative agencies to establish property assessment standards for tax purposes and to equalize assessments.

Substitute Administration. In a few states a state agency may operate a local agency until the local unit establishes standards of performance acceptable to the state. This is called *substitute administration*. In fifteen states, a state agency may act as a receiver if a local government defaults on its financial obligations.

15

METROPOLITAN AREAS

The United States Bureau of the Budget (with the advice of the Federal Committee on Standard Metropolitan Statistical areas) defines a *standard metropolitan statistical area* (SMSA), except in New England, as "a county, or group of contiguous counties, which contains at least one city of 50,000 inhabitants or more or 'twin cities' with a combined population of at least 50,000." (See pp. 280–281.) The smaller of the twin cities must have a population in excess of 15,000. In New England, "a population density of at least 100 persons per square mile is used as the measure of metropolitan character." The New England measurement is the more realistic by far: compare, for instance, the compact SMSA which centers in Portland, Maine, with the thousands of square miles of ranchland, mountains—and the Mohave Desert—of San Bernardino County, California which became a SMSA by virtue of the fact that it contained one city with a population of more than 50,000 located near its southwestern corner. (See Appendix, p. 282.)

Between 1950 and 1960 the population of standard metropolitan statistical areas increased about 23 million. The populations of the central cities increased only about 5.6 million while the population of the outlying areas increased over 17 million. The population increase in standard metropolitan statistical areas between 1950 and 1960 accounted for approximately 85 per cent of the total population increase in the United States. In 1960, approximately 66 per cent of the total population of the United States lived in 212 standard metropolitan areas, which contained more than 15,000 units of local government. New York City, Newark, and Jersey City are central cities in the New York metropolitan area; approximately thirteen million persons reside in this area, which is the largest metropolitan area in the U.S. and which is part of the continuous urban area along the Atlantic Coast between Portsmouth, N.H. and the southern suburbs of Washington, D.C. Other many-city concentrations (megalopolis) are developing in southern California and on the southwestern shores of Lake Michigan. (See pp. 283, 284.)

PROBLEMS OF METROPOLITAN AREAS

The growth of metropolitan areas has created many governmental problems. Since there is no central government, co-ordination of governmental activities in a metropolitan area commonly is lacking. The problems of the principal or central city are intensified by the fact that it has no control over the development of its suburbs; the city line is the limit of its jurisdiction in most cases, yet many of the city's most important services, such as water supply and sanitation facilities, often are extramural.

Conflicts of Authority. Because a metropolitan area encompasses a number of government units, disputes inevitably arise concerning which unit is responsible for the performance of a particular governmental function. Conflicts between city and county officials are common: the city, which contains the bulk of the population of the county and pays most of the taxes, feels hampered by county officials. The responsibility or blame for poor governmental services often is shifted from one governmental unit to the other.

Duplication of Services. Each governmental unit within a metropolitan area faces common governmental problems. The performance of the same functions by different governmental units within a metropolitan area is costly and wasteful: equipment is not fully utilized and extra employees are required for the separate performance of the same duties. Furthermore, each governmental unit may have different standards for the services it performs. The solution to this problem would be less difficult if the officials of all governmental units within a metropolitan area would co-operate with each other, but, of course, in practice they rarely do.

Inadequacy of Services. Local governmental units surrounding the principal city often neglect to provide the most basic governmental services or provide services which are frequently poor in quality. In many instances the central city could readily and better perform these services for its suburbs. In fact the need for better water supplies and better sewage facilities has often induced suburbs to agree to be annexed by the central city.

Lack of Planning. The lack of metropolitan planning is a serious problem. A metropolitan area is an economic whole and therefore planning should be comprehensive. Though cities and counties within the metropolitan area frequently maintain planning agencies, there is no permanent agency charged with the responsibility of making long-range plans for the whole area.

Financial Problems. Many local governmental units located within a metropolitan area have acute financial problems. Taken in its entirety the metropolitan area has adequate financial resources, but its separate governmental units may lack sufficient funds to undertake needed functions. "Suburbanitis," which impels people to migrate from central cities to the surrounding areas results in the decrease of property values in the central city and the shrinkage of its income, while the cost of city government remains the same or increases. The suburbanites who work in the principal central city continue to receive many governmental services from it, yet they usually cannot be compelled to pay taxes to the central city. On the other side of the picture, the suburbs also experience financial difficulties; their tax rates and debts increase significantly owing to the rapid increase in their populations which in turn require extensive capital outlays for new schools, streets, and other facilities. Far from being inexpensive havens, the suburbs are often places where people pay dearly for poor governmental service.

Other Problems. Several other serious problems are associated with metropolitan areas. Because of the rapid growth of metropolitan areas and the consequent increase in the number of automobiles in use, traffic and parking problems multiply faster than new highways and parking facilities can be constructed to accommodate them. Crime rates tend to increase with increases in population density, necessitating larger, more alert, and better trained police forces. Health problems sometimes become acute: Epidemics of contagious diseases do not respect boundary lines and there may not be a metropolitan area health agency with adequate authority to take corrective action. The multiplicity of overlapping local governmental units within a metropolitan area is responsible in part for the long ballot which confuses the voters. Furthermore, the governmental services of the smaller units are likely to be inefficient because they cannot afford expert administrators.

POSSIBLE SOLUTIONS
OF METROPOLITAN PROBLEMS

Many plans have been utilized in an attempt to solve the various metropolitan problems. A discussion of the eight major plans follows.

Annexation. In the courses of their histories all large cities have attempted to solve metropolitan problems by expanding their boundaries to include surrounding areas. In 1959 alone, 532 cities, with populations in excess of 5,000, annexed territory. *Annexation* has three principal advantages. (1) The structure of government is simplified: one government instead of two or more governments is in charge of the area. (2) Duplication of services is eliminated and the number of governmental employees can be reduced. (3) Responsibility is consolidated: the opportunity to shift responsibility to another governmental unit is eliminated. (4) When the principal central city gains control over the annexed territory, services can be improved.

Annexation, although favored by the central city, is commonly opposed by suburbs. If a referendum on the question is required by state law, the voters in the suburbs will often prevent annexation. It may be argued that taxes will be increased; that the suburb's problems will be neglected by the city; that the city's political machine has a reputation for inefficiency and corruption; and that the suburb has no obligation to a central city. Moreover, local pride is involved: the suburbs do not wish to lose their separate political identities. Though state authorities may not hesitate to interfere in individual cities, they are reluctant to force two or more cities to consolidate against their will. Annexation is, of course, no solution when a metropolitan area spreads from one state to another.

Federation. *Federation* of the units in a metropolitan area creates a relationship similar to that which exists between the national government and the states: it is a compromise between complete consolidation and the present conglomeration of political units. Thus far, federation has not been adopted by any metropolitan area in the United States. A proposal to federate Allegheny County and Pittsburgh was defeated by a referendum in 1929.

In 1953 Toronto, Canada, adopted a federal plan in which the governing body is a metropolitan council composed of twenty-five members: twelve from Toronto, one from each of the twelve suburban cities, and a chairman appointed by the provincial government. The council is responsible for regional functions such as water supply, sewage disposal, planning, and streets and highways. Authorities have called the Toronto plan incomplete, because control of public safety, libraries, building regulations, and certain health and welfare functions were not transferred to the metropolitan council.

The borough plan in New York City, adopted in 1898, should not be confused with metropolitan federation. Under this plan, the five boroughs, each consisting of territory consolidated in the greater city, possess no legislative powers. A borough president, elected by the people of each borough, is the chief administrative officer. Boroughs are responsible for the care of their public buildings, the construction and maintenance of their sewers and streets, and the enforcement of their buildings regulations. All other matters are under the control of the government of the greater city.

Functional Consolidation. *Functional consolidation* is an intergovernmental arrangement whereby a single service formerly provided by departments of two or more local governmental units is provided by one agency. This device permits the merger of certain governmental functions without annexation. Typical of the services provided by functional consolidation are public health, prisons, elections, property assessment, tax collection, libraries, planning, sewage disposal, airports, recreation, and water supply.

Functional consolidation has three principal advantages: (1) It is easily achieved either by a state law or by an intergovernmental agreement. (2) It may provide certain expensive services to local governmental units which otherwise could not afford them. (3) It is flexible: functions can be consolidated as needed.

Improvement of County Government. Dade County, Florida, voters in 1957 approved a new county charter which provided for the creation of a metropolitan government: a commission-manager type of county government. Broad powers of home rule were given to the commission; it is empowered to determine standards of services and policy in a number of functional areas, including long-range planning, police and fire protection, slum clearance, transportation facilities, and sewage, surface drainage, and water systems. If a municipality in the county fails to supply services which meet the prescribed standards, the county may provide the services.

City-County Consolidation. Many governmental functions performed by cities and counties are the same. Thus, the *consolidation* of a city government and a county government simplifies the governmental structure and eliminates duplication. It also centers responsibility and increases popular control of government.

In 1854 the city of Philadelphia was given the same boundaries as the county and many county powers, but the consolidation was incomplete because Philadelphia County was retained as a separate governmental unit to execute certain duties. City-county consolidation has not been a popular method for solving the problems of metropolitan areas; in the twentieth century only one city, Baton Rouge, has adopted it (1947).

City-County Separation. A central city may be detached from the county and allowed to perform both city and county functions. *Separation* of the city and the county is a distinct advantage to the central city because it eliminates duplication, centers responsibility, increases popular control of government, and shortens the ballot. City-county separation may, however, impose hardships on the county. Because of the loss of its most valuable territory and its chief source of revenue, the county may be unable to support a county government. A solution to this problem might be the consolidation of the rural area of the old county with an adjoining county.

In 1851, Baltimore and Baltimore County were separated. Later, cities in Virginia with populations in excess of 10,000 were separated from their counties.

Extramural Jurisdiction. By special grant of the state legislature a city is permitted to exercise limited jurisdiction beyond its borders. For example, the legislature may authorize a city to acquire land beyond its borders for the protection of its water supply or the location of a hospital, airport, or other facility. A city also may be granted police power over territory a mile or more beyond its borders. Usually *extramural jurisdiction* does not extend far enough nor is it adequate. Central cities have not been granted jurisdiction over many important regional matters. Though extramural jurisdiction is opposed by some as undemocratic interference with other localities, the principle might be responsibly employed for the benefit of both the suburbs and the central city.

Special District Plan. A metropolitan *special district* is a governmental unit which is responsible for supplying one or more extraordinary services in a central city and part or all of the remainder of the metropolitan area. The special district is superimposed over existing units of local government which continue to perform their other regular governmental functions. Many such districts have been created. One of the most noteworthy is the Port of New York Authority which was formed by an interstate compact between New York and New Jersey. This Authority operates bridges, tunnels, airports, and truck, grain, railroad freight, bus, and marine terminals. Most metropolitan special districts are devoted to a single function, such as water supply, sewage disposal, park administration, and housing projects. Special districts are dependent chiefly on rents, sales, service charges, and tolls for financial support.

Metropolitan special districts have two major advantages: (1) They have permitted a degree of centralization while allowing local governmental units to retain home rule. (2) They can be given additional governmental functions to perform as the need arises. (3) They provide an effective means of solving certain problems of a metropolitan area which includes portions of two or more states. A major disadvantage of the plan is the creation of another governmental unit in an area that may already have too many governmental units.

Metropolitan special districts have difficulty in resolving two problems: (1) in determining the representation of local governmental units on the governing body of the special district and (2) in co-ordinating the activities of the special district with the activities of the local governmental units. The governing bodies in less than one-fifth of the metropolitan special districts are popularly elected; in other districts members of the governing bodies are either appointed or hold office by virtue of posts they hold in other governmental units. For example, the members of the Metropolitan District Commission in Massachusetts are appointed by the governor with the approval of the governor's council.

16

PUBLIC PROTECTION, HEALTH, AND WELFARE

Among the most important functions of government are public protection, public health, and public welfare. Under modern conditions the problems associated with these functions have become increasingly complex. For their solution they require the combined efforts of local, state, and federal governments.

PUBLIC PROTECTION

Public protection includes the enforcement of laws, the preservation of public order, and the protection of life and property both from criminal elements in the population and from natural dangers such as fire, flood, and other disasters. Under normal conditions the services of the police and the fire-fighting forces are sufficient, but in an emergency it may be necessary to call upon the military forces of the state to take temporary command of the situation. (See increasing cost of protection, pp. 290–291.)

The National Guard. Since the early days of the United States there has been in each state an organized and armed force called the state militia. With the enactment of the National Defense Act of 1916 these state units were placed under strict federal regulation and were named the National Guard. The officers and men of this organization are paid and equipped by the federal government; during wartime the National Guard may be called into the service of the United States. When it is not in the federal service, the National Guard units serve as the militia in the individual states; thus, the governor may call upon the National Guard units to enforce state laws, suppress insurrections, and patrol areas which have suffered disasters. The National Guard has been used frequently to preserve order during strikes.

The State Police. Though Massachusetts created a small state police force in 1865, Pennsylvania established in 1905 the first modern state police force—that is, one which patrolled the entire

174

state daily. All the states have been compelled by the rapid increase in the use of the automobile to create either a state highway patrol or a police force. In twelve states the highway patrol has authority to enforce only the motor vehicle laws and regulations; in the other states the state police is charged with the responsibility of general law enforcement in rural areas and sometimes in incorporated places. Relations of the state police with local police forces sometimes require tact in order to avoid offense to local pride. Prior to entering a local government unit to make arrests, members of the state police often notify the local police authorities and attempt to obtain their co-operation.

State police forces are organized along military lines: The administrative officer is called the *chief, commander,* or *superintendent,* and the force is divided into units headed by *captains, lieutenants,* and *sergeants.* Each of the larger units is assigned to a specified area. Though a few states have boards of control which select the superintendents, most of the state police forces are directly responsible to the governor. Several states have created bureaus of investigation either as independent offices or as units within the state police organization to assist local police officers in making investigations.

The Municipal Police. Early American cities relied on voluntary night watchmen for protection during the night. As the populations grew and the complexity of city life increased, trained round-the-clock protectors became a necessity. In 1844 New York City established the first daytime police patrol. Nowadays the functions of the municipal police are the enforcement of state laws and municipal ordinances, the maintenance of order, and the regulation of traffic.

Though the police forces in a few large cities are under the control of state or local commissions, most police forces are directly responsible to the municipal executive who appoints the police chief. In the larger cities the chief is assisted by deputy chiefs, captains, lieutenants, and sergeants. For convenience in administration, large cities are divided into police precincts, each with a "station house," which is the center of police activity for that precinct. Members of the force are commonly assigned to the foot patrol, the motor patrol, or traffic direction, or to bureaus of investigation, juvenile aid, or statistics. The patrolman, who is the private of the police force, is assigned a definite area to patrol known as a *beat;* he may cover his beat on foot or by automobile or motorcycle (or even helicopter in certain areas). By means of the two-way radio connection with the station house the motor patrols may be directed to proceed quickly to the places where they are needed in residential and manufacturing districts. In many ways, however, the foot patrol is regarded as superior in downtown areas. Juvenile bureaus have recently been created or enlarged as a result of increasing crimes by youthful hoodlums. In 1958 New York City created a special force of one hundred juvenile bureau policemen to patrol trouble spots and gather information on gang activities.

Noteworthy recent trends in police administration are the establishment of research and planning units, the telephone alarm system, and increased emphasis on the training of patrolmen. In 1911 Detroit established the first school for the systematic training of new patrolmen. The Federal Bureau of Investigation, in co-operation with state and local police forces, has established training institutes throughout the country for the training of patrolmen for small cities. A number of universities have also provided programs in police work. Unfortunately, relatively low salaries and unsatisfactory political conditions remain in many communities, making it difficult to recruit competent candidates for the police force.

Criminal Prosecution. The *prosecuting attorney*—called in some states the *district attorney,* the *state's attorney,* or the *county solicitor*—is, almost everywhere, elected by the voters of the county to take charge of criminal prosecutions. The prosecuting attorney investigates crimes, orders arrests, draws up indictments for submission to the grand jury, or files informations formally accusing persons of crimes. When a case is tried, he conducts the prosecution on behalf of the state. In the performance of his duties he often reflects the prevailing attitude of the local community toward the enforcement of state laws. Usually the prosecuting attorney is not subject to direction by the attorney general of the state.

The Correctional System. Every state operates a *correctional system* composed of prisons and reformatories of various types. In 1960 about 185,000 prisoners were confined in correctional institutions; of these about 35,000 were in the states of California and New York. In recent years the states have spent large sums in constructing new prisons and reformatories, yet crowding in correctional institutions continues to be a problem.

In the past, the same department sometimes administered the correctional system and public welfare. The present trend is to place these functions in two separate departments, since the relief of poverty and the rehabilitation of criminals present different problems and require separate means of treatment. In some states all correctional institutions are under the control of one board; in others, there is a different board of control for each correctional institution.

The early theory of imprisonment was based on punishment and the closely related purpose of deterring others from committing crimes. In the nineteenth century, revulsion against the barbarous conditions in prisons led to a reform movement which emphasized rehabilitation rather than punishment. Today, only those prisoners who are habitual criminals are imprisoned permanently. Implementation of the more modern theory requires the staffing of correctional institutions by professional administrators who are thoroughly trained in the fields of sociology and psychiatry.

The parole system is an important adjunct to the rehabilitation process. More than 55 per cent of the approximately 68,000 prisoners released from state correctional institutions every year are paroled, subject to continued good behavior. In several states a prisoner is not paroled unless a job is waiting for him. The use of the indefinite sentence with a minimum and a maximum term is strongly recommended by prison authorities in order to allow correctional experts to base the duration of imprisonment on the prisoner's character and behavior.

Idleness is a major problem in correctional institutions, and in most institutions some sort of manufacturing program is set up to combat it. Prison manufacture, however, is opposed by business concerns and labor unions and, as a result, goods made in most state prisons may not be sold on the market and may be used only in other state institutions. Besides dealing with the problem of idleness, prison manufacturing programs also are valuable in teaching prisoners trades which may be useful to them after their release. In addition, many correctional institutions have developed educational programs, through which inmates may complete their schooling.

Youth service programs have been established in California, Illinois, Massachusetts, Minnesota, Texas, and Wisconsin. The agencies in charge of these activities strive to prevent delinquency and are responsible for the supervision of children committed to them by the courts.

Fire Protection. Fires in the United States annually cause approximately twelve thousand deaths and property damage in excess of one and one-half billion dollars. Years ago the principal emphasis in *fire protection* was given to extinguishing fires; in recent years equal or greater attention is given to preventive measures.

Forty-three states have state fire marshals or officials performing similar duties. They are heads of separate departments in five states; they are subordinates of the departments of insurance in twenty-two states, of the state police departments in seven states, of the departments of public safety in five states, of the auditors in Montana and West Virginia, of the commerce department in Ohio, and of the director of safety in New York. Almost everywhere the state fire marshal supervises local fire prevention activities. Municipal fire chiefs are usually appointed deputy state fire marshals. Several states have established boards, of which the state fire marshals are members, to co-ordinate municipal fire departments in the event of enemy attacks or widespread disasters.

The principal functions of the state fire marshal are to prevent fires by eliminating or reducing fire hazards. Members of his staff inspect buildings and issue corrective orders when violations of fire regulations are found. They also assist in public educational programs which are conducted through public media and in the schools. After a fire of undetermined or suspicious origin has occurred the state fire marshal conducts an investigation to find out whether or not the crime of arson has been committed.

Civil Defense. A new public safety activity which originated during World War II consists of measures taken by civilian agencies to reduce the effects of enemy attacks and to rehabilitate areas following such attacks. The Federal Civil Defense Act of 1950 declared that *civil defense* is primarily a responsibility of state and local governments. However, in 1958 Congress enacted a new law which declared "the responsibility for civil defense shall be vested jointly in the Federal Government, and the several States and their political subdivisions." Every state now has a civil defense law, and forty-one states have authorized their civil defense agencies to act in the event of natural disasters as well as in enemy attacks. Nearly all the states have signed interstate civil defense and disaster compacts. Large cities have also created civil defense agencies. Because civil defense problems are broad in scope, the state and local agencies work closely with each other and with departments such as education, fire, health, police, and public works. The best response to civil defense activities has been among the inhabitants of large industrial areas, but the difficulty of developing public interest in civil defense remains a major problem.

PUBLIC HEALTH

A century ago nearly all *public health* functions were performed by local officials who were primarily concerned with quarantine and the isolation of persons afflicted with contagious diseases. The discovery of the germ theory of disease about 1870 resulted in greatly expanded activity by both local and state authorities. Phenomenal progress has been made in protecting public health. In both urban and rural areas sanitary conditions have been improved; contagious diseases have been controlled and epidemics prevented. Health conditions are generally favorable in the United States. The annual death rate had been reduced, in 1960, to 9.1 per thousand persons, and life expectancy has steadily lengthened. In spite of these and other improvements many problems remain which require the unremitting attention of public health authorities. (See pp. 286–287.)

State Health Departments. Massachusetts in 1869 was the first state to create a state board of health; by 1909 every state had set up state health departments. The state board of health usually consists of three to fifteen members. Their principal functions are to study public health problems, establish standards, and make and enforce regulations concerning water supplies, sanitation, and communicable diseases. Members of the board meet only a few times a year, and they are either unsalaried or paid on a per diem basis. The administration of the state department is generally directed by a full-time health commissioner. In nearly all the states the commissioner is appointed by the governor; in the remaining few he is chosen by the state board of health and subject to its general oversight.

The states spend approximately $500 million annually for public health services and another $600 million for mental health programs (see increasing public health expenditures, p. 290), and employ about 60,000 persons to carry out their activities. A major problem in public health work is the shortage of trained personnel, owing partly to low salary scales.

The state department of public health institutes and supervises programs to control (1) tuberculosis, (2) venereal disease, (3) cancer, (4) heart disease, (5) water pollution, (6) air pollution, and (7) radiation; provides services for (8) maternal and child health, and (9) crippled children; enforces (10) state food and drug acts; and promotes (11) scientific research, (12) dental health, and (13) mental health. Some public health functions are performed by officials in other departments—for example, by the commissioner of pure food and drugs and by the state veterinarian.

The most extensive direct activity of the state health department is in mental health. Every state provides hospitals for the treatment of mental disease. At present these hospitals have more than half a million patients. The number has increased every year since 1945 and will probably continue to do so, since increased longevity is a major factor in the increase in the number of patients.

State health departments co-ordinate local health agencies and establish minimum standards. The amount of control varies: in some states the state health department has the power to appoint, direct, and remove local health officers; in other states it acts in an advisory capacity and provides financial and technical assistance to local health departments.

Local Health Departments. Most of the actual administration of public health must be performed at the local level. The city health department is headed by a board or an administrator or both. Board members are generally appointed by the municipal executive, and some members of the board must be physicians. In large cities the public health departments are subdivided into bureaus of communicable diseases, child health, public health education, sanitation, vital statistics, and visiting nurses. New York in 1877 was the first city to employ visiting nurses. Many cities operate public hospitals for medical and surgical care of afflicted persons. (See p. 291 for increasing expenditures.)

In small communities a physician is often employed on a part-time basis as health commissioner. The present trend is toward the consolidation of city and rural areas into relatively large public health units. These large units eliminate duplication in administration and raise standards of public health.

PUBLIC WELFARE

Public welfare administration is concerned with the relief of poverty and with measures to prevent persons from becoming public charges. The causes of poverty are manifold and complicated. Some causes, like shiftlessness and lack of foresight to provide for the future, are traceable to individual defects of mind or character, health, education, and environment (family, milieu). Other causes are clearly social and economic. For instances, changes in processes of manufacture or in demand for certain products, and recessions and depressions, resulting in prolonged unemployment. Old age, physical and mental handicaps, and long illnesses are frequent causes of poverty, especially among persons who have never been the recipients of large incomes.

In earlier periods private charity and local institutions for the care of the indigent were considered sufficient. Under modern conditions of concentrated populations and industrial organization, they are clearly inadequate. Especially since 1935, much of the financial burden of public welfare programs has been borne by the state and federal governments. Today local, state, and federal governments co-operate in welfare work, and many private organizations, such as the Red Cross, the Salvation Army, and religious organizations operate private programs for the relief of poverty and destitution. In the eastern states public welfare is largely administered by municipalities. In other sections, it is administered directly by the state, and only the largest cities have welfare departments. Whether the state or the city is the principal unit in the administration of public welfare, the organizational form is a commission, or a single administrator, or a combination of both. (See public welfare items, pp. 290–291.)

Indoor and Outdoor Relief. The traditional classification of welfare work has been into *indoor relief* (institutional care) and *outdoor relief* (aid to persons who live at home). In most cases outdoor relief is preferable because it (1) avoids the expense of building and operating institutions; (2) permits indigent persons to live with their families; and (3) does not subject them to the humiliation of entering a poorhouse. Once a person is on the relief rolls, there is a tendency for him to remain there even when the need for aid no longer exists.

Relief of the Aged. Approximately 16 million people—8 per cent of the population—are more than sixty-five years old. A fixed retirement age and an increasing life span combine to throw many older people out of work when they are still capable of earning salaries. More serious problems arise when old people are physically or mentally ill and when the resources of their families are limited. To provide a long-range solution for the problem Congress in 1935 passed the Social Security Act requiring from both employers and employees compulsory contributions, used to provide monthly payments to the employees on their retirement. This system of old-age insurance is administered by the federal government. For older persons who were not employed in 1935 or who were ineligible to participate in the plan, Congress provided grants-in-aid for a state-administered system of old-age assistance.

Unemployment Compensation. The Social Security Act of 1935 practically forced the states to provide for *unemployment compensation*. It levied a payroll tax of 3 per cent on employers of four or more persons, with the proviso that taxes paid to a state for unemployment compensation might offset up to 90 per cent of the federal payroll tax. The amounts of unemployment payments and the periods during which they are paid vary widely from state to state. Even in the more financially liberal states, they are hardly ever sufficient to tide a worker over an extended period of unemployment.

Child Welfare Services. A separate division within the department of public welfare is devoted to *child welfare services*. Special attention is given to children who have been deprived of their natural parents. The trend is away from institutional care and toward the placement of childen in foster homes. The division selects foster homes with care and provides for supervision of them by trained social workers. Public child-welfare agencies also assist in placing children for adoption and set standards for adoption agencies. Special programs have been designed to assist mentally retarded and physically handicapped children. Child-welfare agencies are giving increasing importance to the prevention of juvenile delinquency. Several states have created youth authorities which operate parole services and training schools and conduct preventive programs.

17

SCHOOLS, LIBRARIES, AND MUSEUMS

Education is the most expensive service which state and local governments provide. In a democracy an educated electorate is essential to the proper conduct of political, social, and economic affairs. Moreover, in modern life equal and full opportunities for education are necessary for the development of the individual. As a consequence, public schools and universities are maintained by the state for the formal education of its citizens. After formal education ceases, libraries and museums provide opportunities for research, general reading, and cultural development.

SCHOOLS

Well into the nineteenth century and almost everywhere in the country education was considered to be a private function. The New England states were exceptions. For example, Massachusetts in 1647 required each town of more than fifty families to employ a teacher to educate the children of the town. A Connecticut law in 1813 provided that reading, writing, and arithmetic must be taught to children employed in factories. In 1821 the first public high school was established in Boston, Massachusetts. In 1852, under the first compulsory school attendance law enacted in this country, Massachusetts required all children under fourteen years of age to attend public school at least twelve weeks each year. School attendance up to the age of sixteen is now compulsory in forty-six states.

State governments operate only the institutions of higher education and special schools; local authorities operate the public schools under state supervision. The legislature commonly specifies that certain subjects are to be taught in the public schools throughout the state. Twenty-four states provide for uniformity of textbooks throughout the state. The desirability of uniformity in curriculum and textbook adoption is questionable since it limits experimentation designed to improve the educational process.

Enrollment and Expenditures. Public school enrollment in 1961 exceeded thirty-eight million and has been increasing at a rate of more than one million pupils a year. In the same year, there were close to one and one-half million teachers in the public schools of the United States. The especially rapid rise in enrollment since World War II and the relative shortage of qualified teachers have created an educational crises in many areas: Classrooms are overcrowded; many schools operate two sessions a day; and approximately 80,000 persons teaching in public schools cannot meet the qualifications for standard teaching certificates.

In 1961 expenditures for public education and capital expenditures for new schools and equipment exceeded $10 billion and $4 billion, respectively. An estimated 60,000 classrooms have been constructed each year, yet the classroom shortage is still acute. (See Appendix, pp. 284–285, for annual public school and per pupil expenditures in the states.)

Finances. The property tax provides more than 50 per cent, on a nation-wide average, of public school revenues. Its importance as a source of funds has always varied—it furnishes approximately 13 per cent of public school revenue in Delaware as compared to 95 per cent in Nebraska—but recently it has been decreasing. The varying financial resources of local units of school administration have led, however, to inequalities in the standards of local education. Thus, it was inevitable that state funds would have to be used to subsidize local education and to correct these inequalities. In recent years revenue from state income and sales taxes has assumed greater importance in financing education. It has been distributed by the states in the form of grants to aid local school units; these grants of approximate $3 billion annually—providing from 4 per cent of public school expenditures in New Hampshire to 85 per cent in Delaware—furnish on an average 50 per cent of the total cost of operating local school systems. Twenty-three states also assist local school districts in their construction costs.

Administrative Organization. Among the states three principal variations exist in the organization of educational administration: (1) In a few states a superintendent of education administers the state's program without the aid of a board of education. (2) In a small number of other states the superintendent is assisted by a board of education whose consent may be required for the performance of a few specific acts. (3) In many states the board of education is paramount and conducts the administration through a superintendent and other officers whom it appoints. The superintendent of education is popularly elected in more than twenty states, appointed by the board of education in over twenty more, and appointed by the governor in five. The members of the board of education are appointed by the governor in almost forty states and are popularly elected in several others.

Higher Education. All but a few states maintain state universities. Every state maintains an agricultural and mechanical college and one or more institutions for the training of teachers. In 1961 more than three and one-half million students were enrolled in public and private institutions of higher education; enrollment varied from approximately 2,000 students in Alaska to 368,000 students in California. It is estimated that the number of students in institutions of higher education will double within ten to twelve years and the amount spent in 1961, three and one-half billion dollars, for all kinds of both public and private higher education, will probably double within ten to fifteen years. New capital expenditures at state institutions of higher education have totalled approximately 600 million dollars annually. Many states are preparing for the approaching crisis in higher education by inaugurating state-wide surveys of the problem.

The development of a co-ordinated program of higher education in a state is facilitated by a board which governs all institutions of higher education. This situation exists in thirteen states, but in most states institutions of higher education have separate boards of control. The state legislature exercises by means of appropriations a large measure of control over state colleges and universities.

Many states have an adequate number of students to justify maintaining academic programs in all fields; others do not. As a result, interstate compacts have been used to pool the educational resources of several states in a region so as to better fulfill student needs. For this purpose fourteen southern states in 1948 formed the Southern Regional Education Board; similar interstate compacts have been ratified by the western states and the New England states. Consequently, students attending a state university which lacks, for example, a college of architecture may attend the architectural college of one of the states co-operating in the regional plan for higher education. These compacts are especially important in high-cost professional fields such as medicine and dentistry.

Massachusetts established in 1956 a novel educational assistance program: the Massachusetts Higher Education Assistance Corporation insures up to 80 per cent of all noncollateral loans from banks to students to assist them in financing their educations. The law creating the corporation authorized commercial banks to make loans to minors. Since the loans are guaranteed by the corporation—with money contributed by financial institutions, corporations, and individuals—the interest rate on the loans is lower and the repayment period is longer than on ordinary personal loans. The repayment record has been excellent. Several other states including Maine and New York have followed the lead of Massachusetts and have established similar corporations.

Supervision of Local Units. The state educational authorities spend the major portion of their energies in supervising the work of local boards of education and the operation of primary, elementary, and secondary schools. Among other activities of the state authorities are the study of the financial resources and needs of localities and the allotment to them of available funds; the establishment of requirements for teacher certification; the formulation of curricula for various schools and grades; the administration of special programs for children who are mentally retarded, or deaf, or blind; the publication of study manuals; the determination of standards of educational performance; the periodic inspections of schools; and the enforcement of standards.

The extent of state supervisory authority varies greatly— from investigation and advice in some states to thoroughgoing control in others. In Delaware the state education department is responsible for direct administration throughout the state, with the exception of Wilmington and the larger towns.

Local School Units. Four units of local government are responsible for administration of the educational system in the various states—the school district, the township, the town, and the county.

The central states have led the way in reducing the number of school districts by replacing small rural schools with consolidated or regional schools. As a result of consolidation the number of districts in the United States decreased from 127,244 in 1933 to approximately 45,000 in 1960. Nevertheless, there are still too many small school districts with low educational standards, because they cannot afford to erect adequate buildings or employ qualified teachers. Urban school districts are larger and maintain higher standards than do rural school districts. Each urban school district is governed by a board of education or a school committee which is independent of the municipal government. The school committee selects a full-time superintendent to administer the educational program. In many cities the school committee has the power to fix the tax rate for the support of the school system.

The township is responsible for education in Indiana, New Jersey, and Pennsylvania. Township administration of education is an improvement over the school district plan because the township is larger in area than the school district and can afford to construct and maintain better facilities and employ better qualified teachers.

In New England towns, the town school committee is the unit which administers the educational system. This committee, which is popularly elected, selects the superintendent of schools and decides educational policies.

The county educational system existing in twelve states has the advantages of developing uniform educational standards throughout the county and equalizing educational opportunities. A board of education, either popularly elected or appointed by the governor, supervises the county school system, hires all school personnel, determines salaries, selects textbooks, and decides other educational matters. The board selects a county superintendent of schools to administer the system.

Forty states have a county superintendent of schools and thirty states have a county board of education in addition to district or township school committees. The county superintendent of schools in almost every state is popularly elected. His powers, however, are not the same everywhere; in some states he possesses little authority, but in others his authority is relatively broad. The traditional functions of county superintendents of schools are administrative and supervisory, with increasing attention to providing greater services to school districts and formulating educational policy on matters of county-wide concern.

LIBRARIES

Although public library systems were known in ancient civilizations, libraries in this country were generally private until early in the nineteenth century.

In 1961 the approximately 7,500 public library systems in the fifty states operated in excess of 11,000 central libraries and branches and 900 bookmobiles. More than twenty states grant funds to local governments to improve local library services.

The Library Services Act enacted by Congress in 1956 has had, and is continuing to have, a major impact on the development of public libraries in rural areas. Under the provisions of this Act federal grants, which must be matched by state and/or local funds, are made in order to provide public library facilities in rural areas. Almost all the states are participating in this program, which is effective until 1966.

State Libraries. Every state has some type of state library agency, the name and functions of which vary from state to state.

The state library contains official records and other archives of the state; federal, state, and local government publications; and material useful to the legislative reference service, which is sometimes housed in the state library building. In many states, it holds the state law library for use by the supreme court and the attorney general. The state library provides reference and research services, issues publications, and makes loans to libraries within the state. Extension services include the operation of bookmobiles and assistance in the establishment of local libraries. Several states operate regional libraries in parts of the state where local library service is inadequate. Many special services are provided by the state library, including the installation and maintenance of libraries in correctional and mental health institutions, the demonstration of new developments in library services, the recruitment of librarians, and, in the fourteen states requiring it, the certification of librarians.

County Libraries. Library legislation and the efforts of state library agencies have encouraged the establishment and strengthening of county libraries in recent years. Ohio, for example, in 1947 adopted a law which stipulates that new public libraries must be organized as county libraries. In spite of recent efforts, including the extensive use of bookmobiles to serve rural areas, county-wide library service is lacking in approximately two-thirds of the states.

A county library usually is under the control of a board of trustees appointed by the county board; the board of trustees determines the policies of the library, supervises library operation, and employs a librarian to administer the library.

Local Libraries. New Hampshire in 1770 created the first state library and the town of Peterborough, in the same state, in 1833 established the first town-supported library. The Boston Public Library, founded in 1848, was the first municipal library to be established by a state law.

The library in a city, town, township, or village commonly is under the control of a board, although the executive in some communities appoints a librarian, rather than a board, to take charge of the library. Although the library facilities in small communities often are inadequate or nonexistent, the library facilities in larger cities tend to be excellent, and in many places include branch libraries or bookmobiles for general or special purposes. The large library system provides special-reference services for businessmen, government officials, and others. Brookline, Massachusetts, was the first (1890) of many municipalities to establish a children's library service. Special collections of such items as phonograph records, paintings, maps, films, and books for the blind have been set up in many city libraries.

MUSEUMS

The first public museum in the United States was established in 1773 in Charleston, South Carolina. Until recently most museums were private or semiprivate institutions located in large centers of population. By comparison state museums have been of secondary importance, but they are growing both in number and in quality.

More than one-third of the museums in cities are municipally operated and most of the others receive contributions from the city government in the form of land, buildings, or annual appropriations. Museums have been organized within the school systems of a few cities including Cleveland and St. Louis. Generally they are under the control of a separate board appointed by the local executive. In addition to regular and special exhibitions, museums frequently offer conferences, lectures, and instruction in various subjects.

18

PUBLIC WORKS

Many diverse subjects are embraced within the broad category of public works—highways and other facilities for transportation, water supply and other public utilities, public buildings (especially those used for public gatherings), public parks, street cleaning, sewage and refuse disposal, and many others. The most important common characteristics of public works are: (1) they are public improvements; (2) they are built and maintained by government for public use, with, or without payment of a fee; and (3) their construction and maintenance are primarily engineering problems, rather than primarily problems of health, education, or other function.

Though a few states place all public works within one department, the more general rule is to disperse them among several agencies. The great majority of municipalities concentrate the construction and maintenance of all public works in a single department. The extent of public works activity varies greatly from city to city depending on whether or not a city has embarked on a program of public ownership of water, gas, electricity, or other utilities.

HIGHWAYS

Until the end of the nineteenth century local governments were primarily responsible for constructing and maintaining highways. These early roads were in many places poorly constructed and impassable during heavy rains. With the development and increased use of the automobile it became essential to replace existing roads with modern highway systems. In 1891 New Jersey provided the first state aid for highways. Since that date the states have assumed primary responsibility for the improvement and maintenance of highways, though similar road projects are found in all levels of government. Owing to the fact that highway use is well over 700 billion vehicle-miles a year and is increasing constantly, the largest public works programs in the states and localities are the construction and maintenance of highways.

State and Local Highway Departments. In the twenty-five years between 1890 and 1915 the majority of the states organized highway departments. The Federal Road Act of 1916, which offered grants-in-aid for ·the construction of highways induced many of the remaining states to create highway departments.

Most commonly the state highway department is organized under the control of the highway commission, but this state department may also be headed by one individual. In Massachusetts the division of highways is located within the public works department.

A municipality may have either a streets department or a streets bureau located within a department of public works. Large cities commonly have a department of public works headed by one person. In some cities the public works department is under the control of a commission which determines policy and selects a director to administer the department.

Construction and Maintenance. Federal, state, and local expenditures for highways annually total in excess of $9 billion. The states have assumed responsibility for approximately 60 per cent of the cost of constructing, maintaining, and policing all highways. After education, highways make the second largest demand on state funds; in 1959 the states spent $6.5 billion on highways or approximately 28 per cent of total state expenditures. (See Appendix, p. 290.) Local governments contribute 25 per cent of the cost of all highways and are responsible primarily for constructing, with some state aid, urban and rural roads. The federal government provides the remaining 15 per cent of all highways expenditures.

The states administered in 1959 approximately 650,000 road miles of which 380,000 miles are in the state primary system. For the purpose of maintenance, each state usually is divided into highway districts. Each district is supervised by an official who is charged with the responsibility of keeping the roads in his district in good condition.

Finance. State and local highway construction is financed by taxation, by the sale of bonds, and by federal grants. Those who use the highways also contribute to the cost of their upkeep through such sources as license and registration fees and motor fuel taxes. The average state gasoline tax is 5.75 cents per gallon. A majority of states distribute part of the receipts of the gasoline tax to localities.

The Federal Highway Act of 1956 provides federal assistance equal to 90 per cent of the cost of building state highways as part of the interstate highway system. This Act set aside $27.4 billion for a highway construction program over a thirteen-year period. The provisions of this act have greatly alleviated the burden carried by the states.

Toll Roads. In recent years the states have embarked on major programs for the construction of high-speed, limited-access highways. To finance these programs, without directly involving their credit, the states usually created special units of government to issue bonds and charge road tolls. The proceeds of the bonds are utilized to construct the highways; those of the tolls, to retire the outstanding bonds and to maintain the highways. In Colorado, Connecticut, and New Hampshire the state highways departments, not special authorities, are empowered to construct and operate toll roads. Because it provides for the same type of high-speed limited-access freeways as the states have undertaken, the federal highway program (authorized by the Federal Highway Act of 1956) has ended its construction of state toll roads.

Motor-Vehicle Regulation. The rapid rise in motor-vehicle registration (now more than 70,000,000) since the turn of the century has created a severe problem in traffic regulation and safety.

In order to conserve the highways and improve highway safety, the states regulate the types, sizes, and weights of motor vehicles permitted to operate on public highways. In 1961 eighteen states and the District of Columbia also required a periodic inspection of the operating condition of all motor vehicles, but inspection in several states is inadequate for it applies only to brakes and headlights. All states then required an applicant for a driver's license to pass an examination which includes tests of eyesight and hearing, knowledge of state motor-vehicle laws, and driving competence (road test).

The number of persons killed annually in highway accidents is close to 40,000; those injured, near 1,400,000. The traffic figures have been responsible for increasing state efforts to improve highway safety. Newspapers, motion pictures, magazines, posters, and television are utilized to point out the danger of careless driving. Approximately two-thirds of the high schools have driver-education programs; young people with driver training have only one-half as many accidents as young people who lack such training. Radar is used in all states to apprehend speeders, and in forty-five states chemical tests are used to determine intoxication. Several states have abandoned fixed speed limits in favor of reasonable and proper speed limits based on road and traffic conditions. More than half the states use a point system to bar reckless drivers from the highways; under such a system a specified number of points per offense is levied against individuals convicted of violating motor-vehicle regulations; if an individual accumulates a certain number of points, his driver's license is suspended or revoked. The states' programs of education and regulation for improved safety on the highways have been fairly successful; although the number of traffic deaths per year has been increasing, the ratio of deaths per one hundred million vehicle-miles has been decreasing.

OTHER TRANSPORTATION FACILITIES

The development of the motor vehicle has had a profound effect on other forms of transportation. Privately-owned automobiles, trucks, and buses have cut deeply into the traffic formerly carried by railroads and by trolley and bus lines. The greater the congestion of traffic on city streets, the greater is the need for rapid transit facilities. Because of the unprofitableness of trolley and bus lines, the larger cities are more and more being obliged to take them over or to build subways and elevated lines. From a financial standpoint many of the attempted solutions of the problem of traffic congestion are self-defeating, for relief from congestion brings more drivers on the streets. And, when more drivers join the street traffic, there are fewer patrons of the rapid transit system.

Airports. Since airports are of critical importance to the public and are costly to build and operate, they are almost without exception publicly owned. Many municipalities and several counties have taken advantage of offers of federal grants-in-aid to establish airports. Their building and operation—usually outside the city's limits—poses many problems such as acquisition

of land, constant repair of runways, snow removal, proper lighting, construction and maintenance of signal systems, and provision for parking spaces, waiting rooms, and restaurants. Though
the city receives considerable income from rentals and concessions, it must usually expect to devote some of its tax revenues
to airport maintenance.

Terminal Facilities. If a city is located on the seacoast, its
harbor will probably be deepened and the channels marked by
the federal government. The city must often build wharves and
docks for the loading and unloading of goods and passengers and
must operate police and fire boats to protect the waterside.
Every city of considerable size, no matter what its location, finds
it desirable to operate or closely regulate terminal markets for
the wholesale and retail distribution of fresh vegetables, fruit,
and meats.

WATER SUPPLY

Roughly 75 per cent of all cities own and operate their own
water supply systems. The other 25 per cent, which depend on
supplies furnished by private users, take elaborate precautions to
assure the potability and sufficiency of their water supplies. Americans are lavish users of water, and per capita consumption tends
constantly to increase. Industrial use is not entirely to blame:
witness the large quantities of water used in the home in operating disposal units, air conditioners, automatic washing machines,
and dishwashers. Much water is consumed by the city itself in
fighting fires and cleaning streets. Some of the smaller cities,
which depend on wells, are concerned at the apparent lowering
of the water level in the ground. Large cities have been obliged
to go far afield for new sources of water. New York City has found
it necessary to build reservoirs in the upper valley of the Delaware River, and Los Angeles draws a large part of its water supply from the reservoir above Hoover Dam, three hundred miles
away. In order to insure the purity of drinking water, sanitary
engineers and their technicians must maintain a constant vigil.
Heavy chlorination of water drawn from nearby streams and
lakes is essential.

Though some cities still make flat charges against all users of
water and most still charge residential users a flat monthly rate,
an increasing number of cities have installed meters in factories,

stores, and apartment houses. During periods of drought, water department officers prohibit the sprinkling of lawns and may inspect houses for leaky faucets, imposing heavy penalties for violations.

DISPOSAL OF WASTES

Every city faces the problem of disposing of vast quantities of waste material of divers kinds. Because natural channels have been filled up and leveled over, sewers must be constructed to carry away surplus rainwater. In northern cities snow must be plowed out, melted with chemicals, pushed into sewers, or loaded into trucks and hauled to the nearest watercourse. Soot and exhaust fumes must be prevented from entering the air in excessive quantities, lest they mix with water vapor to form choking smog. Sewage must be purified lest it contaminate water and food supplies. Solid wastes of all kinds must be collected and disposed of.

Sewerage Systems. *Sewage* is liquid waste, and a *sewerage system* is the intricate system of pipes, conduits, and facilities for treating sewage. A quarter of all sewage is composed of industrial wastes, some of which, before or after treatment, are discharged directly into a river or harbor. Other sewage flows underground by gravity to low points of discharge. Formerly the same set of conduits served as storm sewers (for rainwater) and sanitary sewers (for removal of household and industrial wastes). During exceptionally heavy rains the combined contents sometimes backed up in cellars; or, when carried to a treatment plant, the great quantity of liquid overtaxed the facilities. The modern practice is to build two entirely separate systems of storm sewers and sanitary sewers. Cities on the seacoast or on large rivers may still discharge sanitary sewage into the water and expect it to be purified by oxidation. Other cities are forced to build plants for sewage treatment by filtration, oxidation, bacterial decomposition, or a combination of several methods. Some cities recover part of the expense of the process by selling the solid residue as fertilizer.

Removal of Solid Wastes. In addition to disposing of liquid wastes, many communities also collect, use, or treat solid wastes, such as ashes, rubbish, and garbage. Ashes are useful for filling land covered by shallow water, or low-lying land subject to flood. Rubbish (remnants of construction materials, bottles, tin cans, old newspapers, and cartons or boxes) may be pressed out and also used as land fill. Garbage (containing quantities of food wastes) is unsatisfactory as land fill because it emits offensive odors, provides breeding places for disease-carrying rats and flies, and is, even after many years, an insubstantial base for buildings. Some of the smaller cities deposit garbage in deep trenches and cover over the trenches at the end of every working day. Other cities have built garbage incinerators or reduction plants. When fired at temperatures of 1200 or more degrees F., the garbage is entirely consumed.

19

LAND POLICIES AND PLANNING

The early settlers of the United States found a land of seemingly unlimited natural resources. In their clearings they exhausted the soil in a few years of intensive cultivation, then abandoned it, repeating the process over and over again. In order to facilitate development of the new country, they destroyed valuable timber and other resources. It was not until the twentieth century that Americans became aware of the need for the conservation of, and careful planning for the future use of, agricultural and urban land, water, forest, and mineral resources.

AGRICULTURE

The farming industry is complicated by a huge number of producers; the inability of farmers to gauge accurately at planting time, the value of their crops when harvested; and the tendency on the part of many farmers to allow their soils to become depleted. All three levels of government—national, state, and local —are engaged in a co-operative effort to give aid to agriculture. The federal government has made available the results of extensive research, has regulated the production and marketing of some basic commodities, and has aided, through soil banks, in restoring the productiveness of land; the states have established departments of agriculture which engage in intensive research and regulatory activities within a smaller area; and the counties have provided means for demonstration of new agricultural processes and for co-operative effort among individual farmers.

State Regulatory Activities. Many activities regulatory of agricultural processes and products have been instituted at the state level. Under the police power of the state, laws have been enacted to control plant and animal diseases and to protect public health against impure food products. State agricultural departments institute quarantines, inspect dairy farms and food processing plants, and enforce the laws by summary action. Thus dairymen who will not or cannot conform to sanitary standards may be prohibited from selling milk, and cows afflicted with bovine tuberculosis and trees and shrubs that harbor dangerous plant parasites may be destroyed. State legislatures authorize the fixing of prices of milk and the inspection and grading of other agricultural products prior to shipment.

Agricultural Experiment Stations. In 1875 Connecticut established the first agricultural experiment station, and in 1887 Congress, through the Hatch Act, authorized federal grants to all the states to enable them to create similar institutions. The station, which is usually located at the state agricultural college, conducts a wide variety of research projects in such areas as plant propagation; seeds, soils, and fertilizers; plant and animal diseases; and horticulture. The research findings are disseminated by the publication of bulletins, by mail in the form of answers to inquiries, and by personal contacts.

The County Agent. In 1906 Texas originated the county agent system which has since been extended to every state. Congress in 1914 began the appropriation of funds to aid states and counties in supporting county agents. Though nominally appointed by the county board and serving at its pleasure, the county agent works under the direction of the agricultural college's extension service. He brings the results of recent agricultural research to the farm community by demonstrating new methods on the farmer's own land. Typical projects are soil conservation, improved seeds, methods of cultivation, new breeds of live stock and poultry, and co-operative marketing.

CONSERVATION

In popular usage, "conservation" often means no more than the withdrawal of publicly owned land from useful development. In actual fact, the term *conservation* means the judicious utilization of natural resources for the purposes for which they are best suited, and it may be applied to privately owned property as well as to public property. It also includes the restoration, wherever possible, of depleted resources in both public and private hands.

Soil Conservation. In 1935 Congress created the Soil Conservation Service and authorized it to co-operate with state and local agencies concerned with maintaining the fertility of soils. The seriousness of the problem of soil erosion has impelled all the states to establish soil-conservation committees with planning and supervisory duties. The federal government supplies technical advice, but effective implementation of the program has rested with officials of local soil-conservation districts working in co-operation with residents of the districts. Conservation district employees instruct landowners in methods of drainage, contour plowing, growing of forage crops, substitution of grazing for cultivation on sloping fields, planting of trees on steep hillsides, and rehabilitation of badly eroded soil.

Water Conservation. Because water consumption is increasing at a swifter rate than population, the development and conservation of water resources have emerged as urgent problems. State agencies have been established for the purposes of controlling floods and pollution, surveying and conserving surface and subterranean water resources, constructing hydroelectric and irrigation facilities, and regulating the use of water. Many projects are sponsored jointly by the federal government and the states. Co-operative action by neighboring states, through interstate compacts, have been particularly beneficial in flood control and pollution control.

Forests. Forests are essential for both water and soil conservation. During heavy rainfalls the spongy forest floor absorbs much water and thus prevents floods. The later gradual release of the water raises the subterranean water tables and maintains some flow in streams during even severe droughts. Without forests the rain would run off quickly, eroding the land, carrying away irreplaceable topsoil, and choking stream beds. Prolonged deforestation is thought to result in reduced rainfall and other permanent climatic changes.

STATE FORESTRY SERVICES. California, Colorado, Ohio, and New York were (in 1885) the first states to create agencies to administer state forestry activities. Forty-seven states now have forestry organizations. The early agencies were devoted mainly to educational or fire-prevention services. Today forest-management assistance, reforestation, forest-fire control, forest-pest control, and the administration of state forests are typical activities of state forestry agencies.

FIRE PROTECTION. The Weeks Act of 1911 authorized the secretary of agriculture to work with the states in the development of a program to protect public forests from fires, and the

Clarke-McNary Act of 1924 authorized grants to states to assist them in their forest fire control programs. In almost all the states, organized forest-fire control is administered by a forestry department. State forests contain approximately nineteen million acres; Michigan, Minnesota, Pennsylvania, New York, and Washington each have more than one million acres of forests.

State forest-fire protection organizations have confined the area burned to 0.3 per cent of the area protected. Use of the airplane and the radio to detect and report forest fires enables fire-fighters to get to the stricken area quickly; the use of bulldozers and pumper tank trucks has increased the efficiency of fire-fighters. Nevertheless, until the general public is thoroughly imbued with the importance of forest-fire prevention, the problem will not be solved.

FOREST MANAGEMENT. Approximately fifty million acres of land in the United States needs to be reforested. Most states co-operate with the United States forest service in this task by maintaining tree nurseries which distribute each year, at no cost or at a nominal fee, several hundred million trees to landowners for planting. Forest-pest control is also an important function of state forestry agencies. Another function is the enforcement of fire-prevention regulations, such as requiring the owners of land, in cutting marketable timber, to dispose of branches which might otherwise cause fires to spread quickly. More and more, trees are being looked upon as a special kind of crop with periods of growth of twenty, fifty, or even one hundred years.

Mineral Resources. Nearly every state maintains a geological survey either as an independent agency or as a bureau in a department of conservation or as a research division in the state university. Its functions are to make surveys and prepare maps showing the mineral, soil, water, and other natural resources of the state. In several states mining experiment stations study and demonstrate safety measures and methods for extracting ores and utilizing byproducts. Considering the depleted condition of many mineral resources, relatively few laws have been enacted to regulate private exploitation. The most significant conservation measures are limitations placed by state commissions on the number of days per year that oil- and natural-gas production is allowed.

Wildlife Conservation. Wild animals, birds, and fish are the property of the state and may be legally taken only on the conditions established by the state. This is the principle behind the familiar "open" and "closed" seasons and the required hunting and fishing licenses; it also is the basis for the higher license fees charged to nonresident hunters and fishermen.

In some states the protection of fish and game is a function of the conservation department; in many others it is placed under an independent commission which makes needful regulations for the conservation of wild life and appoints a full-time administrator to enforce them. Fish and game wardens patrol portions of the state and arrest violators of the regulations. Most states maintain fish hatcheries from which streams and lakes are stocked with fingerlings. In many areas game has been overprotected; for examples, deer and pheasants exist in such quantities as to destroy farm crops.

Parks and Recreation Areas. In 1865 California established the first state park. In the fifty states today there are approximately 2,400 state parks with a total area of over five million acres, and additional acreage is being added every year. Of special importance is state acquisition of scenic sites which in private hands might be destroyed or exploited in undesirable ways. Annual attendance at state parks exceeds 170 million visitors; receipts from admission and other fees pay approximately 40 per cent of the cost of operating state parks.

Though in many cities parks began with common grazing lands and other plots set aside by the founders for public use (such as military drill and parades), most of the present acreage in municipal parks has been purchased from private owners. The uses of parks are many: semiwoodland areas for hiking and picnicking; beaches with facilities for bathing; artificial lakes for boating in summer and ice-skating in winter; athletic fields for outdoor games; playgrounds for children; horticultural and zoological gardens; sites for dramatic and music festivals. In recent years a number of cities have established community recreation centers with organized programs in dramatics, music, sports, and other recreational activities. Among recent trends are increased interest in programs for older persons, women, and girls. The administration of parks and recreational centers in some cities is combined in a single commission and in others is under separate authorities.

PLANNING AND DEVELOPMENT

In some quarters planning is regarded with disapproval because it is supposed to lead to regimentation and the destruction of free enterprise. More truly, *planning* consists of a series of intelligent estimates as to the course of future development. In fact, planning of some kind is a part of almost every governmental (as well as private) activity. If well done, planning should enable a state or locality to avoid the difficulties and even the disasters that follow unconcerned adherence to traditional patterns. Though city planning may be traced to ancient times, state and regional planning and development programs are of recent origin.

State Planning. There is in every state an agency created to prepare long-range plans for the future. The extent of planning activities varies greatly: in some states they are limited mainly to advertising tourist attractions; in others, they include civil defense, transportation, and industrial development. Competition among states to attract new industries is especially strong. In several states exemptions from property taxes for periods of from five to ten years are offered as inducements to industrial concerns to move their plants to one state from another. With or without state financial assistance, many cities offer to furnish land or buildings free of charge in order to attract new industries. Realizing that industrial development is based on sound local planning, state planning authorities either extend their own services directly or employ outside experts to survey local conditions and advise local authorities.

City Planning. The planning of Washington, D.C. in 1791 by the French engineer L'Enfant and the adoption by New York of a rectangular street pattern for Manhattan Island in 1811 are early examples of city planning in the United States. For the most part, however, cities have been at the mercy of real estate developers whose street plans for suburban areas (later incorporated in cities) paid scant attention to the interests of the larger community. Systematic and continuous city planning is one of the newer municipal activities.

Cities usually have planning commissions or planning directors—sometimes both. In most cities the five or seven members of the planning commission are appointed by the mayor or the city manager, or elected by the council. At present the trend is away from an advisory commission and toward a department of planning which can take measures to enforce its policies. Two subjects of particular interest are (1) the design and location of new public buildings and (2) the "circulatory system," which is concerned with all phases of transportation and the amelioration of tangled traffic conditions resulting from too many automobiles on too few streets.

Zoning. Closely associated with planning is *zoning*, which may be defined as the division of the city into specific areas, or zones, within each of which private property-owners are limited as to the kind of buildings they may erect. The principal kinds of zones are: (1) *commercial*—with subclassifications for retail trade, offices, etc.; (2) *industrial*—including separate areas for heavy and light manufacturing, and distributing plants; and (3) *residential*—further subdivisions for single-family homes and for apartment houses. Because zoning ordinances are seldom retroactive, nonconforming buildings are common in the older parts of a city. For areas that are not built upon, the zoning ordinances and/or subdivision control regulations require the developers to meet minimum requirements in regard to the installation of sewers and water supply systems, the width and surfacing of streets, the height of buildings, the percentage of a tract or lot which may be built upon, the setting back of houses to provide light and air, and the materials used in construction.

Urban Renewal. Slums are a major municipal problem. They result from a chain of circumstances which include: inadequate or no original city plans; the obsolescence of older sections of a city; the tendency of upper- and middle-income groups to move to less congested outlying areas rather than attempt to modernize their homes; the partitioning of the former residences of the well-to-do into single rooms or tiny apartments for the very poor; the filth and squalor which ensue when large numbers of people with low standards of living are crowded together. Often the deterioration is set in motion or hurried by the noise, dust, and fumes of nearby factories or transportation facilities. Though housing codes set standards of sanitation, lighting, ventilation, fireproofing, and maintenance, the enforcement of these requirements is often inadequate.

Cities which have sought to cope with the problem of slum clearance have discovered that private owners were unwilling, without tax exemptions and other guarantees, to take the financial risks of erecting new housing for middle- and lower-income groups; and the cities themselves have faced legal and financial problems in providing the necessary means.

During the past decade Congress has passed several laws to assist cities in eliminating slum conditions. Under the Housing Act of 1954 the federal government will pay two-thirds of the net cost of renewing blighted areas; the remaining one-third must be contributed by the city either in cash or in the form of improvements, such as the construction of new streets and sewers. Buildings that cannot be rehabilitated are to be demolished, and the land prepared for the construction of new structures. In order to become eligible to receive a federal grant, a local government must commit itself to the attainment, within a reasonable time, of the following objectives: (1) adequate local codes and ordinances, effectively enforced; (2) a comprehensive plan for the development of the community; (3) analysis of blighted neighborhoods to determine what needs to be done; (4) adequate administrative organization to carry out urban renewal programs; (5) ability to meet financial requirements; (6) responsibility for obtaining adequate housing for families displaced by urban renewal programs; and (7) citizen participation in urban renewal projects.

20

BUSINESS AND LABOR

The power of the government to regulate industry and industrial relations is manifest in many provisions of the English common law. The states on gaining their independence did not immediately begin legislating on these subjects, because the need for legislation was not apparent. In the course of the last century, however, four important conditions have led to the abandonment of *laissez faire:* (1) change in the methods of manufacturing from the small shop in which the owner worked with a few hands to the giant corporation with tens of thousands of employees; (2) change from a primarily local distributing system to one that is primarily concerned with national and international markets; (3) popular demands for governmental protection against the overweening power of big business and big labor; and (4) development of increased social consciousness. All these were causes of legislation by Congress under the interstate commerce power and by state legislatures under the police power.

REGULATION OF BUSINESS

Though the national government seems to have assumed the lion's share of business regulation, important segments remain under state and local control. These include the regulation of small businesses, with few employees, which do not engage in interstate commerce; dangerous and unhealthy conditions in factories, mines, and shops; weights and measures; banks, insurance companies, and public utilities; and professions and trades. State enforcement may take a number of different forms: inspections, followed by orders to make improvements; punishments by fine or imprisonment; issuance of licenses or permits which may be revoked if conditions are not complied with; or summary closing of an establishment which has engaged in fraudulent practices or whose continued existence endangers public health, morals, or safety. Decisions are made in the first instance by

administrative officers or commissions, subject to appeal in the
courts.

Creation of Corporations. The corporate form of business enterprise offers the advantages of limited liability and perpetual
existence (or at least longevity independent of the lives of the
individual owners). Charters of incorporation are issued, usually
by the secretary of state, upon the fulfillment of conditions established by law. These include a minimum number of incorporators
who are often required, at the beginning of a corporation's existence, to be residents of the state; and a minimum amount of
paid-in capital. Other specifications vary from state to state: in
some states they are purposely vague and general in order to
attract companies to incorporate within the state; in other states
the specifications are rigorous.

A corporation is an artificial person, but not a citizen. It
therefore lacks the privilege, guaranteed to citizens by the constitution of the United States, of moving freely from one state
to another. Unless it is actually engaged in interstate commerce, a
corporation chartered in Delaware, for instance, may be refused
the privilege of doing business in a different state; or its admission may be subject to whatever special fees, taxes, and other
conditions the second state sees fit to impose. In their treatment
of "foreign" corporations (those chartered in other states) state
policies vary: some states are as lenient with them as with their
own "domestic" corporations; other states make it exceedingly
difficult for foreign corporations to enter.

Monopoly and Fair Trade. Commonly, state laws contain
prohibitions of monopolistic practices similar to those of federal
antitrust statutes. To prevent the opposite abuse of cutthroat
competition, many states have enacted price-maintenance, or fair-
trade, laws. According to the usual provisions of such laws, if a
manufacturer signs an agreement with one retailer to maintain
a fixed price for an article, that agreement becomes binding on
all other retailers in the state. When constitutional doubts arose,
Congress enacted laws validating the state laws; but the supreme
courts of a third of the states have declared fair-trade laws unconstitutional.

Blue-Sky Laws. One Kansas legislator has described dishonest
securities-promoters as those who would sell shares in the "blue
sky." In order to curb the activities of such promoters, all but

three states have enacted laws regulating the sale of securities to the public. The usual provisions of the laws are: (1) Before a corporation is permitted to issue securities, it must make a full disclosure of its financial condition and other pertinent facts to a state commission which has the discretion to grant or withhold its consent to the issue. (2) Brokers and dealers are required to be licensed, or at least registered, by the state commission. (3) Fraud and misrepresentation are prohibited under severe penalties. Some state laws are modeled on federal blue-sky laws and provide additional sanctions for their enforcement; others outlaw a somewhat wider range of fraudulent practices.

Regulation of Banks. Every institution engaged in the banking business is chartered by either a state or the federal government. As custodians of depositors' money, banks are subject to strict regulation. Their capitalization, the minimum amount of reserves they must keep on hand, the distribution of their investments and loans, and their methods of conducting business are all governed by regulations made by law. Enforcement is usually under the direction of a commissioner, or, in a few states, of a board. Inspectors make unannounced visits to audit books and determine whether or not the banks' managements and the individual employees have faithfully performed their functions. Failure to conform may result in the dismissal of officers and employees. If a bank is found to be insolvent, it is closed and its assets are liquidated for the benefit of its creditors. Similar supervision is exercised over building and loan associations, credit unions, and small-loan companies.

Regulation of Insurance. Though the insurance business is in interstate commerce, Congress has preferred to leave its regulation almost entirely with the states. For the protection of policyholders, the state insurance commissioner controls the licensing of insurance companies, requires the maintenance of sufficient reserves to cover claims on policies, specifies the type of investments a company may make, licenses insurance agents, and reviews rate schedules, adjusting downward those rates which are deemed excessive.

Public Utility Regulation. Electric power, gas, water, telephone, and transportation companies come within a special classification of businesses affected with a public interest. They are natural monopolies because competition in any of these fields would be uneconomical, if not practically impossible; and they render essential services to the public. Owing to these circumstances they are granted franchises by the state which permit them to use public property, and they are sometimes permitted to use the state's power of eminent domain to obtain routes through private property. In return, public utilities must serve everyone and submit to detailed regulation by the state.

PUBLIC SERVICE COMMISSIONS. Forty-eight states have public service commissions; Oregon and Rhode Island vest the power to regulate in a public utility commissioner. Though a few are elective, most commissions are appointed by the governor with the consent of the senate. The commissioners are almost always chosen for their political prominence rather than for their knowledge of engineering and economics. Their function is to determine policies. Each commission employs a considerable number of experts whose duty is to make continuous studies of the rates charged and the quality of services rendered by the companies.

BASES OF RATE-MAKING. Long ago the Supreme Court of the United States declared that the rates fixed for utilities must be high enough to allow a public utility company to earn a reasonable return on its investment.[1] However, the determination of the value of property for rate-making purposes is by no means easy. Consumers contend that the value is the actual amount of money prudently invested in the property, less depreciation. Utility companies insist on using *reproduction cost* (the amount of money in today's dollars that would be required to build an equivalent plant) as the basis for rate determination. Commission policy has alternated between the two theories and often has attempted a compromise between them. When appeals have been taken from the commissions' determinations, the courts have also wavered—leaving the commissions without any clear guidance.

In addition to problems of investment, the commissions consider questions of operating costs, prescribe particular methods of accounting, require the keeping of records, regulate the issuance of stocks and bonds, and require certain fixed standards in the performance of services.

PUBLIC OWNERSHIP. The alternative to private ownership under regulation is public ownership. Though a few states and many municipalities already own electric utilities, water works,

[1] *Smyth* v. *Ames*, 169 U.S. 466 (1898).

transit systems, grain elevators, docks, or warehouses, the people have been reluctant to accept the principle of public ownership. In part this is due to the average man's difficulty in reaching conclusions on enormously complicated problems amid a welter of claims and counterclaims, and in part to his suspicion that political *management* might not be greatly superior to political *regulation*. It is noteworthy that most municipalities, including practically every large city, own and operate water works. In this case questions of public health and convenience overshadow purely economic considerations.

Regulation of Professions and Trades. Under the police power the states have subjected practically every profession and many trades to regulation, usually in the form of examination and licensure. At the beginning professional associations took the initiative by drafting bills and lobbying them through the legislature. Afterward they brought pressure on appointing authorities to select members of their profession to administer the laws. Because established practitioners were generally exempted from the examination requirement, the suspicion has been expressed that the association has had an ulterior motive, that of keeping the profession from becoming too numerous. On the ground of protection of health, however, the licensing of physicians, chiropractors, druggists, embalmers, food-processors, barbers, and beauticians can be amply justified. So can the licensing of electricians for the protection of homes and working places, and of places of amusement for safeguarding public morals. All these and many others need to be controlled in order to protect the public against impostors and the ill-trained or irresponsible.

In two-thirds of the states the laws are administered by a separate board for each profession. In the remaining one-third, all the licensing agencies are brought together into a department of licenses. Much of the work of licensing people engaged in trades devolves upon municipal governments.

LABOR

Though federal activities concerning labor have assumed vast proportions, the regulations by the states, under their police powers, cover essential portions of the field. Beginning with protection of the health and safety of employees, state labor legislation was extended to protect workers from exploitation by greedy employers and later assumed the more positive function of promoting the welfare of labor. Every state has an administrative office, commonly called a "department of labor," which issues regulations, makes inspections, and takes the initiative in the enforcement of the laws.

Industrial Health and Safety. The states have given much attention to the physical conditions of factories, offices, mines, stores, and farms. To protect against fires, the buildings must be of fireproof construction, with firewalls, fire escapes, and sprinkler systems; to prevent accidents, protective devices are required over moving parts of machinery; to protect health, good lighting, adequate ventilation, protection against dust and gases, clean rest rooms, and satisfactory facilities for meals are necessary. Through diligent efforts, the incidence of disease and of industrial accidents has greatly decreased.

Workmen's Compensation. When industrial accidents occur, who should bear the cost? An early theory held that the question should be answered in individual cases by the courts. When sued by an employee, an employer, under the common law, could plead three possible defenses; (1) contributory negligence—the accident had been caused (or contributed to) by the carelessness of the employee himself; (2) the fellow-servant doctrine—the accident had been caused by the carelessness of another workman, who should pay the damages; (3) assumption of risk—when he accepted the job, the employee knew it was dangerous, and the higher than usual wages he received constituted a sort of advance compensation for possible injury. In taking the case to law an employee faced heavy expenses; the result was uncertain; even if he won his case, he might suffer long delays and heavy expenses if the employer appealed to a higher court. Under such circumstances the common-law remedies were clearly inadequate.

Under more humane laws, first enacted by New York in 1911 and later copied in other states, compensation for industrial accidents was considered one of the costs of doing business, to be passed on, like other expenses, to the consumer. The employer was deprived of his common-law defenses and was compelled to insure himself against accidents to his employees. The state administers an unemployment insurance fund into which the employer pays contributions at low rates. If an accident occurs the employee or his widow receives speedy compensation as determined by an unemployment compensation board; the amount depends on the nature and extent of the injury. Maximum payments per week varied in 1960 from about $30 to about $150; in one-quarter of the states, they exceeded $40 per week. Total disability benefits range from 50 per cent to 97½ per cent of total wages, according to the number of dependents.

Child Labor Legislation. More than a century ago several of the northern industrial states began to pass statutes to protect children from greedy parents and employers. The failure of other states to follow their example led to a movement for federal protection of child labor which finally succeeded in 1938. State laws are still important, however, both in prohibiting child labor in intrastate commerce and in regulating the details of all employment of children. All states have now established maximum daily and weekly working hours for children. Nearly every state has either entirely prohibited or rigidly limited the employment of minors at night and in occupations where safety or moral hazards are present. The employment of girls is more carefully restricted than the employment of boys. The minimum age at which children can be hired is usually fixed at fourteen or sixteen years.

Wages and Hours Laws. In order to protect women nearly every state limits their daily and weekly working hours. Many states require one day of rest in seven, prohibit night work in certain industries, limit the hours of night work in others, and establish minimum wages. About one-third of the states prohibit wage differentials based on sex. The hours of labor of men are subject to fewer state regulations. The most noteworthy laws pertain to work in mines, tunnels, smelters, and other places where prolonged exposure is injurious to the health of the worker; and to industries, like transportation, where excessive fatigue is apt to cause accidents affecting both the worker and the general public.

Unemployment Insurance. Though Wisconsin provided for unemployment insurance in 1932, most of the impetus for state laws on the subject came from the federal Social Security Act of 1935. It levied a payroll tax of 3 per cent for unemployment insurance, but provided that employers might deduct up to 90 per cent of the amount due if they had paid taxes to a state to support a system of unemployment insurance which met federal standards. Only workers registered with the employment service who have been unable to find employment for a specified period of time are eligible to receive benefits. The maximum period during which benefits may be paid is twenty-six weeks. The amount of weekly payments varies from state to state.

Migratory Labor. The migratory laborer whose work is necessary in the harvesting of certain agricultural crops has often been subject to cruel exploitation. In order to combat such exploitation several states have required that farm labor contractors must be licensed. In order to obtain a license, a contractor is obliged to submit information concerning his character and the methods he intends to pursue in conducting his business.

Discrimination in Employment. Since 1945 about a third of the states have enacted laws forbidding employers to discriminate against workers on account of race, color, or creed. The same prohibition applies to discriminations in admitting members to labor unions. Enforcement is by a commission which usually foregoes prosecution of first offenders if they show a willingness to abide by the letter and spirit of the law in the future.

INDUSTRIAL RELATIONS

Provisions of the federal Constitution severely limit the state in regulating industrial relations. Under ordinary conditions it cannot order an employer to pay a certain wage without violating the clause against deprivation of property; nor can it compel an unwilling employee to remain at work without depriving him of his liberty without due process of law. Generally the state acts, not as a supreme legislator, but as an umpire. Amid almost continuous pressures from both labor and capital, the state's legislative and administrative policies at any given time reflect current ideas of fair play and equality of consideration.

The Right to Organize. Under the common law labor unions were regarded as conspiracies among workers for the purpose of injuring an employer. The courts in Massachusetts in 1842 were the first to recognize that a labor union was legal as a means of protecting the interests of its members. Today all states recognize the right of workers to unite in unions and to bargain collectively with their employers. Their gains have been impressive. In some places they have achieved the *closed shop,* in which none but union members may be hired; in other places, they have achieved the *union shop,* in which nonunion workers may be hired, providing they join the union within thirty or sixty days. The closed shop was outlawed in 1947 by the Taft-Hartley Act, yet it remains in effect in certain industries. *Maintenance-of-membership provisions* may require workers to continue as members of the union as long as they remain on a particular job. By means of the *check-off* the employer may be required to collect union dues through payroll deductions. On the other hand, employers have sometimes induced legislatures to pass *right-to-work laws,* which allow workers to be hired without the requirement of being or becoming union members. The time is long since past when an employer, by means of a *"yellow-dog" contract,* could legally require a newly hired worker to promise not to join a union.

Strikes and Boycotts. Commonly, the state laws permit workers to strike if the purpose is legal and the methods are non-violent. *Sit-down strikes* in which workers occupy an employer's plant against his wishes, *sympathetic strikes* to aid another union, and strikes which occur without regard to the waiting period required by law are usually considered as having an illegal purpose. Destruction of an employer's property, or the use of force (coercion) to prevent other employees from working, or intimidation to prevent the public from patronizing an employer are examples of illegal methods. To avoid the appearance of coercion, the law limits the number of pickets who may carry placards and specifies the distance they must keep away from the entrance to a struck plant or shop.

Primary boycotts, in which employees refuse to buy the products of their employer, are legal; but *secondary boycotts,* in which employees attempt to induce others not to patronize their employer, are illegal.

The State's Role in Labor Disputes. When a strike occurs or is threatened the state conciliation service attempts to bring representatives of the employer and the union together, and state officers may attempt to mediate between the parties by suggesting terms of settlement. Approximately half the states have provided for voluntary arbitration, in which the parties agree to submit their claims to a third party, whose decision shall be final. A few states have provided for compulsory arbitration when a strike would disrupt the service furnished by a public utility.

21

STATE AND LOCAL PERSONNEL MANAGEMENT

Governments are the largest employers in the United States: the federal government employs approximately two and one-third million persons; the fifty state governments employ in excess of one and one-half million persons; and municipalities, towns, townships, and villages employ approximately four and three-quarters million persons. State government monthly payrolls totalled $560 million in January, 1961 compared to $136 million in January, 1947. The monthly payrolls of cities, towns, and villages approximate $1.5 billion dollars. Approximately two-thirds of all state and local government employees work in the fields of education, highways, hospitals, and police protection.

Large cities employ more persons in relation to population and pay higher wages than small cities, towns, townships, and villages; the difference is due both to the greater number of functions performed and to the need for more supervisory personnel (see Appendix, "City Employment and Payrolls for October, 1960," p. 282).

THE MERIT SYSTEM

The United States inherited a spoils system from Great Britain. Both *nepotism*—the appointment of relatives—and *patronage*—the employment of friends or dependents—were freely practiced in the colonial and early national periods. When the American two-party system arose, it became customary for the winners to dismiss incumbents from office and fill the vacant positions from among their own friends and followers. In 1832 the practice was justified in a highsounding statement by Senator William L. Marcy of New York: "To the victor belong the spoils of the enemy." Unfortunately the victors dismissed honest and capable officials as well as "enemy spoilsmen." The appointment of inefficient and often dishonest party hacks contributed to the degeneration of the public service and the corruption of the democratic process.

The Reform Movement. The antithesis of the spoils system is the *merit system,* under which persons seeking public employment must demonstrate their capacity to fill a position before they can be appointed. Advocates of the merit system made little headway until 1881, when the assassination of President James A. Garfield by a disappointed office-seeker shocked the public conscience into action. Within three years Congress passed the Pendleton Act, which is still the fundamental federal law on the subject; the New York legislature created separate civil service commissions for the state and New York City; and Massachusetts established a merit system for the selection of state employees. Between 1905 and 1920 eight other states adopted the merit system. In 1939 Congress stipulated that states and localities would not thenceforth be eligible to receive federal grants-in-aid unless the officials who administered the grants had been chosen under a merit system. Partly in consequence of this legislation the number of states with general civil laws covering all employees has increased to twenty-nine; and the other states have provided a partial merit system coverage for at least those agencies which administer federal funds.

In the cities the conditions are somewhat more satisfactory chiefly because people living under home rule charter provisions have voted to end the spoils system. Approximately 70 per cent of the cities with populations of more than 10,000 and all cities with populations of more than 250,000 select their employees through the merit system. The counties, however, remain the stronghold of the spoils system; only 6 per cent of all counties use the merit system.

The passage of merit-system constitutional amendments and statutes does not automatically guarantee the proper functioning of the merit system. Statutes may be repealed (as they have been in Arkansas and New Mexico); practical politicians have shown considerable dexterity in circumventing the provisions of civil service laws; and spoilmen have even been appointed as members of civil service commissions.

Merit-System Organization. The civil service consists of all governmental employees except officers and enlisted men in the armed forces, and judicial and legislative employees. In the

earlier period, civil service reformers desired to place the administration of the merit system in the hands of a commission.
More recently experts in public administration have pointed
out the advantages of administration by a personnel manager.
THE CIVIL SERVICE COMMISSION. In most states and cities the
merit system is administered by a bipartisan commission of from
two to five members. In the states, appointment is by the governor
with senate approval, and terms of office range from three to ten
years. In large cities the commissioners are usually appointed by
the mayor; in small cities, by the council. Overlapping terms of
three, four, or six years are common. In Massachusetts the state
administers the personnel systems of cities, and in New York the
cities have the option of coming under the state personnel system.

The advantages claimed for the *civil service commission* are:
(1) its bipartisan membership will be on guard to defend the civil
service against spoilsmen of either party; and (2) its plural membership is adapted to the functions of issuing rules and regulations and of hearing appeals.

THE PERSONNEL MANAGER. In Maryland and Rhode Island
and in many cities personnel directors administer the civil service
system. They are generally appointed by the chief executive, or
by the city council, or by the civil service commission. In a few
cities the city manager administers the merit system. The administrative experts who favor a single personnel director point
out that, while commissions were once desirable as defenses
against spoilsmen, the emphasis today should be placed on the
positive aspects of personnel administration. A *personnel director*
is more efficient in cutting red tape, in eliminating delays, and
especially in co-operating with the governor, mayors, and city
managers in the solution of personnel problems. Most of the
states and cities have effected a compromise by employing both
a commission and a personnel director.

PUBLIC PERSONNEL FUNCTIONS

In the beginning of the reform movement, almost the sole
functions of the civil service commission were to examine applicants for jobs and certify the names of the three highest candidates to department heads, who alone had the power to make appointments. These are still important functions. In the course
of experience, however, the simple processes of examination and

certification have developed so many ramifications that merit system authorities now have some influence or control over most aspects of public personnel administration.

Recruitment of Personnel. Every alert civil service agency is aware of the necessity for attracting intelligent and competent persons to the public service. For this purpose newspaper advertisements, radio and television announcements, and notices to schools and colleges are utilized to bring to the attention of qualified applicants the advantages both of the public service and of specific positions.

Examination of Personnel. A great variety of tests must be used in determining the fitness of applicants for different kinds of positions in civil service. For unskilled workers only a physical examination is necessary. For a job a little higher up the scale, a performance test may be required to determine the ability of a person to do the job. When the personnel agency wishes to test the educational qualifications or the intelligence of applicants, it may prepare written examinations of various types, including essay questions or completion, matching, multiple-choice, true-false, and other forms of objective tests. For the highest positions there may be an examination of an applicant's published writings, an evaluation of his scholastic record, an investigation of his previous employment record, and a checking of his references. At all the higher levels personal interviews are important in estimating the personal qualities of candidates and their adaptability for certain kinds of work.

Certification of Personnel. The merit system authority does not make appointments, except to positions on its own staff. It prepares, in advance, eligibility lists for various government positions. When the head of the department concerned notifies the civil service office that a position is vacant, the office usually sends him the names of the three candidates who stand highest on the list; he may appoint any of the persons named. For the first three to six months, the appointment is probationary and may be terminated at the sole discretion of the appointing officer.

Job Classification. For the successful administration of a personnel system the classification of positions according to the nature of work to be done and the responsibilities imposed on the employee is essential. An examination can then be set, not for each separate position, but for all types and grades of jobs that require the same qualifications. Furthermore, transfers from one office to another become possible without a new examination, and salaries can be fixed on the basis of equal pay for equal work.

In the process of classification, specialists survey all positions, hold hearings, and develop a systematic plan for grading all jobs in the civil service. The published results of their work show, for every job, the class title, a description of duties and responsibilities, a specification of qualifications, the salary grade and range, and an indication of the lines of future advancement. The "classified service" is another name for positions under the merit system, to distinguish them from "exempt positions" which are filled by popular election or by political appointment.

Salary Plan. A comprehensive salary plan must be developed in order to secure fairness in compensation and maintain morale at a high level. In the better civil service systems, maximum and minimum pay scales are established for each position and provision is made for periodic increments in the salary for each position up to a specified level. In many states and cities inequities exist in the salary plan. There is constant powerful pressure from employees to have their positions reclassified at a higher level. On the other hand, when general reclassifications are made, it is a customary rule that individuals should continue to receive their former salaries even if their jobs are downgraded.

Training of Personnel. The civil service commission may be charged with the responsibility of installing and maintaining an in-service training program designed to increase the proficiency of the employees and keep them abreast of the latest developments in their fields. In many departments and agencies a cross-training program is utilized which provides training for employees in positions other than their own so that they may qualify for promotion or fill in for employees who are absent.

Promotion and Advancement. *Promotion* is a change in the status of an employee from a position in one class to a position in a higher class with greater duties, responsibilities, and salary; *advancement* is a periodic increment in salary without a change in position. The promotional system may be either closed or open: under a closed promotional system all promotions are made from within the civil service, and outsiders are not considered in filling vacancies, whereas under the open promotional system outsiders as well as regular employees are eligible to fill vacancies.

Administrators agree that the open system is best for the selection of certain types of officials such as city managers and superintendents of schools, but that the closed system, based on rewards for good work, contributes greatly to the maintenance of high morale. In administering the closed system, the personnel authorities depend upon the service record rather than the assembled examination.

The discretion of superiors, examinations, efficiency ratings, and seniority are the usual bases for making promotions. An efficiency rating system requires supervisors to rate their subordinates on characteristics such as attitude, knowledge of work, co-operation, and judgment; these ratings can be valuable only if they are carefully prepared. The seniority system is easy to administer, but does not insure the selection of the most competent individuals for positions of higher responsibility. A system of promotion-potential ratings is used in California, Michigan, and Wisconsin: an employee's preparation for advancement, not his ability to perform his present position, is rated. In many states and cities political connections still appear to be the most important single factor in determining promotions.

Discipline of Personnel. In order to maintain efficiency in the civil service, some forms of disciplinary action—suggestion, reprimand, transfer, lowered efficiency ratings, suspension, or removal may be necessary. It is a sound principle that discipline should be administered by supervisory officers, subject to possible intervention by the civil service commission to protect the employee from mistreatment. An administrator's power of removal is absolute in many states, counties, and municipalities; in others it is subject to review by a commission or by the courts. In Chicago, an administrative officer may only suspend an employee. The civil service commission alone has the power to remove him.

Retirement of Personnel. A sound retirement system contributes to high morale in an organization because employees are assured of a steady income upon retirement, and the public service is not encumbered with superannuated employees. Most of the states have general retirement programs for their state personnel, and several states have such programs at least for employees in certain categories. The cities with a population in excess of one-half million have established retirement systems for all employees, and approximately 85 per cent of the cities with a population in excess of 10,000 have established a retirement system for all or some of their employees. In 1950 the federal social security act was amended to extend coverage to government employees not covered by a state or local retirement plan: by 1961 forty-eight states had adopted enabling legislation authorizing eligible public employees to come under the federal social security program. More than two million state and local employees are covered by social security.

Eligibility for retirement is based upon age, or years of service, or a combination of age and years of service: it is generally agreed that age should be the principal basis for retirement.

Pension plans are contributory or non-contributory. Under a contributory system, the employees pay all or part of the cost of the retirement system; their contributions range from 1.5 to 6 per cent of their wages or salaries. Under the noncontributory system the governmental unit assumes the entire cost of the retirement system. Methods of managing the retirement funds vary. The cash-disbursement plan provides for the use of current contributions to pay the current cost of the system. The only sound method of financing the retirement system is the actuarial reserve plan. On the basis of the average life expectancy of the employees and the size of the pensions, a pension fund can be established which will adequately meet future obligations. For most state and local retirement funds the reserves are inadequate.

The administration of state and local retirement systems is customarily entrusted to a board composed equally of representatives of the government and of public employees. Half the members are appointed by the chief executive of the governmental unit, and the other half are elected by the public employees. It is desirable to have the government finance officer represented on the board and essential to provide for frequent fund audits.

PROBLEMS OF PUBLIC PERSONNEL ADMINISTRATION

Public personnel administration on the state and local levels is beset with several major problems. In many governmental units the basic objectives of merit and career systems have not been accomplished.

Coverage of Personnel. The coverage of the merit system is inadequate; many state and local positions with routine duties continue to be filled by election or political appointment. At the local level many units of government are unable to finance a merit system. Two alternatives are available: first, small local governmental units with few employees could be abolished and their functions transferred to counties; and second, states could extend their facilities to localities. In New York and New Jersey civil service facilities are available without cost to the localities. In Maryland and Ohio the localities must reimburse the state for the cost of state provided personnel services.

Provisional Appointments. Eligible lists occasionally are not available for a particular position; in the absence of an eligible list a provisional appointment may be made until an examination can be held and an eligible list prepared. If the civil service agency is efficient and possesses foresight, provisional appointments should be few in number. Unfortunately, in many states and cities provisional appointments are frequent and, in the course of time, may become permanent.

Political Activity. In return for protection against partisan dismissal, civil service employees are required, by state and local laws, to refrain from pernicious political activities. In addition, the Hatch Acts passed by Congress in 1939 and 1940 limit the partisan activities of employees paid in whole or in part from federal funds. Though the dividing line between innocent and pernicious partisanship is hardly ever made clear, the general principle is that an employee retains the political privileges of a citizen but must refrain from public political activity. He has the right to vote and to express his opinions privately, but he may not serve on a party committee, participate in a campaign, or express partisan opinions publicly.

Employee Organizations. Associations of public employees began in the nineteenth century and have since expanded in number and activity. Some of the public employees' organizations have become affiliated with outside labor groups. Numerous agreements concerning wages, hours, and conditions of work have been negotiated between government agencies and employees' unions.

In several states the laws severely limit the freedom of some employees—particularly of firemen and policemen—to organize. The right of public employees to strike is hotly debated. Some states have enacted no-strike laws; and many public employees' unions, in their policy declarations, have renounced the strike as a weapon in labor disputes. When a strike would endanger the public safety it should be prohibited by law; but the law should contain provisions for fair and just consideration of the grievances of public employees. The enforcement of no-strike legislation is difficult; to consider but one situation, what should be done when large numbers of employees fail to report to work, giving illness as an excuse?

Other Problems. Personnel programs on the state and local levels are hampered by giving veterans' "preference" over non-veterans, and by residence, age, and sex requirements. Veterans' preference originated at the turn of the century and was given great impetus by World War I; veterans commonly are given a bonus of five points on examinations and disabled veterans may receive a bonus of ten points and be placed above equally qualified non-veterans. Veterans' preference laws are based upon the theory that former soldiers have proved their loyalty to their country by defending it. Though freely admitting that veterans deserve to be rewarded, many public administration experts feel that the reward should not be at the expense of the efficiency of the civil service; if it is desirable to reward veterans, other methods can be found.

In spite of the fact that more competent individuals might be found elsewhere, many governmental positions are open only to residents of the governmental unit. Only California and Maryland do not prescribe residence requirements as a condition for employment in the state government. Nearly all cities have residence requirements, but in most council-manager cities the council may select a manager without regard to his residence.

The minimum- and maximum-age requirements often are too restrictive: high minimum age requirements discourage many competent young men and women from considering a career in the public service and a high maximum age often attracts individuals who are too old to make a career in the civil service. Experience requirements exclude recent college graduates and others who are exceptionally competent. Sex requirements based on antiquated notions of male superiority bar qualified women from certain positions.

22

STATE AND LOCAL FINANCE

The rise in expenditures of all governmental units since the early 1930's has been phenomenal: in 1960 these units spent approximately $153 billion annually. General federal expenditures in that year approximated $97 billion; general state expenditures, $27 billion; and total general expenditures of all local governments were $29 billion. Municipal expenditures amounted to approximately $14 billion dollars. The budget of New York City nowadays is larger than the annual budget of the federal government prior to World War I.

The great rise in state and local governmental expenditures has four causes: (1) Population growth. (2) Inflation, which since the 1930's has substantially increased total dollar expenditures. (3) Demands of citizens in recent years for new governmental services and the expansion of old services. (Prior to 1875 the principal functions of government were education, protection of life and property, and the operation of the government; in recent years industrialization and urbanization have created problems which citizens expect governments to solve.) (4) The trend toward greatly increased capital outlays for highways, water-supply and sewerage systems, schools and colleges, and charitable and correctional institutions.

A classification of state and local expenditures reveals that education, highways, and public welfare are the most expensive governmental functions. In 1959 states spent approximately $3.3 billion and local governments over $14 billion for education. In that same year state expenditures for highways approximated $6.5 billion, and local expenditures for highways totaled over $3 billion. Also, state and local expenditures for public welfare totaled over $4 billion. (See Appendix, pp. 290, 291.)

THE BUDGET

Financial planning is of recent origin. Prior to the early 1900's systematic financial procedure was lacking in all governmental units. Each department transmitted its requests for funds directly to the legislature and sent representatives to try to secure favorable action from legislative committees and individual members. Logrolling was common; departments bargained for support wherever they could. Recurrent economy waves in the legislature commonly took the form of a fixed-percentage, across-the-board cut in requests.

The chaotic financial condition of state and local governments gave rise to a reform movement; New York City in 1907 was one of the first governmental units to install a budget system and its lead was followed by California and Wisconsin in 1911. By 1923 every state provided for some type of budget system.

A budget is a comprehensive financial document which sets forth a balanced estimate of proposed expenditures and anticipated revenues for a specified future period of time. If properly prepared, it will contain information on the debt position. Many so-called budgets, are expenditure plans only and fail to consider either revenue or debts.

Types of Budgets. Current, capital, and performance budgets are the three major types of budgets. A *current budget* provides for regularly recurring expenditures. A *capital budget* provides for expensive nonrecurring capital improvements which have a life span of several years, such as the construction of highways and large buildings. Items are listed according to priority so that the financial burden of the improvements is relatively uniform each year; the priority listing is reviewed annually. A capital budgeting program has four major advantages: the advance planning of capital projects is assured, the tax rate in localities remains relatively stable, the need to borrow large sums in any one year is obviated, and the credit rating of the government is maintained. A *performance budget* focuses attention on the cost of separate governmental services and eliminates useless itemization of salaries or things to be purchased; all proposed appropriations are supported by detailed work data.

Budget-Making Authorities. Budgets are also popularly classified according to the particular authority—legislative, executive, or a combination of both—responsible for their preparation. The *legislative budget* is prepared by a standing committee of the legislature which sits in the interim between sessions. This method is sometimes justified on the ground that it maintains unimpaired the legislature's control over finances; but it places budget preparation in the hands of those who are neither familiar with the needs of departments nor responsible for their administration. The legislative budget is employed in Arkansas and many local government units. The *joint budget* is prepared by a commission composed of representatives of the legislative and executive branches. Though it familiarizes legislative members with financial problems, it has the disadvantage of dividing responsibility and resulting in political bargains. It is used in North Dakota and South Carolina. Under the *board plan,* the budget is prepared by an ex officio board composed of the chief executive and a number of other officers. This system has all the defects of a plural executive division of responsibility: compromise, delay, and, often, failure to present a united front. The board plan is in effect in five states and in many local units of government. The *executive budget* is prepared under the direct supervision of the governor, mayor, or manager, who has the responsibility for proposing taxes and the allocation of the proceeds for the best interests of the government and the people as a whole. Besides insuring fairness, the executive budget is a means whereby the chief executive may exert control over all phases of the government. This system has proved itself so far superior to other methods that it is presently in use in a great majority of the states and larger cities.

Budgetary Procedure. It is customary, especially in the preparation of the executive budget, for the preliminary stages to be handled by a budget director who has charge of a bureau or office.

SUBMITTAL OF ESTIMATES. Department and agency heads are provided, several months prior to the beginning of the fiscal year, with forms by the budget bureau and are directed to prepare their request for funds, with supporting data, by a specified date. Within each department, bureau chiefs and others recommend the inclusion of items; the whole estimate is commonly reviewed by a department or agency budget officer for conformity with established principles. The head of the department must take the responsibility for recommending expenditures for his department. For preparation of estimates of revenue and for figures on the debt, the budget director frequently relies on the auditor or controller.

Review of Estimates. After the estimates have been submitted the budget director conducts hearings, at which agency and department heads personally are called upon to explain and defend their estimates. If his own investigations indicate that the estimates have been padded or that duplication and waste exist, the budget director may return the estimates to the department with instructions to reduce or eliminate certain items.

Consolidation of Estimates. Department heads have the right to appeal to the budget director's superior. Conferences may be called to iron out disagreements. At the end, the budget director makes the necessary adjustments, consolidates the estimates, and submits the entire budget to his superior. If the superior approves, the document is printed and transmitted to the legislature.

Legislative Action on the Budget. Upon the receipt of the budget by the state legislature it is referred to the appropriate committees of the two houses which then hold open or closed hearings. Administrative officials are summoned to explain and justify their requests for funds, and private individuals and representatives of organizations are permitted to express their views on the budgetary requests. Frequently the legislature accepts the judgment of its committees with few or no amendments.

In 1941 the California legislature created a joint legislative budget committee and authorized it to hire a legislative auditor and staff to keep the state's financial program under surveillance and make recommendations to the legislature. The auditor participates in budget hearings held by the division of budget and accounts and investigates the actual performance of agencies included in the budget. More than one-third of the states have followed California's lead.

In some cities the council makes use of a committee for the consideration of the budget; in others the council acts on the budget as a committee of the whole, with relatively informal procedures. County boards usually do not use committees for the consideration of the budget.

In most states and cities the legislative body may revise the executive budget in any manner it wishes, but the legislature in Maryland, New York, Nevada, and West Virginia and the city council in New York, Boston, and a number of other cities may only delete or reduce budgetary items; they may not add new items or increase amounts. If the legislative body in many governmental units decides to increase appropriations, it must provide for the raising of a corresponding amount of additional revenue by levying taxes.

Whether detailed or lump-sum appropriations should be utilized is debatable. Detailed, or "segregated," appropriations, which reflect a distrust of the chief executive, specify precisely how the funds shall be expended and eliminate certain abuses that have been associated with lump-sum appropriations. However, limiting the discretion of the administrators introduces rigidity into the financial system and in this way results in inefficiencies.

Administration of Appropriations. After appropriations have been made, various devices are utilized to see that funds are expended according to law. Collectively, these devices are called by some writers "budget execution."

ALLOTMENTS. Until recently it has been the usual practice for legislatures to make lump-sum appropriations and for department and agency heads to determine how and when the funds were to be spent. If the funds became exhausted before the end of the fiscal year it was customary to request the legislature to make supplementary, or "deficiency," appropriations. To exercise tighter control over expenditures and to eliminate requests for supplementary appropriations, the chief executive often uses an allotment system. In a quarterly system, only one-fourth of the annual appropriations may be drawn upon each quarter. Sometimes allotments are broken down into categories such as materials, personnel, and capital expenditures. Some flexibility is introduced into the allotment system by permitting (with the approval of the chief executive) the transfer of funds from one of the categories to another and the advance withdrawal of funds.

ACCOUNTING SYSTEMS. The efficacy of financial control depends to a large extent upon whether the accrual or the cash system is used. The *accrual system* provides for the recording of financial obligations as they are incurred and accurately records the current financial position of the government. Under the *cash system,* expenditures are recorded when payments are made by the government; many governmental units have experienced financial difficulties as the result of using the cash system because they were unaware of the current status of their obligations.

CURRENT AUDIT. The *current audit,* or *pre-audit,* occurs when a voucher is presented to a comptroller for payment. Before he approves it, the comptroller must ascertain that the proposed expenditure is covered by an appropriation made by law, that the purpose is constitutional, and that the amount is available under the periodic allotment. Current auditing permits the chief executive to initiate corrective action if needed.

CENTRAL PURCHASING. *Central purchasing* is a relatively new development which provides for all governmental purchases to be made by a central purchasing agency. Prior to the adoption of central purchasing each administrative department and agency purchased its own supplies; this decentralized system of purchasing became associated with extravagance and waste. In 1897 Iowa established a board to control purchases for state charitable and penal institutions; in 1911 Oklahoma became the second state to adopt central purchasing; and now more than forty-five states use a central office for all or part of their purchases. Fewer than half the municipalities utilize central purchasing for all or part of their purchases, and relatively few counties have adopted it. Certain supplies, such as small items and perishable items, commonly are exempt from the requirement of central purchasing. In some governmental units central purchasing has been destroyed by exemptions.

As compared with purchasing by each department or agency, purchasing by a central agency has five major advantages: (1) it buys supplies in quantity at lowered costs; (2) it has better facilities for testing the quality of available supplies; (3) its central warehousing, delivery, and distribution of supplies provides greater economies; (4) its personnel costs are lower because it needs fewer employees; and (5) it more completely regulates expenditures, since accounting control is closer and favoritism is reduced.

THE POST-AUDIT. *Post-auditing* is a financial control device utilized to insure that public funds have been properly expended; it is a thorough study of the books of all departments and agencies. The post-audit should be conducted by an agency independent of the executive branch. In state and local governments the auditor is either appointed by the legislative body or popularly elected. Auditors elected by the people frequently lack the necessary technical qualifications to carry out their responsibilities. In many localities post-auditing is neglected or carelessly done.

TAXATION

Beginning with Adam Smith in 1776, numerous authors have set forth the characteristics which a good tax should possess. Among these are: (1) *Equity*—The tax burden should be placed with some consideration of the taxpayer's ability to pay and the benefits he will derive from the taxation. (2) *Certainty*—Every taxpayer should know in advance what his tax liability will be. (3) *Convenience*—The time, place, and method of collection should be fixed so as to cause the average taxpayer the least possible trouble. (4) *Economy*—The cost of administering a tax should not exceed 5 per cent of the gross amount collected. (5) *Stability of yield*—Dependable yields in both good years and bad facilitate intelligent fiscal planning. (6) *Conservation of tax sources*—A tax should not be confiscatory or have the effect of driving away business and investment capital.

No one tax has all these desirable characteristics. It is necessary for fiscal authorities to construct a tax system combining the favorable aspects of several different taxes. Unfortunately, it must be said of many state and local tax systems that they, like Topsy, "just growed."

Per capita state tax collections vary from about $100 to about $238; the average per capita tax collection in all states is slightly in excess of $169. Comparison of state tax data can be misleading because the distribution of governmental services between state and local units, the scope and quality of services, and the resources vary considerably from state to state. (See pp. 288–289.)

Small amounts of income are received by state and local governments from the sale of public property, admissions to public parks, fines, and forfeitures. Somewhat larger sums are received from fees for the issuance of licenses and for other services rendered by state and local officials. Special assessments to pay part or all the cost of improvements that directly benefit the property holder are essential to help defray the expenses of constructing boulevards, parks, and sewerage systems. A large and apparently increasing porportion of state revenue comes from federal grants-in-aid. Similarly, much local revenue is from state grants-in-aid.

By far the greatest source of the revenue of all governments is taxation. (See Appendix, pp. 269, 288–289, 290–293.)

Constitutional Aspects of Taxation. A tax is a compulsory contribution exacted by public authority from private or corporate persons for the support of government, or for regulation, or for the promotion of certain social objectives. It may be collected without reference to benefits derived by the taxpayer.

The taxing power of the state and national governments is implicit in sovereignty. It may be exercised at the discretion of the legislature, subject to numerous restrictions contained in federal and state constitutions.

FEDERAL CONSTITUTIONAL LIMITATIONS. The federal Constitution contains numerous expressed and implied limitations on the taxing power of the states. It makes no mention of local governments, but they, as creatures of the state, are governed by the same restrictions. No state may levy tonnage taxes or duties on imports or exports except for the purpose of executing its inspection laws; nor unduly restrain interstate commerce by taxation; nor impose taxes that arbitrarily discriminate between individuals, denying them equal protection of law; nor, without the consent of congress, tax instrumentalities of the federal government.

The last-named limitation prohibits the states from taxing bonds issued by the federal government or the interest paid on such bonds. Under the same constitutional interpretation, a reciprocal protection from federal taxation is extended to property owned by state and local governments and to the principal and interest of their bond issues. The purpose is to preserve the federal system by preventing the states and the federal government from interfering with each other.

STATE CONSTITUTIONAL LIMITATIONS. State constitutions generally prohibit inequalities or discrimination in taxation of individuals or classes of property. As a corollary, no public funds may be spent for the benefit of a private individual or group of persons. Exceptions are made for the attainment of a few worthy objectives: in most states the constitution specifically exempts from taxation property used for religious, charitable, educational, or scientific purposes. State constitutional limitations are readily enforceable: any taxpayer is qualified to bring suit against a public officer to enjoin the wrongful collection of taxes or the misapplication of funds.

STATE LIMITS ON LOCAL TAXATION. Local governments lack an inherent power to tax; they derive their fiscal powers from state constitutions, from statutes, and from charters. Though the states have always conferred on cities and counties the power to levy taxes on property, the grants have been hedged with many restrictions—concerning methods of assessment, maximum tax rates, and purposes for which the proceeds of certain taxes might be used. The states have also permitted cities to levy excises on certain articles and collect fees for the performance of special services. A few states, notably Pennsylvania in 1947, have given local units general grants to levy any taxes not levied by the state.

Types of State and Local Taxes. The most common types of state and local taxes are property, gross receipts and sales, excise, income, death and gift, and franchise and license taxes.

PROPERTY TAX. The general property tax is a tax on real property and tangible and intangible personal property and is an ad valorem tax; that is, a rate is established per $100 or $1000 of assessed valuation. Though the tax theoretically falls equally upon all property owners, many classes of property (charitable, educational, governmental, religious, and other nonprofit property) are tax-exempt. Furthermore, a number of states and localities grant new industrial firms a property-tax exemption for a specified number of years and in some taxing jurisdictions each owner is granted a homestead exemption of a few hundred dollars.

On the state level, there has been a shift from the property tax to new sources of revenue. Prior to World War I the general property tax accounted for over 50 per cent of the total revenue of the states, but in 1960 it produced only about 3.5 per cent of the total revenue of the states, or over $600 million. All states, except Oklahoma, Rhode Island, and Tennessee, levy a property tax. Because of low yields and difficulties of administration, states have been relinquishing the property tax to local governments.

The largest and oldest source of local revenue is the general tax on property which provided in excess of $14 billion in 1960, or approximately 40 per cent of total local revenue. County governments received about $2 billion from property taxes in that year or about 45 per cent of their total revenues.

Three major problems are associated with property taxation.

First, the real property tax is attacked on the ground that it is unsound in principle because real property ownership no longer reflects accurately the ability to pay, as it did in the past, for certain classes of property are more productive of income than others. For example, intangibles, such as stocks, bonds, and other similar evidences of ownership, are a major source of income today.

Second, the administration of taxes on intangible and personal property is weak. Evasion is common, since intangibles can be easily hidden. A tax on intangibles can be, and is, evaded by investing funds in tax exempt securities and establishing a legal residence in a locality which has a low tax rate. A number of state and local governments have attempted to solve the problem of evasion by establishing a lower property-tax rate for intangibles. Self-assessment of personal property is common: owners write the value of their property on a tax form and transmit the form to the tax collector with a signed affidavit that the form is accurate to the best of their knowledge.

Third, assessment—the assigning of value to property by an assessor—is unfair in many taxing jurisdictions. The evaluation of property requires technical knowledge of a high order which a popularly-elected assessor rarely possesses. Furthermore, salaries paid to assessors and their assistants often are too low to attract competent personnel. To correct inequities between individuals, boards of equalization hear appeals brought by taxpayers. Real and personal property generally are undervalued; this would be no problem if all property were uniformly underassessed, but different classes of property commonly are assessed at a different percentage of true value. Inequities between taxing districts are common.

In several states the state tax commission has been empowered to supervise the assessment of property in localities; standards have been raised considerably in some of these states. To strengthen assessment practices, several states hold training institutes for assessors and provide them with assessment manuals. In Oregon only appraisers approved by the state civil service commission are allowed to assess property. Assessment practices could be greatly strengthened if assessment districts were enlarged; many counties or other assessment districts are too small to support a competent staff with the necessary equipment.

GROSS RECEIPTS AND SALES TAXES. States received in 1960 $4.3 billion or 23.9 per cent of their total tax revenue from gross receipts and sales taxes. The same taxes yielded over $1.1 billion to local government units. West Virginia, in 1921, was the first state to adopt a general sales tax and its lead has been followed by about three-fourths of the states and over 1,400 cities and counties. The greatest number of adoptions occurred during the great depression of the 1930's. The state governments in California, Illinois, Mississippi, and New Mexico collect locally imposed sales taxes. Most of the proceeds from sales taxes are received by municipalities.

Sales taxes are advocated by individuals and groups who wish to afford tax relief to owners of real estate. They are opposed by others on the ground that they are regressive—they bear most heavily upon people in the lower-income groups. The exemption of food and medicine from the sales tax lessens its regressivity, because these items account for a large proportion of the expenditures of low-income groups. At least two states and many cities impose a special tax on meals served in restaurants.

EXCISE TAXES. An *excise* is a tax collected from the manufacturer or wholesaler of an article of commerce. In 1960 forty-six states levied excise taxes on cigarettes (two to eight cents a pack); seventeen states on other tobacco products; and all states levied excise taxes on gasoline (three to eight cents a gallon). In the same year, the excise taxes on all tobacco products produced over $900 million; on motor fuels they totaled over $3.3 billion. Some cities levy a motor fuel tax directly but most of the local governments' income from this source comes from state-sponsored shared taxes. The proceeds of motor fuel taxes usually are restricted to highway purposes.

About two-thirds of the states levy on distilled spirits an excise tax varying from seventy-five cents to three dollars a gallon. In 1960 the total tax-yield on alcoholic beverage sales and licenses was about $730 million.

INCOME TAXES. Income taxes are taxes on net income after certain deductions and exemptions, allowed by law, have been subtracted from gross income. Wisconsin, in 1911, was the first state to adopt an income tax. More than thirty states levy an income tax, with rates varying from 8 per cent on incomes under $1,000 in Iowa to 11.6 per cent on incomes over $8,000 in

Oregon; twenty-nine states levy a graduated income tax with increasing tax rates as the amount of income rises. In seventeen states the income tax is collected under withholding laws, but only three states (Louisiana, Massachusetts, and Missouri) compensate the employer for his services in withholding the tax. State individual income taxes yielded in excess of $2.2 billion in 1960 or over 12 per cent of total state tax revenue.

New York City adopted an income tax in 1934, but abandoned it primarily because of jurisdictional disputes. In 1939 Philadelphia levied an income tax of 1.5 per cent on all income earned in the city. A gross income tax is levied by about 700 local governments in five states and yields more than $230 million annually.

More than thirty-five states levy a corporation income tax; twenty states allow the deduction of federal taxes in computing net corporate income. Rates vary from 1 per cent on incomes under $1,000 in Arizona and on incomes under $3,000 in Arkansas to 8.4 per cent on the income of national and state banks in Minnesota. State corporation income taxes yielded in excess of $1 billion in 1960, approximately 6 per cent of total state tax revenue. Local corporation income taxes yield less than $10 million annually. The income tax generally is considered to be the tax which most accurately reflects ability to pay, but heavy federal income taxes limit severely the amount of taxes which the state and the city governments can derive from taxing incomes.

DEATH AND GIFT TAXES. In 1885 New York adopted an inheritance tax; death and gift taxes presently are levied by every state except Nevada. The federal government in 1924 enacted a statute which permits 80 per cent of the state inheritance tax to be deducted and applied against federal inheritance and estate taxes; this law induced states to adopt inheritance and estate taxes in order to capture the funds that otherwise would go to the federal government. The rates of state inheritance and estate taxes generally are progressive, and the rate varies with the amount of the inheritance and with the relationship of the beneficiary to the deceased. Relatively large exemptions are allowed and, consequently, so-called "death taxes" are paid only by a small number of individuals. Gift taxes are levied to prevent evasion of inheritance and estate taxes by making gifts prior to death. Death and gift taxes produced approximately $420 million in 1960 or about 2.3 per cent of total state tax revenue.

FRANCHISE AND LICENSE TAXES. All states levy franchise and license taxes. A corporation is required to pay an organization fee when it is chartered by the state, and a franchise tax is levied on corporations annually for the privilege to operate. Drivers' licenses and motor vehicle licenses produced approximately $1.5 billion in 1960. Chain stores are licensed in sixteen states and amusement centers are licensed in thirty-four states. Licenses to hunt and fish are required in all states. State revenue from licenses totaled more than $2 billion in 1960, approximately 11 per cent of total state revenue.

Local governments receive a substantial sum annually from franchise and license taxes. In the year 1960 this sum exceeded $734 million.

BORROWING

Few governments rely exclusively on taxes to finance their expenditures. A turnpike should not be built in stretches of five or ten miles a year; nor should the construction of a new central high school in a small city be spread over a five-year period. Rather, it is good sense to borrow the money for the construction as soon as the improvement is needed and sound plans are made to amortize the loan. When war, earthquake, or flood strikes, borrowing is a necessary means toward swift reconstruction. The principal dangers to be avoided in borrowing are spreading the repayment over too long a period, inadequate provision for repayment, and, above all, yielding to the temptation of meeting current expenses by borrowing rather than by levying the additional taxes needed to pay for them.

Debt Limitations. Unless restricted by state constitutions legislatures may authorize borrowing at their discretion. Debt limitations first appeared in state constitutions as a result of fiscal abuses which culminated in the panic of 1837. Huge debts had been authorized for the construction of canals and other internal improvements. When the panic temporarily dried up the sources of ordinary revenue the states found it difficult to meet their obligations, and eight states defaulted on the interest payments on their bonds. To avoid similar difficulties in the future, states amended their constitutions so as to prohibit incurring debts except in war-time emergencies. After the Civil War and again during the 1930's, financial stringencies resulted in defaults, which in turn resulted in the reimposition of debt limitations.

Five types of debt limitations commonly are found in state constitutions: (1) The maximum size of the debt is specified and may be exceeded only with the approval of the voters. (2) A maximum debt limit is prescribed which may be exceeded only for specified purposes. (3) Constitutions commonly contain restrictions relative to the purposes for which funds may be borrowed. (4) Constitutions often stipulate that the debt of a locality may not exceed a specified percentage of the assessed valuation of property located within it. (5) In many states the government is forbidden to assume the obligations of private organizations or to purchase stock of private corporations.

The desirability of debt limitations is questionable, since they provide a false sense of security for bondholders and taxpayers. Relatively extensive debt limitations did not prevent governmental units from defaulting on their bonds during the 1930's. Furthermore, debt limitations introduce an element of rigidity which hampers financial planning.

The total debt of state and local governments exceeds $56 billion; the total debt of each state varies from $487,000 in South Dakota to $1.9 billion in New York. Sixteen states have no state debts. The debt of local governments approximates $37 billion, more than one-half of this amount being municipal debt.

Methods of Borrowing. Government units usually borrow by issuing bonds with maturity dates of ten to fifty years. Experts agree that the life of bonds issued to finance capital improvements should not exceed the useful life of the capital improvements. State and local governments issue two types of bonds—sinking-fund and serial bonds.

SINKING-FUND BONDS. *Sinking-fund bonds* provide for making annual payments to a special reserve fund which, together with the interest earned by investing the fund, will be equal to the face value of the bonds on their maturity date: the investment of the sinking fund, as payments are made into it, reduces the cost of borrowing. These bonds have become discredited in many areas because of the dishonesty and mismanagement associated with them: some governments have failed to build up adequate funds by making periodic payments, and parts of a sinking fund frequently were lost by poor investments. Consequently, the sinking fund proved to be inadequate when the outstanding bonds matured.

SERIAL BONDS. The trend in state and local finance is toward the use of serial bonds. The straight serial-bond plan provides for a specified percentage of the bonds to become due annually; these bonds and the interest on the unpaid principal are paid each year. The serial-annuity plan provides for an equal payment each year to retire the bond issue; payments on the principal are the smallest during the first year of the issue because interest payments are largest this year. During each succeeding year, principal payments are increased as interest payments on the unpaid balance decrease, so that the annual payments are equal. Serial bonds lower the cost of borrowing, since interest is paid only on the unpaid principal. Furthermore, serial bonds—in contrast to sinking-fund bonds—are not subject to tampering.

Many bonds issued by state and local governments contain a "call provision" which enables the issuing government to take advantage of any future reductions in the interest rate in the money market. The bond indenture specifies that the bonds may be retired at the option of the issuing government after a specified period of time at par or at a small premium. In this way they allow governments to refund their debts at a lower interest rate.

INTERGOVERNMENTAL PAYMENTS

Largely as a result of the drying up of revenue from the property tax, there is a constant shifting of funds from richer to poorer governments. The national government makes grants-in-aid to the states; the states, in turn, make grants to local government units, with or without conditions, and also share the proceeds of taxes with the local units. (See pp. 294, 295.)

Grants-in-Aid. The federal government has been making substantial grants to state and local governments since the early 1900's. Federal grants-in-aid to state and local governments in 1959 exceeded $7.1 billion.

State grants-in-aid to local governments totaled approximately $8.2 billion in 1959, accounting for 30 per cent of total state expenditures. Grants-in-aid are an important state control device; a state, for example, will not make a grant to a local government for school construction unless the local government complies with state schooling building requirements.

Proponents cite six major advantages of grants-in-aid: (1) They permit the collection of certain taxes by governmental units which have the most efficient tax collection facilities. (2) Through grants poorer governments are aided in carrying out their financial responsibilities, yet they retain their independence. (3) Grants have great value as a device for relieving the financial difficulties of recipient governments during emergency periods. (4) The conditions attached to grants-in-aid have tended to raise the quality of the services provided by recipient units. (5) Grants help to equalize the costs of governmental services among the various governmental units. (6) They also permit the establishment of new governmental services.

Grants-in-aid are attacked on three principal grounds: (1) They are centralizing devices which weaken self government; recipient governments become so dependent upon grants that their self-reliance is destroyed. (2) State grants to localities permit many inefficient local units to survive which should be abolished or consolidated with others. (3) Efficiently organized localities are taxed by the state to secure revenue for grants to inefficient localities.

Shared Taxes. State taxes the proceeds of which are shared with localities should be distinguished from grants-in-aid, which are appropriated from the general revenue of the state. The receipt of *shared taxes* by localities is not conditional upon meeting state requirements.

APPENDIX

TABLES AND CHARTS

APPENDIX

Federalism in the United States

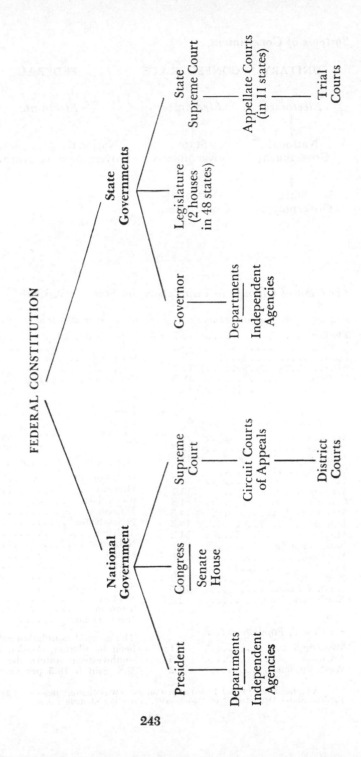

Systems of Government

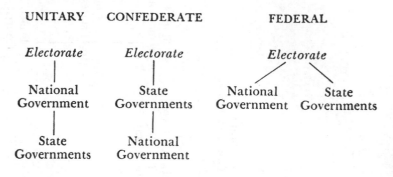

UNITARY	CONFEDERATE	FEDERAL
Electorate	*Electorate*	*Electorate*
National Government	State Governments	National Government / State Governments
State Governments	National Government	

Per Cent of Change in Population, by State, 1950-1960 *

Increase of 40 per cent or more

Florida	78.7
Nevada	78.2
Alaska	75.8
Arizona	73.7
California	48.5
Delaware	40.3

Increase of 10 per cent or more

Washington	19.9
Virginia	19.5
Indiana	18.5
Oregon	16.3
Illinois	15.7
Wisconsin	15.1
Georgia	14.5
Minnesota	14.5
Kansas	14.3
Montana	14.2
New Hampshire	13.8
Wyoming	13.6
Idaho	13.3
New York	13.2
South Carolina	12.5
North Carolina	12.2

Per Cent of Population Loss

Mississippi	− 0.1
Arkansas	− 6.5
West Virginia	− 7.2

Increase of 20 per cent or more

New Mexico	39.6
Colorado	32.4
Maryland	32.3
Utah	29.3
Connecticut	26.3
Hawaii	26.6
New Jersey	25.5
Texas	24.2
Michigan	22.8
Louisiana	21.4
Ohio	22.1

Increase up to 10 per cent

Massachusetts	9.8
Missouri	9.2
Rhode Island	8.5
Tennessee	8.4
Pennsylvania	7.8
Alabama	6.7
Nebraska	6.5
Maine	6.1
Iowa	5.2
Oklahoma	4.3
South Dakota	4.3
Kentucky	3.2
Vermont	3.2
North Dakota	2.1

The greatest population gains have been in Florida, Alaska, and the southwestern states; the average U.S. gain is 18.5 per cent.

* Adapted from "Final Population Counts" (Washington: Bureau of the Census [United States Department of Commerce], November 15, 1960), p. 6.

Area, Population, and Per Capita Income, by State, 1960

State or Territory	Area (sq. mi.) *	Population *	Per Capita Income †
Alabama	51,060	3,266,740	$1,409
Alaska	571,065	226,167	2,550
Arizona	113,575	1,302,161	1,959
Arkansas	52,499	1,786,272	1,322
California	156,573	15,717,204	2,661
Colorado	103,884	1,753,947	2,123
Connecticut	4,899	2,535,234	2,817
Delaware	1,987	446,292	2,946
Florida	54,252	4,951,560	1,980
Georgia	58,274	3,943,116	1,553
Hawaii	6,412	632,772	2,139
Idaho	82,708	667,191	1,782
Illinois	55,930	10,081,158	2,610
Indiana	36,185	4,662,498	2,102
Iowa	56,032	2,757,537	1,953
Kansas	82,048	2,178,611	1,994
Kentucky	39,863	3,038,156	1,514
Louisiana	45,106	3,257,022	1,575
Maine	31,012	969,265	1,768
Maryland	9,874	3,100,689	2,343
Massachusetts	7,867	5,148,578	2,444
Michigan	57,019	7,823,194	2,253
Minnesota	80,009	3,413,864	1,962
Mississippi	47,223	2,178,141	1,162
Missouri	69,138	4,319,813	2,145
Montana	145,736	678,767	1,955
Nebraska	76,612	1,411,330	1,981
Nevada	109,788	285,278	2,745
New Hampshire	9,014	606,921	2,010
New Jersey	7,521	6,066,782	2,608
New Mexico	121,510	951,023	1,833
New York	47,939	16,782,304	2,736
North Carolina	49,067	4,556,155	1,485
North Dakota	69,457	632,446	1,526
Ohio	40,972	9,706,397	2,328
Oklahoma	68,887	2,328,284	1,786
Oregon	96,248	1,768,687	2,171
Pennsylvania	45,007	11,319,366	2,222
Rhode Island	1,058	859,488	2,156
South Carolina	30,272	2,382,594	1,332
South Dakota	76,378	680,514	1,476
Tennessee	41,762	3,567,089	1,521
Texas	262,840	9,579,677	1,908
Utah	82,339	890,627	1,848
Vermont	9,276	389,881	1,789
Virginia	39,780	3,966,949	1,816
Washington	66,709	2,853,214	2,271
West Virginia	24,079	1,860,421	1,635
Wisconsin	54,705	3,951,777	2,116
Wyoming	97,411	330,066	2,149
District of Columbia	61	763,956	....

* Bureau of the Census, United States Department of Commerce.
† Survey of Current Business (Washington: United States Department of Commerce, August, 1960), p. 13.

State Constitutions *

State or Commonwealth	Number of Constitutions and Dates of Adoption	Date of Present Constitution	Estimated Number of Words	Number of Amendments
Alabama	1819; 1861; 1865; 1868; 1875; 1901	1901	57,000	140
Alaska	1956	1959	12,000	
Arizona	1912	1912	15,000	42
Arkansas	1836; 1861; 1864; 1868; 1874	1874	21,500	49
California	1849; 1879	1879	75,000	327
Colorado	1876	1876	20,000	59
Connecticut	1818(a)	1818	6,741	52(b)
Delaware	1776; 1792; 1831; 1897	1897	20,000	73(c)
Florida	1839; 1861; 1865; 1868; 1886	1886	30,000	106
Georgia	1777; 1789; 1798; 1861; 1865; 1868; 1877; 1945	1945	25,000	30(d)
Hawaii	1950(e)	1959	11,412	
Idaho	1890	1890	13,492	55
Illinois	1818; 1848; 1870	1870	17,000	13
Indiana	1816; 1851	1851	7,816	18
Iowa	1846; 1857	1857	7,997	19
Kansas	1859	1859	8,052	45(f)
Kentucky	1792; 1799; 1850; 1891	1891	21,500	19
Louisiana	1812; 1845; 1852; 1861; 1864; 1868; 1879; 1898; 1913; 1921	1921	201,423	376
Maine	1820	1820	9,000	84
Maryland	1776; 1851; 1864; 1867	1867	23,722	89
Massachusetts	1780	1780	28,760	81
Michigan	1835; 1850; 1908	1908	15,323	66
Minnesota	1858	1858	14,991	85
Mississippi	1817; 1832; 1869; 1890	1890	15,302	35
Missouri	1820; 1865; 1875; 1945	1945	30,000	8
Montana	1889	1889	26,000	28
Nebraska	1866; 1875	1875	16,550	79
Nevada	1864	1864	16,700	51
New Hampshire	1776; 1784(g)	1784	10,900	37(g)
New Jersey	1776; 1844; 1947	1947	12,500	4
New Mexico	1911	1912	22,400	43
New York	1777; 1801; 1821; 1846; 1868; 1894	1894	45,000	133
North Carolina	1776; 1868	1868	12,000	112
North Dakota	1889	1889	19,797	70
Ohio	1802; 1851	1851	15,417	67
Oklahoma	1907	1907	35,940	42
Oregon	1859	1859	25,000	104
Pennsylvania	1776; 1790; 1838; 1873	1873	15,092	59
Rhode Island	1843(a)	1843	6,650	35
South Carolina	1776; 1778; 1790; 1865; 1868; 1895	1895	30,063	231

State Constitutions (cont.) *

State or Commonwealth	Number of Constitutions and Dates of Adoption	Date of Present Constitution	Estimated Number of Words	Number of Amendments
South Dakota	1889	1889	24,545	63
Tennessee	1796; 1835; 1870	1870	9,460	8
Texas	1845; 1861; 1866; 1869; 1876	1876	43,000	140
Utah	1896	1896	13,261	29
Vermont	1777; 1786; 1793	1793	8,000	43
Virginia	1776; 1830; 1851; 1868; 1902	1902	23,101	91
Washington	1889	1889	36,422	35
West Virginia	1863; 1872	1872	22,000	29
Wisconsin	1848	1848	10,717	61
Wyoming	1890	1890	21,500	22
Puerto Rico	1952	1952	9,000	2

(a) Colonial Charters with some alterations, in Connecticut (1662) and Rhode Island (1663) served as the first constitutions for these states.

(b) In 1955, 47 earlier amendments were recodified and incorporated in the constitution. Five amendments have been adopted since 1955.

(c) Amendments do not require popular ratification.

(d) Figure does not include amendments of a local nature.

(e) Four sections of the constitution of the State of Hawaii were affected by 3 propositions adopted by the people in accordance with Public Law 86-3, 86th Congress, providing for admission.

(f) If a single proposition amends more than one section of the constitution, it may be counted as more than a single amendment.

(g) The constitution of 1784 was extensively amended, rearranged and clarified in 1793. Figures show proposals and adoptions since 1793.

* Adapted from *The Book of States, 1960-1961*, XIII (Chicago: The Council of State Governments, 1960), 12.

State Organization under Model State Constitution

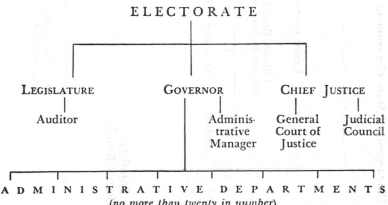

ELECTORATE

LEGISLATURE — Auditor

GOVERNOR — Administrative Manager

CHIEF JUSTICE — General Court of Justice — Judicial Council

ADMINISTRATIVE DEPARTMENTS
(*no more than twenty in number*)

247

Unreorganized State Governmental Structure

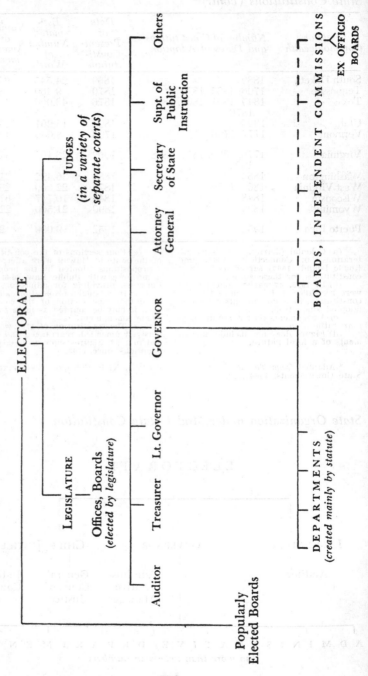

ELECTORATE

Popularly Elected Boards

Auditor Treasurer Lt. Governor GOVERNOR Attorney General Secretary of State Supt. of Public Instruction Others

LEGISLATURE

Offices, Boards
(elected by legislature)

JUDGES
(in a variety of separate courts)

DEPARTMENTS
(created mainly by statute)

BOARDS, INDEPENDENT COMMISSIONS

EX OFFICIO BOARDS

NATIONAL CONVENTION

Senatorial Campaign Committee *(Responsible to the Party Conference in the Senate)*	NATIONAL COMMITTEE NATIONAL CHAIRMAN	Congressional Campaign Committee *(Responsible to the Party Conference in the House)*

STATE CONVENTION

	STATE COMMITTEE STATE CHAIRMAN	
District Senatorial Committee	Congressional District Committee	Judicial District Committee

	County Committee County Chairman	
City Committee		Town (Town- ship, Borough, Village, etc.) Committee

Ward Committee		
	Precinct Committee	
	Precinct Captains	

	Electorate	

U. S. Citizen Living in	Mini-mum Age	Residence in State	Residence in County	Residence in District	Literacy Test
Alabama	21	2 yrs.	1 yr.	3 mo.	
Alaska	19	1 yr.		30 da.	(5)
Arizona	21	1 yr.	30 da.	30 da.	x
Arkansas	21	12 mo.	6 mo.	1 mo.	
California (8)	21	1 yr.(9)	90 da.(9)	54 da.	x
Colorado	21	1 yr.	90 da.	15 da.(10)	
Connecticut	21	1 yr.		6 mo.	x
Delaware	21	1 yr.	3 mo.	30 da.	x
Florida	21	1 yr.	6 mo.		
Georgia	18	1 yr.	6 mo.		(12)
Hawaii	20	1 yr.		3 mo.	x(13)
Idaho	21	6 mo.	30 da.		
Illinois	21	1 yr.	90 da.	30 da.	
Indiana	21	6 mo.	60 da.(15)	30 da.	
Iowa	21	6 mo.	60 da.	10 da.	
Kansas	21	6 mo.	30 da.(15)	30 da.	
Kentucky	18	1 yr.	6 mo.	60 da.	
Louisiana	21	1 yr.	1 yr.	3 mo.(16)	(17)
Maine	21	6 mo.	3 mo.	3 mo.	x
Maryland	21	1 yr.	6 mo.	6 mo.	
Massachusetts	21	1 yr.		6 mo.(18)	x
Michigan	21	6 mo.		30 da.	
Minnesota (8)	21	6 mo.		30 da.	
Mississippi	21	2 yrs.		1 yr.(20)	x
Missouri	21	1 yr.(23)	60 da.	60 da.	
Montana	21	1 yr.	30 da.		
Nebraska	21	6 mo.	40 da.	10 da.	

NOTE: no state has property qualifications for voting in a general election. Some states have property qualifications for voting on bond issues or special assessments.

(1) Poll or head taxes are levied in many other states. Those listed here provide that payment of the poll tax is a prerequisite for voting.
(2) All states which have permanent registration, except Alabama, Delaware, Florida, Maine, Mississippi, Nebraska, New Hampshire and South Dakota, make it subject to cancellation for failure to vote at certain specified intervals.
(3) Must pay all poll taxes owed for the two years next preceding election at which person offers to vote. Persons who have honorably served in the military service of the United States while the United States is engaged in hostilities, whether war is declared or not, are exempt from payment of poll taxes.
(4) Registration is permanent unless removed for cause.

(5) Must be able to read or speak the English language.
(6) Municipal election.
(7) Except for irrigation district elections.
(8) Must have been citizen 90 days.
(9) Persons who have resided in the state for at least 54 days may vote for Presidential electors if, immediately prior to moving to the state, they were qualified electors in another state or would have been eligible to vote in such other state at the time of such election. Such persons must meet all other qualifications for voting.
(10) City or town, 30 days.
(11) All except certain minor elections.
(12) Under 1949 act, all voters must reregister and pass literacy test. Those failing test may qualify by answering 10 of 30 oral questions prescribed by law.
(13) English or Hawaiian language.
(14) For all state and federal elections.
(15) Township.

* Adapted from *The Book of the States, 1960-1961*, XIII (Chicago: The Council of

the States and Territories *

Poll Tax(1)	Permanent(2) All Areas	Permanent(2) Some Areas	Periodic All Areas	Periodic Some Areas	Frequency	All Elections	Some Elections
(3)	x(4)					x	
		x				(6)	
	x					(7)	
x							
	x					x	
	x						(11)
	x					x	
	x					x	
	x					x	
	x(4)					x	
	x					x	
	x					x	
	x						(14)
	x						(11)
		x		x	4 yrs.		(11)
		x		x		x	
	x					x	
		x		x	4 yrs.	x	
	x					x	
		x		x		x	
	x					x	
	x					x	
		x		x		(19)	
(21)	x(4)					x(22)	
		x		x	4 yrs.	x	
	x						(11)
		x		x	6 yrs.		(11)

(16) Municipality, four months.
(17) Literacy test required, but exception allowed if person can pass certain specified requirements.
(18) In city or town.
(19) Except school district elections.
(20) Ministers of the Gospel and their wives may vote after six months' residence.
(21) Assessed upon citizens 21 to 60 years of age except those specifically exempted.
(22) Registration is for all elections of state and county, but voter must be registered in municipality also to vote in municipal elections.
(23) When voting for Presidential and Vice Presidential electors only 60 days' residence required.
(24) A person who became entitled to vote after January 1, 1922, must be able, except for physical disability, to read and write English.
(25) No residence requirements when voting for Presidential and Vice Presidential electors.

(26) Six months if previously an elector or native of the United States.
(27) Ministers of the Gospel, teachers in public schools, and their spouses may vote after six months' residence.
(28) Ownership of property is an alternative to literacy.
(29) No elector who has changed his residence from one county or precinct to another loses his right to vote in his former county or precinct until he acquires voting residence in the new one.
(30) Constitution provides for registration in cities over 10,000, but no system exists. Poll tax receipts determine eligibility of voters aged 21 to 60 years; exemption certificates determine eligibility for those over 60 in cities over 10,000, and for certain others.
(31) Must owe no past due taxes.
(32) Except in some cities.
(33) All elections except special elections.
(34) Precinct.

State Governments, 1960), 20-21.

U. S. Citizen Living in	Minimum Age	State	Residence in County	District	Literacy Test
Nevada	21	6 mo.	30 da.	10 da.	
New Hampshire	21	6 mo.		6 mo.	x
New Jersey	21	6 mo.	60 da.		
New Mexico	21	12 mo.	90 da.	30 da.	
New York (8)	21	1 yr.	4 mo.	30 da.	(24)
North Carolina	21	1 yr.		30 da.	x
North Dakota	21	1 yr.	90 da.	30 da.	
Ohio	21	1 yr.(25)	40 da.	40 da.	
Oklahoma	21	1 yr.	6 mo.	30 da.	
Oregon	21	6 mo.		30 da.	
Pennsylvania	21	1 yr.(26)		2 mo.	x
Rhode Island	21	1 yr.		6 mo.	
South Carolina	21	2 yrs.(27)	1 yr.	4 mo.	(28)
South Dakota	21	1 yr.	90 da.(29)	30 da.(29)	
Tennessee	21	12 mo.	3 mo.		
Texas	21	1 yr.	6 mo.	6 mo.	
Utah (8)	21	1 yr.	4 mo.	60 da.	
Vermont	21	1 yr.		3 mo.(15)	
Virginia	21	1 yr.	6 mo.	30 da.	x
Washington	21	1 yr.	90 da.	30 da.	x
West Virginia	21	1 yr.	60 da.		
Wisconsin	21	1 yr.(25)		10 da.	
Wyoming	21	1 yr.	60 da.	10 da.	x
Guam	18	2 yrs.		90 da.(34)	
Puerto Rico	21	1 yr.		1 yr.	
Virgin Islands	21	1 yr.		60 da.	x

NOTE: no state has property qualifications for voting in a general election. Some states have property qualifications for voting on bond issues or special assessments.

(1) Poll or head taxes are levied in many other states. Those listed here provide that payment of the poll tax is a prerequisite for voting.
(2) All states which have permanent registration, except Alabama, Delaware, Florida, Maine, Mississippi, Nebraska, New Hampshire and South Dakota, make it subject to cancellation for failure to vote at certain specified intervals.
(3) Must pay all poll taxes owed for the two years next preceding election at which person offers to vote. Persons who have honorably served in the military service of the United States while the United States is engaged in hostilities, whether war is declared or not, are exempt from payment of poll taxes.
(4) Registration is permanent unless removed for cause.

(5) Must be able to read or speak the English language.
(6) Municipal election.
(7) Except for irrigation district elections.
(8) Must have been citizen 90 days.
(9) Persons who have resided in the state for at least 54 days may vote for Presidential electors if, immediately prior to moving to the state, they were qualified electors in another state or would have been eligible to vote in such other state at the time of such election. Such persons must meet all other qualifications for voting.
(10) City or town, 30 days.
(11) All except certain minor elections.
(12) Under 1949 act, all voters must reregister and pass literacy test. Those failing test may qualify by answering 10 of 30 oral questions prescribed by law.
(13) English or Hawaiian language.
(14) For all state and federal elections.
(15) Township.

* Adapted from *The Book of the States, 1960-1961,* XIII (Chicago: The Council of

States and Territories (cont.)*

Poll Tax(1)	Permanent(2) All Areas	Some Areas	Periodic All Areas	Some Areas	Frequency	All Elections	Some Elections
	x					x	
	x					x	
	x					x	
	x					x	
		x		x	Annual		x
	x					x	
		x		x		x	
	x					(19)	
	x					x	
	x					x	
	x					x	
			x		Decennial	x	
	x						x
	x					x	
(21)	(30)	(30)	(30)	(30)	Annual		
	x						(11)
			x		Ea. elec.		x
(31)	(32)					x	
	x					(7)	
	x					(33)	
		x				x	
			x		Ea. gen. elec.		x
	x					x(22)	
	x					x	

(16) Municipality, four months.
(17) Literacy test required, but exception allowed if person can pass certain specified requirements.
(18) In city or town.
(19) Except school district elections.
(20) Ministers of the Gospel and their wives may vote after six months' residence.
(21) Assessed upon citizens 21 to 60 years of age except those specifically exempted.
(22) Registration is for all elections of state and county, but voter must be registered in municipality also to vote in municipal elections.
(23) When voting for Presidential and Vice Presidential electors only 60 days' residence required.
(24) A person who became entitled to vote after January 1, 1922, must be able, except for physical disability, to read and write English.
(25) No residence requirements when voting for Presidential and Vice Presidential electors.

(26) Six months if previously an elector or native of the United States.
(27) Ministers of the Gospel, teachers in public schools, and their spouses may vote after six months' residence.
(28) Ownership of property is an alternative to literacy.
(29) No elector who has changed his residence from one county or precinct to another loses his right to vote in his former county or precinct until he acquires voting residence in the new one.
(30) Constitution provides for registration in cities over 10,000, but no system exists. Poll tax receipts determine eligibility of voters aged 21 to 60 years; exemption certificates determine eligibility for those over 60 in cities over 10,000, and for certain others.
(31) Must owe no past due taxes.
(32) Except in some cities.
(33) All elections except special elections.
(34) Precinct.

State Governments, 1960), 20-21.

| | Salary and Daily Pay Plans | | | | |
| | Regular session | | | Special session | |
State	Amount per Day	Max. No. Days Pay	Salary Calculated for Biennium	Pay per Day	Max. No. Pay Days
Alabama	$10	36 L(a)		$10	36 L
Alaska			$ 6,000(b)		
Arizona			3,600(b,d)		
Arkansas	20	60 C	2,400(e)	6	15 C
California			12,000(b)		
Colorado	20	120 C	4,800(b,h)	20	None
Connecticut			2,000		
Delaware			6,000		
Florida			2,400		
Georgia	10	40 C(b)		10	70 C(i)
Hawaii			4,000(j)	(j)	
Idaho	10	60 C		10	20 C
Illinois			12,000(k)		
Indiana			3,600		
Iowa	30			30	None
Kansas	5	90(b,l)		5	30 L

Abbreviations: L—Legislative days; C—Calendar days

(a) In practice the legislature meets for 18 weeks. Legislators receive $210 a week in combined daily salary and expense allowance, a total of $3,780 for each regular biennial session.

(b) Annual sessions.

(c) Plus excess baggage allowance.

(d) Plus $20 per day salary (limited to $1,800 in a year) for special sessions and interim committee meetings; $9 per day subsistence for days required to attend interim committee meetings, plus 8c a mile or first class public carrier.

(e) Speaker of the house receives $2,700.

(f) 15c a mile for interim committee meetings and $20 a day for maximum of 60 days for interim committee meetings.

(g) Actual and necessary expenses.

(h) Legislators receive $100 a month during biennium plus $2,400 per biennium, paid at rate of $20 a day during regular and special sessions with remainder paid as a lump sum. Legislators also receive $20 per day, not to exceed $600 in any calendar year, while not in session, for attendance at legislative meetings, plus actual and necessary traveling expenses.

(i) 70-day limit on special sessions called by governor; 30-day limit on sessions convened by legislature except for impeachment proceedings.

(j) $2,500 per general session; $1,500 per budget session.

(k) This salary became effective at the 1959 session. This is an increase from $10,000 a biennium except that holdover senators continue to receive the old salary until present terms expire.

(l) 90 days biennial total: 60-day regular session, 30-day budget session.

(m) Legislators are paid for Sundays and holidays during session, consequently compensation period usually is 72 to 74 days.

		Additional Compensation for Legislators		
		Travel Allowance		
Senate Term	House Term	Amount per Mile	No. of Trips during Session	Additional Expense Allowances
4	4	10c	1 round trip	$20 per day(a)
4	2	15c	1 round trip(c)	$40 per day
2	2	8c		$9 per day subsistence for those from outside capital(d)
4	2	5c	1 round trip	
4	2	5c(f)	1 round trip	$19 per day(f)
4	2	(g)	1 round trip	None during session(h)
2	2	10c	Each day	$500 expense allowance
4	2	15c	Unlimited mileage	$25 stationery and supplies
4	2	10c	Weekly round trip	$15 per day
2	2	10c	1 round trip	$5 per day
4	2			$32.50 per day for those from Oahu; $45 for those from outer islands
2	2	10c	1 round trip	Additional $15 a day for max. of 60 days for committeemen
4	2	10c	Weekly round trip	$50 for postage and stationery
4	2	6c	Weekly round trip	
4	2	7c	1 round trip	
4	2	15c	1 round trip	$7 per day

(n) This salary becomes effective in 1961. It is an increase from $1,400 a biennium in Maine and from $6,000 in Pennsylvania.
(o) In terms of fixed amounts for each legislator.
(p) Determined at each session in Massachusetts. In Pennsylvania $500, or $750 if longer than one month.
(q) Within 40-mile radius, $10 per week expense allowance, plus 7c a mile daily to amount to not less than $4.50 a week; outside 40-mile radius, $38.50 per week living expenses plus 7c a mile for one round trip per week.
(r) Plus one extra round trip each 7 days at 6c a mile.
(s) 10c a mile for daily commuting or $15 per day if living in capital.
(t) 20c per mile for first 45 miles, 8c for next 25 miles, 6c for next 25 miles, 5c over 95 miles.
(u) Legislators receive $15 for first 75 legislative days, including intervening non-legislative days, for regular or special session, otherwise $100 a month.
(v) Effective in 1960.
(w) For all members elected in 1958. Following 1960 elections all legislators will receive $7,200. Until then all holdover senators elected prior to 1958 will receive $4,800 a biennium.
(x) 10c a mile for one round trip; thereafter, 7c a mile for first 2,000 miles per month, 6c a mile for each additional mile once a week during the session.
(y) For legislators filing affidavit regarding necessity of establishing temporary residence at capital during regular or special session.
(z) Minimum $10.
(aa) Unicameral legislature, 2-year term.

* Adapted from *The Book of the States, 1960-1961*, XIII (Chicago: The Council of State Governments, 1960) 37-39.

State	Salary and Daily Pay Plans				
	Regular session			Special session	
	Amount per Day	Max. No. Days Pay	Salary Calculated for Biennium	Pay per Day	Max. No. Pay Days
Kentucky	25	60 L(m)		25	None
Louisiana	50	90 C(b,l)		50	30 C
Maine			1,600(n)	10	None
Maryland			3,600(b)		
Massachusetts			10,400(b)	(p)	None
Michigan			8,000(b)		
Minnesota			4,800	25	None
Mississippi			3,000	22.50	None
Missouri			3,000		
Montana	20	60 C		20	60 C
Nebraska			1,744		
Nevada	25	60 C		25	20 C
New Hampshire			200	3	15 C

Abbreviations: L—Legislative days; C—Calendar days

(a) In practice the legislature meets for 18 weeks. Legislators receive $210 a week in combined daily salary and expense allowance, a total of $3,780 for each regular biennial session.

(b) Annual sessions.

(c) Plus excess baggage allowance.

(d) Plus $20 per day salary (limited to $1,800 in a year) for special sessions and interim committee meetings; $9 per day subsistence for days required to attend interim committee meetings, plus 8c a mile or first class public carrier.

(e) Speaker of the house receives $2,700.

(f) 15c a mile for interim committee meetings and $20 a day for maximum of 60 days for interim committee meetings.

(g) Actual and necessary expenses.

(h) Legislators receive $100 a month during biennium plus $2,400 per biennium, paid at rate of $20 a day during regular and special sessions with remainder paid as a lump sum. Legislators also receive $20 per day, not to exceed $600 in any calendar year, while not in session, for attendance at legislative meetings, plus actual and necessary traveling expenses.

(i) 70-day limit on special sessions called by governor; 30-day limit on sessions convened by legislature except for impeachment proceedings.

(j) $2,500 per general session; $1,500 per budget session.

(k) This salary became effective at the 1959 session. This is an increase from $10,000 a biennium except that holdover senators continue to receive the old salary until present terms expire.

(l) 90 days biennial total: 60-day regular session, 30-day budget session.

(m) Legislators are paid for Sundays and holidays during session, consequently compensation period usually is 72 to 74 days.

		Additional Compensation for Legislators		
		Travel Allowance		
Senate Term	House Term	Amount per Mile	No. of Trips during Session	Additional Expense Allowances
4	2	15c	1 round trip	$10 per day, not to exceed $600; $50 in lieu of stationery
4	4	10c	8 round trips and 4 round trips during budget session	$150 per month while legislature not in session
2	2	5c	Weekly round trip	Small allowance for postage, telephone, etc.
4	4	20c(o)		$2,400 per biennium
2	2	7c(q)	Each day(q)	$1,000 per biennium; weekly exp. allow. according to distance from capital(1)
2	2	10c	Monthly round trip	$2,000 per biennium; plus allow. for postage, telephone, etc.
4	2	15c	1 round trip	In 1959, $12 per day for those who have to leave home to attend; $8 per day for others
4	4	10c	1 round trip(r)	
4	2	10c	1 round trip	$10 per day
4	2	7c	1 round trip	
(aa)	(aa)	8c	1 round trip	$100 postage allowance
4	2	10c	Daily commuting(s)	$15 per day(s); $60 for postage, etc.
2	2	(t)	Daily round trip(t)	

(n) This salary becomes effective in 1961. It is an increase from $1,400 a biennium in Maine and from $6,000 in Pennsylvania.

(o) In terms of fixed amounts for each legislator.

(p) Determined at each session in Massachusetts. In Pennsylvania $500, or $750 if longer than one month.

(q) Within 40-mile radius, $10 per week expense allowance, plus 7c a mile daily to amount to not less than $4.50 a week; outside 40-mile radius, $38.50 per week living expenses plus 7c a mile for one round trip per week.

(r) Plus one extra round trip each 7 days at 6c a mile.

(s) 10c a mile for daily commuting or $15 per day if living in capital.

(t) 20c per mile for first 45 miles, 8c for next 25 miles, 6c for next 25 miles, 5c over 95 miles.

(u) Legislators receive $15 for first 75 legislative days, including intervening non-legislative days, for regular or special session, otherwise $100 a month.

(v) Effective in 1960.

(w) For all members elected in 1958. Following 1960 elections all legislators will receive $7,200. Until then all holdover senators elected prior to 1958 will receive $4,800 a biennium.

(x) 10c a mile for one round trip; thereafter, 7c a mile for first 2,000 miles per month, 6c a mile for each additional mile once a week during the session.

(y) For legislators filing affidavit regarding necessity of establishing temporary residence at capital during regular or special session.

(z) Minimum $10.

(aa) Unicameral legislature, 2-year term.

* Adapted from *The Book of the States, 1960-1961*, XIII (Chicago: The Council of State Governments, 1960) 37-39.

State	Regular session Amount per Day	Regular session Max. No. Days Pay	Salary Calculated for Biennium	Special session Pay per Day	Special session Max. No. Days Pay
	Salary and Daily Pay Plans				
New Jersey			10,000(b)		
New Mexico	20	60 C		20	30 C
New York			15,000(b)		
North Carolina	15	120 C		15	25 C
North Dakota	5	60 L		5	None
Ohio			10,000		
Oklahoma	15	75 L(u)	3,950(u)	15	75 L(u)
Oregon			1,200		
Pennsylvania			12,000(b,n)	(p)	
Rhode Island	5	60 L(b)			
South Carolina			2,000(b)	25	40 L
South Dakota			1,800	10	None
Tennessee	10	75 C		10	20 C
Texas	25	120 C		25	30 C
Utah			1,000		
Vermont			1,750		
Virginia			1,080	30(v)	30(v)
Washington			2,400	10	
West Virginia			3,000(b)		
Wisconsin			7,200(w)		
Wyoming	12	40 C		12	None

Abbreviations: L—Legislative days; C—Calendar days

(a) In practice the legislature meets for 18 weeks. Legislators receive $210 a week in combined daily salary and expense allowance, a total of $3,780 for each regular biennial session.

(b) Annual sessions.

(c) Plus excess baggage allowance.

(d) Plus $20 per day salary (limited to $1,800 in a year) for special sessions and interim committee meetings; $9 per day subsistence for days required to attend interim committee meetings, plus 8c a mile or first class public carrier.

(e) Speaker of the house receives $2,700.

(f) 15c a mile for interim committee meetings and $20 a day for maximum of 60 days for interim committee meetings.

(g) Actual and necessary expenses.

(h) Legislators receive $100 a month during biennium plus $2,400 per biennium, paid at rate of $20 a day during regular and special sessions with remainder paid as a lump sum. Legislators also receive $20 per day, not to exceed $600 in any calendar year, while not in session, for attendance at legislative meetings, plus actual and necessary traveling expenses.

(i) 70-day limit on special sessions called by governor; 30-day limit on sessions convened by legislature except for impeachment proceedings.

(j) $2,500 per general session; $1,500 per budget session.

(k) This salary became effective at the 1959 session. This is an increase from $10,000 a biennium except that holdover senators continue to receive the old salary until present terms expire.

(l) 90 days biennial total: 60-day regular session, 30-day budget session.

(m) Legislators are paid for Sundays and holidays during session, consequently compensation period usually is 72 to 74 days.

# of State Legislators (cont.) *

Additional Compensation for Legislators

Travel Allowance

Senate Term	House Term	Amount per Mile	No. of Trips during Session	Additional Expense Allowances
4	2		State railroad pass	
4	2	10c	1 round trip	Stationery, postage, telephone and telegraph allowance
2	2	(g)	Weekly round trip	$1,000 expense allow. for 1960 session
2	2	7c	1 round trip	$8 per day subsistence
4	2	10c	1 round trip	$20 per day
4	2	10c	Weekly round trip	Postage and stationery
4	2	10c	1 round trip	Postage, stationery, telephone, telegraph allowance; shipping supplies
4	2	10c	1 round trip	Postage, stationery; shipping supplies
4	2	10c	Weekly round trip	
2	2	8c		
4	2	7c	Weekly round trip	$7.50 per day for max. of 40 days
2	2	5c	1 round trip	
2	2	16c	1 round trip	$5 per day
4	2	10c	1 round trip	Small exp. allow. determined at session
4	2	10c	1 round trip	$5 per day
2	2	20c	1 round trip	Stationery
4	2	7c	1 round trip	
4	2	10c	1 round trip	$25 per day
4	2	10c	1 round trip	
4	2	(x)	Rate-distance ratio(x)	$175 monthly expense allowance(y)
4	2	8c	1 round trip	$12 per day

(n) This salary becomes effective in 1961. It is an increase from $1,400 a biennium in Maine and from $6,000 in Pennsylvania.

(o) In terms of fixed amounts for each legislator.

(p) Determined at each session in Massachusetts. In Pennsylvania $500, or $750 if longer than one month.

(q) Within 40-mile radius, $10 per week expense allowance, plus 7c a mile daily to amount to not less than $4.50 a week; outside 40-mile radius, $38.50 per week living expenses plus 7c a mile for one round trip per week.

(r) Plus one extra round trip each 7 days at 6c a mile.

(s) 10c a mile for daily commuting or $15 per day if living in capital.

(t) 20c per mile for first 45 miles, 8c for next 25 miles, 6c for next 25 miles, 5c over 95 miles.

(u) Legislators receive $15 for first 75 legislative days, including intervening nonlegislative days, for regular or special session, otherwise $100 a month.

(v) Effective in 1960.

(w) For all members elected in 1958. Following 1960 elections all legislators will receive $7,200. Until then all holdover senators elected prior to 1958 will receive $4,800 a biennium.

(x) 10c a mile for one round trip; thereafter, 7c a mile for first 2,000 miles per month, 6c a mile for each additional mile once a week during the session.

(y) For legislators filing affidavit regarding necessity of establishing temporary residence at capital during regular or special session.

(z) Minimum $10.

(aa) Unicameral legislature, 2-year term.

* Adapted from *The Book of the States, 1960-1961,* XIII (Chicago: The Council of State Governments, 1960) 37-39.

Voting Statistics for 1960 (in Thousands) *

State	Presidential Electors Total	Presidential Electors Percent for Majority Party	U.S. Senator Total	U.S. Senator Percent for Majority Party	U.S. Representative Total	U.S. Representative Percent for Majority Party	Governor Total	Governor Percent for Majority Party
Alabama	570	D–56.9	554	D–70.2	438	D–89.0		
Alaska	61	R–50.9	60	D–63.4	59	D–57.6		
Arizona	398	R–55.5			377	R–52.3	397	R–59.3
Arkansas	429	D–50.2	377	D–100.0	70	D–82.9	422	D–69.2
California	6,507	R–50.1			6,193	D–53.9		
Colorado	736	R–54.6	728	R–53.5	715	D–51.7		
Connecticut	1,223	D–53.7			1,216	D–53.5		
Delaware	196	D–50.6	195	R–50.7	195	D–50.3	195	D–51.7
Florida	1,544	R–51.5			1,248	D–69.0	1,419	D–59.8
Georgia	733	D–62.6	576	D–100.0	574	D–95.6		
Hawaii	185	D–50.0			183	D–74.3		
Idaho	300	R–53.8	292	R–52.3	290	D–54.8		
Illinois	4,757	D–50.0	4,633	D–54.6	4,635	D–51.1	4,674	D–55.5
Indiana	2,135	R–55.0			2,122	R–51.3	2,129	D–50.4
Iowa	1,274	R–56.7	1,238	R–51.9	1,226	R–54.1	1,237	R–52.1
Kansas	929	R–60.4	889	R–54.6	871	R–54.2	923	R–56.0
Kentucky	1,124	R–53.6	1,089	R–59.2	913	D–59.0		
Louisiana	808	D–50.4	542	D–79.8	519	D–85.2	507	D–80.5
Maine	422	R–57.0	417	R–61.6	409	R–56.5	417	R–52.7
Maryland	1,055	D–53.6			981	D–59.4		
Massachusetts	2,469	D–60.2	2,418	R–56.2	2,259	D–61.0	2,417	R–52.9
Michigan	3,318	D–50.9	3,227	D–51.7	3,222	D–50.9	3,256	D–50.6
Minnesota	1,542	D–50.6	1,537	D–57.5	1,515	D–50.2	1,550	R–50.6
Mississippi	298	(a)	266	D–91.8	258	D–98.1		
Missouri	1,934	D–50.3	1,880	D–53.2	1,843	D–57.7	1,887	D–58.0

State	%	Votes	%	Votes	%	Votes	%	Votes
Montana	R-51.1	278	D-50.7	277	D-51.1	272	R-55.1	280
Nebraska	R-62.1	613	R-58.9	599	R-56.5	581	R-52.3	599
Nevada	D-51.2	107	R-60.3	288	D-57.7	104	R-55.5	291
New Hampshire	R-53.4	296			R-58.2	285	R-52.0	306
New Jersey	D-50.0	2,773	R-55.7	2,665	R-51.2	2,659		
New Mexico	D-50.2	311	D-63.4	301	D-58.8	301		
New York	D-52.5	7,291			D-47.9	7,024		
North Carolina	D-52.1	1,369	D-61.4	1,291	D-60.4	1,302	D-54.4	1,350
North Dakota	R-55.4	278			R-53.1	256	D-49.4	275
Ohio	R-53.3	4,162			R-54.1	3,847		
Oklahoma	R-59.0	903	D-54.8	864	D-54.7	839		
Oregon	R-52.6	775	D-54.6	756	D-51.2	762		
Pennsylvania	D-51.1	5,007			D-52.2	4,954		
Rhode Island	D-63.6	406	D-68.9	400	D-68.6	392	D-56.9	401
South Carolina	D-51.2	387	D-100.0	330	D-100.0	328		
South Dakota	R-58.2	306	R-52.4	305	R-56.1	301	R-50.7	305
Tennessee	R-52.9	1,052	D-71.8	829	D-68.4	643		
Texas	D-50.5	2,312	D-58.0	2,254	D-82.4	2,040	D-72.8	2,251
Utah	R-54.8	375			D-50.7	369	R-52.7	371
Vermont	R-58.6	167			R-57.2	166	R-56.4	165
Virginia	R-52.4	771	D-81.4	622	D-64.2	640		
Washington	R-50.7	1,242			R-57.5	1,125	D-51.3	1,216
West Virginia	D-52.7	838	D-55.3	828	D-57.1	820	D-54.0	827
Wisconsin	R-51.8	1,729			R-50.9	1,663	D-51.6	1,728
Wyoming	R-55.0	140	R-56.4	139	R-52.2	135		

NOTE: D = Democratic, R = Republican. Majority party vote refers to the party vote representing either a majority or a plurality for the victorious party.

(a) Unpledged Democratic elector vote, who later agreed to support Harry F. Byrd.

* Adapted from *Statistical Abstract of the United States, 1961* (Washington: U.S. Government Printing Office, 1961), pp. 349, 351, 354, 357.

Representation in State Legislatures *

NOTE: Figures in 3rd and 7th cols. show how many people would be represented by each legislator if states were evenly apportioned on a strict population basis. This theoretical situation bears comparison with the actual present-day figures in columns 4, 5, 8 and 9, showing extremes of overrepresentation and underrepresentation. All statistics are based on the 1950 Federal Census.

State	Year of Last Adjustment (1)	Lower House				Upper House			
		Total Membership (2)	Average Population per Representative (3)	Smallest Population per Representative (4)	Largest Population per Representative (5)	Total Membership (6)	Average Population per Senator (7)	Smallest Population per Senator (8)	Largest Population per Senator (9)
Alabama	1901	106	28,884	8,027	79,846	35	87,478	18,018	558,928
Alaska	1959	40	2,706	1,187	3,972	20	5,412	3,424	26,602
Arizona	1910	80	9,357	6,402	27,767	28	26,735	4,672	165,385
Arkansas	1951	100	19,095	5,978	32,614	35	54,357	43,114	65,562
California	1951	80	132,327	62,975	200,750	40	264,656	14,014	4,151,687
Colorado	1953	65	20,386	9,362	27,843	35	37,860	18,438	56,602
Connecticut	1941	280	7,195	130	88,699	36	55,758	24,309	122,931
Delaware	1897	35	9,088	1,321	35,762	17	18,711	3,496	57,179
Florida	1945	95	29,171	2,199	165,028	38	72,929	10,413	495,084
Georgia	1950	205	16,803	2,494	157,857	54	63,788	16,237	473,572
Idaho	1917	59	9,976	918	17,865	44	13,379	918	70,649
Illinois	1955	177	49,221	39,809	68,655	58	150,210	17,063	383,803
Indiana	1921	100	39,342	15,674	68,353	50	78,684	39,592	122,717
Iowa	1911	108	24,269	8,753	113,005	50	52,421	21,173	226,010
Kansas	1886	125	15,242	2,010	74,097	40	47,631	20,018	222,290
Kentucky	1942	100	29,448	12,890	50,373	38	77,495	51,992	104,254
Louisiana	1921	101	26,569	6,244	79,118	39	68,808	25,326	158,236
Maine	1951	151	6,051	2,372	11,090	33	27,690	16,053	42,300
Maryland	1922	123	19,049	6,136	44,894	29	80,793	12,272	269,362
Massachusetts	1948	240	19,544	2,870	28,675	40	117,263	92,216	164,334
Michigan	1953	110	57,925	32,469	94,994	34	187,405	61,008	396,001

State	Year¹								
Minnesota	1913	131	22,767	7,290	107,246	67	44,513	16,878	153,455
Mississippi	1916	140	16,383	4,966	57,235	49	44,468	17,869	99,910
Missouri	1951	157	25,189	4,777	48,432	34	116,313	87,559	136,687
Montana	1925	94	6,287	1,026	10,366	56	10,554	1,026	55,875
Nebraska ²	1935					43	30,826	21,579	40,998
Nevada	1951	47	3,406	614	6,037	17	9,417	614	50,205
New Hampshire	1915	399	1,336	16	2,179	24	22,218	12,051	34,368
New Jersey	1941	60	80,589	34,423	135,910	21	230,254	34,423	905,949
New Mexico	1955	66	12,385	3,013	16,186	32	21,974	3,013	45,673
New York	1954	150	94,960	14,066	167,226	58	244,887	146,666	344,547
North Carolina	1941	120	33,849	5,048	71,220	50	81,239	48,375	197,052
North Dakota	1931	113	5,484	3,180	16,609	49	12,909	5,405	38,766
Ohio	1957	139	59,303	10,759	98,920	33	240,807	163,335	395,551
Oklahoma	1907	121	18,457	4,589	46,479	44	50,758	15,898	251,286
Oregon	1954	60	26,230	12,740	48,313	30	50,711	26,317	67,362
Pennsylvania	1921	210	49,991	4,944	77,106	50	209,960	78,181	442,516
Rhode Island	1940	100	7,919	732	14,810	44	19,315	732	55,060
South Carolina	1919	124	17,073	9,577	23,173	46	46,022	9,577	108,152
South Dakota	1951	75	8,703	4,046	21,044	35	19,198	10,450	35,455
Tennessee	1901	99	33,250	3,948	75,134	33	99,748	40,416	208,255
Texas	1951	150	51,408	29,192	100,837	31	248,748	136,756	806,701
Utah	1955	64	10,934	364	15,437	25	27,554	9,642	45,812
Vermont	1793	246	1,505	49	33,155	30	12,592	3,406	17,027
Virginia	1952	100	33,187	19,218	60,994	40	82,967	55,637	135,449
Washington	1958	99	24,030	12,994	39,383	49	48,550	18,935	82,732
West Virginia	1951	100	21,335	5,119	37,540	32	62,672	30,646	119,814
Wisconsin	1951	100	34,346	18,840	51,657	33	104,078	73,301	128,970
Wyoming	1931	56	5,188	2,481	7,943	27	11,174	2,481	23,831

¹ Year of last adjustment may mean complete redistricting or merely slight adjustments in existing district lines. Data from individual states as of March 1959.
² Nebraska has only senate.

* Adapted from *The Congressional Record*, June 29, 1960, pp. 13828-9.

State or Other Jurisdiction	Years Held	Limitations on Length		Special Sessions	
		Regular	Special	Leg. May Call	Leg. May Determine Subject
Alabama	Odd	36 L	36 L	No	(bb)
Alaska	Annual	None	30 C	Yes	Yes (b)
Arizona	Annual	63 C (c)	20 C (c)	(y)	Yes
Arkansas	Odd	60 C	15 C (d)	No	(d)
California	Annual (e)	120 C (f) 30 C	None	No	No
Colorado	Annual (e)	120 C (c)	None	No	No
Connecticut	Odd	150 C (g)	None	Yes	Yes
Delaware	Annual (e)	90 L, 30 L	30 C	No	Yes
Florida	Odd	60 C (h)	20 C (i)	(i)	Yes (i)
Georgia	Annual	40 C	(j)	(k) (aa)	Yes
Hawaii	Annual (e)	60 C (1)	30 C (1)	Yes (m)	Yes
Idaho	Odd	60 C (c)	20 C	No	No
Illinois	Odd	None (n)	None	No	No
Indiana	Odd	61 C	40 C	No	Yes
Iowa	Odd	None (o)	None	No	Yes
Kansas	Annual (e)	60 L (c), 30 C	30 L (c)	No	Yes
Kentucky	Even	60 L	None	No	No
Louisiana	Annual (e)	60 C, 30 C	30 C	(z)	No (p)
Maine	Odd	None	None	No	Yes
Maryland	Annual (e)	90 C	30 C	No	Yes
Massachusetts	Annual	None	None	Yes	Yes
Michigan	Annual	None	None	No	No
Minnesota	Odd	90 L	None	No	Yes
Mississippi	Even	None	None	No	No
Missouri	Odd	150 C (g)	60 C	No	No
Montana	Odd	60 C	60 C (c)	No	No

L = Legislative days; C = Calendar days.

(a) Legislature meets quadrennially on second Tuesday after election for purpose of organizing.

(b) Unless governor calls and limits.

(c) Indirect restriction on session length. Legislator's pay ceases but session may continue.

(d) Governor may convene general assembly for specified purpose. After specific business is transacted, a 2/3 vote of members of both houses may extend sessions up to 13 days.

(e) Alternate year budget sessions are held, all except the Louisiana session meeting in the even-numbered years.

(f) Exclusive of Saturdays and Sundays.

(g) Approximate length of session. Connecticut session must adjourn by first Wednesday after first Monday in June, Missouri's by May 31, and Puerto Rico's by April 30.

(h) Length of session may be extended by 30 days, but not beyond Sept. 1, by 3/5 vote of both houses.

(i) Twenty per cent of the membership may petition the Secretary of State to poll the legislature; upon affirmative vote of 3/5 of both houses an extra session, no more than 30 days in length, may be called. Extra sessions called by the governor are limited to 20 days.

(j) Seventy-day session limit except for impeachment proceedings if governor calls session; 30-day limit if legislature convenes itself.

(k) Thirty-day limit.

(l) General sessions, odd years 60 days; budget sessions, even years 30 days. Governor may extend any session for not more than 30 days. Sundays and holidays shall be excluded in computing the number of days of any session.

* Adapted from *The Book of the States, 1960-1961*, XIII (Chicago: The Council of

Sessions °

State or Other Jurisdiction	Years Held	Limitations on Length		Special Sessions	
		Regular	Special	Leg. May Call	Leg. May Determine Subject
Nebraska	Odd	None	None	(y)	No
Nevada	Annual	60 C (c)	20 C (c)	No	No
New Hampshire	Odd	None	15 C (c)	Yes	Yes
New Jersey	Annual	None	None	(q)	Yes
New Mexico	Odd	60 C	30 C (r)	Yes (r)	Yes (r)
New York	Annual	None	None	No	No
North Carolina	Odd	120 C (c)	25 C (c)	No	Yes
North Dakota	Odd	60 L	None	No	Yes
Ohio	Odd	None	None	No	No
Oklahoma	Odd	None	None	No (s)	No
Oregon	Odd	None	None	No	Yes
Pennsylvania	Annual (e)	None	None	No	No
Rhode Island	Annual	60 L (c)	None	No	No
South Carolina	Annual	None	None	No	Yes
South Dakota	Odd	60 C	None	No	Yes
Tennessee	Odd	75 C (c)	20 C (c)	No	No
Texas	Odd	120 C (c)	30 C	No	No
Utah	Odd	60 C	30 C	No	No
Vermont	Odd	None	None	No	Yes
Virginia	Even	60 C (c, t)	30 C (c, t)	(y)	Yes
Washington	Odd	60 C	None	No	Yes
West Virginia	Annual (e)	60 C (u) 30 C (u)	None	(y)	No
Wisconsin	Odd	None	None	No	No
Wyoming	Odd	40 C	None	No	Yes
Guam	Annual	60 C (v)	14 C	No	No
Puerto Rico	Annual	111 C (g, w)	20 C	No	No
Virgin Islands	Annual	60	15 (x)	No	No

(m) Legislature may convene in special session on 45th day after adjournment to act on bills submitted to the governor less than ten days before adjournment if governor notifies the legislature he plans to return them with objections.
(n) By custom legislature adjourns by July 1, since all bills passed after that day are not effective until July 1 of following year.
(o) Custom and pay limit session to 100 calendar days.
(p) Unless legislature petitions for session, or may be extended by vote of 3/4 elected members of each house.
(q) Petition by majority members of each house to governor, who then "shall" call special session.
(r) Limitation does not apply if impeachment trial is pending or in process. Legislature may call 30-day "extraordinary session" if governor refuses to call session when requested by 3/5 of legislature.
(s) Governor may convene senate alone in special session.
(t) May be extended up to 30 days by 3/5 vote of each house, but without pay.
(u) Must be extended by governor until general appropriation passed; may be extended by 2/3 vote of legislature.
(v) Organic Act specifies legislature may meet for 60 days during each year, statutes specify legislature shall meet for 30 days twice each year.
(w) Session may be extended by adoption of joint resolution.
(x) No special session may continue longer than 15 calendar days and the aggregate for the year may not exceed 30.
(y) Petition 2/3 members.
(z) Petition 2/3 members elected each house.
(aa) Petition 3/5 members.
(bb) Two-thirds vote those present.

State Governments, 1960), 40-41.

Legislative Procedure: Standing Committees and Hearings *

State	House Committees Appointed by Speaker	Senate Committees Appointed by	Standing Committees at most recent Regular Session			Range in Size of Committees			Hearings Open to Public
			House	Senate	Joint	House	Senate	Joint	
Alabama	x	President	17	30	0	7–15	3–21		Dis.
Alaska	(a)	(a)	10	10	0	5–7	3–5		Dis.
Arizona	x	President	21	21	0	15	7–11		Dis.
Arkansas	x	President	68	25	1	5–28	5–10	12	Dis.
California	x	Comm. on Rules	26	20	1	6–28	5–13		Yes
Colorado	x	Resolution	18	20	1	3–19	3–20	6	Dis.
Connecticut	x	Pres. pro tem	0	0	28			(b)	Yes
Delaware	x	Pres. pro tem	22	22	0	5	5		Dis.
Florida	x	President	54	38	1	5–25	7–13	6	Yes(c)
Georgia	x	President	24	16	0	5–15	5–35		Dis.
Hawaii(d)	x	President(e)	26	18	0	5–11	3–10		Dis.
Idaho	x	President	20	22	3	3–11	5–11		Dis.
Illinois	x	Comm. on Comms.	23	23	0	6–41	3–29	9–18	Yes
Indiana	x	President	43	39	2	4–16	6–11	8–12	Dis.
Iowa	x	President	40	32	2	7–46	1–27	9	Dis.
Kansas	x	President	43	30	1	3–23	5–11	12	Dis.
Kentucky	x	President	15	18	0	11–34	9–16(f)		Dis.
Louisiana	x	President	16	17	0	16–20	6–17		Dis.
Maine	x	President	7	3	24	4–16	3–12	7–10	Yes
Maryland	x	President	14	14	3	5–35	3–15	6–10	Yes
Massachusetts	x	President	6	4	31	3–15	3–8	15	Yes
Michigan	x	Comm. on Comms.	47	20	0	5–15	5–7		Dis.
Minnesota	x	Comm. on Comms.	39	20	0	5–29	10–23		Yes
Mississippi	x	Lt. Governor	50	46	5	5–33	3–26	5–13	Dis.
Missouri	x	Pres. pro tem	45	26	1	4–41	5–13	14	Dis.
Montana	x	Comm. on Comms.	36	36	0	5–18	3–11		Dis.
Nebraska	(g)	Comm. on Comms.	(g)	14	(g)	(g)	1–8	(g)	Yes

State		By whom appointed	No. house	No. senate	No.	House range	Senate range		
Nevada	x	President	27	19	0	5-13	3-5		Dis.
New Hampshire	x	President	25	18	1	5-21	3-7	9	Yes
New Jersey	x(h)	President	16	16	4	7	5-7	12	Dis.
New Mexico	x	Comm. on Comms.	16(i)	7(i)	0	7-14	7-11		Dis.
New York	x	Pres. pro tem	36	28	0	15-20	6-25		Dis.
North Carolina	x	President	43	32	4	8-62	6-26		Yes
North Dakota	x	Comm. on Comms.	21	18	0	3-22	3-17		Dis.
Ohio	x	Pres. pro tem	22	13	4	7-23	7-11	4	Yes
Oklahoma	x(k)	(1)	39	40	0	3-30	2-28		Dis.
Oregon	x	President	20	21	1	6-11	5-7	14	Yes
Pennsylvania	x	Pres. pro tem	32	22	0	15-20	9-24		Dis.
Rhode Island	x	Named in rules	15	17	6	8-17	5-10	8	Dis.
South Carolina	x	Elected(m)	8	36	4	5-27	5-18	6-15	Dis.
South Dakota	x	President	50	27	0	3-15	3-15		Dis.
Tennessee	x	Speaker	17	17	0	17-33	11-17		Dis.
Texas	x	President	43	24	0	5-21	5-21	28	Yes
Utah	x	President	22	15	1	5-17	5-7	6-56	Yes
Vermont	x	Special comm.	18	18	3(n)	5-15	3-6		Yes
Virginia	x	Elected	34	21	3	NA	NA	NA	Dis.(o)
Washington	x	President	31	33	0	6-51	3-32		Dis.
West Virginia	x	President	25	29	3	10-25	3-18	5	Dis.
Wisconsin	x	Comm. on Comms.(p)	23	11	2	3-11	3-10	5-14	Yes
Wyoming	x	President	18	16	1	7-10	2-5		Dis.

Abbreviations: Dis.—discretionary; NA—information not available.

(a) Nominated by committee on committees and elected by house and senate respectively.
(b) Not more than 7 senators nor 25 representatives.
(c) Senate committees sometimes meet in executive session.
(d) 1959 territorial legislature.
(e) Except 4 select committees made up of senators from each of the 4 counties.
(f) Only 1 committee has more than 9 members.
(g) Unicameral legislature.
(h) Standing committee on committees advises him.

(i) Only 12 consider legislation; 4 are procedural.
(j) Also the committee on committees.
(k) Confirmed by house.
(l) Senate elects senate standing committees. Appointments to temporary and special committees are made by the senate presiding officer.
(m) Special committees are appointed.
(n) Corresponding committees of each house usually meet jointly.
(o) Final vote by a house committee must be in open session.
(p) Confirmation by senate.

* Adapted from *The Book of the States, 1960-1961,* XIII (Chicago: The Council of State Governments, 1960), 45.

Route of Bill through State Legislature *

| | The House of Representatives (formal session) | | | | | | The Senate | | | Administrative Officials | | |
| | Introducing Member | Staff of the Chief Clerk of the House | | | Speaker of the House | House Standing Committee | Committee of the Whole House | The Senate | Secretary of the Senate | President of the Senate | State Printer | Secretary of State | The Governor |
		Chief Clerk	Reading Clerk	Other Clerks									
	Introduction of Bill		First Reading	Record of First Reading							Printing of Bill		
			Second Reading	Record of Second Reading	Reference to Standing Committee	Consideration by Standing Committee							
		Reading of Report of Standing Committee		Record of Report of Standing Committee			Consideration by Committee of the Whole House						
		Reading of Report of Committee of the Whole		Record of Report of Committee of the Whole									
				Third Reading Roll Call and Vote									
				Record of Third Reading and Vote									
		Certification						Procedure followed Similar to that in House	Certification				
				Reading of Message from Senate									
				Record of Bill's Return from Senate									
		Signature of Chief Clerk of House.			Signature of Speaker of the House								
											Printing of Bill on Parchment	Preparation of Correct Copy for Enrollment	
									Signature of Secretary of Senate	Signature of President of Senate			Signature of the Governor

* Adapted from *The Life of a Bill* (Lawrence [Government Research Center]: University of Kansas, 1961), p. 16-17.

State Tax Collections 1950-1960 *

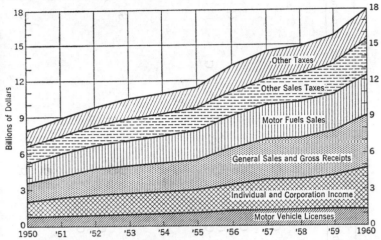

* Adapted from *State Tax Collections in 1960* (Washington [Bureau of the Census]: U. S. Government Printing Office, 1960), p. 1.

Distribution of Metropolitan Population between Central Cities and Surrounding Areas *

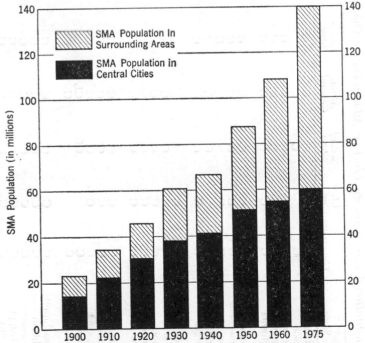

* Adapted from *Guiding Metropolitan Growth* (New York: Committee on Economic Development, August, 1960), p. 8.

Constitutional and Statutory Elective Administrative Officials *

State	Governor	Lt. Gov.	Sec. of State	Attny. General	Treasurer	Auditor	Controller	Education	Agriculture	Labor	Insurance
Alabama	C	C	C	C	C	C		C	C		
Alaska	C		C	C	C						
Arizona	C		C	C	C			C			
Arkansas	C	C	C	C	C	C					
California	C	C	C	C	C		C	C			
Colorado	C	C	C	C	C						
Connecticut	C	C	C	C	C		C				
Delaware	C	C		C	C	C					
Florida	C		C	C	C	SL	C	C	C		
Georgia	C	C	C	C	C		C	C	C	C	C
Hawaii	C	C	C		C	CL					
Idaho	C	C	C	C	C	C		C			
Illinois	C	C	C	C	C	C		C			
Indiana	C	C	C	S	C	C		C			
Iowa	C	C	C	C	C	C			S		
Kansas	C	C	C	C	C	C		C			
Kentucky	C	C	C	C	C	C	C	C	C		S
Louisiana	C	C	CL	CL	CL			C	C		
Maine	C				CL	SL			SL		
Maryland	C			C	C		C				
Massachusetts	C	C	C	C	C	C		C			
Michigan	C	C	C	C	C	C					
Minnesota	C	C	C	C	C	C					
Mississippi	C	C	C	C	C	C					
Missouri	C	C	C	C	C	C		C	S		S

Montana	C	C	C	C	C	C
Nebraska	C	C	C	C	C	C
Nevada	C	C	CL	CL	C	
New Hampshire	C	CL				
New Jersey	C	C	C			
New Mexico	C	C	C	C	C	
New York	C	C	C	C	C	C
North Carolina	C	C	C	C	C	C
North Dakota	C	C	C	C	C	C
Ohio	C	C	C	C	C	
Oklahoma	C	C	C	C	C	C
Oregon	C	C	C	S	S	S
Pennsylvania	C	C	C	C	C	
Rhode Island	C	C	C	C	C	
South Carolina	C	C	C	S	S	SL
South Dakota	C	SL	CL	C	SL	
Tennessee	SL	C	CL	C	C	
Texas	C	C	C	C	S	
Utah	C	C	C	C		
Vermont	C	C	C	C		
Virginia	C	C	C	C	CL	CL
Washington	C	C	C	C	S	S
West Virginia	C	C	C	C	S	S
Wisconsin	C	C	C	C	C	
Wyoming	C	C	C	C		

C = Constitutional L = Elected by Legislature S = Statutory

* Adapted from *The Book of the States, 1960-1961* XIII (Chicago: The Council of State Governments, 1960), 124-125.

Classification of Courts and Terms of Judges *

State or Jurisdiction	Appellate Courts		Chancery Court	Other Major Trial Courts	Courts of Limited Jurisdiction †			
	Court of Last Resort	Intermediate Appellate Court			Probate Court	County Court	Municipal Court	Justice, Magistrate or Police Court
Alabama	6	6		6	6			4
Alaska	10			6				
Arizona	6			4				4
Arkansas	8		6	4		2	2–4	2
California	12	12		6			6	6
Colorado	10			6		4		2
Connecticut	8			8	4		4	4
Delaware	12		12	12	4		2–4	4
Florida	6	6		4–6	4	4	2–4	4
Georgia	6	6		4–8	4		1–4	4
Hawaii	7			6				
Idaho	6			4	2		2	2
Illinois	9	3		6	4	4	6	4
Indiana	6	4		4–6	4		4	4
Iowa	6			4			4	2
Kansas	6			4	2	2	2	2
Kentucky	8			6		4		4
Louisiana	14	12		6	4		4–8	4
Maine	7			7	4		4	
Maryland	15			15			8	2
Massachusetts	Life			Life	Life		Life	
Michigan	8			6	4		6	4
Minnesota	6			6	4		4	2
Mississippi	8		4	4		4		4
Missouri	12	12		4–6	4			4

272

	To age 70	7 yrs. with reappointment for life	To age 70 / life	To age 70		To age 70	To age 70 / 3
Montana	6		4			2	2
Nebraska	6		4			4	2
Nevada	6		4			4	2
New Hampshire	To age 70		Life		4	To age 70	2
New Jersey	7 yrs. with reappointment for life						To age 70 / 3
New Mexico	8		6	2			2
New York	14	5	6–14	6			4
North Carolina	8		8		2–4	2	2–6
North Dakota	10	6	6		2		4
Ohio	6		6	6	4	6	
Oklahoma	6		4	2	2	2	2
Oregon	6		6	6	6	6	6
Pennsylvania	21	10	10	10	10	10	5
Rhode Island	Life		Life				
South Carolina	10		4	4	4	4	2
South Dakota	6	8	4		2	4	2
Tennessee	8	8	8				6
Texas	6	6	4		4		4
Utah	10		6	2		6	4
Vermont	2		2			2	2
Virginia	12	8	8		4		4
Washington	6		4				4
West Virginia	12		8		6	6	4
Wisconsin	10		6		6	2–6	2
Wyoming	8		6				2
Puerto Rico	To age 70		12				4

† In addition, several states have established a number of specialized courts of limited jurisdiction, among them, juvenile courts, domestic relations courts, small claims courts, workmen's compensation courts, courts of industrial relations, and land courts.

* Adapted from *The Book of the States, 1960–1961*, XIII (Chicago: The Council of State Governments, 1960), 104.

State	Regular Term (in years)	Maximum Consecutive Terms Allowed by Constitution	Annual Salary
Alabama	4	(a)	$25,000
Alaska	4	2	25,000
Arizona	2		18,500
Arkansas	2		10,000
California	4		40,000
Colorado	4		20,000
Connecticut	4		15,000
Delaware	4	2	17,500
Florida	4	(a)	22,500
Georgia	4	(a)	12,000(d)
Hawaii	4		25,000
Idaho	4		12,500
Illinois	4		30,000
Indiana	4	(a)	15,000
Iowa	2		20,000
Kansas	2		16,500
Kentucky	4	(a)	18,000
Louisiana	4	(a)	18,000
Maine	4		10,000(e)
Maryland	4	2	15,000
Massachusetts	2		20,000
Michigan	2		22,500
Minnesota	2(b)		19,000
Mississippi	4	(a)	15,000
Missouri	4	(a)	25,000

(a) Governor cannot succeed himself.
(b) Four-year term effective with election in 1962.
(c) Nomination for third successive term prohibited by state law.
(d) Minimum: Acts 1953 provided a minimum salary for elected officials with an

Forms of Government in Cities with 5,000 or more People *

Population Group	Number of Cities Covered	Mayor-Council Number	Mayor-Council Per Cent	Commission Number	Commission Per Cent	Council-Manager Number	Council-Manager Per Cent
Over 500,000	20	16	80.0	0	0.0	4	20.0
250,000 to 500,000	30	13	43.3	5	16.7	12	40.0
100,000 to 250,000	80	30	37.5	11	13.8	39	48.8
50,000 to 100,000	190	67	35.3	27	14.2	96	50.5
25,000 to 50,000	388	132	34.0	51	13.1	205	52.8
10,000 to 25,000	1,005	499	49.7	101	10.0	405	40.3
5,000 to 10,000	1,257	838	66.7	66	5.2	353	28.1
All cities over 5,000	2,970ª	1,595	53.7	261	8.8	1,114	37.5

ª Not included in this table are Washington, D. C., 15 cities with town-meeting government, 19 with representative town-meeting government, and 43 other cities for which no information was obtained.

* From *The Municipal Year Book, 1961* (Chicago: The International City Managers' Association, 1961), p. 76.

and Salaries of Governors *

State	Regular Term (in years)	Maximum Consecutive Terms Allowed by Constitution	Annual Salary
Montana	4		12,500
Nebraska	2		11,000
Nevada	4		18,000
New Hampshire	2		15,000
New Jersey	4	2	30,000
New Mexico	2	2	17,500
New York	4		50,000
North Carolina	4	(a)	15,000
North Dakota	2		10,000(f)
Ohio	4		25,000
Oklahoma	4	(a)	15,000
Oregon	4	2	17,500
Pennsylvania	4	(a)	35,000
Rhode Island	2		15,000
South Carolina	4	(a)	15,000
South Dakota	2	2(c)	13,000
Tennessee	4	(a)	12,000
Texas	2		25,000
Utah	4		12,000
Vermont	2		12,500
Virginia	4	(a)	20,000
Washington	4		15,000
West Virginia	4	(a)	17,500
Wisconsin	2		20,000
Wyoming	4		15,000

automatic increase of $800 for each four years of service.
  (e) Effective 1963—$15,000.
  (f) Plus $1,500 unaudited expense account.

   * Adapted from *The Book of the States, 1960-1961* XIII (Chicago: The Council of State Governments, 1960), 122, 126.

Typical County Government Organization

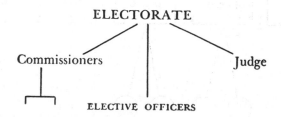

Town-Manager Plan

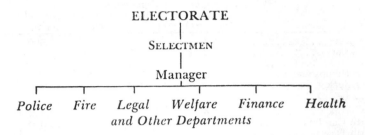

ELECTORATE
|
SELECTMEN
|
Manager

Police   Fire   Legal   Welfare   Finance   Health
and Other Departments

Commission Form of Government *

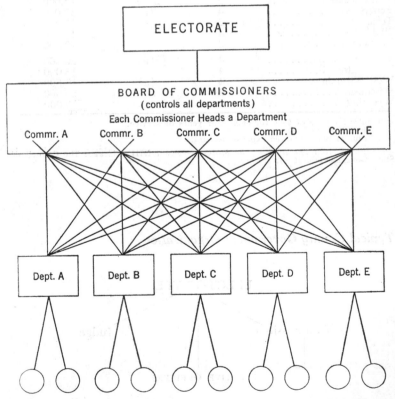

ELECTORATE

BOARD OF COMMISSIONERS
(controls all departments)
Each Commissioner Heads a Department

Commr. A   Commr. B   Commr. C   Commr. D   Commr. E

Dept. A   Dept. B   Dept. C   Dept. D   Dept. E

* Adapted and reprinted with permission from *Forms of Municipal Government* (New York: National Municipal League, 1961), p. 5.

Council-Manager Form of Government

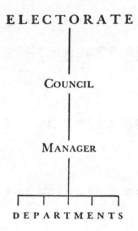

ELECTORATE

Council

Manager

DEPARTMENTS

Weak Mayor-Council Form of Government *

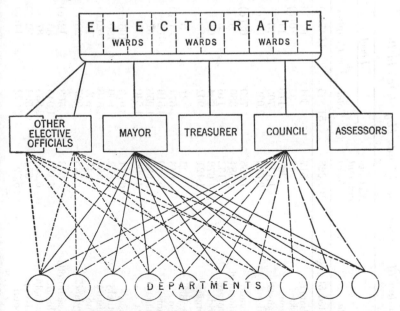

ELECTORATE

WARDS   WARDS   WARDS

| OTHER ELECTIVE OFFICIALS | MAYOR | TREASURER | COUNCIL | ASSESSORS |

DEPARTMENTS

* Adapted and reprinted with permission from *Forms of Municipal Government* (New York: National Municipal League, 1961), p. 3.

Number of Governmental Units (by State) in 1957 *

State	All Government Units(a)	Local Governments except School Districts					School Districts	Other Public School Systems(b)
		Total	Counties	Munici-palities	Town-ships	Special Districts		
United States	102,328	51,833	3,047(c)	17,183	17,198(d)	14,405	50,446	2,467
Alabama	617	504	67	318	0	119	112	0
Alaska	42	33	0(c)	31	0	2	8	21
Arizona	367	116	14	52	0	50	250	3
Arkansas	1,127	703	75	374	0	254	423	0
California	3,879	2,038	57(c)	331	0	1,650	1,840	0
Colorado	1,666	729	62(c)	246	0	421	936	0
Connecticut	384	380	8	33	152	187	3	167
Delaware	132	116	3	49	0	64	15	2
Florida	672	604	67	310	0	227	67	0
Georgia	1,121	992	159	508	0	255	198	0
Hawaii	22	21	3	1	0	17	0	1
Idaho	843	674	44(c)	199	0	431	168	0
Illinois	6,510	4,516	102	1,181	1,433	1,800	1,993	0
Indiana	2,989	1,958	92	544	1,009	313	1,030	0
Iowa	4,906	1,240	99	942	0	199	3,665	0
Kansas	6,214	3,073	105	610	1,550	808	3,140	0
Kentucky	822	600	120	323	0	157	221	0
Louisiana	584	516	62(c)	237	0	217	67	0
Maine	645	636	16	42	471	107	8	476
Maryland	328	327	23(c)	149	0	155	0	24
Massachusetts	573	568	12(c)	39	312	205	4	349
Michigan	5,160	1,945	83	498	1,262	102	3,214	0
Minnesota	6,298	2,833	87	826	1,828	92	3,464	15
Mississippi	672	592	82	262	0	248	79	82
Missouri	5,307	2,072	114(c)	803	328	827	3,234	0

Montana	1,503	353	56(c)	123	0	174	1,149	0
Nebraska	6,658	1,715	93	534	478	610	4,942	0
Nevada	110	92	17	17	0	58	17	0
New Hampshire	545	324	10	12	222	80	220	9
New Jersey	1,217	727	21	333	233	140	489	74
New Mexico	317	221	32	77	0	112	95	0
New York	4,189	2,524	57(c)	611	932	924	1,664	6
North Carolina	624	623	100	412	0	111	0	173
North Dakota	3,968	1,969	53	356	1,392	168	1,998	0
Ohio	3,667	2,498	99	915	1,335	160	1,168	0
Oklahoma	2,332	688	77	506	0	105	1,643	0
Oregon	1,526	799	36	213	0	550	726	0
Pennsylvania	5,073	2,655	66(c)	991	1,564	34	2,417	441
Rhode Island	91	90	0(c)	7	32	51	0	39
South Carolina	503	395	46	235	2	112	107	0
South Dakota	4,808	1,519	64(c)	306	1,080	69	3,288	0
Tennessee	560	545	95	255	0	195	14	137
Texas	3,485	1,692	254	793	0	645	1,792	7
Utah	398	357	29	210	0	118	40	0
Vermont	409	392	14	68	238	72	16	242
Virginia	367	366	98(c)	228	0	40	0	130
Washington	1,577	1,105	39	252	69	745	471	0
West Virginia	362	306	55	219	0	32	55	0
Wisconsin	5,731	1,972	71	547	1,276	78	3,758	90
Wyoming	489	242	23(c)	86	0	133	246	0
District of Columbia	2	2	0	1	0	1	0	1

(a) Includes federal government and the 50 states not shown in distribution by type.
(b) Includes other local public school systems operated as part of state, county, municipal, or township governments and not included with the independent school district figure.
(c) Excludes areas corresponding to counties but having no organized county government.
(d) Includes "towns" in the six New England states, New York, and Wisconsin.

* Adapted from *The Municipal Year Book, 1961* (Chicago: The International City Managers' Association, 1961), p. 16.

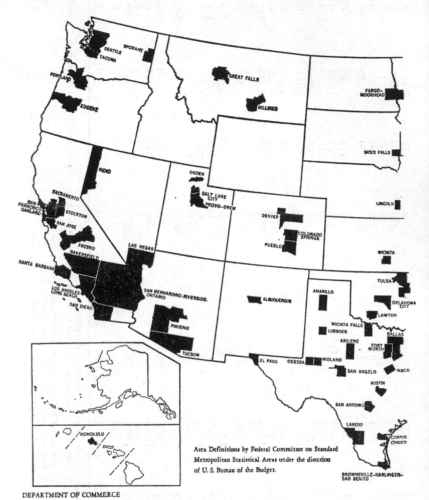

Area Definitions by Federal Committee on Standard
Metropolitan Statistical Areas under the direction
of U. S. Bureau of the Budget.

DEPARTMENT OF COMMERCE

* Adapted from *Standard Metropolitan Statistical Areas* (Washington [Bureau of

The Largest Standard Metropolitan Statistical Areas †

Standard Metropolitan Statistical Area	1960 Population	1950 Population	Per Cent Increase
New York	10,602,382	9,555,943	11.0
Los Angeles–Long Beach	6,668,975	4,367,911	52.7
Chicago	6,171,517	5,177,868	19.2
Philadelphia (Pa.–N.J.) *	4,301,283	3,671,048	17.2
Detroit	3,743,447	3,016,197	24.1
San Francisco–Oakland	2,725,841	2,240,767	21.6
Boston	2,566,732	2,410,572	6.5
Pittsburgh	2,392,086	2,213,236	8.1
St. Louis (Mo.–Ill.) *	2,046,477	1,719,288	19.0
Washington (D.C.–Md.–Va.) *	1,967,682	1,464,089	34.4
Cleveland	1,786,740	1,465,511	21.9
Baltimore	1,707,462	1,405,399	21.5
Newark	1,682,882	1,468,458	14.6
Minneapolis–St. Paul	1,474,149	1,151,053	28.1
Buffalo	1,301,604	1,089,230	19.5
Houston	1,236,704	806,701	53.3
Patterson–Clifton–Passaic (N.J.)	1,183,514	876,232	35.1
Seattle	1,098,741	844,572	30.1
Milwaukee	1,184,806	956,948	23.8
Dallas	1,071,003	743,501	44.0
Cincinnati (O.–Ky.) *	1,067,669	904,402	18.1
Kansas City (Mo.–Kans.) *	1,034,150	814,357	27.0
Atlanta	1,010,577	726,989	39.0
San Diego	1,000,856	556,808	79.7

* This standard metropolitan statistical area spans territory in 2 states.

† Adapted from *The Municipal Yearbook, 1961* (Chicago: The International City Managers' Association, 1961), p. 162.

City Employment and Payrolls for October, 1960 *

NOTE: Because of rounding detail may not add to totals.

Population Group	Number of Cities a	Full- and Part-Time Employees		Average Monthly Earnings of Full-Time Employees	
		Total Number b	Monthly Payroll b (in thousands)	City Operated Schools	All Other
Total, all cities	18,043	1,691,947	$538,447.2	$502	$387
Cities over 1,000,000	5	396,649	178,768.4	573	453
500,000 to 1,000,000	17	205,188	85,802.4	527	417
300,000 to 500,000	21	111,162	43,124.1	480	385
200,000 to 300,000	18	63,451	23,704.1	480	362
100,000 to 200,000	69	136,539	50,482.7	487	367
50,000 to 100,000	180	155,987	57,616.2	493	372
25,000 to 50,000	365	146,736	50,365.2	472	354
Less than 25,000	17,368	476,235	93,584.1	405	311

a Preliminary as of April, 1960.

b Includes school information only for those school systems which are operated as part of the general city government.

From *The Municipal Year Book, 1961* (Chicago: The International City Managers' Association, 1961), p. 162.

Interstate Metropolitan Areas in 1960 *

Metropolitan Area	State Territory Included ᵃ	Number of County Areas	Population
New York	New York–Northeastern New Jersey ᵇ	13ᶜ	14,759,429
Chicago	Illinois–Northwestern Indiana ᵈ	8	6,794,461
Philadelphia	Pennsylvania–New Jersey	8	4,342,897
St. Louis	Missouri–Illinois	6	2,060,103
Washington	District of Columbia–Maryland–Virginia	7	2,001,897
Cincinnati	Ohio–Kentucky	3	1,071,624
Kansas City	Missouri–Kansas	4	1,039,493
Portland	Oregon–Washington	4	821,897
Providence–Pawtucket	Rhode Island–Massachusetts	8	816,148
Louisville	Kentucky–Indiana	3	725,139
Allentown–Bethlehem–Easton	Pennsylvania–New Jersey	3	492,168
Omaha	Nebraska–Iowa	3	457,873
Wilmington	Delaware–New Jersey	2	366,157
Chattanooga	Tennessee–Georgia	2	283,169
Duluth–Superior	Minnesota–Wisconsin	2	276,596
Davenport–Rock Island–Moline	Iowa–Illinois	2	270,058
Huntington–Ashland	West Virginia–Kentucky–Ohio	4	254,780
Columbus	Georgia–Alabama	3	217,985
Augusta	Georgia–South Carolina	2	216,639
Evansville	Indiana–Kentucky	2	199,313
Wheeling	West Virginia–Ohio	3	190,342
Lawrence–Haverhill	Massachusetts–New Hampshire	2	187,601
Steubenville–Weirton	Ohio–West Virginia	3	167,756
Fall River	Massachusetts–Rhode Island	2	138,156
Fargo–Moorhead	North Dakota–Minnesota	2	106,027
Texarkana	Texas–Arkansas	2	91,657

ᵃ The state containing the central city (or containing the most populous central city when there are two or more) is listed first.

ᵇ A "standard consolidated area," consisting of four standard metropolitan statistical areas (New York, Newark, Jersey City, and Paterson-Clifton-Passaic) plus Middlesex and Somerset Counties, N. J.

ᶜ Counting New York City as a single area, rather than in terms of its five component "counties."

ᵈ A "standard consolidated area," consisting of two standard metropolitan statistical areas (Chicago and Gary-Hammond-East Chicago).

* From "Government Structure, Organization, and Planning in Metropolitan Areas" (Washington: U. S. Government Printing Office, 1961), p. 13.

Per Cent of State Population Included in Standard Metropolitan Statistical Areas in 1960 *

State or Jurisdiction	Per Cent in SMSA's	State or Jurisdiction	Per Cent in SMSA's
District of Columbia	100.0	Louisiana	50.0
California	86.5	Indiana	48.1
Rhode Island	86.2	Wisconsin	46.3
New York	85.5	Georgia	46.0
Massachusetts	85.2	Tennessee	45.8
Hawaii	79.1	Oklahoma	43.9
New Jersey	78.9	Nebraska	37.6
Maryland	78.2	Kansas	37.4
Pennsylvania	77.9	Kentucky	34.1
Connecticut	77.6	Iowa	33.2
Illinois	76.9	South Carolina	32.2
Nevada	74.2	West Virginia	30.9
Michigan	73.1	New Mexico	27.6
Arizona	71.4	North Carolina	24.6
Ohio	69.5	Montana	22.6
Delaware	68.9	Maine	19.7
Colorado	68.0	Arkansas	19.1
Utah	67.5	New Hampshire	17.7
Florida	65.6	South Dakota	12.7
Texas	63.4	North Dakota	10.6
Washington	63.1	Mississippi	8.6
Alabama	63.0	Alaska	0.0
Missouri	57.9	Idaho	0.0
Minnesota	51.3	Vermont	0.0
Virginia	50.9	Wyoming	0.0
Oregon	54.0		

* From "Government Structure, Organization, and Planning in Metropolitan Areas" (Washington: U. S. Government Printing Office, 1961), p. 6.

Estimated Public School and Per Pupil Expenditures: 1958-59 *

State or Other Jurisdiction	Total Current Expense (in thousands)	Current Expense per Pupil a	Total Capital Outlay (in thousands)	Total Expenditures d (in thousands)
Alabama	$ 114,000	$164.00	$ 19,000	$ 133,000
Alaska	17,500	520.00	3,000	20,500
Arizona	78,078	331.65	13,500	91,578
Arkansas	74,500	201.00	19,000	93,500
California	1,250,000	390.00	500,000	1,750,000
Colorado	120,000	355.00	28,000	148,000
Connecticut	156,000	380.00	45,000	201,000
Delaware	28,000	420.00	10,000	38,000
Florida	242,574	295.00	107,561	350,135
Georgia	207,500	208.00	40,000	247,500
Hawaii	34,500	275.00	6,500	41,000
Idaho	37,000	270.00	10,000	47,000
Illinois	565,000	410.00	210,000	775,000
Indiana	270,000	325.00	70,000	340,000
Iowa	180,000	346.00	50,000	230,000

284

Estimated Public School and Per Pupil Expenditures: 1958-59 (cont.) *

State or Other Jurisdiction	Total Current Expense (in thousands)	Current Expense per Pupil[a]	Total Capital Outlay (in thousands)	Total Expenditures[d] (in thousands)
Kansas	130,000	330.00	40,000	170,000
Kentucky	115,000	205.00	31,000	146,000
Louisiana	196,000	330.00	65,000	261,000
Maine	43,500 [b]	255.00 [b]	6,000 [b]	49,500 [b]
Maryland	190,583	366.00	76,323	266,906
Massachusetts	290,000	375.00	70,000	360,000
Michigan	550,000	375.99	250,000	800,000
Minnesota	214,000	358.00	100,000	314,000
Mississippi	81,500	181.00	18,000	99,500
Missouri	219,000	335.00	70,000	289,000
Montana	48,582	373.00	9,000	57,582
Nebraska	73,000	290.00	15,000	88,000
Nevada	20,092	410.00	7,500	27,592
New Hampshire	29,684	326.00	5,989	35,673
New Jersey	409,000	463.00	140,000	549,000
New Mexico	79,380	390.00	8,000	87,380
New York	1,280,000	535.00	612,000	1,892,000
North Carolina	225,000 [b]	220.00 [b]	45,000 [b]	270,000 [b]
North Dakota	37,500	310.00	8,500	46,000
Ohio	505,000	330.00	180,000	685,000
Oklahoma	130,000	279.00	32,000	162,000
Oregon	136,000	413.00	35,000	171,000
Pennsylvania	645,000	370.00	228,500	873,500
Rhode Island	44,000 [b]	380.00 [b]	4,200 [b]	48,200 [b]
South Carolina	110,000 [b]	215.00 [b]	36,000 [b]	146,000 [b]
South Dakota	43,000	333.00	9,500	52,500
Tennessee	147,942	205.00	30,000	177,942
Texas	530,000	308.00	115,000	645,000
Utah	57,300	280.00	27,000	84,300
Vermont	22,000	305.00	10,500	32,500
Virginia	185,000	245.00	60,000	245,000
Washington	212,000	375.00	60,000	272,000
West Virginia	98,500	225.00	9,600	108,100
Wisconsin	220,000	360.00	85,000	305,000
Wyoming	28,000	435.00	10,000 [b]	38,000 [b]
District of Columbia	44,330	434.43	8,920	53,250
Total	$10,764,545	$340.00 [c]	$3,650,093	$14,414,638

Research Division, National Education Association, *Estimates of School Statistics, 1958-59*, December, 1958. Tables 10 and 13, pp. 27 and 30. Except where otherwise indicated the estimates are based on information from state departments of education and education associations.

[a] Current expense per pupil in average daily attendance.

[b] Estimated by National Education Association Research Division.

[c] Total excludes Hawaii.

[d] Since a significant percentage of the children in states such as Massachusetts and Rhode Island attend private schools, these figures are not always a good indication of the total expenditures for education.

* Adapted from *The Book of the States, 1960-61*, XIII (Chicago: The Council of State Governments, 1960), 297.

Amounts Expended for Public Health Services (by State) in 1958 *

State	Totals Expended	State Funds	Local Funds	Private Agencies' Funds	Total Federal Funds
Alabama	6,265,537	2,148,588	2,201,413	46,276	1,869,260
Alaska	3,121,636	541,915	90,730	39,465	2,449,526
Arizona	1,875,611	520,296	884,025	23,271	448,019
Arkansas	3,159,633	1,386,916	657,793	1,199	1,113,725
California	42,609,014	16,210,088	22,224,296	450,408	3,724,222
Colorado	3,843,737	849,243	2,154,962		839,532
Connecticut	5,521,762	3,062,706	1,273,387	352,287	833,382
Delaware	1,099,220	765,632		5,856	327,732
Florida	13,020,431	7,784,124	3,715,308	12,099	1,508,900
Georgia	11,965,300	5,760,844	4,291,151	18,053	1,895,252
Hawaii	4,470,021	2,862,452		90,997	1,516,572
Idaho	1,404,716	588,617	313,718	8,482	493,899
Illinois	16,155,517	6,450,541	7,379,398		2,325,578
Indiana	5,863,742	2,471,729	1,936,272	197,842	1,257,899
Iowa	3,119,209	1,687,366	347,661	187,734	896,448
Kansas	3,557,401	1,380,324	1,397,357		779,720
Kentucky	6,596,953	3,358,128	1,596,370	58,797	1,583,658
Louisiana	8,127,949	4,104,210	2,564,173	9,528	1,450,038
Maine	1,777,969	1,336,251			441,718
Maryland	11,282,226	5,859,774	4,232,369	16,344	1,173,739
Massachusetts	13,549,630	9,815,641	1,919,220	68,077	1,746,692
Michigan	19,075,973	7,259,634	9,234,595	390,257	2,191,487
Minnesota	5,629,986	2,321,369	1,855,927	42,942	1,409,748
Mississippi	4,661,508	1,954,349	1,275,283	11,146	1,420,720
Missouri	8,562,947	2,657,340	4,214,844	237,160	1,453,603

Montana	1,222,119	492,473	218,737	10,000	500,909
Nebraska	1,800,508	554,114	702,968	38,503	504,923
Nevada	794,542	308,462	96,561	13,514	376,005
New Hampshire	1,105,791	771,753		3,550	330,488
New Jersey	12,477,359	3,292,389	7,885,352	50,000	1,249,618
New Mexico	2,112,858	921,964	490,747	15,000	685,147
New York	76,327,223	44,206,204	27,692,270	594,415	3,834,334
North Carolina	10,698,075	3,434,990	4,890,968	13,883	2,358,234
North Dakota	1,405,033	399,514	509,074	30,000	466,445
Ohio	18,944,860	3,840,343	11,232,134	1,423,888	2,448,495
Oklahoma	4,586,821	2,254,954	1,204,578	34,244	1,093,045
Oregon	4,418,977	1,576,103	2,194,890	3,011	644,973
Pennsylvania	27,389,839	16,870,534	6,368,755	976,395	3,183,155
Rhode Island	1,587,845	1,089,022			498,823
South Carolina	5,129,406	2,633,108	1,071,148		1,425,150
South Dakota	987,667	362,738	181,289	83,226	360,414
Tennessee	8,260,812	3,740,753	2,433,562	138,330	1,948,167
Texas	17,087,673	7,432,158	6,467,563		3,187,952
Utah	1,961,002	774,475	585,973	62,587	537,967
Vermont	1,502,120	1,088,872		26,573	386,675
Virginia	11,554,602	5,419,400	4,455,281	353,498	1,679,921
Washington	7,340,798	1,617,715	4,525,554		844,031
West Virginia	3,403,001	1,334,896	1,118,637	21,639	927,829
Wisconsin	7,723,949	2,496,992	4,090,617	58,803	1,077,537
Wyoming	759,191	251,191	160,736	12,000	335,264
Totals	$453,734,478	$214,445,203	$164,337,646	$6,415,110	$68,536,519

* Adapted from *The Book of the States, 1960-1961* XIII (Chicago: The Council of State Governments, 1960), 346-347. [Reported to the U. S. Public Health Service and Children's Bureau by state health departments and other state agencies.]

State Tax Collections (in Thousands of Dollars), by Major Source and by States, 1960 *

State	Total	Sales and gross receipts	Licenses	Individual income	Corporation net income	Property	Death and gift	Severance	Poll	Document and stock transfer	Other
States Using Tax	50	50	50	33	37	45	49	29	10	15	10
Total	18,017,359	10,498,189	2,485,015	a 2,213,813	a 1,180,151	607,246	419,162	420,744	9,578	109,183	74,278
Alabama	274,239	193,973	21,583	31,879	9,674	13,156	705	1,567	377	1,266	
Alaska	27,110	7,954	5,798	8,903	1,692	b 542	54	1,449	718		59
Arizona	164,153	104,637	13,750	10,000	6,833	28,470	463	5,165			
Arkansas	158,118	112,971	20,784	9,774	8,862	321	241	1,184			
California	2,124,369	1,287,861	176,824	245,797	240,064	125,459	47,180				
Colorado	192,542	100,710	26,434	34,542	10,723	10,646	6,638	2,811			38
Connecticut	238,124	165,843	24,576		30,773	12	16,920				
Delaware	70,776	17,585	16,390	26,393	7,478	1,842	1,088				
Florida	521,682	394,114	84,182			18,629	5,488	43		19,226	
Georgia	369,080	281,517	25,231	36,442	23,634	1,275	981				
Hawaii	124,230	87,756	1,460	28,778	5,649		587				
Idaho	68,999	24,171	15,448	20,195	5,778	2,572	751	84			
Illinois	836,372	690,306	123,121			918	22,027				
Indiana	399,379	330,498	50,275			9,967	7,563	353	723		
Iowa	265,787	163,646	50,728	36,671	3,807	3,641	7,294	421			
Kansas	206,622	133,485	28,606	24,000	8,434	7,949	3,727	356			
Kentucky	228,507	111,945	21,134	51,686	20,240	17,080	5,302			764	
Louisiana	452,705	224,530	37,980	12,500	18,331	14,880	7,311	137,173			
Maine	86,929	66,765	15,282			1,650	3,229				
Maryland	343,577	188,269	31,768	85,010	20,381	12,101	4,987		3	31	
Massachusetts	491,123	175,115	113,659	151,728	e 28,539	270	20,535			1,277	1,030
Michigan	913,920	613,608	163,934			51,170	12,124	792			d 72,292

288

Minnesota	351,923	123,900	54,235	89,328	39,840	22,518	7,335	14,558		209
Mississippi	194,300	141,409	15,466	7,639	13,460	4,448	666	10,778		434
Missouri	312,895	194,939	53,785	37,659	10,000	11,224	5,259	29		
Montana	64,868	29,990	8,527	10,707	4,671	6,247	1,775	2,951	195	
Nebraska	91,253	50,679	11,478			27,173	374	1,354		179
Nevada	43,478	33,568	7,841			1,841		49	1,444	
New Hampshire	41,757	24,762	9,433	1,581	27,690	2,366	2,093	78		17
New Jersey	365,232	203,793	110,428		[a]	2,700	20,621			71
New Mexico	123,206	75,110	15,586	[a]7,101	256,309	8,234	676	16,482		
New York	1,961,008	614,013	201,621	756,364	51,516	3,474	71,611			57,616
North Carolina	459,373	240,859	57,314	91,814	1,414	11,155	6,644			
North Dakota	60,760	35,550	13,000	4,796		3,220	278	2,502		
Ohio	872,723	652,382	164,956	16,780	12,166	46,691	8,694	32,969		
Oklahoma	275,379	160,774	46,294	94,641	22,442	21	6,396	659		
Oregon	208,099	44,982	40,831		142,086	1,656	4,523			20,518
Pennsylvania	1,029,478	644,432	169,665				51,121			
Rhode Island	86,095	64,309	9,494	31,642	8,419	1,042	3,873			1,321
South Carolina	234,990	162,218	18,374		18,797	[b]3	1,596	466		446
South Dakota	52,828	40,955	10,082	5,218	395	[b]9	927			1,500
Tennessee	304,587	218,224	52,954		21,392	37,498	4,844			230
Texas	777,863	387,025	156,760	16,234	5,671	8,087	11,500	182,000	2,850	
Utah	103,460	58,859	9,723	11,373	2,219	339	1,017	3,869	790	65
Vermont	43,414	19,197	8,763	77,314	31,715	13,170	733		1,706	3,643
Virginia	291,664	115,530	43,073			34,017	5,176	272		
Washington	460,770	378,566	37,996	139,324	59,057	390	9,422	235	772	769
West Virginia	179,919	151,851	24,097			30,423	2,430	95		379
Wisconsin	426,234	129,050	54,025			6,750	14,039			
Wyoming	41,460	24,004	10,267				344			81

a Combined corporation and individual income taxes for New Mexico are tabulated with individual income taxes.

b Back taxes only; not included with number of states using tax.

c Corporation taxes measured in part by net income.

d Business Activities Tax.

* From "State Tax Collections in 1960" (Washington: Bureau of the Census [United States Department of Commerce], 1961), p. 5.

State Direct Expenditures (in Millions) *

Selected Years 1902–1959 [a]

Year	Total	General Expenditures								Insurance Trust	Liquor Stores
		Total General	Education	Highways	Welfare [b]	Health & Hospitals	Re-sources	General Control	Other [c]		
1902	$ 136	$ 134	$ 17	$ 74	$ 10	$ 32	$ 9	$ 23	$ 39	$	$ 2
1913	301	297	55	26	16	53	14	38	95		
1922	1,085	1,031	164	303	38	125	61	69	271	54	
1932	2,028	1,965	278	843	74	215	119	114	322	63	
1942	3,563	2,769	391	790	523	299	159	164	443	505	288
1952	10,790	8,653	1,494	2,556	1,410	1,132	539	361	1,161	1,413	723
1959	22,585	17,466	3,242	6,414	2,007	1,967	976	619	2,243	4,259	860

[a] Data for 1959 include Alaska. [b] Principally categorical public assistance.
[c] Includes police, housing and community redevelopment, miscellaneous veterans services, Employment Security Administration, nonhighway transportation, interest, and other and unallocable expenditures.

State Tax Collections (in Millions) by Source *

Selected Years 1902–1960

Year	Total	Sales or Gross Receipts	Motor Fuels Sales	Tobacco Products Sales	Alcoholic Beverages Sales & Licenses	Motor Vehicle & Operators' Licenses	Indi-vidual Income	Corpora-tion Income	Prop-erty	Death and Gift	Other
1902	$ 156								82		74
1913	301				2	5			140		154
1922	947		13			152	43	58	348	66	267
1932	1,890	7	527	19	1	335	74	79	328	148	353
1942	3,903	632	940	130	313	431	249	269	264	110	502
1952	9,857	2,229	1,870	449	519	924	913	838	370	211	1,262
1959	15,848	3,697	3,058	675	684	1,492	1,764	1,001	566	347	2,171
1960	18,017	4,303	3,332	919	733	1,566	2,214	1,180	607	419	2,324

* From Facts and Figures on Government Finance, 1960–1961 (New York: Tax Foundation, Inc., 1961), pp. 156, 172–173, respectively.

Selected Years 1902–1959

Year	Total	Education b	Highways	Public Welfare	Health & Hospitals	Police & Fire	General Control	Other c
1902	$ 879	238	171	27	28	90	118	207
1913	1,767	522	393	36	55	164	173	424
1922	4,187	1,541	991	81	133	344	244	853
1932	5,800	2,033	898	370	241	513	356	1,389
1942	6,421	2,195	700	702	292	590	414	1,528
1952	17,444	6,824	2,094	1,378	1,053	1,419	832	3,844
1958	29,257	13,046	3,060	1,874	1,704	2,269	1,274	6,030
1959 a	31,421	14,041	3,178	2,012	1,874	2,396	1,384	6,535

a 1959 data include Alaska. b Principally elementary and secondary schools.
c Includes natural resources, sanitation, recreation, interest on general debt, housing and community redevelopment, nonhighway transportation, correction, local libraries, general public buildings, and other general government.

Local Revenue (in Millions) by Source *

Selected Years 1902–1959

Year	Total	Property	Sales & Gross Receipts	Net Income	License & Other	Charges & Misc.	Utility & Liquor Stores	Insurance Trust	Intergovernmental From States	Intergovernmental From Federal
1902	914	624			80	94	60	2	52	4
1913	1,755	1,192	3		113	232	116	16	91	6
1922	4,148	2,973	20		76	476	266	39	312	9
1932	6,192	4,159	26		89	605	463	68	801	10
1940	7,724	4,170	130	19	178	510	717		1,654	278
1952	19,398	8,282	627	93	465	2,205	2,184	262	5,044	237
1958	31,202	13,514	1,079	215	652	3,885	3,153	471	7,828	404
1959	33,423	14,417	1,150	230	734	4,202	3,451	500	8,250	489

* From Facts and Figures on Government Finance, 1960–1961 (New York: Tax Foundation, Inc., 1961), pp. 221, 231, respectively.

Trend of Federal, State, and Local Tax Receipts (in Millions) *
Selected Years 1902-1960 [a]

Year		Total	Federal	State	Local
1902	....	$ 1,373	$ 513	$ 156	$ 704
1913	........,..	2,271	662	301	1,308
1922	....	7,387	3,371	947	3,069
1927	....	9,451	3,364	1,608	4,479
1932	....	7,977	1,813	1,890	4,274
1934	....	8,854	2,942	1,979	3,933
1936	....	10,606	3,882	2,641	4,083
1938	....	14,188	5,877	3,834	4,477
1940	....	14,243	5,583	4,157	4,503
1942	....	22,962	13,351	4,979	4,632
1944	....	52,050	41,953	5,390	4,707
1946	....	49,018	37,887	5,971	5,160
1948	....	54,584	40,180	7,802	6,602
1950	......•...	54,799	37,853	8,958	7,988
1952	....	84,801	64,036	11,295	9,470
1953	....	89,778	67,496	11,922	10,360
1955	....	87,915	63,291	12,735	11,889
1956	....	100,025	72,340	14,690	12,995
1957	....	107,693	77,362	16,041	14,290
1958	....	108,593	76,716	16,412	15,465
1959 [b]	....	110,209	76,178	17,495	16,536
1960 [b]	....	126,600	88,400	20,200	18,000

[a] Includes social insurance taxes.
[b] 1960 estimated by Tax Foundation; data include Alaska beginning in 1959 and Hawaii in 1960.

* From *Facts and Figures on Government Finance, 1960-1961* (New York: Tax Foundation, Inc., 1961), p. 21.

Trend of State and Local Tax Receipts *
Selected Years 1902-1960

Year	State (Millions)	State (Per Capita)	Local (Millions)	Local (Per Capita)
1902	$ 156	2	$ 704	9
1913	301	3	1,308	14
1922	947	9	3,069	28
1932	1,890	15	4,274	34
1942	4,979	37	4,632	35
1952	11,295	74	9,470	62
1959	17,495	101	16,536	95
1960	20,200	114	18,000	102

* From *Facts and Figures on Government Finance, 1960-1961* (New York: Tax Foundation, Inc., 1961), pp. 21-22.

Trend of Federal, State, and Local Expenditures (in Millions) °
Selected Years 1902–1960 ª

Year	Total	Federal	State	Local
1902	$ 1,660	$ 572	$ 179	$ 909
1913	3,215	970	372	1,873
1922	9,297	3,763	1,261	4,273
1927	11,220	3,533	1,882	5,805
1932	12,437	4,266	2,562	5,609
1934	12,807	5,941	2,532	4,334
1936	16,758	9,165	3,144	4,449
1938	17,675	8,449	3,955	5,271
1940	20,417	10,061	4,545	5,811
1942	45,576	35,549	4,456	5,571
1944	109,947	100,520	4,062	5,365
1946	79,707	66,534	6,162	7,011
1948	55,081	35,592	9,531	9,959
1950	70,334	44,800	12,774	12,761
1952	99,847	71,568	13,330	14,948
1953	110,054	79,990	14,095	15,969
1955	110,717	73,441	17,400	19,876
1956	115,796	75,991	18,379	21,426
1957	125,463	81,783	20,405	23,274
1958	134,931	86,054	23,338	25,539
1959 ᵇ	145,748	93,531	25,106	27,111
1960 ᵇ	153,000	97,000	27,000	29,000

ª Grants-in-aid are counted as expenditures of the first disbursing unit. Total expenditures are shown as defined by the Bureau of the Census including insurance trust expenditures.
ᵇ 1960 estimated by Tax Foundation; data include Alaska beginning in 1959 and Hawaii in 1960.

* From *Facts and Figures on Government Finance, 1960-1961* (New York: Tax Foundation, Inc., 1961), p. 18.

Typical State Revenue Rates *

Tax	Basis	Rate
Motor fuel	gallon	5½%
Malt beverages	gallon	6½%
Alcoholic beverages	gallon	30¢–$2.25
Cigarettes	package	6¢
Meals	$1.00 or more	5%
Earned income	net inc. taxable	3.075%
Interest, dividends, gains	net inc. taxable	7.380%
Annuities	net inc. taxable	1.845%
Corporations	(1)	(1)
National banks and trust cos.	net income	8%
Savings banks	average deposit	½%
Insurance companies	gross premiums	2%
Public utilities	net income	4.92%
Racing	total wagered	3½–8¾%
Inheritance	appraised value	1.23–18.45%

(1) Total of $6.15 per $1,000 of corporate excess or value of Massachusetts tangibles plus 6.765% of net income allocable to the Commonwealth; with certain minimum measures.

* Adapted from *Massachusetts State Budget in Brief* (Boston: Budget Bureau of the Commonwealth of Massachusetts, 1961), p. 26.

Federal Aid (in Millions) to State, Local Governments *

State	1939	1949	1959
Total	$518.3	$1,848.5	$6,306.5
Alabama	8.2	35.5	131.5
Alaska	.5	1.9	36.5
Arizona	4.5	15.5	70.1
Arkansas	6.3	27.6	90.7
California	37.9	145.5	552.7
Colorado	10.6	33.4	99.4
Connecticut	5.1	15.3	63.8
Delaware	1.4	3.7	14.4
Florida	6.4	41.8	142.9
Georgia	7.7	45.9	154.3
Hawaii	1.5	8.0	19.2
Idaho	4.5	10.7	43.6
Illinois	24.0	92.6	272.3
Indiana	15.2	34.1	97.2
Iowa	13.1	33.9	110.1
Kansas	8.4	29.1	100.3
Kentucky	7.6	31.3	124.3
Louisiana	7.3	60.9	198.0
Maine	4.6	11.2	41.2
Maryland	6.0	17.8	85.1
Massachusetts	21.7	57.2	157.1
Michigan	18.4	74.9	201.5
Minnesota	15.7	41.6	127.7
Mississippi	5.9	29.7	108.7
Missouri	14.9	66.5	205.5
Montana	3.8	14.9	49.0
Nebraska	8.0	18.8	49.5
Nevada	3.1	7.5	26.7
New Hampshire	2.0	6.9	24.9
New Jersey	9.6	33.2	100.0
New Mexico	3.9	15.0	78.5
New York	41.9	116.2	451.2
North Carolina	10.2	38.7	140.5
North Dakota	4.5	12.6	43.1
Ohio	25.9	75.5	318.2
Oklahoma	14.1	60.0	177.0
Oregon	6.7	25.9	93.7
Pennsylvania	30.9	94.3	319.6
Rhode Island	2.6	9.0	30.9
South Carolina	5.8	25.9	79.3
South Dakota	5.2	13.7	35.6
Tennessee	8.9	44.6	137.8
Texas	25.3	117.3	353.7
Utah	5.4	12.9	50.2
Vermont	2.0	6.1	18.3
Virginia	7.0	21.3	108.9
Washington	10.9	44.1	138.9
West Virginia	5.9	19.1	77.7
Wisconsin	14.0	39.2	104.8
Wyoming	3.7	12.2	49.2

* From *Facts and Figures* on *Government Finance, 1960-1961* (New York: Tax Foundation, Inc., 1961), p. 90.

Federal Aid to State and Local Governments by Form of Aid, 1961 *

Form of Aid and Function	Millions
Total Aid to State and Local Governments	$7,122.8
Grants-in-Aid	6,811.5
Veterans Services and Benefits	8.2
Labor and Welfare	3,297.3
Public Assistance	2,083.0
Labor and Manpower	303.5
Education	319.5
Health	300.2
Other Welfare	291.1
Agriculture and Agricultural Resources	314.8
Natural Resources	33.5
Commerce and Housing	3,111.6
Transportation and Communication	2,807.7
Housing and Community Development	303.9
General Government	46.0
Shared Revenue	123.9
Natural Resources	100.1
General Government	23.8
Loans and Repayable Advances (net of collections)	187.4
Labor and Welfare	.7
Agriculture and Agricultural Resources	1.1
Natural Resources	19.8
Commerce and Housing	145.2
General Government	20.6

* From *Facts and Figures on Government Finance, 1960-1961* (New York: Tax Foundation, Inc., 1961), p. 89.

MODEL STATE CONSTITUTION (Sixth Edition)*

PREAMBLE

We, the people of the State of ...., recognizing the rights and duties of this state as a part of the federal system of government, re-affirm our adherence to the Constitution of the United States of America; and in order to assure the state government power to act for the good order of the state and the liberty, health, safety and welfare of the people, we do ordain and establish this Constitution.

ARTICLE I: Bill of Rights

Section 1.01. Freedom of Religion, Speech, Press, Assembly and Petition. No law shall be enacted respecting an establishment of religion, or prohibiting the free exercise thereof, or abridging the freedom of speech or of the press, or the right of the people peaceably to assemble and to petition the government for a redress of grievances.

Section 1.02. Due Process and Equal Protection. No person shall be deprived of life, liberty or property without due process of law, nor be denied the equal protection of the laws, nor be denied the enjoyment of his civil rights or be discriminated against in the exercise thereof because of sex, race, national origin, religion or ancestry.

Section 1.03. Searches and Seizures and Interceptions.

(a) The right of the people to be secure in their persons, houses, papers and effects, against unreasonable searches and seizures shall not be violated, and no warrants shall issue, but upon probable cause, supported by oath or affirmation, and particularly describing the place to be searched and the persons or things to be seized.

(b) The right of the people to be secure against unreasonable interception of telephone, telegraph and other electronic means of communication [, and against unreasonable interception of oral and other communications by electric or electronic methods,] shall not be violated, and no orders and warrants for such interceptions shall issue but upon probable cause supported by oath or affirmation that evidence of crime may be thus obtained, and particularly identifying the means of communication, and the person or persons whose communications are to be intercepted.

(c) Evidence obtained in violation of this section shall not be admissible in any court against any person.

Section 1.04. Self-Incrimination. No person shall be compelled to give testimony which might tend to incriminate him.

Section 1.05. Writ of Habeas Corpus. The privilege of the writ of habeas corpus shall not be suspended, unless when in cases of rebellion or invasion the public safety may require it.

Section 1.06. Rights of Accused Persons.

(a) In all criminal prosecutions, the accused shall enjoy the right to a speedy and public trial, to be informed of the nature and cause of the

* Prepared by the Committee on State Government of the National Municipal League and reprinted with permission from the League.

accusation, to be confronted with the witnesses against him, to have compulsory process for obtaining witnesses in his favor, and to have the assistance of counsel for his defense. In prosecutions for felony, the accused shall also enjoy the right of trial by an impartial jury of the county [or other appropriate political subdivision of the state] wherein the crime shall have been committed, or of another county, if a change of venue has been granted, and he shall have the right to have counsel appointed for him.

(b) All persons shall, before conviction, be bailable by sufficient sureties, but bail may be denied to persons charged with capital offenses or offenses punishable by life imprisonment, giving due weight to the evidence and to the nature and circumstances of the event. Excessive bail shall not be required, nor excessive fines imposed, nor cruel or unusual punishment inflicted.

(c) No person shall be twice put in jeopardy for the same offense.

Section 1.07. Political Tests for Public Office. No oath, declaration or political test shall be required for any public office or employment other than the following oath or affirmation: "I do solemnly swear (or affirm) that I will support and defend the Constitution of the United States, and the constitution of the state of ...., and that I will faithfully discharge the duties of the office of .... the best of my ability."

ARTICLE II: POWERS OF THE STATE

Section 2.01. Powers of Government. The enumeration in this constitution of specified powers and functions shall be construed neither as a grant nor as a limitation of the powers of state government, but the state government shall have all of the powers not denied by this constitution or by or under the Constitution of the United States.

ARTICLE III: SUFFRAGE AND ELECTIONS

Section 3.01. Qualifications for Voting. Every citizen of the age of [ ] years and a resident of the state for three months shall have the right to vote in the election of all officers that may be elected by the people, and upon all questions that may be submitted to the voters; but the legislature may by law establish 1) minimum periods of local residence, not exceeding three months, 2) a reasonable literacy test to determine ability, except for physical cause, to read and write English, and 3) disqualifications for voting for mental incompetency or conviction of felony.

Section 3.02. Legislature to Prescribe for Exercise of Suffrage. The legislature shall by law define residence for voting purposes, insure secrecy in voting, and provide for the registration of voters, absentee voting, the administration of elections and the nomination of candidates.

ARTICLE IV: THE LEGISLATURE

Section 4.01. Legislative Power. The legislative power of the state shall be vested in the legislature.

Section 4.02. Composition of the Legislature. The legislature shall be composed of a single chamber consisting of one member to represent each legislative district. The number of members shall be prescribd by law, but shall not be less than .... nor exceed .... Each member of the legislature shall be a qualified voter of the state, and shall be at least .... years of age.

Bicameral Alternative: Section 4.02. *Composition of the Legislature.* The legislature shall be composed of a senate and an assembly. The number of members of each house of the legislature shall be prescribed by law, but the number of assemblymen shall not be less than ...... nor exceed ......, and the number of senators shall not exceed one-third, as near as may be, the number of assemblymen. Each assemblyman shall represent one assembly district, and each senator shall represent one senate district. Each member of the legislature shall be a qualified voter of the state, and shall be at least ...... years of age.

Section 4.03. *Election of Members.* The members of the legislature shall be elected by the qualified voters of the state for a term of two years.

Bicameral Alternative: Section 4.03. *Election and Term of Members.* Assemblymen shall be elected by the qualified voters of the state for a term of two years, and senators for a term of six years. One-third of the senators shall be elected every two years.

Section 4.04. *Legislative Districts.*

(a) For the purpose of electing members of the legislature, the state shall be divided into as many districts as there shall be members of the legislature. Each district shall consist of compact and contiguous territory. All districts shall be so nearly equal in population that the district with the greatest population shall not exceed the district with the least population by more than [   ] per cent thereof. In determining the population of each district, inmates of such public or private institutions as prisons or other places of correction, hospitals for the insane, or other institutions housing persons who are disqualified from voting by law shall not be counted.

(b) Immediately following each decennial census, the governor shall appoint a board of [   ] qualified voters to make recommendations within 90 days of their appointment concerning the redistricting of the state. The governor shall publish the recommendations of the board when received. The governor shall promulgate a redistricting plan within 90 to 120 days after appointment of the board, whether or not it has made its recommendations. The governor shall accompany his plan with a message explaining his reasons for any changes from the recommendations of the board. The governor's redistricting plan shall be published in the manner provided for acts of the legislature and shall have the force of law upon such publication. Upon the application of any qualified voter, the supreme court, in the exercise of original exclusive and final jurisdiction, shall review the governor's redistricting plan and shall have jurisdiction to make orders to amend the plan to comply with the requirements of this constitution, or, if the governor has failed to promulgate a redistricting plan within the time provided, to make one or more orders establishing such a plan.

Bicameral Alternative: *Section 4.04. Legislative Districts.*

(a) For the purpose of electing members of the assembly, the state shall be divided into as many districts as there shall be members of the assembly. Each district shall consist of compact and contiguous territory. All districts shall be so nearly equal in population that the district with the greatest population shall not exceed the district with the least population by more than [ ] per cent thereof. In determining the population of each district, inmates of such public or private institutions as prisons or other places of correction, hospitals for the insane, or other institutions housing persons who are disqualified from voting by law shall not be counted.

(b) For the purpose of electing members of the senate the state shall be divided into as many districts as there shall be members of the senate. Each senate district shall consist of three assembly districts which together form a compact and contiguous territory.

(c) Immediately following each decennial census, the governor shall appoint a board of [ ] qualified voters to make recommendations within 90 days of their appointment concerning the redistricting of the state. The governor shall publish the recommendations of the board when received. The governor shall promulgate a redistricting plan within 90 to 120 days after appointment of the board, whether or not it has made its recommendations. The governor shall accompany his plan with a message explaining his reasons for any changes from the recommendations of the board. The governor's redistricting plan shall be published in the manner provided for acts of the legislature and shall have the force of law upon such publication. Upon the application of any qualified voter, the supreme court, in the exercise of original exclusive and final jurisdiction, shall review the governor's redistricting plan and shall have jurisdiction to make orders to amend the plan to comply with the requirements of this constitution, or, if the governor has failed to promulgate a redistricting plan within the time provided, to make one or more orders establishing such a plan.

Section 4.05. Time of Election. Members of the legislature shall be elected at the regular election in each odd numbered year, beginning in 19. . . .

Section 4.06. Vacancies. When a vacancy occurs in the legislature, it shall be filled as provided by law.

Section 4.07. Compensation of Members. The members of the legislature shall receive an annual salary and such allowances as may be prescribed by law, but any increase or decrease in the amount thereof shall not apply to the legislature which enacted the same.

Section 4.08. Sessions. The legislature shall be a continuous body during the term for which its members are elected. It shall meet in regular sessions annually as provided by law. It may be convened at other times by the governor, or, at the written request of a majority of the members, by the presiding officer of the legislature.

Bicameral Alternative: *Section 4.08. Sessions.* The legislature shall be a continuous body during the term for which members of the assembly are elected. The legislature shall meet in regular sessions annually as provided by law. It may be convened at other times by the governor, or, at the written request of a majority of the members of each house, by the presiding officers of both houses.

Section 4.09. Organization and Procedure. The legislature shall be the final judge of the election and qualifications of its members, and may by law vest in the courts the trial and determination of contested elections of members. It shall choose its presiding officer from among its members, and it shall employ a secretary to serve for an indefinite term. It shall determine its rules of procedure; it may compel the attendance of absent members, discipline its members and, with the concurrence of two-thirds of all the members, expel a member, and it shall have power to compel the attendance and testimony of witnesses and the production of books and papers either before the legislature as a whole or before any committee thereof. The secretary of the legislature shall be its chief fiscal administrative and personnel officer, and shall perform such duties as the legislature may prescribe.

Bicameral Alternative: *Section 4.09. Organization and Procedure.* Each house of the legislature shall be the final judge of the election and qualifications of its members, and the legislature may by law vest in the courts the trial and determination of contested elections of members. Each house of the legislature shall choose its presiding officer from among its members, and it shall employ a secretary to serve for an indefinite term, and each house shall determine its rules of procedure; it may compel the attendance of absent members, discipline its members and, with the concurrence of two-thirds of all the members, expel a member, and it shall have power to compel the attendance and testimony of witnesses and the production of books and papers either before such house of the legislature as a whole or before any committee thereof. The secretary of each house of the legislature shall be its chief fiscal, administrative and personnel officer, and shall perform such duties as each such house of the legislature may prescribe.

Section 4.10. Legislative Immunity. For any speech or debate in the legislature, the members shall not be questioned in any other place.

Section 4.11. Special Legislation. The legislature shall pass no special or local act when a general act is or can be made applicable, and whether a general act is or can be made applicable shall be a matter for judicial determination.

Section 4.12. Transaction of Business. A majority of all the members of the legislature shall constitute a quorum to do business, but a smaller number may adjourn from day to day and compel the attendance of absent members. The legislature shall keep a journal of its proceedings which shall be published from day to day. The legislature shall prescribe the methods of voting on legislative matters, but a record vote, with the yeas and nays entered in the journal, shall be taken on any question on the demand of one-fifth of the members present.

Bicameral Alternative: *Section 4.12.* [Refer to "each house of the legislature" instead of "the legislature", wherever appropriate.]

Section 4.13. Committees. The legislature may establish such committees as may be necessary for the efficient conduct of its business. When a committee to which a bill has been assigned has not reported on it, one-third of all the members of the legislature shall have power to relieve it of further consideration. Adequate public notice of all committee hearings, with a clear statement of all subjects to be considered at each hearing shall be published in advance.

Bicameral Alternative. *Section 4.13.* [Refer to "each house of the legislature" instead of "the legislature", wherever appropriate.]

Section 4.14. Bills; Single Subject. The legislature shall enact no law except by bill, and every bill except bills for appropriations and bills for the codification, revision or rearrangement of existing laws shall be confined to one subject. All appropriation bills shall be limited to the subject of appropriations. Legislative compliance with the requirements of this section is a constitutional responsibility not subject to judicial review.

Section 4.15. Passage of Bills. No bill shall become a law unless it has been printed and upon the desks of the members in final form at least three days prior to final passage, and the majority of all the members has assented to it. The yeas and nays on final passage shall be entered in the journal. The legislature shall provide for the publication of all acts, and no act shall become effective until published as provided by law.

Bicameral Alternative: *Section 4.15.* [Refer to "each house of the legislature" instead of "the legislature", wherever appropriate.]

Section 4.16. Action by the Governor.

(a) When a bill has passed the legislature, it shall be presented to the governor, and, if the legislature is in session, it shall become law if the governor either signs or fails to veto it within fifteen days of presentation. If the legislature is in recess, or if the session of the legislature has expired during such fifteen-day period, it shall become law if he signs it within thirty days after such adjournment or expiration. If the governor does not approve a bill, he shall veto it and return it to the legislature either within fifteen days of presentation if the legislature is in session, or upon the reconvening of the legislature from its recess. Any bill so returned by the governor shall be reconsidered by the legislature and if, upon reconsideration two-thirds of all the members shall agree to pass the bill, it shall become law.

(b) The governor may strike out or reduce items in appropriation bills passed by the legislature, and the procedure in such cases shall be the same as in case of the disapproval of an entire bill by the governor.

Bicameral Alternative: *Section 4.16.* [Refer to "each house of the legislature" instead of "the legislature", wherever appropriate.]

Section 4.17. Post-Audit. The legislature shall appoint an auditor to serve at its pleasure. The auditor shall conduct post-audits as prescribed by law and shall report to the legislature and to the governor.

Section 4.18. Impeachment. The legislature may impeach the governor, the heads of principal departments, judicial officers, and such other officers of the state as may be made subject to impeachment by law, by a two-thirds vote of all the members, and shall provide by law procedures for the trial and removal from office, after conviction, of officers so impeached. No officer shall be convicted on impeachment by a vote of less than two-thirds of the members of the tribunal hearing the charges.

Bicameral Alternative: *Section 4.18.* [Refer to "each house of the legislature" instead of "the legislature", wherever appropriate.]

ARTICLE V: THE EXECUTIVE

Section 5.01. Executive Power. The executive power of the state shall be vested in a governor.

Section 5.02. Election and Qualifications of Governor. The governor shall be elected, at the regular election every other odd numbered year beginning in 19. . ., by the direct vote of the people, for a term of four years beginning on the first day of [December] [January] next following his election. Any qualified voter of the state who is at least . . . . years of age shall be eligible to the office of governor.

Section 5.03. Governor's Messages to the Legislature. The governor shall, at the beginning of each session, and may, at other times, give to the legislature information as to the affairs of the state, and recommend measures he considers necessary or desirable.

Section 5.04. Executive and Administrative Powers.

(a) The governor shall be responsible for the faithful execution of the laws. He may, by appropriate action or proceeding brought in the name of the state, enforce compliance with any constitutional or legislative mandate, or restrain violation of any constitutional or legislative power, duty, or right by an officer, department, or agency of the state or any of its civil divisions. This authority shall not authorize any action or proceeding against the legislature.

(b) The governor shall commission all officers of the state. He may at any time require information, in writing or otherwise, from the officers of any administrative department, office or agency upon any subject relating to their respective offices. He shall be commander-in-chief of the armed forces of the state, except when they shall be called into the service of the United States, and may call them out to execute the laws, to preserve order, to suppress insurrection or to repel invasion.

Section 5.05. Executive Clemency. The governor shall have power to grant reprieves, commutations and pardons, after conviction, for all offenses, and may delegate such powers, subject to such procedures as may be prescribed by law.

Section 5.06. Administrative Departments. All executive and administrative offices, agencies and instrumentalities of the state government, and their respective functions, powers and duties, shall be allocated by law among and within not more than twenty principal departments so as to group them as far as practicable according to major purposes. Regulatory, quasi-judicial and temporary agencies established by law may, but need not, be allocated within a principal department. The legislature shall by law prescribe the functions, powers and duties of the principal departments and of all other agencies of the state, and may from time to time reallocate offices, agencies and instrumentalities among the principal departments, may increase, modify, diminish or change their functions, powers and duties, and may assign new functions, powers and duties to them; but the governor may make such changes in the allocation of offices, agencies and instrumentalities, and in the allocation of such functions, powers and duties, as he considers necessary for efficient administration. If such changes affect existing law, they shall be set forth in executive orders which shall be submitted to the legislature while it is in session, and shall become effective, and shall have the force of law, sixty days after submission, or at the close of the session, whichever is sooner, unless specifically modified or disapproved by a resolution concurred in by a majority of all the members.

Section 5.07. Executive Officers; Appointment. The governor shall appoint and may remove the heads of all administrative departments. All other officers in the administrative service of the state shall be appointed and may be removed as provided by law.

Section 5.08. Succession to Governorship.

(a) If the governor-elect dies, resigns or is disqualified or fails to assume office for any other reason, the presiding officer of the legislature shall serve as acting governor until the governor-elect qualifies and assumes office, or, if the governor-elect dies or resigns or does not assume office within six months, until the unexpired term has been filled by special election and the newly elected governor has qualified. If, at the time the presiding officer of the legislature is to assume the acting governorship, the legislature has not yet organized and elected a presiding officer, the outgoing governor shall hold over until the presiding officer of the legislature is elected.

(b) When the governor is unable to discharge the duties of his office by reason of impeachment or other disability, including but not limited to physical or mental disability, or when the duties of the office are not being discharged by reason of his continuous absence, the presiding officer of the legislature shall serve as acting governor until the governor's disability or absence terminates. If the governor's disability or absence does not terminate within six months, the office of the governor shall be vacant.

(c) When, for any reason, a vacancy occurs in the office of the governor, the unexpired term shall be filled by special election, except when such unexpired term is less than one year, in which event the presiding officer of the legislature shall succeed to the office for the remainder of the term. When a vacancy in the office of the governor is filled by special election, the presiding officer of the legislature shall serve as acting governor from the occurrence of the vacancy until the newly elected governor has qualified. When the presiding officer of the legislature succeeds to the office of governor, he shall have the title, powers, duties and emoluments of that office, and when he serves as acting governor, he shall have the powers and duties thereof, and shall receive such compensation as the legislature shall provide by law.

(d) The legislature shall provide by law for special elections to fill vacancies in the office of the governor.

(e) The supreme court shall have original, exclusive and final jurisdiction to determine absence and disability of the governor or governor-elect and to determine the existence of a vacancy in the office of governor, and all questions concerning succession to the office or to its powers and duties.

ARTICLE VI: The Judiciary

Section 6.01. Judicial Power. The judicial power of the state shall be vested in a unified judicial system, which shall include a supreme court, an appellate court and a general court, and which shall also include such inferior courts of limited jurisdiction as may from time to time be established by law. All courts except the supreme court may be divided into geographical departments or districts as may be provided by law, and into functional divisions and subdivisions as may be provided by law or by judicial rules not inconsistent with law.

Section 6.02. Supreme Court. The supreme court shall be the highest court of the state and shall consist of a chief judge and ... associate judges.

Section 6.03. Jurisdiction of Courts. The supreme court shall have appellate jurisdiction in all cases arising under this constitution and the Constitution of the United States and in all other cases as provided by law. It shall also have original jurisdiction in cases arising under sections 4.04(b) and 5.08(e) of this constitution, and in all other cases as provided by law. All other courts of the state shall have original and appellate jurisdiction as provided by law, which jurisdiction shall be uniform in all geographical departments or districts of the same court. The jurisdiction of functional divisions and subdivisions shall be as provided by law or by judicial rules not inconsistent with law.

Section 6.04. Appointment of Judges; Qualification; Tenure; Retirement; Removal.

(a) The governor shall nominate, and, by and with the advice and consent of the legislature, appoint the chief judges and associate judges of the supreme, appellate and general courts. The governor shall give ten days' public notice before sending a judicial nomination to the legislature or before making an interim appointment when the legislature is not in session.

Alternative (a) (Nomination by Nominating Commission). The governor shall fill a vacancy in the offices of the chief judges and associate judges of the supreme, appellate and general courts from a list of nominees presented to him by the appropriate judicial nominating commission. If the governor fails to make an appointment within sixty days from the day the list is presented, the appointment shall be made by the chief judge or by the acting chief judge from the same list. There shall be a judicial nominating commission for the supreme court, and one commission for the nomination of judges for the court sitting in each geographical department or district of the appellate court. Each judicial nominating commission shall consist of seven members, one of whom shall be the chief judge of the supreme court, who shall act as chairman. The members of the bar of the state in the geographical area for which the court or the department or district of the court sits shall elect three of their number to be members of such a commission, and the governor shall appoint three citizens not members of the bar, from among the residents of the same geographical area. The terms of office and the compensation for members of a judicial nominating commission shall be as provided by law. No member of a judicial nominating commission shall hold any other public office or office in any political party or organization, and no member of such a commission shall be eligible for appointment to a state judicial office so long as he is a member of such a commission and for (five) (three) (two) years thereafter.

(b) No person shall be eligible for judicial office in the supreme court, appellate court and general court unless he has been admitted to practice law before the supreme court for at least [   ] years. No person who has been appointed to judicial office in the supreme court, appellate court or general court shall hold any other paid office, position of profit or employment under the state, its civil divisions, or the United States. Any judge of the supreme court, appellate court or general court who becomes a candidate for an elective office shall thereby forfeit his judicial office.

(c) The judges of the supreme court, appellate court and general court shall hold their offices for initial terms of seven years and upon reappointment shall hold their offices during good behavior. They shall be retired upon attaining the age of seventy years and may be pensioned as may be provided by law. The chief judge of the supreme court may from time to time appoint retired judges to such special assignments as may be provided by the rules of the supreme court.

(d) The judges of the supreme court, appellate court and general court shall be subject to impeachment, and any such judge impeached shall not exercise his office until acquitted. The supreme court may also remove judges of the appellate and general courts for such cause and in such manner as may be provided by law.

(e) The legislature shall provide by law for the appointment of judges of the inferior courts, and for their qualifications, tenure, retirement and removal.

(f) The judges of the courts of this state shall receive such salaries as may be provided by law, which shall not be diminished during their term of office.

Section 6.05. Administration. The chief judge of the supreme court shall be the administrative head of the unified judicial system. He may assign judges from one geographical department or functional division of a court to another department or division of that court, and he may assign judges for temporary service from one court to another. The chief judge shall, with the approval of the supreme court, appoint an administrative director to serve at his pleasure and to supervise the administrative operation of the judicial system.

Section 6.06. Financing. The chief judge shall submit an annual consolidated budget for the entire unified judicial system, and the total cost of the system shall be paid by the state. The legislature may provide by law for the reimbursement to the state of appropriate portions of such cost by political subdivisions.

Section 6.07. Rulemaking Power. The supreme court shall make and promulgate rules governing the administration of all courts. It shall make and promulgate rules governing practice and procedure in civil and criminal cases in all courts. These rules may be changed by the legislature by a two-thirds vote of all the members.

ARTICLE VII: Finance

Section 7.01. State Debt. No debt shall be contracted by or in behalf of this state unless such debt shall be authorized by law for projects or objects distinctly specified therein.

Section 7.02. The Budget. The governor shall submit to the legislature, at a time fixed by law, a budget estimate for the next fiscal year setting forth all proposed expenditures and anticipated income of all departments and agencies of the state, as well as a general appropriation bill to authorize the proposed expenditures, and a bill or bills covering recommendations in the budget for new or additional revenues.

Section 7.03. Expenditure of Money.

(a) No money shall be withdrawn from the treasury except in accordance with appropriations made by law, nor shall any obligation for the payment of money be incurred except as authorized by law. The appropriation for each department, office, or agency of the state, for which appropriation is made, shall be for a specific sum of money, and no appropriation shall allocate to any object the proceeds of any particular tax or fund or a part or percentage thereof, except when required by the federal government for participation in federal programs.

(b) All state and local expenditures, including salaries paid by the legislative, executive and judicial branches of government, shall be matters of public record.

ARTICLE VIII: LOCAL GOVERNMENT

Section 8.01. Organization of Local Government. The legislature shall provide by general law for the government of counties, cities and other civil divisions, and for methods and procedures of incorporating, merging, consolidating and dissolving such civil divisions and of altering their boundaries, including provisions

(1) for such classification of civil divisions as may be necessary, on the basis of population or on any other reasonable basis related to the purpose of the classification;

(2) for optional plans of municipal organization and government so as to enable a county, city or other civil division to adopt or abandon an authorized optional charter by a majority vote of the qualified voters voting thereon;

(3) for the adoption or amendment of charters by any county or city for its own government, by a majority vote of the qualified voters of the city or county voting thereon, including methods and procedures for the selection of charter commissions, and for framing, publishing, disseminating and adopting such charters or charter amendments, and for meeting the expenses connected therewith.

Alternative for self-executing home rule powers: (3) for the adoption or amendment of charters by any county or city, in accordance with the provisions of section 8.02 concerning home rule for local units.

Section 8.02. Powers of Counties and Cities. A county or city may exercise any legislative power or perform any function which is not denied to it by its charter, is not denied to counties or cities generally, or to counties and cities of its class, and is within such limitations as the legislature may establish by general law. This grant of home rule powers shall not include the power to enact private or civil law governing civil relationships except as incident to an exercise of an independent county or city power, nor shall it include power to define and provide for the punishment of a felony.

Alternative provisions for self-executing home rule powers:

Section 8.02. Home Rule for Local Units.

(a) Any county or city may adopt or amend a charter for its own government, subject to such regulations as are provided in this constitution and may be provided by general law. The legislature shall provide one or more optional procedures for nonpartisan election of five, seven or nine charter commissioners and for framing, publishing, and adopting a charter or charter amendments.

(b) Upon resolution approved by a majority of the members of the legislative authority of the county or city or upon petition of ten per cent of the qualified voters, the officer or agency responsible for certifying public questions shall submit to the people at the next regular election

not less than sixty days thereafter, or at a special election if authorized
by law, the question "Shall a commission be chosen to frame a charter
or charter amendments for the county (or city) of ....?"
An affirmative vote of a majority of the qualified voters voting on the
question shall authorize the creation of the commission.

(c) A petition to have a charter commission may include the
names of five, seven or nine commissioners, to be listed at the end of the
question when it is voted on, so that an affirmative vote on the question
is a vote to elect the persons named in the petition. Otherwise, the petition or resolution shall designate an optional election procedure provided by law.

(d) Any proposed charter or charter amendments shall be published by the commission, distributed to the qualified voters and submitted to them at the next regular or special election not less than thirty
days after publication. The procedure for publication and submission
shall be as provided by law or by resolution of the charter commission
not inconsistent with law. The legislative authority of the county or city
shall, on request of the charter commission, appropriate money to provide for the reasonable expenses of the commission and for the publication, distribution and submission of its proposals.

(e) A charter or charter amendments shall become effective if approved by a majority of the qualified voters voting thereon. A charter
may provide for direct submission of future charter revisions or amendments by petition or by resolution of the local legislative authority.

Section 8.03. Powers of Local Units. Counties shall have such powers
as shall be provided by general or optional law. Any city or other civil division may, by agreement, subject to a local referendum and the approval of
a majority of the qualified voters voting on any such question, transfer to
the county in which it is located any of its functions or powers, and may revoke the transfer of any such function or power, under regulations provided by general law; and any county may, in like manner, transfer to another county or to a city within its boundaries or adjacent thereto any of its
functions or powers, and may revoke the transfer of any such function or
power.

Section 8.04. County Government. Any county charter shall provide the
form of government of the county and shall determine which of its officers
shall be elected and the manner of their election. It shall provide for the
exercise of all powers vested in, and the performance of all duties imposed
upon, counties and county officers by law. Such charter may provide for the
concurrent or exclusive exercise by the county, in all or in part of its area,
of all or of any designated powers vested by the constitution or laws of this
state in cities and other civil divisions; it may provide for the succession by
the county to the rights, properties and obligations of cities and other civil
divisions therein incident to the powers so vested in the county, and for the
division of the county into districts for purposes of administration or of taxation or of both. No provision of any charter or amendment vesting in the
county any powers of a city or other civil division shall become effective
unless it shall have been approved by a majority of those voting thereon
(1) in the county, (2) in any city containing more than 25 per cent of the
total population of the county, and (3) in the county outside of such city
or cities.

Section 8.05. City Government. Except as provided in sections 8.03 and 8.04, each city is hereby granted full power and authority to pass laws and ordinances relating to its local affairs, property and government; and no enumeration of powers in this constitution shall be deemed to limit or restrict the general grant of authority hereby conferred; but this grant of authority shall not be deemed to limit or restrict the power of the legislature to enact laws of statewide concern uniformly applicable to every city.

ARTICLE IX: PUBLIC EDUCATION

Section 9.01. Free Public Schools; Support of Higher Education. The legislature shall provide for the maintenance and support of a system of free public schools open to all children in the state, and shall establish, organize and support such other public educational institutions, including public institutions of higher learning, as may be desirable.

ARTICLE X: CIVIL SERVICE

Section 10.01. Merit System. The legislature shall provide for the establishment and administration of a merit system in the civil service of the state and of its civil divisions.

ARTICLE XI: INTERGOVERNMENTAL RELATIONS

Section 11.01. Intergovernmental Cooperation. Nothing in this constitution shall be construed 1) to prohibit the cooperation of the government of this state with other governments, or 2) the cooperation of the government of any county, city or other civil division with any one or more other governments in the administration of their functions and powers, or 3) the consolidation of existing civil divisions of the state. Any county, city or other civil division may agree, except as limited by general law, to share the costs and responsibilities of functions and services with any one or more other governments.

ARTICLE XII: CONSTITUTIONAL REVISION

Section 12.01. Amending Procedure; Proposals.

(a) Amendments to this constitution may be proposed by the legislature or by the initiative.

(b) An amendment proposed by the legislature shall be agreed to by record vote of a majority of all of the members which shall be entered on the journal.

(c) An amendment proposed by the initiative shall be incorporated by its sponsors in an initiative petition which shall contain either the full text of the amendment proposed, or an adequate summary, and which shall be signed by qualified voters equal in number to at least ... per cent of the total votes cast for governor in the last preceding gubernatorial election. Initiative petitions shall be filed with the secretary of the legislature.

(d) An amendment proposed by the initiative shall be presented to the legislature, if it is in session, and if it is not in session, when it convenes or reconvenes. If the proposal is agreed to by a majority vote of all the members, such vote shall be entered on the journal, and the proposed amendment shall be submitted for adoption in the same manner as amendments proposed by the legislature.

(e) The legislature may provide by law for a procedure for the withdrawal by its sponsors of an initiative petition at any time prior to its submission to the voters.

Section 12.02. Amendment Procedure; Adoption.

(a) The question of the adoption of a constitutional amendment shall be submitted by the secretary of the legislature to the voters at the first [regular or special] state-wide election held no less than two months after it has been agreed to by the vote of the legislature, and, in the case of amendments proposed by the initiative which have failed to receive such legislative approval, not less than two months after the end of the legislative session.

(b) Each proposed constitutional amendment shall be submitted to the voter by a ballot title which shall be descriptive but not argumentative or prejudicial, and which shall be prepared by the legal department of the state, subject to review by the courts. Any amendment submitted to the voters shall become a part of the constitution only when approved by a majority of the votes cast thereon. Each amendment so approved shall take effect thirty days after the date of the vote thereon, unless the amendment itself otherwise provides.

Section 12.03. Constitutional Conventions.

(a) The legislature, by an affirmative record vote of a majority of all the members, may at any time submit the question "Shall there be a convention to amend or revise the constitution?" to the qualified voters of the state. If the question of holding a convention is not otherwise submitted to the people at some time during any period of fifteen years the secretary of the legislature shall submit it at the general election in the fifteenth year following the last submission.

(b) The legislature, prior to a vote on the holding of a convention, shall provide for a preparatory commission to assemble information on constitutional questions to assist the voters, and if a convention is authorized the commission shall be continued for the assistance of the delegates. If a majority of the qualified voters voting on the question of holding a convention approves it, delegates shall be chosen at the next regular election not less than three months thereafter unless the legislature shall by law have provided for election of the delegates at the same time that the question is voted on or at a special election.

(c) Any qualified voter of the state shall be eligible to membership in the convention and one delegate shall be elected from each existing legislative district. The convention shall convene not later than one month after the date of the election of delegates and may recess from time to time.

(d) No proposal shall be submitted by the convention to the voters unless it has been printed and upon the desks of the delegates in final form at least three days on which the convention was in session prior to final passage therein, and has received the assent of a majority of all the delegates. The yeas and nays on any question shall, upon request of one-tenth of the delegates present, be entered in the journal. Proposals of the convention shall be submitted to the qualified voters at the first regular or special state-wide election not less than two months after final action thereon by the convention, either as a whole or in such parts and with such alternatives as the convention may determine. Any constitutional revision submitted to the voters in accordance with this section shall require the approval of a majority of the qualified voters voting thereon, and shall take effect thirty days after the date of the vote thereon, unless the revision itself otherwise provides.

Section 12.04. *Conflicting Amendments or Revisions.* If conflicting constitutional amendments or revisions submitted to the voters at the same election are approved, the amendment or revision receiving the highest number of affirmative votes shall prevail to the extent of such conflict.

Bicameral Alternative: Appropriate changes to reflect passage by two houses must be made throughout this article.

ARTICLE XIII: SCHEDULE

Section 13.01. *Effective Date.* This constitution shall be in force from and including the first day of ...., 19..., except as herein otherwise provided.

Section 13.02. *Existing Laws, Rights and Proceedings.* All laws not inconsistent with this constitution shall continue in force until they expire by their own limitation or are amended or repealed, and all existing writs, actions, suits, proceedings, civil or criminal liabilities, prosecutions, judgments, sentences, orders, decrees, appeals, causes of action, contracts, claims, demands, titles and rights shall continue unaffected except as modified in accordance with the provisions of this constitution.

Section 13.03. *Officers.* All officers filling any office by election or appointment shall continue to exercise the duties thereof, according to their respective commissions or appointments, until their offices shall have been abolished or their successors selected and qualified in accordance with this constitution or the laws enacted pursuant thereto.

Section 13.04. *Choice of Officers.* The first election of governor under this constitution shall be in 19.... The first election of members of the legislature under this constitution shall be in 19....

Section 13.05. *Establishment of the Legislature.* Until otherwise provided by law, members of the legislature shall be elected from the following districts: The first district shall consist of [The description of all the districts from which the first legislature will be elected should be inserted in similar language].

Bicameral Alternative: refer to "assembly districts" and "senate districts".

Section 13.06. *Administrative Reorganization.* The governor shall submit to the legislature orders embodying a plan for reorganization of administrative departments in accordance with section 5.06 of this constitution prior to .... [date]. These orders shall become effective as originally issued or as they may be modified by law on [a date three months later] unless any of them are made effective at earlier dates by law.

Section 13.07. *Establishment of the Judiciary.*

(a) The unified judicial system shall be inaugurated on September 15, 19.... Prior to that date the justices, judges and principal ministerial agents of the judicial system shall be designated or selected and any other act needed to prepare for the operation of the system shall be done in accordance with this constitution.

(b) The judicial power vested in any court in the state shall be transferred to the unified judicial system and the justices and judges of the [here name all the courts of the state except justice of the peace courts] holding office on September 15, 19..., shall become justices and judges of the unified judicial system and shall continue to serve as such for the remainder of their respective terms and until their successors shall have qualified. The justices of the [here name the highest court of the state] shall become justices of the supreme court, and the judges of the other courts shall be assigned by the chief justice to appropriate service in the other departments of the judicial system, due regard being had to their positions in the existing judicial structure and to the districts in which they had been serving.

APPENDIX

ARTICLE   : LEGISLATIVE INITIATIVE AND REFERENDUM

Section   .01. Legislative Initiative.

(a) The people reserve to themselves the power to propose laws, and to enact or reject such laws at the polls. This reserved power is the initiative.

(b) The sponsors of an initiative petition shall incorporate therein either the full text of the law proposed, or an adequate summary. The petition shall be signed by qualified voters equal in number to at least . . .* per cent of the total votes cast for governor in the last preceding gubernatorial election. Initiative petitions shall be filed with the secretary of the legislature. If the proposed law is not enacted into law at the next ensuing session of the legislature, the question of the adoption of the proposed law shall be submitted by the secretary of the legislature to the qualified voters at the first regular election held not less than sixty days after the end of the session which fails to enact the proposal. The legislature may provide by law for a procedure by which the sponsors may withdraw an initiative petition at any time prior to its submission to the people.

(c) Each law proposed by the initiative shall be submitted to the qualified voters by a ballot title which shall be descriptive but not argumentative or prejudicial, and which shall be prepared by the legal department of the state, subject to review by the courts. Any initiative proposal submitted to the voters shall become law only when approved by a majority of the votes cast thereon, and shall take effect thirty days after the date of the vote thereon, unless the proposal itself otherwise provides.

(d) The initiative shall not be used to enact laws making or repealing appropriations of public funds, dedicating revenues, creating courts or defining their jurisdiction or prescribing their rules, naming or designating any person to hold a public office, or to enact or abrogate special or local laws.

(e) No law adopted by the initiative by the vote of the qualified voters under this section shall be repealed or amended by the legislature

* A percentage less than that provided in Section 12.01 for the constitutional initiative.

within a period of three years of adoption except by a two-thirds vote of all of the members.

Section   .02. *Referendum on Legislation.*

(a) Any bill failing of passage by the legislature may be submitted to referendum by order of the governor, either in its original form or with such amendments as were considered by the legislature as he may designate. Any bill which, having passed the legislature, is returned thereto by the governor with objections and, upon reconsideration, is not approved by a two-thirds vote of all the members but is approved by at least a majority thereof, may be submitted to referendum by a majority of all the members. Bills thus submitted to referendum shall be voted on at the next succeeding regular election occurring at least sixty days after action is taken to submit them, unless the legislature shall provide for their submission at an earlier date.

(b) The legislature may provide, by a vote of the majority of all the members, that a law shall not become effective until it is submitted to a referendum and is approved by a majority of the qualified voters voting thereon.

Section   .03. *Conflicting Legislative Proposals.* If conflicting provisions of law submitted to the voters at the same election are approved, the provision receiving the highest number of affirmative votes shall prevail to the extent of such conflict.

BIBLIOGRAPHY

The books in this bibliography are listed by chapter topic. See the beginning of the Outline for treatments of these topics in the standard textbooks.

1—Introduction

The American Assembly. *The Forty-Eight States: Their Tasks as Policy Makers and Administrators* (New York: Columbia University Graduate School of Business, 1955).

Anderson, William. *The Units of Government in the United States* (Chicago: Public Administration Service, 1949).

The Book of the States (Chicago: The Council of State Governments, published biennially).

Graves, W. Brooke, and Others. *American State Government and Administration: A State by State Bibliography* (Chicago: The Council of State Governments, 1949).

Smelser, Marshall. *American Colonial and Revolutionary History,* "College Outline Series" (New York: Barnes & Noble, Inc., 1950).

——. *American History at a Glance,* "Everyday Handbooks" (New York: Barnes & Noble, Inc., 1961).

Syrett, Harold C., ed. *American Historical Documents,* "College Outline Series" (New York: Barnes & Noble, Inc., 1960).

The Municipal Yearbook (Chicago: International City Managers Association, published annually).

U. S. Department of Commerce, Bureau of the Census. *Governments in the United States in 1957* (Washington: U. S. Government Printing Office, 1957).

2—National-State Relations

Anderson, William. *The Nation and the States, Rivals or Partners?* (Minneapolis: University of Minnesota Press, 1955).

——. *Intergovernmental Relations in Review* (Minneapolis: University of Minnesota Press, 1960).

Barnes, William R., ed., *The Constitution of the United States and the Declaration of Independence* (New York: Barnes & Noble, Inc., 1956).

Benson, George C. S. *The New Centralization* (New York: Rinehart & Co., Inc., 1941).

Blundred, R. H., and Hanks, D. W. *Federal Services to Cities and Towns* (Chicago: American Municipal Association, 1950).

Clark, Jane P. *The Rise of a New Federalism; Federal-State Coopera-*

APPENDIX

tion in the United States (New York: Columbia University Press, 1938).

The Commission on Intergovernmental Relations *A Report to the President for Transmittal to the Congress* (Washington: U. S. Government Printing Office, 1955).

Federal Grants-In-Aid (Chicago: The Council of State Governments, 1949).

Jensen, Merrill, ed. *Regionalism in America* (Madison: University of Wisconsin Press, 1951).

Krout, John A. *United States to 1865,* "College Outline Series" (New York: Barnes & Noble, Inc., 1962).

——. *United States since 1865,* "College Outline Series" (New York: Barnes & Noble, Inc., 1961).

Macmahon, Arthur W., ed. *Federalism: Mature and Emergent* (Garden City, N.Y.: Doubleday & Co., Inc., 1955).

Maxwell, James A., *The Fiscal Impact of Federalism in the United States* (Cambridge: Harvard University Press, 1946).

Sayre, Wallace S. *American Government,* "College Outline Series" (New York: Barnes & Noble, Inc., 1962).

Syrett, Harold C. *American Historical Documents,* "College Outline Series" (New York: Barnes & Noble, Inc., 1960).

The Future Role of the States (New York: National Municipal League, 1962).

White, Leonard D. *The States and the Nation* (Baton Rouge: Louisiana State University Press, 1953).

3—Interstate Relations

Anderson, William. *Federalism and Intergovernmental Relations* (Chicago: Public Administration Service, 1946).

Barnes, William R., ed., *The Constitution of the United States and the Declaration of Independence* (New York: Barnes & Noble, Inc., 1956).

Bird, Frederick L. *A Study of the Port of New York Authority* (New York: Dun & Bradstreet, 1948).

Interstate Compacts, 1783–1956 (Chicago: The Council of State Governments, 1955).

Jackson, Robert H. *Full Faith and Credit: The Lawyer's Clause of the Constitution* (New York: Columbia University Press, 1945).

Maxwell, James A. *The Fiscal Impact of Federalism in the United States* (Cambridge: Harvard University Press, 1946).

Tax Barriers to Trade (Philadelphia: Tax Institute, 1941).

The Handbook of Interstate Crime Control (Chicago: The Council of State Governments, 1955).

Thursby, V. V. *Interstate Cooperation: A Study of the Interstate Compact* (Washington: Public Affairs Press, 1953).

Zimmerman, Frederick L., and Mitchell, Wendell. *The Interstate Compact since 1925* (Chicago: The Council of State Governments, 1951).

4—State Constitutions

A Manual for Constitutional Conventions (New York: National Municipal League, 1961).

Barnes, William R., ed., *The Constitution of the United States and the Declaration of Independence* (New York: Barnes & Noble, Inc., 1956).

Constitutional Studies (Chicago: Public Administration Service, 1955). [Prepared for the use of members of the Alaska constitutional convention.]

Constitutions of the States and the United States (Albany: New York State Constitutional Convention Committee, 1938).

Dealey, James Q. *Growth of American State Constitutions from 1776 to the End of the Year 1914* (Boston: Ginn & Co., 1915).

Graves, W. Brooke, ed. *Major Problems in State Constitutional Revision* (Chicago: Public Administration Service, 1960).

Hoar, Roger S. *Constitutional Conventions: Their Nature, Powers, and Limitations* (Boston: Little, Brown & Co., 1917).

How to Study Your State Constitution (New York: National Municipal League, 1961).

Jacobsen, G. A., and Lipman, M. H. *Political Science, "College Outline Series"* (New York: Barnes & Noble, Inc., 1956).

Krout, John A. *United States to 1865, "College Outline Series"* (New York: Barnes & Noble, Inc., 1962).

Model State Constitution (New York: National Municipal League, 1962).

Rankin, Robert S. *The Bill of Rights* (New York: National Municipal League, 1960).

Salient Issues of Constitutional Revision (New York: National Municipal League, 1961).

Sayre, Wallace S. *American Government, "College Outline Series"* (New York: Barnes & Noble, Inc., 1962).

Smelser, Marshall. *American Colonial and Revolutionary History, "College Outline Series"* (New York: Barnes & Noble, Inc., 1950).

Spiro, Herbert J. *Government by Constitution: the Political Systems of Democracy* (New York: Random House, 1959).

Sturm, Albert L. *Major Constitutional Issues in West Virginia* (Morgantown: Bureau for Government Research, West Virginia University, 1961).

———. *Methods of State Constitutional Reform* (Ann Arbor: The University of Michigan Press, 1954).

The Book of the States (Chicago: The Council of State Governments, published biennially).

5—Suffrage and Elections

Albright, S. D. *The American Ballot* (Washington: American Council on Public Affairs, 1942).

Burdick, Eugene, and Brodbeck, A. J. *American Voting Behavior* (New York: Free Press of Glencoe, Inc., 1958).

Ewing, Cortes, A. M. *Primary Elections in the South* (Norman: University of Oklahoma Press, 1953).

Harris, Joseph P. *Election Administration in the United States* (Washington: The Brookings Institution, 1934).

Holland, L. M. *The Direct Primary in Georgia* (Urbana: University of Illinois Press, 1949).

Jacobsen, G. A., and Lipman, M. H. *Political Science,* "College Outline Series" (New York: Barnes & Noble, Inc., 1956).

Litchfield, E. H. *Voting Behavior in a Metropolitan Area* (Ann Arbor: The University of Michigan Press, 1941).

McGovney, Dudley O. *The American Suffrage Medley* (Chicago: University of Chicago Press, 1949).

Registration for Voting in the United States (Chicago: The Council of State Governments, 1941).

Sayre, Wallace S. *American Government,* "College Outline Series" (New York: Barnes & Noble, Inc., 1962).

Scammon, R. M. *America Votes* (New York: The Macmillan Co., 1956).

Voting in the United States (Chicago: The Council of State Governments, 1940).

6—Political Parties and Pressure Groups

Allen, Robert S., ed. *Our Fair City* (New York: Vanguard Press, 1947).

Blaisdell, R. C. *American Democracy under Pressure* (New York: The Ronald Press Co., 1957).

Bone, Hugh A. *American Politics and the Party System* (New York: McGraw-Hill Book Co., 1949).

Ewing, Cortez A. M. *Primary Elections in the South: A Study in Uniparty Politics* (Norman: University of Oklahoma Press, 1953).

Farley, James A. *Behind the Ballots* (New York: Harcourt, Brace, 1938).

Fenton, John H. *Politics in the Border States* (New Orleans: The Hauser Press, 1957).

Flynn, Edward J. *You're the Boss* (New York: The Viking Press, Inc., 1947).

Ford, Pamela. *Regulation of Campaign Finances* (Berkeley: University of California Press, 1955).

Jacobsen, G. A., and Lipman, M. H. *Political Science,* "College Outline Series" (New York: Barnes & Noble, Inc., 1956).

Heard, Alexander. *A Two-Party South?* (Chapel Hill: University of North Carolina Press, 1952).

Herring, Pendleton. *The Politics of Democracy* (New York: Rinehart & Co., Inc., 1940).

Key, V. O., Jr. *American State Politics: An Introduction* (New York: Alfred A. Knopf, Inc., 1956).

——. *Politics, Parties, and Pressure Groups* (New York: The Crowell-Collier Publishing Co., 1960).

——. *Southern Politics in State and Nation* (New York: Alfred A. Knopf, Inc., 1949).

Kornhauser, Arthur, and Others. *When Labor Votes: A Study of Auto Workers* (N.Y.: University Books, Inc., 1956).

Latham, Earl. *The Group Basis of Politics* (Ithaca: Cornell University Press, 1952).

Lockard, Duane. *New England State Politics* (Princeton: Princeton University Press, 1959).

Lubell, Samuel. *The Future of American Politics* (New York: Harper & Brothers, 1952).

McKean, Dayton D. *The Boss: The Hague Machine in Action* (Boston: Houghton Mifflin Co., 1940).

Merriam, Robert B., and Goetz, Rachel M. *Going into Politics: A Guide for Citizens* (New York: Harper & Brothers, 1957).

Model Direct Primary Election System (New York: National Municipal League, 1951).

Peterson, Virgil W. *Barbarians in Our Midst* (Boston: Little, Brown & Co., 1952).

Price, Hugh D. *The Negro in Southern Politics* (New York: New York University Press, 1957).

Sayre, Wallace S. *American Government*, "College Outline Series" (New York: Barnes & Noble, Inc., 1962).

Truman, David B. *The Governmental Process* (New York: Alfred A. Knopf, Inc., 1953).

7—Direct Legislation and the Recall

Bird, F. L., and Ryan, F. M. *The Recall of Public Officers: A Study of the Operation of the Recall in California* (New York: The Macmillan Co., 1930).

Crouch, W. W. *The Initiative and Referendum in California* (Los Angeles: Haynes Foundation, 1950).

La Palombara, Joseph G. *The Initiative and Referendum in Oregon 1938–1949* (Corvallis: Oregon State College Press, 1950).

Pollock, James K. *Direct Government in Michigan* (Ann Arbor: The University of Michigan Press, 1940).

The Book of the States (Chicago: The Council of State Governments, published biennially).

8—The State Legislature

American Legislatures: Structure and Procedures (Chicago: The Council of State Governments, 1955).

Baker, Gordon E. *Reapportionment* (New York: National Municipal League, 1960).

——. *Rural Versus Urban Political Power* (New York: Random House, 1955).

Breckenridge, A. C. *One House for Two: Nebraska's Unicameral Legislature* (Washington: Public Affairs Press, 1957).

Buck, Arthur E. *Modernizing Our State Legislatures* (Philadelphia: American Academy of Political and Social Science, 1936).

Chamberlain, Joseph P. *Legislative Processes: National and State* (New York: Appleton-Century, 1936).

Fordham, Jefferson B. *The State Legislative Institution* (Philadelphia: University of Pennsylvania Press, 1959).

Greenfield, Margaret. *Legislative Reapportionment* (Berkeley: University of California Press, 1951).

Neuberger, Richard L. *Adventures in Politics: We Go to the Legislature* (New York: Oxford University Press, Inc., 1954).

Sears, Kenneth. *Methods of Reapportionment* (Chicago: University of Chicago Press, 1952).

Siffin, William J. *The Legislative Council in the American States* (Bloomington: Indiana University Press, 1959).

State Regulation of Lobbying (Chicago: The Council of State Governments, 1951).

Walker, Harvey. *Law Making in the United States* (New York: The Ronald Press Co., 1949).

Weeks, O. Douglas. *Research in the American State Legislative Process* (Ann Arbor: J. W. Edwards, 1947).

Zeller, Belle (ed.). *American State Legislatures* (New York: Thomas Y. Crowell Co., 1954).

9—The Governor

Jensen, Christen. *The Pardoning Power in the American States* (Chicago: University of Chicago Press, 1922).

Lipson, Leslie. *The American Governor: From Figurehead to Leader* (Chicago: University of Chicago Press, 1939).

Public Authorities in the States (Chicago: The Council of State Governments, 1953).

Ransone, Coleman B., Jr. *The Office of Governor in the United States* (University, Ala.: University of Alabama Press, 1956).

Rich, Bennett M. *The Governor* (New York: National Municipal League, 1960).

Scace, Homer E. *The Organization of the Executive Office of the Governor* (New York: Institute of Public Administration, 1950).

Smith, Alfred E. *Up To Now* (New York: The Viking Press, Inc., 1929).

Strain, Jack W. *The Chief Executive* (Oklahoma City: Report of the Constitutional Survey Committee, 1948).

10—State Administrative Organization

Barnard, Chester J. *Organization and Management* (Cambridge: Harvard University Press, 1948).

Bollens, John C. *Administrative Reorganization in the States Since 1939* (Berkeley: University of California Press, 1947).

Buck, Arthur E. *The Reorganization of State Governments in the United States* (New York: Columbia University Press, 1938).

Gaus, John M. *Reflections on Public Administration* (University, Ala.: University of Alabama Press, 1947).

Gulick, Luther, and Urwick, L. *Papers on the Science of Administration* (New York: Institute of Public Administration, 1937).

Heady, Ferrel. *The Structure of Administration* (New York: National Municipal League, 1961).

Lepawsky, Albert. *Administration* (New York: Alfred A. Knopf, Inc., 1949).

Pfiffner, John M. *Public Administration* (New York: The Ronald Press Co., 1946).

Redford, Emmette S. *Ideal and Practice in Public Administration* (University, Ala.: University of Alabama Press, 1958).

Reorganizing State Governments (Chicago: The Council of State Governments, 1950).

Simon, Herbert A. *Administrative Behavior* (New York: The Macmillan Co., 1950).

Waldo, Dwight. *The Administrative State* (New York: The Ronald Press Co., 1948).

11—The State Judiciary

Aumann, Francis R. *The Instrumentalities of Justice: Their Forms, Functions, and Limitations* (Columbus: Ohio State University Press, 1956).

Courts of Last Resort in the Forty-Eight States (Chicago: The Council of State Governments, 1950).

Frank, Jerome. *Courts on Trial: Myth and Reality in American Justice* (Princeton: Princeton University Press, 1949).

— and Frank, Barbara, with Harold M. Hoffman. *Not Guilty* (Garden City, N. Y.: Doubleday & Co., Inc., 1957).

Haynes, Ewan. *The Selection and Tenure of Judges* (Newark: National Conference of Judicial Councils, 1944).

Keeney, Barnaby C. *Judgment by Peers* (Cambridge: Harvard University Press, 1949).

Mayers, Lewis. *The American Legal System* (New York: Harper & Brothers, 1955).

Mitchell, Wendell. *Relations Between the Federal and State Courts* (New York: Columbia University Press, 1950).

Pound, Roscoe. *Criminal Justice in America* (New York: Henry Holt and Co., 1945).

Sayre, Wallace S. *American Government,* "College Outline Series" (New York: Barnes & Noble, Inc., 1962).

Trial Courts of General Jurisdiction in the Forty-Eight States (Chicago: The Council of State Governments, 1951).

Vanderbilt, Arthur T. *Judges and Jurors: Their Functions, Qualifications and Selection* (Boston: Boston University Press, 1956).

——. *Minimum Standards of Judicial Administration* (New York: National Conference of Judicial Councils, 1949).

——. *Men and Measures in the Law* (New York: Alfred A. Knopf, Inc., 1949).

12—Rural Local Government

Bollens, John C. *Special District Governments in the United States* (Berkeley: University of California Press, 1957).

Burchfield, Laverne. *Our Rural Communities* (Chicago: Public Administration Service, 1947).

Commission on Intergovernmental Relations. *Local Government* (Washington: U. S. Government Printing Office, 1955).

Lancaster, Lane W. *Government in Rural America* (New York: D. Van Nostrand Co., Inc., 1952).

Model County Charter (New York: National Municipal League, 1956).

Sayre, Wallace S. *American Government,* "College Outline Series" (New York: Barnes & Noble, Inc., 1962).

Snider, Clyde F. *Local Government in Rural America* (New York: Appleton-Century-Crofts, Inc., 1957).

Wager, Paul W., ed. *County Government Across the Nation* (Chapel Hill: University of North Carolina Press, 1950).

Weidner, Edward W. *The American County: Patchwork of Boards* (New York: National Municipal League, 1946).

13—Municipal Government

A Guide for Charter Commissions (New York: National Municipal League, 1960).

Baker, Benjamin. *Urban Government* (Princeton: D. Van Nostrand Co., Inc., 1958).

Bromage, Arthur W. *Councilmen at Work* (Ann Arbor: George Wahr Publishing Co., 1954).

Chicago Home Commission. *Modernizing a City Government* (Chicago: University of Chicago Press, 1954).

Childs, Richard S. *Civic Victories* (New York: Harper & Brothers, 1952).

Elliot, C. B. *The Principles of the Law of Municipal Corporations* (Chicago: Callaghan and Co., 1925).

Guideposts on Assuming a City Manager Position (Chicago: International City Managers Association, 1957).

MacCorkle, Stuart. *The City Manager's Job* (Austin: University of Texas, 1958).

Maddox, Russell W. *Extraterritorial Powers of Municipalities in the United States* (Corvallis: Oregon State College Press, 1955).

Model City Charter (New York: National Municipal League, 1962).

Morlan, Robert L., ed. *Capital, Courthouse, and City Hall* (Boston: Houghton Mifflin Co., 1960).

Robson, William A., ed. *Great Cities of the World* (New York: The Macmillan Co., 1955).

Sayre, Wallace S. *American Government,* "College Outline Series" (New York: Barnes & Noble, Inc., 1962).

―― and Kaufman, Herbert. *Governing New York City* (New York: Russell Sage Foundation, 1960).

Stewart, Frank M. *A Half Century of Municipal Reform* (Berkeley: University of California Press, 1950).

Stone, Harold A.; Price, Don K.; and Stene, Kathryn H. *City Manager Government in the United States: A Review after Twenty-Five Years* (Chicago: Public Administration Service, 1940).

The Municipal Yearbook (Chicago: International City Managers Association, published annually).

The Technique of Municipal Administration (Chicago: International City Managers Association, 1947).

Woodbury, Coleman, ed. *The Future of Cities and Urban Redevelopment* (Chicago: University of Chicago Press, 1953).

14—State and Local Relations

City-State Relations (Philadelphia: Institute of Local and State Government, 1937).

Dillon, J. F. *Commentaries on the Law of Municipal Corporation* (Boston: Little, Brown & Co., 1911).

McMillan, T. E., Jr. *State Supervision of Municipal Finance* (Austin: University of Texas Institute of Public Affairs, 1953).

Mott, Rodney L. *Home Rule for America's Cities* (Chicago: American Municipal Association, 1949).

Pontius, Dale. *State Supervision of Local Government* (Washington: American Council on Public Affairs, 1942).

State-Local Relations (Chicago: The Council of State Governments, 1946).

The States and the Metropolitan Problem (Chicago: The Council of State Governments, 1957).

15—Metropolitan Areas

Bollins, John C. *The Problem of Government in the San Francisco Bay Region* (Berkeley: University of California Press, 1948).

Jones, Victor. *Metropolitan Government* (Chicago: University of Chicago Press, 1942).

Lyon, Leverett, ed. *Governmental Problems in the Chicago Metropolitan Area* (Chicago: University of Chicago Press, 1957).

Owen, Wilfred. *The Metropolitan Transportation Problem* (Washington: The Brookings Institution, 1956).

Simon, Herbert A. *Fiscal Aspects of Metropolitan Consolidations* (Berkeley: University of California Press, 1943).

Sweeney, Stephen B., and Blair, George S., eds. *Metropolitan Analysis: Important Elements of Study and Action* (Philadelphia: University of Pennsylvania Press, 1958).

The Municipal Yearbook (Chicago: International City Managers Association, published annually).

The States and the Metropolitan Problem: A Report to the Governors' Conference (Chicago: The Council of State Governments, 1956).

Whyte, W. H., Jr. and the Editors of *Fortune. The Exploding Metropolis* (Garden City, N. Y.: Doubleday & Co., Inc., 1958).

Wood, Robert C. *Suburbia, Its People and Their Politics* (Boston: Houghton Mifflin Co., 1959).

16—Public Protection, Health, and Welfare

Burns, Eveline M. *Social Security and Public Policy* (New York: McGraw-Hill Book Co., 1956).

Camp, Irving. *Our State Police* (New York: Dodd, Mead, 1953).

Chute, Charles L., and Bell, Marjorie. *Crime, Courts, and Probation* (New York: The Macmillan Co., 1956).

Corson, John J., and McConnell, John W. *Economic Needs of Old People* (New York: Twentieth Century Fund, 1956).

Drake, J. T. *The Aged in American Society* (New York: The Ronald Press Co., 1958).

Ehlers, Victor M., and Steel, E. W. *Municipal and Rural Sanitation* (New York: McGraw-Hill Book Co., 1943).

Hiscock, Ira V. *Community Health Organization* (New York: The Commonwealth Fund, 1950).

Lemkau, Paul V. *Mental Health in Public Health* (New York: McGraw-Hill Book Co., 1949).

Leonard, V. A. *Police Organization and Management* (Brooklyn: Foundation Press, 1951).

Linford, Alton A. *Old Age Assistance in Massachusetts* (Chicago: University of Chicago Press, 1949).

Meyer, Harold D., and Brightbill, C. K. *Community Recreation* (Englewood Cliffs, N. J.: Prentice-Hall, Inc., 1956).

Municipal Fire Administration (Chicago: International City Managers Association, 1950).

Municipal Police Administration (Chicago: International City Managers Association, 1950).

Mustard, Harry S. *An Introduction to Public Health* (New York: The Macmillan Co., 1953).

"New Goals in Police Administration," *Annals of the American Academy of Political and Social Science* (Philadelphia: January, 1954).

Smith, Bruce. *Police Systems in the United States* (New York: Harper & Brothers, 1949).

Stevenson, Marietta. *Public Welfare Administration* (New York: The Macmillan Company, 1938).

Straus, Nathan. *Two-Thirds of a Nation* (New York: Alfred A. Knopf, Inc., 1952).

The States and Their Older Citizens (Chicago: The Council of State Governments, 1955).

Wilson, C. W. *Police Administration* (New York: McGraw-Hill Book Co., 1950).

Wyatt, Laurence. *Intergovernmental Relations in Public Health* (Minneapolis: University of Minnesota Press, 1951).

17—Schools, Libraries, and Museums

Beach, Fred F., and Will, Robert F. *The State and Education: The Structure and Control of Public Education at the State Level* (Washington [U. S. Department of Health, Education and Welfare, Office of Education]: Government Printing Office, 1955).

Conant, James B. *The American High School Today* (New York: Mc-Graw-Hill Book Co., 1959).

Garceau, Oliver. *The Public Library in the Political Process* (New York: Columbia University Press, 1949).

Hagman, Harlan L. *The Administration of American Public Schools* (New York: McGraw-Hill Book Co., 1951).

Higher Education in the Forty-Eight States (Chicago: The Council of State Governments, 1952).

Joeckel, Carleton B. *Government of the American Public Library* (Chicago: University of Chicago Press, 1945).

Millett, John D. *Financing Higher Education in the United States* (New York: Columbia University Press, 1952).

Morlan, Robert L. *Intergovernmental Relations in Education* (Minneapolis: University of Minnesota Press, 1950).

Pittenger, B. F. *Local Public School Administration* (New York: Mc-Graw-Hill Book Co., 1951).

Reeves, Charles E. *School Boards: Their Status, Functions and Activities* (New York: Prentice-Hall, Inc., 1954).

Remmlein, Madaline K. *The Law of Local Public School Administration* (New York: McGraw-Hill Book Co., 1953).

The Forty-Eight State School Systems (Chicago: The Council of State Governments, 1949).

United States Office of Education. *The State and Nonpublic Schools* (Washington: U. S. Government Printing Office, 1958).

18—Public Works

Federal Works Agency, Public Roads Administration. *Highway Practice in the United States of America* (Washington: U. S. Government Printing Office, 1949).

Gomez, R. A. *Intergovernmental Relations in Highways* (Minneapolis: University of Minnesota Press, 1950).

Hebden, Norman, and Smith, Wilbur S. *State-City Relationships in Highway Affairs* (New Haven: Yale University Press, 1950).

Municipal Public Works Administration (Chicago: International City Managers Association, 1950).

Stone, Donald C. *The Management of Municipal Public Works* (Chicago: Public Administration Service, 1939).

19—Land Policies

Baker, Gladys. *The County Agent* (Chicago: University of Chicago Press, 1939).

Bartholomew, Harland. *Land Uses in American Cities* (Cambridge: Harvard University Press, 1955).

Branch, Melville C. *Aerial Photography in Urban Planning and Research* (Cambridge: Harvard University Press, 1948).

Chapin, F. Stuart, Jr. *Urban Land Use Planning* (New York: Harper & Brothers, 1957).

Gallion, Arthur B. *The Urban Pattern: City Planning and Design* (New York: D. Van Nostrand Co., Inc., 1950).

Gulick, Luther. *American Forest Policy: A Study of Government and Economic Control* (New York: Duell, Sloan & Pearce, Inc., 1951).

Hillman, Arthur. *Community Organization and Planning* (New York: The Macmillan Co., 1950).

Lewis, Harold M. *Planning the Modern City* (New York: John Wiley & Sons, Inc., 2 vols., 1949).

Local Planning Administration (Chicago: International City Managers Association, 1948).

Model State and Regional Planning Laws (New York: National Municipal League, 1955).

National Resources Committee. *The Future of State Planning* (Washington: U. S. Government Printing Office, 1938).

Parson, Ruben L. *Conserving American Resources* (Englewood Cliffs, N. J.: Prentice-Hall, Inc., 1955).

Rodgers, Cleveland. *American Planning* (New York: Harper, 1947).

Smith, Guy H., ed. *Conservation of Natural Resources* (New York: John Wiley & Sons, Inc., 1950).

Walker, Robert A. *The Planning Function in Urban Government* (Chicago: University of Chicago Press, 1950).

Webster, Donald H. *Urban Planning and Municipal Public Policy* (New York: Harper & Brothers, 1958).

Woodbury, Coleman, ed. *The Future of Cities and Urban Redevelopment* (Chicago: University of Chicago Press, 1953).

20—Business and Labor

Anderson, Ronald A. *Government Regulation of Business* (Chicago: South-western Publishing Co., 1950).

Bernstein, M. H. *Regulating Business by Independent Commissions* (Princeton: Princeton University Press, 1955).

Dimock, Marshall E. *Business and Government* (New York: Holt, Rinehart & Winston, Inc., 1960).

Killingsworth, Charles C. *State Labor Relations Acts: A Study of Public Policy* (Chicago: University of Chicago Press, 1948).

Mund, Vernon A. *Government and Business* (New York: Harper & Brothers, 1960).

Occupational Licensing Legislation in the States (Chicago: The Council of State Governments, 1952).

Taylor, George W. *Government Regulation of Industrial Relations* (New York: Prentice-Hall, Inc., 1948).

Torpey, William G. *Public Personnel Management* (New York: D. Van Nostrand Co., Inc., 1953).

Witney, Fred. *Government and Collective Bargaining* (Philadelphia: J. B. Lippincott Co., 1951).

21—State and Local Personnel Management

Betters, Paul V. *The Personnel Classification Board* (Washington: The Brookings Institution, 1931).

Crouch, Winston W., and Jamieson, Judith N. *The Work of Civil Service Commissions* (Chicago: 1955).

Kaplan, H. Eliot. *The Law of Civil Service* (Albany: Bender, 1958).

Merit System Installation (Chicago: Public Administration Service, 1941).

Merriam, Lewis. *Public Service and Special Training* (Chicago: University of Chicago Press, 1936).

Model State Civil Service Law (New York: National Municipal League, 1953).

Mosher, W. E.; Kingsley, J. D.; and Stahl, O. G. *Public Personnel Administration* (New York: Harper & Brothers, 1950).

Municipal Personnel Administration (Chicago: International City Managers Association, 1950).

Position Classification in the Public Service (Chicago: Civil Service Assembly of the United States and Canada, 1942).

Powell, Norman J. *Personnel Administration in Government* (New York: Prentice-Hall, Inc., 1956).

Recruiting Applicants for the Public Service (Chicago: Civil Service Assembly of the United States and Canada, 1942).

Retirement Plans for Public Employees (Chicago: Municipal Finance Officers Association, 1946).

Roethlisberger, F. J. *Management and Morale* (Cambridge: Harvard University Press, 1947).

Spero, Sterling. *Government as Employer* (New York: Remsen Press, 1948).

Stahl, O. Glenn. *Public Personnel Administration* (New York: Harper & Brothers, 1956).

The Municipal Yearbook (Chicago: International City Managers Association, published annually).

Torpey, William G. *Public Personnel Management* (New York: D. Van Nostrand Co., Inc., 1953).

22—State and Local Finance

Anderson, William, and Durfee, Waite D., Jr. *Intergovernmental Fiscal Relations* (Minneapolis: University of Minnesota Press, 1956).

Blough, Roy, and Others. *Tax Relations Among Governmental Units* (New York: Tax Policy League, Inc., 1938).

Buck, Arthur E. *Public Budgeting* (New York: Harper & Brothers, 1929).

Burkhead, Jesse V. *Government Budgeting* (New York: John Wiley & Sons, Inc., 1956).

Commission on Intergovernmental Relations. *The Administration and Fiscal Impact of Federal Grants-in-Aid* (Washington: U. S. Government Printing Office, 1955).

———. *Twenty-Five Federal Grants-in-Aid Programs* (Washington: U. S. Government Printing Office, 1955).

Due, John F. *Sales Taxation* (Urbana: University of Illinois Press, 1952).

Federal Grants-in-Aid (Chicago: The Council of State Governments, 1949).

Financial Planning for Governments (Chicago: Municipal Finance Officers' Association, 1949).

Groves, Harold M. *Financing Government* (New York: Henry Holt and Co., 1952).

Hansen, Alvin H., and Perloff, Harvey S. *State and Local Finance in the National Economy* (New York: W. W. Norton & Co., Inc., 1944).

Kilpatrick, Wylie. *State Supervision of Local Budgeting* (New York: National Municipal League, 1939).

Miskesell, R. M. *Governmental Accounting* (Chicago: Richard D. Irwin, Inc., 1951).

Municipal Finance Administration (Chicago: International City Managers Association, 1949).

Penniman, Clara, and Heller, Walter W. *State Income Tax Administration* (Chicago: Public Administration Service, 1959).

Sigafoos, Robert A. *The Municipal Income Tax: Its History and Problems* (Chicago: Public Administration Service, 1955).

EXAMINATION QUESTIONS

Part I: True-False Questions

Place the letter *T* or the letter *F* at the left of each question.

_____ 1. In a confederate form of government, one central government wields supreme power over all territorial divisions within a state.

_____ 2. The lack of uniformity in state laws is a characteristic of the federal form of government.

_____ 3. The early state constitutions provided for the primacy of the governor.

_____ 4. A federal government is one in which the national government possesses all governmental powers.

_____ 5. The philosophy of natural rights was incorporated into early state constitutions.

_____ 6. The states exhibit basic similarities in their governmental structure.

_____ 7. The powers of the federal government have been expanding in recent years.

_____ 8. The federal Constitution enumerates state powers.

_____ 9. The federal Constitution contains restrictions on state powers.

_____ 10. Affirmative state action is necessary before the federal Constitution can be amended.

_____ 11. The implied powers of the federal government are enumerated in the federal Constitution.

_____ 12. Concurrent powers are governmental powers exercised by both the federal government and the state governments.

_____ 13. The federal Constitution may be amended to deprive a state of its equal suffrage in the United States Senate without the consent of the state.

_____ 14. A state with the consent of Congress may enter into a political compact with another state.

_____ 15. The police power of a state has been used to erect interstate trade barriers.

_____ 16. Amendments to the federal Constitution may be proposed by a vote of three-fourths of the states.

_____ 17. Congress may impose upon a territory conditions with which it must comply before it is admitted to the union.

_____ 18. Suits between states are tried in the United States Supreme Court.

328

_____ 19. Congress has defined the full faith and credit obligations of the states.

_____ 20. The privileges and immunities clause applies to "beneficial services."

_____ 21. Rendition is mandatory.

_____ 22. The constitution of New Hampshire permits constitutional amendments to be proposed only by a constitutional convention.

_____ 23. The Model State Constitution provides for a unicameral legislature.

_____ 24. A constitutional convention is a unicameral body.

_____ 25. The constitutions of all states provide for the constitutional initiative.

_____ 26. Aliens may at present vote in some state elections.

_____ 27. Corrupt practices acts make illegal the bribing of judges.

_____ 28. Most qualifications for voting are found in the state constitution.

_____ 29. All primary elections are partisan.

_____ 30. The Massachusetts ballot prevents voters from voting a straight ticket.

_____ 31. A system of limited voting is designed to give representation to minority groups.

_____ 32. A pressure group is an organization that seeks to secure control of a government by nominating its candidates for office.

_____ 33. The direct primary is an election.

_____ 34. The open primary is the most common form of primary.

_____ 35. Pressure groups perform no legitimate functions.

_____ 36. Decentralization of party control is a distinguishing feature of American political parties.

_____ 37. Direct legislation permits voters to reverse actions of a legislature.

_____ 38. The indirect initiative allows citizens, by means of petitions, to propose bills which must be considered by the legislature.

_____ 39. The referendum allows citizens to recall a public official from office prior to the expiration of his term.

_____ 40. The presiding officer of a state senate is always the lieutenant governor.

_____ 41. Every governor possesses the veto power.

_____ 42. The item veto may be used to veto only items in appropriation bills.

_____ 43. A legislative council studies legislative problems between sessions.

_____ 44. The state constitution prescribes the qualifications for membership in the legislature.

—— 45. The governor in every state may call a special session of the legislature.

—— 46. Revenue bills must originate in the upper house.

—— 47. In every state the lieutenant governor succeeds to the governorship in the event of the governor's removal from office.

—— 48. All executive power is vested in a governor by the state constitution.

—— 49. The governor possesses legislative powers.

—— 50. A reprieve absolves a person of the guilt of a crime.

—— 51. Functional integration means large departments with many different functions.

—— 52. Common law was developed by the courts.

—— 53. In the United States justice is dispensed by a dual system of courts.

—— 54. Magistrates courts have general jurisdiction.

—— 55. The petit jury determines guilt or innocence in criminal cases.

—— 56. Conviction of a felony is usually followed by a penitentiary sentence.

—— 57. Jury trials are not held in a supreme court.

—— 58. The Model State Constitution provides for the popular election of the chief justice of the supreme court.

—— 59. In every state the principal subdivisions are called counties.

—— 60. The lack of an executive is a major weakness of county government.

—— 61. Separation of powers is not found in counties.

—— 62. Counties are quasi-municipal corporations.

—— 63. In theory the New England town is an example of indirect democracy.

—— 64. The relationship between a city and a state is unitary.

—— 65. The optional charter system secured a degree of uniformity while permitting some flexibility.

—— 66. A city is liable for its contracts whether they are concerned with governmental or private functions.

—— 67. Historically the mayor has been a strong official.

—— 68. The weak-mayor plan diffuses responsibility.

—— 69. The chief charge directed against the council-manager plan is that it fails to develop policy leaders in the council.

—— 70. A quasi-municipal corporation may be created by the legislature without the consent of a majority of the residents of the area.

___ 71. A quasi-municipal corporation has relatively little ordinance-making power.

___ 72. The general charter is the oldest type of charter.

___ 73. A metropolitan area is not a governmental unit.

___ 74. Functional consolidation has been used in an attempt to solve the problems of metropolitan areas.

___ 75. A city with extramural jurisdiction may exercise limited jurisdiction beyond its borders.

___ 76. The governor is commander in chief of the national guard during peacetime.

___ 77. Zoning refers to the division of the city into areas and the development of special regulations for each area.

___ 78. Indoor relief aids persons who live at home.

___ 79. Fair-trade laws are price maintenance laws.

___ 80. States may not limit the hours of private employees.

___ 81. Civil service laws require all applicants for public positions to take assembled examinations.

___ 82. A higher percentage of the population is publicly employed in large cities than in small cities.

___ 83. State and local laws restrict the political activities of their employees.

___ 84. A performance budget is a type of capital budget.

___ 85. The trend in state and local finance is toward the use of serial bonds.

___ 86. The accrual system of accounting provides for the recording of financial obligations as they are incurred.

___ 87. Federal property may be taxed by states without the consent of Congress.

___ 88. State governments have priority in tax claims.

___ 89. The item veto may be overriden in the same manner as a regular veto.

___ 90. From the fiscal standpoint education, highways, and public welfare are the most important state functions.

___ 91. Indoor relief is more expensive than outdoor relief.

___ 92. The merit system does not cover all positions in a state or local government.

___ 93. Conditions are attached to shared taxes.

___ 94. Veterans' preference has strengthened the merit system.

___ 95. The commission form of government originated in Galveston, Texas.

___ 96. Judicial review of legislation is unconstitutional in a few states.

—— 97. A school district is a special district.

—— 98. A governor possesses both executive and legislative powers.

—— 99. A governor may remove county officials for cause.

—— 100. Debt limitations are intended to prevent governments from defaulting on their financial obligations.

See page 341 for answers to the questions in Part I of this examination.

Part II: Essay Questions

1. Compare the respective advantages and disadvantages of the confederate, unitary, and federal forms of government.

2. Analyze the weaknesses of the Articles of Confederation and Perpetual Union.

3. Trace the historical development of state government.

4. Describe the differences and similarities of the states.

5. Account for the expansion of the powers of the federal government.

6. What powers are possessed by state governments?

7. Discuss the limitations on state powers contained in the federal Constitution.

8. What is meant by the police power?

9. List and briefly discuss the federal Constitution's guarantees to states.

10. Fully discuss the procedure for admitting new states to the Union.

11. What is meant by the sentence, "The citizens of each state shall be entitled to all privileges and immunities of citizens in the several states?"

12. Discuss interstate rendition.

13. Discuss methods by which interstate trade barriers may be removed.

14. List and briefly describe the obligations of the states to the Union.

15. What were the chief characteristics of the early state constitutions?

16. Trace the development of state constitutions.

17. Describe the contents of a state constitution.

18. How may state constitutions be amended?

19. What are the advantages of a constitutional commission?

20. Critically analyze the major provisions of the Model State Constitution.

21. Describe the extension of the suffrage up to 1860.

22. List the present suffrage requirements in your state.

23. Briefly describe the functions of political parties.

24. Describe the development of our present day two-party system.

25. What are the functions of minor parties?

26. Describe the organization of a political party.

27. By what methods may an individual be nominated as a candidate for public office.

28. Criticize the direct primary.

29. Evaluate direct legislation.

30. Evaluate the recall.

31. Do you favor unicameralism or bicameralism? Why?

32. Trace the steps followed by a bill in a typical state legislature.

33. List the powers the legislature may use to control state administration.

34. Evaluate the performance of the Nebraska unicameral legislature.

35. List and briefly describe the powers of a state legislature.

36. Trace the historical development of the office of governor.

37. What powers does a governor possess?

38. Discuss the principles of administrative reorganization.

39. Describe the administrative reorganization movement.

40. Distinguish between common law and equity; between constitutional law and statutory law.

41. How are judges selected?

42. List and describe proposed reforms in the administration of justice.

43. Criticize the justice of the peace system.

44. Describe the functions of county governments.

45. What are the functions of county boards?

46. List and briefly describe the reforms that have been proposed for county governments.

47. Describe the principal forms of municipal government.

48. Discuss the defects of the weak-mayor plan of municipal government.

49. Evaluate the commission form of municipal government.

50. Compare the structure of the council-manager form of municipal government with that of the strong-mayor-and-council plan.

51. Explain the differences between municipal and quasi-municipal corporations.

52. To what extent are local governments supervised by departments or agencies of state government?

53. What are the most pressing problems of metropolitan areas?
54. What are the possible solutions for the problems of metropolitan areas?
55. Describe the organization of a state department of public health.
56. Trace the development of the merit system.
57. What are the public personnel functions?
58. Describe the major problems of public personnel administration.
59. Account for the great rise in governmental expenditures since 1900.
60. Describe budgetary procedure.
61. Criticize the real property tax.
62. Evaluate grants-in-aid as a means of administrative control.
63. What are the major advantages of central purchasing?
64. List the major constitutional limitations on state and local taxing powers.
65. Describe the agencies that have been established to aid legislators.
66. Clearly differentiate between the impeachment process and the recall as devices to remove public officials from office.
67. Explain how the joint committee system speeds up the legislative process?
68. In what respect does an advisory opinion differ from a declaratory judgment?
69. Assess the arguments for and against a sales tax.
70. What services are rendered by a state government to agriculture?
71. What principal activities of state governments are concerned with labor?
72. How does a candidate get his name on a primary election ballot?
73. What bases for rate-making are used by state public utility commissions?
74. Trace the historical evolution of forms of local rural government.
75. Describe the principal means by which states have sought to control municipal governments.
76. Carefully define municipal home rule.
77. What arguments might be adduced in favor of the establishment of a state department to supervise the work of local governments?
78. Describe the organization of a state police system.

79. What should be the relationship between state police and the police forces maintained by cities?

80. What is the legal position of the organized state militia (1) in peacetime and (2) in wartime?

81. Describe the principal functions of the state fire marshal.

82. What is the role of the state in social security administration?

83. Criticize the operation of the jury system.

84. Describe the relationships between state and local health departments.

85. Describe state organization for the administration of education.

86. Describe the organization and powers of local school boards.

87. Describe the financing of the highway system.

88. Comment on the statement: "Highway congestion is turning the downtown sections of cities into desert wastes."

89. Discuss the extent of municipal ownership of public utilities.

90. Discuss planning at the state and local level.

91. Discuss licensing as a means of government control.

92. Discuss state regulation of banking and insurance.

93. Discuss state and national laws for the protection of investors in securities.

94. Trace the development of workmen's compensation.

95. Why may civil service reform be called an "unfinished business?"

96. What are the advantages of a civil service commission over a personnel manager, and vice versa?

97. Explain the declining importance of property taxes in financing state and local governments.

98. Comment on the fairness, or equity, of different taxes used by state and local governments.

99. Discuss advantages and disadvantages of pay-as-you-go as compared to borrowing in financing municipal improvements.

100. Discuss the financial problems of municipal governments resulting from the exodus from city to suburbia.

Part III: Identification Topics

Identify and explain the following terms:

1. Federalism
2. Articles of Confederation
3. Separation of powers
4. Implied power
5. Police power
6. Concurrent powers

7. Ex-post-facto law
8. Grant-in-aid
9. Reserved power
10. Interstate compact
11. Full faith and credit
12. Republican form of government
13. Interstate rendition
14. Constitutional convention
15. Constitutional commission
16. Model State Constitution
17. Suffrage
18. Grandfather clause
19. Australian ballot
20. Corrupt practices acts
21. Short ballot
22. Caucus
23. Precinct captain
24. Preprimary convention
25. Open primary
26. Plurality
27. Pressure group
28. Lobbyist
29. State central committee
30. Direct legislation
31. Recall
32. Optional referendum
33. Indirect initiative
34. Statutory initiative

35. Bicameralism
36. Gerrymander
37. Select committee
38. Standing committee
39. Engrossment
40. Item veto
41. Pocket veto
42. Legislative council
43. Reviser of Statutes
44. Split session
45. Reapportionment
46. Calendar
47. Committee of the whole
48. Conference committee
49. Reprieve
50. Commutation of sentence
51. Constitutional officer
52. Functional integration
53. Rider
54. Impeachment
55. Secretary of state
56. Jurisdiction
57. Common law
58. Equity
59. Misdemeanor
60. Civil case
61. Grand jury
62. Judicial council
63. Magistrates' court
64. Probate court
65. Judicial review
66. Petit jury

67. County board
68. Chief administrative officer plan
69. Representative town meeting
70. *Ad hoc* districts
71. Strong mayor
72. Municipal corporation
73. Dillon's rule
74. Governmental function
75. Special charter
76. Home rule
77. Substitute administration
78. Metropolitan area
79. Metropolitan federation
80. Extramural jurisdiction
81. Parole system
82. Indoor relief
83. Unemployment insurance
84. County agent
85. Youth authorities
86. Licensure
87. Spoils system
88. Classified service
89. Taxpaying qualification
90. Office-group ballot
91. Nonpartisan primary
92. Attorney general
93. Comptroller
94. Preaudit

95. Prosecuting attorney	104. White primary	116. Hatch acts
96. Optional-charter plan	105. Indiana ballot	117. Veterans' preference
97. Workmen's compensation	106. Third reading	118. Unassembled examinations
98. Picketing	107. Code	119. Provisional appointments
99. Public utility	108. Stay of execution	120. Allotments
100. Assembled examination	109. Coroner	121. Capital budget
101. Service record	110. Court of record	122. Current audit
102. Party circle	111. Prudent Investment Theory	123. Sinking fund bonds
103. Personal registration	112. Nepotism	124. Post audit
	113. "Blue sky" laws	125. Shared taxes
	114. Primary boycott	
	115. Arbitration	

Other items for identification may be found in the Index.

Part IV: Multiple Choice Questions

In each of the following cases select the statement that does *not* correctly complete the main statement.

1. A confederacy suffers from all but one of the following disadvantages:
   a. a state may discriminate against citizens of other states
   b. a state has complete freedom to adapt its governmental system to its own special environment
   c. a state does not have to abide by the decisions of the national government
   d. a state may withdraw from the confederacy whenever it desires

2. The federal Constitution grants Congress all but one of the following powers:
   a. the power to tax
   b. the power to regulate commerce
   c. the power to declare war
   d. the power to consolidate states

3. The state governments possess
   a. delegated powers
   b. reserved powers
   c. implied powers
   d. none of the above

4. A state government may do all but one of the following things:
   a. levy a sales tax

b. levy an inheritance tax
c. tax federal property
d. tax corporations

5. The federal Constitution contains all but one of the following restrictions on state powers:
   a. states are forbidden to enter into a confederation
   b. states are forbidden to coin money
   c. states are forbidden to levy income taxes
   d. states are forbidden to pass bills of attainder

6. The early state constitutions possessed all but one of the following characteristics:
   a. the constitution was detailed
   b. the suffrage was restricted
   c. the legislature was strong
   d. private rights were protected

7. Home rule allows
   a. a state to govern its own affairs
   b. a county to annex territory
   c. a city to draft, adopt, and amend its charter
   d. a town to levy taxes

8. The recall permits voters
   a. to defeat laws passed by the legislature
   b. to pass laws
   c. to remove elected officials from office
   d. to shorten the governor's term of office

9. The majority leader in the House of Representatives
   a. refers bills to committee
   b. appoints committees
   c. administers the rules of the house
   d. defends his party's policies against attack

10. "Blue sky" laws
    a. regulate the sale of municipal bonds
    b. regulate public utilities
    c. regulate the sale of securities by corporations
    d. regulate artificial rain-making

11. In terms of expenditures the most important state function is
    a. public welfare
    b. education
    c. highways
    d. public protection

12. Interstate compacts must be approved by
    a. the Congress
    b. the Senate

      c. the President

      d. the Supreme Court

13. Dillon's rule provides that

      a. the secretary of state must issue charters to cities

      b. municipal corporations possess limited powers

      c. counties possess broad powers

      d. a city is liable for torts committed by its employees

14. Corrupt practices acts

      a. limit the political activities of public employees

      b. regulate lobbying

      c. prohibit graft

      d. regulate campaign finances

15. Engrossment refers to

      a. addition of amendments to a bill

      b. provision for new items not included in the executive budget

      c. introduction of a bill

      d. preparation of the final draft of a legislative act

16. The referendum permits

      a. referring a bill to a committee

      b. delegation of power by a governor

      c. the legislature to defeat bills proposed by the governor

      d. the voters to prevent laws passed by the legislature from becoming effective

17. County agricultural agents are paid from

      a. county, state, and federal funds

      b. county funds alone

      c. receipts from special taxes

      d. collections at the source

18. All but one of the following have been proposed as solutions for the problems of metropolitan areas

      a. city-county consolidation

      b. optional-charter system

      c. annexation

      d. functional consolidation

19. The legal relationship between a state and a city is

      a. confederate

      b. unitary

      c. federal

      d. none of the above

20. A governor may

      a. impeach a legislator

      b. veto a proposed amendment

c. grant a reprieve

d. increase an item in an appropriation bill

See page 341 for the answers to the questions in Part IV.

Part V: Association Test

Each word or phrase in column B is in some way associated with a word or phrase in column A. In each blank space to the left of column B place the number (from 1 to 12) which is assigned to its pair in column A. Follow the same procedure in the second dozen pairs. When you have completed these exercises, compare your results with those given in the key on page 341.

A	B
1. Residual powers	____ Federal Constitution
2. Initiative	____ Legislative declaration of guilt
3. Philadelphia convention	____ Quasi-municipal corporation
4. Exemption of states from suit	____ Nominations
5. A county	____ Federal government
6. Literacy tests	____ Campaign funds
7. Corrupt Practices Acts	____ A city
8. Delegated powers	____ Legislative organization
9. Bill of attainder	____ State governments
10. Special charter	____ Disenfranchisement of Negroes
11. The direct primary	____ The Eleventh Amendment
12. Unicameral	____ Direct legislation

A	B
1. Speaker	____ Appropriation bills
2. Auditor	____ Justice of the peace
3. Unicameral legislature	____ A township
4. Minor trial court	____ Presiding officer
5. Grand jury	____ Administrative reorganization
6. Napoleonic Code	____ Act of legislature
7. Item veto	____ Direct democracy
8. Rural local government	____ Constitutional elective officer
9. Municipal corporation	____ Nebraska
10. Functional consolidation	____ Indictment
11. New England town	____ A city
12. Statute	____ Louisiana

Solutions to Examination Questions

Answers to the true-false questions appearing on pages 328–332.

1. F	26. F	51. F	76. T
2. T	27. F	52. T	77. T
3. F	28. T	53. T	78. F
4. F	29. F	54. F	79. T
5. T	30. F	55. T	80. F
6. T	31. T	56. T	81. F
7. T	32. F	57. T	82. T
8. F	33. T	58. T	83. T
9. T	34. F	59. F	84. F
10. T	35. F	60. T	85. T
11. F	36. T	61. T	86. T
12. T	37. T	62. T	87. F
13. F	38. T	63. F	88. F
14. T	39. F	64. T	89. T
15. T	40. F	65. T	90. T
16. F	41. F	66. T	91. T
17. T	42. T	67. F	92. T
18. T	43. T	68. T	93. F
19. F	44. T	69. T	94. F
20. F	45. T	70. T	95. T
21. F	46. F	71. T	96. F
22. T	47. F	72. F	97. T
23. T	48. F	73. T	98. T
24. T	49. T	74. T	99. T
25. F	50. F	75. T	100. T

Answers to multiple-choice questions appearing on pages 337–340.

1. b	2. d	3. b	4. c	5. c
6. a	7. c	8. c	9. d	10. c
11. b	12. a	13. b	14. d	15. d
16. d	17. a	18. b	19. b	20. c

These figures should appear opposite the terms in the first B column in Part V (p. 340):

3	9	5	11	8	7
10	12	1	6	4	2

These figures should appear opposite the terms in the second B column in Part V:

7	4	8	1	10	12
11	2	3	5	9	6

INDEX

103–104; debate on the floor, 103; engrossment and passage, 103; executive action, 104–105; in committee, 102–103; introduction and first reading, 102; reference, 102; route of bill, 268

Legislators, 98–99, 254–259: compensation of, 98–99, 254–259; occupational distribution of, 99; privileges and immunities of, 99; qualifications of, 98; terms of office of, 98, 254–259

Legislature, 95–107, 116, 262–263: adjournment of, 116; organization of, 99–101; powers of, 95–96; procedure of, 101–105; sessions, 97–98; representation in, 262–263; structure of, 96–99

Legislature, organization of, 99–101: committees, 100–101; officers, 100; party organization, 101; presiding officers, 99–100

Legislature, structure of, 96–99: apportionment, 97; bicameral, 96; gerrymandering, 97; unicameral, 96

Libraries, 189–190: county, 190; local, 190; state, 189

Library Services Act, 189

License powers, trade barriers and, 34

Licenses, 34

License taxes, 237

Lieutenant governor, 100, 111, 121

Literacy test, 52, 53, 55

Little Hoover commissions, 125

Lobbyists, 83, 85

Local committee, 71

Local government, 9–11, 18–19, 40, 140–148, 157–166: creation of, 159–163; development of, 9–11; extension of, 40; importance of, 11; legal status of, 157–159; legislative control of, 163–165; rural, 140–148; state administrative supervision of, 165–166; state control of, 18–19

Local government, rural, 140–148, 159–160: county, 140–145; creation of units, 159–160; New England town, 145–146; special districts, 147–148; township, 146–147

Local units of government, 157–163: charters, 160–163; classification of, 157–158; creation of rural, 159–160; creation of urban, 160–163; liability of, 159; powers of, 158–159

Lockport, N. Y., 59

Long ballot, 144

Los Angeles County, 68, 92, 145, 196

Louisiana, 40, 43, 45–46, 57, 62, 129, 140

Louisville, 59

Machines, political, 72–73

Machines, voting, 59–60

Magistrates' courts, 132–133

Maine, 25, 40, 46, 52, 110, 113, 121–122, 134, 146, 187

Maintenance-of-membership provisions, 215

Majority nomination, 75–76

Majority party, 69

Mandatory referendum, 88

Maryland, 5, 51, 57, 96, 97, 132, 134, 218, 223–224, 228

Massachusetts, 5, 25, 37–38, 40, 42–43, 51–52, 54, 56, 74, 85, 89, 95, 100, 104, 108, 113, 116, 120, 134–135, 146, 161, 174, 178–179, 184, 187, 193, 214, 217–218, 236

Massachusetts ballot, 59

Massachusetts Higher Education Assistance Corporation, 187

Mayor, 150–154, 156: strong, 151, 153–154; weak, 152–153

McCulloch v. Maryland, 13, 13fn.

Medical examiner, county, 143

Megalopolis, 168, 283

Merit system, 216–222: advancement, 220–221; certification, 219; civil service commission, 218; discipline, 221; examination, 219; job classification, 219–220; merit-system organization, 217–218; Pendleton Act, 217; personnel manager, 218; promotion, 220–221; recruitment, 219; reform movement, 217; retirement, 221–222; salary plan, 220; training, 220

Metropolitan areas, 167–173, 280–281, 282, 283, 284: interstate, 283; problems of, 168–169; solutions to problems, 170–173; SMSAs, 280–281, 282, 284

Metropolitan District Commission, 173

Metropolitan problems, 168–169, 269; conflicts of authority, 168; duplicate and inadequate services, 168; financial, 169; planning, 168–169; population distribution, 269

Metropolitan proposals, 170–173: annexation, 170; consolidation, 171, 172; extramural jurisdiction, 172–173; federation, 170–171; improvement of county, 171–172; special district plan, 173

Michigan, 40, 54, 68, 142, 162, 165, 202, 221

Migratory labor, 214

Militia, 174

Mineral resources, 202

Minnesota, 54, 178, 202, 236

Minor political parties, function of, 70

Mississippi, 8, 47, 55, 62, 100, 110, 112, 130, 235

Missouri, 27–28, 57, 100, 132, 135, 148, 161

Missouri v. Illinois, 28fn.

Model state constitution, 48–49, 110, 247, 296ff.: state organization and, 247

Monopoly, fair trade and, 208

Montana, 95, 178

Motor-vehicle registration, 194

Municipal corporations, 157–159: liability of, 159; powers of, 158–159

Municipal courts, 132–133

Municipal government, 149–156, 274, 282; charters, 149–150; city council, 150, 151–152; forms of, 152–156, 274;